WHAT BECAME OF THE SEATTLE, WASHINGTON, LABOR MOVEMENT after its famous general strike of February 1919? This book examines the fate of the Seattle American Federation of Labor (AFL) in the decade 1919–29 as a case study of the decline of the U.S. labor movement nationwide in the 1920s. It explores in detail the use of consumer tactics – boycotts, co-operatives, labor-owned businesses, and promotion of the union label – by Seattle's AFL unions. All these tactics have been central to the labor movement since its inception, yet we know little of their history.

Gender dynamics were central to Seattle trade unions' use of consumer tactics, as union members, mostly male, sought to persuade the female members of their families to "shop union." Housewives, though, had their own concerns as workers in the home whose job it was to manage their families' consumption. In analyzing consumer tactics, this book redefines labor history to include housework as well as waged work. It pulls back to examine the sexual division of labor and gender dynamics of the Seattle AFL movement as a whole, including both male and female union members and the members of their families. The book additionally shows race dynamics to have been central to the unions' politics of consumption. Built by white workers who excluded African-American and Asian-American workers, Seattle's AFL unions used boycotts and union-label promotion to attack Japanese-owned businesses and to force workers of color out of the labor market.

Purchasing Power

Purchasing Power
Consumer Organizing, Gender, and the Seattle Labor Movement, 1919–1929

DANA FRANK

University of California, Santa Cruz

CAMBRIDGE
UNIVERSITY PRESS

Published by the Press Syndicate of the University of Cambridge
The Pitt Building, Trumpington Street, Cambridge CB2 1RP
40 West 20th Street, New York, NY 10011-4211, USA
10 Stamford Road, Oakleigh, Melbourne 3166, Australia

First published 1994

Printed in the United States of America

Library of Congress Cataloging-in-Publication Data
Frank, Dana.
Purchasing power : consumer organizing, gender, and the
Seattle labor movement, 1919–1929 / Dana Frank.
p. cm.
Includes index.
ISBN 0-521-38367-6 (hc). – ISBN 0-521-46714-4 (pb)
1. Trade-unions – Washington (State) – Seattle – Political activity –
History – 20th century. 2. Labor movement – Washington (State) –
Seattle – Political activity – History – 20th century. 3. Boycotts –
Washington (State) – Seattle – History – 20th century. I. Title.
HD8085.S413F7 1993
331.89'3 – dc20   93-567
                                                              CIP

A catalog record for this book is available from the British Library.

ISBN 0-521-38367-6 hardback
ISBN 0-521-46714-4 paperback

For my parents,
Carolyn and Joseph Frank

Contents

Acknowledgments

First, I want to thank the many people in Seattle who welcomed me to the city and to the collective project of understanding its history, and who supported this project through its many rounds of research. Above all I want to express my deepest thanks to Cathy Buller and John Veith, who generously and with great humor and warmth opened their house to me year after year. Thanks also to the many people who helped me in my research: Richard Berner; Robert Burke; Sarah Sharbach; Ruth Vincent and the staff of the Wing Luke Asian Museum; Richard Engeman, Carla Rickerson, and the staff of the Special Collections Division at the University of Washington Library; and, most important, Jo Lewis, Karyl Winn, and the staff of the University of Washington Manuscripts Collection, especially Janet Ness, whose friendship and labor made this such an enjoyable project. I owe a great thanks to Jan Eckstadt and Local #76 of the American Federation of Musicians for opening up their archival materials, photocopying machine, and office for my research. A great number of people at the Seattle Public Library have helped this project over the years, and I am indebted to them for their support. My special thanks to Doug Honig for sharing his own work with me and for years of conversations about Seattle labor history. Thanks also to Ross Rieder and the Pacific Northwest Labor History Association for welcoming me into the labor history community so generously.

Staff members of archives throughout the country made my research possible, and I want to thank the many people at the State Historical Society of Wisconsin; the Archives of Labor and Urban Affairs at the Walter Reuther Library, Wayne State University; the New York Public Library Manuscript Collection; and the Washington State Historical Society who contributed their labors to this project. I also want to extend my great thanks to all the library workers who helped me, especially the Interlibrary Loan staffs at the University of California, Santa Cruz; the University of Washington; the University of Missouri–St. Louis; the State University of New York at Binghamton; and Yale University. I especially want to thank the members of Locals 34 and 35, Federation of University

Employees, Hotel Employees and Restaurant Employees, who not only did much of the labor of the early stages of this book but also kept clearly before me quite how moving and inspiring union struggles in the present can be. Thanks also to all the librarian members of my own local, #2199 of the American Federation of Teachers.

I was fortunate to receive many generous grants, and I want to express my deep gratitude to all those who funded the research and writing of this book: National Endowment for the Humanities Fellowships for College Teachers; American Historical Association Albert Beveridge Grants; Woodrow Wilson Doctoral Dissertation Fellowships in Women's Studies; Yale University Program on Non-Profit Organizations John D. Rockefeller 3rd Fellowships; Henry Kaiser Family Grants from the Walter Reuther Library, Wayne State University; University of Missouri–St. Louis Weldon Springs Grants and Faculty Research Grants; Yale University American Studies Program travel grants; and the University of California, Santa Cruz, Academic Senate and Humanities Division Research Grants.

I want to thank Rieko Terai, Curtis Eberhard, Stephen Crane, and Takashi Fujitani for translations of materials in Japanese. I am also grateful to Cheryl Van Der Veer, Nona Williams, Zoe Sodja, and especially Ilene Fineman for the labor they contributed to this book.

My greatest thanks go to my family – Carolyn Frank, Joseph Frank, Laura Frank, and Leona Frank – for their support, patience, and enthusiasm for many years, sustaining me, as always, with their love. My special thanks to Laura Frank for designing the wonderful cover.

I also want to thank members of my tremendously supportive extended family in California, who have watched and cheered on this project for ten years, have supported me through the best and worst of times, and who together make up a wonderful political and personal community. My deepest thanks to Frank Bardacke, Joe Chrastil, Gerri Dayharsh, Eleanor Engstrand, Marge Frantz, Jean Ingebritsen, Steve McCabe, Wendy Mink, Mary Beth Pudup, Judy Shizuru, Susan Stewart, Helen Wallis, and the American Studies Program at the University of California, Santa Cruz.

My great thanks also to friends from New Haven who have sustained me with friendship, advice, historical insights, and comradeship: Marjorie Becker, Susan Besse, George Chauncey, Dan Letwin, Cookie Polan, and Karin Shapiro. I also thank Jeanne Boydston and Molly Ladd-Taylor for teaching me many years ago to take seriously housework as a form of labor.

Many friends and colleagues have also helped me along with the way with advice, information, and support. My thanks to Jim Barrett, John Bloom, Louis Gerteis, Yuji Ichioka, Temma Kaplan and the Barnard study group on women's protest movements, Regina Kunzel, Joe McCartin, Angela Miller, Neville Kirk, Bill Tabb, and John Works.

I want to express my great thanks to three professors who helped make my graduate education exciting and whose advice and support shaped immeasurably the dissertation upon which this book is in part based. Jean-Christophe Agnew helped me develop the theoretical implications of this project and challenged me to rethink its deeper analytical and narrative framework. Emilia Da Costa read the dissertation with great insight and humor. I want to give special thanks to Nancy Cott, who not only, along with Emilia Da Costa, served as an all-important role model but who also has sustained me for many years with her intellectual acuity, mastery of women's history, and great support for my work at every stage.

Many people have read and commented upon parts of this book in its various incarnations, and I want to express my gratitude for their advice and support. My thanks to Ava Baron, Jeremy Brecher, David Brody, Edmund G. Burke III, Melvyn Dubofsky, Steve Fraser, Takashi Fujitani, Martha Hodes, Kimberly Phillips, David Sweet, and the Women's History Reading Group at UCSC.

For years of comradeship, input, and support, I want to express my particular thanks to David Anthony, Cecelia Bucki, Ileen DeVault, Toni Gilpin, and Gerda Ray. My special thanks to David Brundage and Nelson Lichtenstein, who not only read and commented upon much of the manuscript but who have also been wonderful colleagues and friends.

At the center of this book lies the influence of David Montgomery. I have been fortunate to serve an apprenticeship with this consummate master of labor history and to continue to share with him in the political project of figuring out the place of history in bringing about a more just society. He has given generously of his time and intellectual insights for twelve years, including careful readings of both the dissertation and the book manuscript. He has shared with me an understanding of labor history that underlies this book at every turn. And he has taught me a vision of working-class empowerment and self-management that will always sustain my political life.

Cambridge University Press blessed me with Shelton Stromquist, an ideal reader. His tremendous understanding of the deep rhythms and goals of this book continues to amaze me. He understood from the first what I was trying to do, and I owe him a great debt for his advice and support throughout the revision process. My editor at Cambridge, Frank Smith – that rarest of rare things, a real editor – read the entire manuscript with great care and has been helpful, accessible, and enjoyable to work with at every turn. I am very grateful to him for both his advice and his support for my book. And I want to thank Eric Newman, my copy editor, for all his excellent advice and careful labors.

Finally, I especially want to thank a few friends whose love, enthusiasm, and support have sustained me through years of painstaking work on this project. My great thanks to Beth Haas, with whom it was always a delight to share writing books together; to Karin Stallard, who not only contributed insightful criticisms to the manuscript but whose tremendous support always came as part of a larger package of wisdom and love; and to Priscilla Murolo, comrade and sister since the first days of graduate school. I want to express my deepest gratitude to Eric Arnesen, who not only sustained me with years and years of friendship but who also, with limitless generosity, read the entire manuscript and commented upon it closely; and to Julia Greene, whose advice on the manuscript strengthened it immensely and whose support, insight, and friendship made our years of labor history comradeship such a great pleasure.

Introduction

LET ME BEGIN WITH A WARNING: This story does not have a happy ending. In 1919, when the story starts, the Seattle American Federation of Labor (AFL) had established itself as a power to be reckoned with for the city's employers. Trade-union activism reached beyond factories and building sites to include weekly mass meetings in the streets, twenty consumer and producer cooperatives, and a dozen organizations of working-class housewives. The unions owned their own savings and loan, their own film production company, and a daily newspaper with a circulation of 100,000.

By 1929, when the story ends, all that was dead. The independent institutions had collapsed. Women's roles in the movement, whether as trade unionists or as their wives, had shrunk to the subservient or dependent. Business unionist leaders dominated the movement in contented collaboration with the city's elite. And rank-and-file union members, rather than attend meetings, stayed home.

All over the country, the 1920s brought defeat, disillusionment, and conservatism to the labor movement. Selig Perlman, studying the AFL in 1928, described it as "a curious blending of 'defeatism' with complacency."[1] At the end of the decade, J.B.S. Hardman reflected: "1919 seems to have happened ages ago. The language that was used then no longer sounds familiar to our ears. The emotions that overwhelmed people in those momentous days fail to excite us today. The world has grown not only older but old."[2]

The task of this book is to explain that transformation, to understand how and why the U.S. labor movement, after nationwide militancy in the war years, fell so precipitously in the 1920s. We have few studies of decline. The generation of historians that produced what we call the "new" labor history that has flourished since the 1960s focused, more often, on periods of upswing. We have many insightful analyses of the labor movement in the 1880s, the 1910s, and the 1930s, the times of expansion and triumph in U.S. labor history, and few studies focusing directly on defeat or incremental decline. My own interest in times of decline stems directly from the experience of my exact political generation. I came of age in the mid-1970s and knew I was living in a time not of expansion, like the 1960s, but of contraction. By the time I took up labor history in 1980 the labor movement itself had entered a period of dramatic decline, as employers' demands for concessions and a hostile government combined to devastate many U.S. trade unions. For many in my intellectual generation, while we continue to take inspiration from stories of past victories, our questions also concern defeat. As a result, this tale of Seattle labor begins in February 1919, at the peak of the AFL movement, and descends from there.[3]

Like the 1890s, the 1920s decade until very recently was one of the least popular, most obscure topics in U.S. labor history. In the most widely used bibliography of labor history the twenties are subsumed under the category "World War I and the Golden Aftermath." Most studies, whether local or national, pass over the decade with a brief mention, skipping with palpable relief from the mass strikes of 1919 to the Great Depression. Some of the best analyses of the period were written in the late 1920s. The more recent studies that analyze the decade offer such a diverse array of interpretations and historical dynamics that it has been difficult to construct a single chronology.[4]

Understanding the labor movement in the 1920s means confronting the twentieth-century American Federation of Labor, a topic still more unpopular. While historians have learned a great deal about the Congress of Industrial Organizations (CIO), we know little about the AFL after World War I. Yet the AFL was the only form of organized labor in most towns during the 1920s, and in the 1930s its total membership was far larger than that of the CIO. It grew as fast as the CIO in the World War II era, counted twice as many members in the late 1940s and early 1950s, and in many respects provided the model that the merged AFL-CIO would follow in the post–World War II era. The apparent story of organized labor's decline in the 1920s is one of triumph for AFL business unionists, those who eschewed larger social transformations and defined unionism in its narrowest sense of delivering services to the membership. Business unionists rose to near-complete domination of the labor movement in the decade both at the local level, as in Seattle, and nationwide. To grasp the nature of that victory is central to understanding the 1920s.[5]

Business unionists' rise to power in the Seattle AFL was always challenged and by no means inevitable. Socialists, Japanese- and African-American workers, white female workers, and rank-and-file white male workers all opposed conservative business unionists' increasing dominance of the AFL in the 1920s. Part of the story of this book concerns the gradual silencing of their alternative visions of what the labor movement might be.

The defeat of dissenting voices can be understood only by paying careful attention to political–economic forces. At the conclusion of World War I, the federal government shut down the immense shipyards that underlay the Seattle labor movement's wartime strength, glutting the local labor market and dispersing militant rank-and-file workers. Repression drove radicals underground or out of town. As the tide began to turn economically, the city's employers mounted a massive open shop drive against the AFL locals that soon brought the movement to its knees. The depression of 1921 did the rest of the work. Working-class institutions founded in the boom times of 1919 collapsed. Those trade unions that survived granted sweeping concessions. When the smoke cleared in 1922–23, the survivors came from the local-market sector of the Seattle economy. Business unionist leaders from this sector in the next two years purged any remaining radicals, brought the local movement in line with the national AFL of Samuel Gompers, and offered peace and collaboration to the city's employers.

The story of Seattle illuminates an important distinction between unions in the mass production sector and those in the local-market sector of the economy. The latter came to dominate the AFL throughout the country in the second half of the decade, both in cities such as Chicago that boasted large mass production sectors and in cities like Seattle that after the war lacked one altogether. Relations between labor and capital in the building trades, local transportation, printing, and skilled service work were distinct from those simultaneously evolving in mass production, far away from the world of well-funded welfare programs and employee representation programs. This was a world of innumerable small firms dependent on a local community for both their labor supply and for their market, vulnerable to consumer campaigns and dependent on workers with a long tradition of craft unionism. Unions and employers alike were open to mutually beneficial cooperative agreements once the challenge of radical industrial unionism had been repressed.[6]

Many scholars in trying to explain labor's quiescence in the 1920s have invoked cultural factors. In the most well-known formulation, Stuart Ewen argued that the rise of mass-market advertising offered a new sphere of fulfillment to working people in the 1920s, who chose "consumerism" over activism. Ewen, in turn, drew on Robert and Helen Lynd's classic 1929 study of Muncie, Indiana, *Middletown*, which identified new forms of leisure and spending that had supplanted older patterns of trade-union and community involvement.[7] Recent studies of working-class culture in the 1920s have disputed such claims. Lizabeth Cohen, especially, demonstrates that Chicago workers incorporated the allures of mass culture into their own independent styles of shopping and spending. Cohen and others argue that by the early 1930s mass culture could be absorbed into new forms of working-class activism. Mass consumption and active trade unions were not necessarily mutually exclusive.[8]

Aware of the arguments of Ewen and the Lynds, I began this study interested in the relationship between consumption and conservatism in the 1920s. Hoping to dispute them, I imagined that I would find a wealth of heretofore-unknown working-class rank-and-file activism in late 1920s Seattle. I never found it. Instead, I found exactly the same apathy about trade unionism the Lynds described in Muncie. But the causes I found for that apathy were very different. Seattle workers, exactly like those in Muncie, drove around in shiny new Fords rather than attend union meetings. But they did so not just because the Ford offered so very much but because the meetings offered so very little. And those meetings offered so little because of the complex dynamics of labor and capital in the postwar years.

Consumption was nonetheless crucial to the story of labor in the 1920s. My examination of Seattle revealed an extensive sphere of grassroots activism in which workers used consumption politically as part of the labor movement. Through boycotts, cooperatives, labor-owned businesses and promotion of the union label and shop card, they politicized relations of consumption in service to trade unions. Class conflict took place on two fronts: not just at the waged workplace, over relations of production, but in the sphere of consumption as well. Production and consumption were inseparable.[9]

The relationship between politicized consumption on the one hand and the trade unions' shift toward relative conservatism on the other proved both intimate and complex. Consumer organizing activities within the AFL were neither simply "radical" nor "conservative" but defy easy political categorization. They were part and parcel of the AFL movement in all its periods and strategic forms. In the period of upswing and radicalism immediately after the war, a critical mass of strength at the point of production spilled over into multiple campaigns to politicize consumption. Unionists constructed a profusion of independent institutions through which members and their families could shop at "their own" businesses and, they hoped, transform the structures of U.S. society. Consumer organizing tactics were equally central to the transition years of 1920–23, when the unions turned to boycotts, especially, in a defensive posture. The postwar depression's destruction of their independent institutions carried down the creative vision and will to experiment of the movement as a whole. The business unionist conservatives who controlled the movement by mid-decade proved as interested in consumer organizing as those they supplanted and elevated a consumer tactic, the union label, to the top of their own tactical list. Whatever the exact nature of the movement, politicized consumption was central to the story.

Consumer tactics were popular in working-class communities throughout the country in the post–World War I era. Cooperatives founded in 1919–20 ranged from Finnish cooperatives in the Great Lakes area, to a "Citizens Cooperative Laundry" in Little Rock, Arkansas, to railroad workers' food cooperatives and citywide chains in New York, San Francisco, and Cincinnati. Workers in Tampa, Florida, alone belonged to twenty-three cooperatives. Boycotts continued as a mainstay of local trade-union activity. In the middle and second half of the decade, union label promotion rose to strategic prominence throughout the country, in part because of a concerted campaign by the national-level AFL, which organized "Trade Union Promotional Leagues" to promote union-made products in cities nationwide.[10]

Consumer tactics have been at the core of the labor movement in all periods of U.S. history, their importance often underestimated. Workers organized cooperatives throughout the nineteenth and early twentieth centuries and would turn to them again in the 1930s. Boycotts were vital to the ability of both the Knights of Labor and AFL to mobilize working-class communities in the late nineteenth century. Two Supreme Court decisions restrained organized labor's use of the boycott and national "unfair" lists after 1908, but city-level central labor councils continued to promote local boycotts, and the AFL to this day publishes a "We Don't Patronize" list. The United Farm Workers revived the tactic most vigorously with nationwide grape and lettuce boycotts in the 1970s. Union label and shop-card promotion has been equally important to the labor movement. Label promotion began in the late nineteenth century in the cigar and hat industries, and by 1908 it had spread to sixty-eight AFL internationals, marking a vast array of goods and services. The label lives on today in the garment workers' exhortations to "look for the union label" and in the autoworkers' slogan "Buy American – Buy Union." The politics of consumption, in sum, have been central to class conflict and working-class self-organization throughout U.S. history, in periods of both expansion and retrenchment.[11]

Consumer organizing also offers an opening for the construction of a gendered labor history. Feminist historians have challenged the field of labor history to integrate women into the larger, male-centered narrative of U.S. labor and working-class history. We are trying not only to "add" women but also to ask how the main story itself is gendered, how gender is part of the story whether or not women are present. Ava Baron, Alice Kessler-Harris, Mari Jo Buhle, and others have underscored that in order to do so, we need to rethink the very concepts and frameworks through which we discuss the history of work, working people, and their organizations.[12]

Working-class consumption was anything but gender-neutral. In the sexual division of labor in the working-class family of the 1920s, it was a sphere assigned to women, especially those not working for wages. Theorists have spoken of the assigned labors of housewives as "the reproduction of the labor force," that is, feeding, clothing, and nurturing waged workers, as well as rearing a new generation of workers through the labor of child care. Part of housewives' work was to shop and spend wisely the money supplied by wage-earning members of their households. Consumption, in other words, was housewives' job. It was a form of work. In discussing consumption here, I am trying to reconceptualize "labor" and therefore "labor history" to include not just the labor that happens at workplaces in which employers pay wages in exchange for workers' labor power but also the unwaged work that people perform within the household economy, the sphere popularly understood as "housework."[13]

The unions' consumer organizing tactics inhabited an intersection between those two forms of labor, a meeting point between the sexual division of labor in the home and capitalist relations of production at the waged workplace. Trade unions emerged out of wage–work relations. But once they chose to politicize consumption, they also sought to change the way housewives performed their unwaged labors of consumption.

The Seattle AFL movement in the post–World War I decade employed two very different though overlapping forms of consumer organizing, and the distinction between the two highlights the nature of this intersection between waged work and housework. In the first type, the politicization of consumption involved a restructuring of the economics of consumption itself – that is, the process through which goods and services are distributed. Seattle workers' consumer cooperatives of 1918–21 were the most popular example of this sort. They sought to "eliminate the middleman," lower prices, and offer working-class families the opportunity to shop at "their own stores." They offered a rest room for tired women shoppers and delivery of groceries to working-class homes. Cooperatives were thus designed to address the workplace concerns of housewives as well as those of wage-earning men and women.

The second type of consumer organizing was far more common. In these, such as boycotts and promotion of the union label, trade-union members sought to shape workers' shopping and saving habits in order to affect relations between employer and employee at the waged workplace. Labors of consumption, here, were subordinated to the concerns of those earning wages, who built and sustained trade unions and then turned to these consumer tactics the better to strengthen their position in relation to their employers. Such campaigns involved an intensification of housewives' labor as consumers. Assiduous pro-union consumption meant more time spent shopping, a restricted supply of available commodities and services, and, usually, higher prices, necessitating more labor in order to balance the household budget. Deep within the consumer organizing strategies of the Seattle AFL lay an inherent contradiction between the workplace concerns of working-class housewives and the concerns of trade-union members who worked for pay. Working-class housewives' identification of their own concerns with those of wage earners in their families as part of a family economy could in part alleviate this tension. But for the most part the wives of union men proved unwilling to speed up their own labors on behalf of a "working class" movement not of their own making. As a result, the AFL unions' efforts to mobilize consumption on behalf of a "class" agenda would always be limited by their inability to grasp the workplace concerns of female members of their class.

These dynamics have been invisible in part because labor history's own conceptual framework has marginalized consumption. As Mari Jo Buhle has put it, "[T]he narrative baseline remains production relations, traditionally defined." Housework and the labors of reproduction enter the story only on the subordinated edges of the analysis.[14] We are trapped, in other words, inside the very same assumptions as those of our male subjects in the trade-union movement, who assumed that the primary sphere of labor was that of production. Our concepts date back to Karl Marx, who himself was a product of a particular working-class movement in the mid–nineteenth century that defined "class interests" in male terms. "Marx's concept of 'class interests' did not represent [women's] essential needs as the class members who raised children and maintained families," Harold Benenson observes. "Rather these needs could only find indirect expression (through some connection with the productive realm)." Marx's analysis was implicitly a "two-tiered conception of men's (direct) versus women's (mediated) relation to the interest of the working class."[15] The story of consumer organizing by the labor movement offers one way to rethink the nature of class conflict in gendered terms. If working people and their unions challenged the power of organized capital through the politicization of consumption, they did so in ways that would benefit working-class men and women very differently.

This gendered analysis of consumer organizing contributes as well to our understanding of the earlier, still salient question of women's roles in the labor movement. First, it adds the wives of unionized men to the story. It was their labors as consumers that trade unionists most actively sought to influence through consumer campaigns. Wives, in turn, should not be overgeneralized. Some were married to men in the leadership, others to rank-and-file men only marginally in contact with their union locals. Some had become housewives after their own careers as trade-union activists; others were hostile to the trade unions that drew their men off to mysterious meetings. They might be socialists, place their faith in conservative business unionism, or identify their class interests in subordination to the trade-union movement. Still others dropped out rather than embrace a subservient role.[16]

Despite these differences, remarkably similar patterns emerged when wives did choose to involve themselves in the AFL movement. They organized, by and large, in organizations separate from those of men. One of their primary concerns was to establish an independent physical space for their meetings and social events. In their activities they mixed support work for the unions, such as petition gathering or supplementing picket lines, with events addressing their own concerns as workers in the home, such as swapping recipes, improving their cooking methods, or decorating pleasant rooms downtown in which to rest while shopping. They were also committed to the concerns of wage-earning women. They agitated, for example, in support of the minimum wage for women in 1920. Their activities offer a rare glimpse into the political visions of working-class housewives. Most often, they spoke of their ideal as "homelike," a term they applied both to their own activities and to meeting rooms, to the spirit they wished to bring to the movement as a whole, and to the ideal society they hoped their activism would usher in.

Wives' activism sheds new light on the role of women who were themselves trade-union members. Female unionists were equally diverse. They were careful to distinguish themselves from the wives and differed with them over issues such as married women's right to work. At the same time female unionists also functioned in many ways as the "wives" of the movement, serving the male union members in a manner that replicated the sexual division of labor in the family. They established styles of sociability that duplicated those of the wives and that were also inseparable from the sexual division of labor: They, too, decorated their own rooms, shared cooking tips, and chose to cook for union events. In other ways, though, trade-union women used their sex-segregated activities as a base from which to challenge the sexual division of labor and to fight for women's equality in the waged workplace. While the presence of wives who accepted a role in which they were subservient to their menfolk highlighted the challenge that wage-earning women brought to the male-dominated trade-union movement, wives' support for women unionists strengthened women unionists' fight for equality in both the movement and at the waged workplace.[17]

I have tried in this study to integrate women unionists into the larger story of the Seattle AFL in the 1920s as well as into the story of labor's consumer tactics. The postwar open shop drive, the economic transformation of the city, the political shift in the movement from left to right, the tensions between leadership and rank and file – all these elements affected unionized men and women differently. All were shaped by both female and male union members, as well as by wives. Gender was embedded in the tactics, institutions, and political ideals through which working-class people challenged their place in an unequal society and simultaneously renegotiated their relations with one another. This is a history of the labor movement, in sum, that interweaves the story of working-class women and men, waged workers and unwaged workers, into a single gendered story.[18]

Just as gender permeated working-class history whether women were present or not, so too did race. David Roediger has issued a challenge to labor historians paralleling the call for a gendered history. "The assumption remains, even as the issue [of race] is raised, that the Black Worker enters the story of American labor as an actor in a subplot which can be left on the cutting-room floor, probably without vitiating the main story," he argues. "What if race is instead part of the very lens through which labor's story must be filmed?"[19] In Seattle, the AFL was built by workers who identified themselves as white and then excluded workers of African or Asian descent from their organizations. Their exclusionary practices were central to the "main" story of class, gender, and organized consumption in 1920s Seattle. Racial exclusion sharply constricted any solidarity the white working class might try to construct, while reinforcing solidarity between some groups of white workers. Like gender, it was part and parcel of AFL unionists' concepts of "the workers" and "the working class" and permeated every tactic they employed, including those involving consumption. AFL unionists often declared boycotts against firms owned by Japanese immigrants or those owned by whites who employed Asian-Americans, and they called upon white workers' sense of racial solidarity to reinforce trade union solidarity. Class identities were constructed in racial terms. To be a "worker," in the Seattle AFL, was to be not only a wage earner but also white.[20]

Yet race relations in the Seattle labor movement were always contested, always in flux. In the same period during which white workers built trade unions walling off workers of color, Japanese- and African-American workers formed their own independent organizations at the waged workplace. Throughout the decade they contested the AFL's exclusionary policies, aided, at times, by white unionists who advocated industrial unionism and criticized the racial premises of the white movement. In a number of cases Japanese- and African-American workers were able to gain a place, if always an unequal one, within the AFL. Their admission was less a product of white workers' antiracist ideologies, however, than of the pragmatic considerations of traditional AFL unionists threatened by the self-organization of African- and Japanese-American workers. These two groups encountered the white labor movement on quite different terms, moreover. "White racism . . . was not a monolithic structure that affected all minority groups in precisely the same ways," Tomás Almaguer argues. "Instead, important differences existed in the ways Anglo Americans viewed and discriminated against different minority groups."[21] African- and Asian-American workers labored in different positions within the Seattle economy, and in turn this difference shaped the ways in which they challenged the AFL. So too did the distinct ways in which they organized within their own communities. "Race," in other words, was no simple, ahistoric matter, nor was it negotiated and interpreted along a single axis.

Gender permeated these dynamics of race and class. African- and Asian-American women and men experienced labor-market discrimination differently, and this placed them in different relationships to the AFL. When combined with the AFL's deep gender biases, this meant that Japanese- and African-American women were pushed far away from the AFL, while white women and some men of color might, under certain circumstances, gain partial entry. Racial exclusion, in other words, was gendered. From the other side, white women, both trade-union members and wives, supported the racial practices of the AFL movement. One of Seattle's strongest proponents of Asian exclusion was Alice Lord, president of the waitresses' local union. Her activities underscore our need to redefine the exclusionary "white working class" to include women as well as men.

These efforts to rethink the race and gender dynamics of labor history have necessitated a careful choice of language in telling this story. No solution is satisfactory. I am employing racial categories, for example, that the groups of people I am discussing in some cases would not have recognized at the time. I use, here, "African-American" to speak of people of African descent. I use "Japanese-American" to speak of both foreign- and native-born people who either immigrated to Seattle from Japan in the first two decades of the century or were the children of those immigrants. I use "white" to speak of people of European descent, of many different ethnic traditions and immigrant nationalities, who identified themselves as white in contradistinction to people of African and Asian descent. My gender analysis has called for a careful choice of words to describe work, working people, and their organizations as well. When I say "worker" I mean people who belonged to the working class, male and female, whether they worked for wages or not. I use "unionist" to embrace both trade-union members and female workers who actively supported the trade unions even though they did not formally belong. I distinguish clearly in my language between "consumption," the activities through which people consume goods and services, and "consumerism," the presumed ideological effects of mass-consumption society.

My choice of Seattle was equally deliberate. Seattle offers a useful case study of the 1920s in part because its general strike of early 1919 served at the time, and has served ever since, as one of the classic examples of working-class radicalism and organizational power immediately following World War I. The Seattle AFL's transformation into a quiescent piece of the national AFL machinery by the end of the 1920s was equally representative of nationwide trends. Using Seattle as a case study also offers an opportunity to correct the regional bias of U.S. labor history, which tends to treat eastern and midwestern patterns as the norm, and those in the West as abnormal. Much in this story is not regionally specific. At the same time, other dynamics were characteristic of cities on the Pacific coast.[22] Seattle's race dynamics, in particular, were specific to the West. The axis of racial negotiation was between whites and Japanese-Americans as much as between whites and African-Americans. The focus on Seattle, then, both illustrates national dynamics and changes the way we understand them. A local study also allows one to analyze the AFL movement of the 1920s without sacrificing the perspectives, voices, and participation of rank-and-file working people. Restricting the story both geographically and temporally made possible an analytical complexity otherwise lost.

Much is left out, nonetheless, that affected the story I tell and was unfortunately outside of the scope of a manageable project. This book intertwines the story of consumer organizing tactics employed by the Seattle AFL with the fate of the overall AFL movement in the period from 1919 to 1929. It does not treat the Industrial Workers of the World (IWW, or "Wobblies"), who were still marginally active in Seattle in the decade, except insofar as their activities affected the story of the AFL. Seattle's AFL unionists were very much involved in electoral politics, and a careful attention to that sphere of activism is necessary to any full analysis of the decade. Equally important, but not fully treated, are dynamics of the shopfloor, whether that of the shipyard or the kitchen. Finally, an extensive analysis of the exact nature of working-class people's daily habits of consumption and the political economy of consumption would illuminate many of the dynamics in this book.

The book proceeds in chapters organized in some cases chronologically, in other cases thematically, that move forward in time while alternating between and connecting different spheres of activity. Many developments occurred simultaneously. In constructing the story I have tried to show how the seeds of later events were sown at the same time as other, seemingly quite different, activities unfolded. Half of the book, as a result, concerns 1919 and 1920 alone, for the rest of the decade can be understood only in context of the changes that were set in motion in the immediate postwar years, and the lag between workers' strategies and the political–economic context in which they sought to employ them.

The book is divided into three sections. Part I depicts the Seattle AFL movement in its expansionary phase, which peaked in late 1919. Chapter 1 sets the stage, using the story of the February 1919 general strike to capture the growing strength of the AFL at the waged workplace, and the tension within it between solidarity and exclusion. The next two chapters explore the ways in which that strength at the point of production spilled over into politicized consumption in a wave of working-class institution building. Chapter 2 analyzes the rise of consumer and producer cooperatives between 1918 and 1920, especially the gender dynamics of their popularity. Chapter 3 looks at labor-owned businesses known at the time as "labor capitalism," through which workers sought to politicize not just spending but also saving their money.

Part II, comprising the middle chapters of the book, analyzes the transformation of that movement by 1924. Chapter 4 returns to the trade unions and, after examining their continued gains and structural innovations after the general strike, describes Seattle's employers' successful counterattack in the open shop drive of late 1919. Chapter 5 carries the story into 1920, showing how the unions, in turn, politicized consumption in defense against organized employers through a citywide boycott of the Bon Marche department store and uses that example to analyze the gender and jurisdictional dynamics inherent in boycotts. Chapter 6 treats the postwar depression, which in Seattle began in 1919 and peaked in 1921, devastating the trade unions and bringing down their independent institutions. Chapter 7 then analyzes the final accommodations of 1921–24 through which the Seattle AFL adapted itself to the postwar economy, changing racial configurations, and the strictures of the national-level AFL.

Part III examines the aftermath: the world of the business unionists who controlled the movement after 1924. It focuses on their single most popular tactic, the union label. Chapter 8 examines the relationships between trade-union officials and employers embedded in label unionism and the local-market sector. Chapter 9 examines the rank and file's lack of interest in pro-union shopping as a window on the movement's dynamics of gender, race, and internal democracy in the second half of the decade.

As this survey of the book's progression suggests, in the last analysis this is a book about organizing. It is about organized workers' creative ideas and organizational efforts in an initial moment of expansion, and their strategic responses to a period of retrenchment and intensified employer hostility. It is about the tension between working-class solidarity and self-imposed barriers to such solidarity. Ultimately, it is about the definition of solidarity itself. And it is about learning from defeats in the past in order to meet the challenges of our own time. In the end, it is about the tension between the U.S. labor movement at its best and the U.S. labor movement at its weakest – between what the AFL-CIO is reduced to today and what a labor movement of the future might yet be.

Part I

Vision

1

Solidarity

THE SEATTLE GENERAL STRIKE of February 1919 was one of the most dramatic examples of working-class solidarity in twentieth-century U.S. history. Sixty-five thousand of the city's workers, from hotel maids to garbage collectors to plasterers to violin players, announced that they would not work until the federal government and local shipyard owners granted wage increases to workers in the city's huge wartime shipyards. The general strike symbolized the tremendous power that Seattle's AFL unions had achieved by the end of World War I, exemplifying the movement as it stood poised to enter the postwar decade. It was a movement defined above all at the point of production. The general strike was, indeed, the quintessential point-of-production tactic. The union members who employed it included not just the skilled craft workers who built the prewar Seattle AFL but also 35,000 new metal trades workers who had flocked to the city during the war and another 20,000 newly organized workers. By the war's end the AFL had expanded its definition of solidarity to embrace over one-fifth of the city's entire population.

Stark limits constrained that expansionary solidarity, however. The Seattle AFL movement developed in constant tension between self-imposed barriers of skill, gender, and race that excluded much of the city's working class and growing pressures to transcend those limits. The war boom, especially the labor shortages it created, strengthened the bargaining power of most working people vis-à-vis their employers. As the AFL locals rose up to seize that sudden opportunity, the key issue would be the extent to which the movement could, even in the moment of its greatest glory, part with its exclusionary heritage.

Before the war

Seattle in 1914, while the largest city in the Pacific Northwest, was not a great manufacturing site. It thrived as shipping center for the natural products of the Northwest. The city's small amount of manufacturing involved processing products from the hinterland, most importantly lumber.

Some logs passed intact to the docks; others, at mills employing anywhere from a dozen to a hundred men and women, became boxes, furniture, doors, window sashes, wood pulp, or paper, in turn supporting a local printing industry. Wheat and other grains passed into cereal and flour mills and then to cracker bakeries. Fish (especially salmon from Alaska) and fruit from the orchards of the Yakima Valley were canned in Seattle. Cattle and hogs met their fate at three meatpacking firms, the largest of which, Frye's, dispatched thousands of animals a day. A final industry, metalworking, drew on abundant coal and metals mined in the region and served the region's extractive industries. A dozen small firms in Seattle produced boilers, machinery, and tools for ships; donkey engines and stump pullers for lumber camps; and by the 1910s steel, stoves, and streetcars. One shipyard, the Seattle Dry Dock and Construction Company, began producing wooden ships in the 1890s.[1]

Seattle differed economically from the manufacturing cities of the upper Midwest and East in these years, though not from other western ones. Pennsylvania's steel mills, for example, employed as many as 8,000 to 10,000 by the 1910s. Textile firms in New England employed up to 40,000 in a single mill. In prewar Seattle, by contrast, only one company, the shipyard, employed over a thousand; two, around 500; and below that, a few others hired one or two hundred. No mass production existed. Instead, three-quarters of the wage-earning people in Seattle worked in the local market, that is, for companies that produced goods and services for local consumption: building construction, transportation, commercial laundries, sales, clerical work, domestic service, bakeries, restaurants, and others.[2]

Seattle's population in turn reflected its relationship to the hinterland. The region's extractive industries, the products of which Seattle processed and shipped, employed tens of thousands of people throughout the Northwest. Lumber, agriculture, salmon fishing, and canning all involved migrant and temporary workers who flowed in an annual cycle into Seattle each winter and out again each spring. Largely single, overwhelmingly male, in many ways alienated from the *politesse* of mainstream society, these casual workers contrasted sharply with the other, more rooted world of working-class Seattle men and women laboring in the local-market sector and in small-scale production, a group that included skilled craft workers as well as a huge range of unskilled workers.[3]

The largest group within Seattle's population was native-born whites born of native parents, counting for 44.6 percent of the city's population in 1910. Of the other roughly half who were white immigrants or the children of immigrants, more than a third were from Canada or the British Isles. Together, these two groups – the native born and British/Canadian – made up two-thirds of the city's population. Within the working class, men of this group dominated skilled work, especially the metal and building trades. Anglo-American women found jobs in clerical, sales, and waitressing work.[4]

Scandinavians, approximately a third of the city's immigrants, counted as the second largest group within the foreign-born, after Britons and Canadians. Most were from Sweden and Norway, in about equal numbers. In 1920, for example, there were 7,191 Norwegians, 8,676 Swedes, 1,879 Danes, and 1,298 Finns. They had followed Northern Pacific Rail links from earlier settlements in the upper Midwest and the Dakotas. In Seattle, the men worked as fishermen, in lumber processing, and in the building trades. Women, Swedes especially, worked as domestic servants.[5]

White immigrants also included 8,000 Germans and Austrians. Men found jobs readily available in the skilled trades. "New immigrant" white settlers, those from southern and eastern Europe, came to Seattle in only small numbers by national standards. Three thousand Italians eked out a bare subsistence as manual laborers largely in construction or in railroad yards, as garbage wagon drivers, or as truck gardeners tending precarious plots of two or three acres on the hillsides of the Rainier and Duwamish Valleys. Several thousand Jews labored as tailors, garment workers, or cigar makers for tiny firms employing both men and women. An earlier wave of German Jews, who had come with capital in hand, had by the prewar years established themselves in retailing and jobbing. Several hundred Greeks and Turks, most of them male, sustained tiny ethnic clusters in the downtown laborers' neighborhoods.[6]

Seattle's white immigrant population, like its economy, differed from that of eastern cities. First, while the white foreign-born and their children counted two-fifths of the city's population by 1920, this was far less than in the East. In Boston, for example, 63 percent of all white residents were foreign-born or the children of the foreign-born. In New York, the total was 68 percent. Second, Seattle's white immigrants and their children were overwhelmingly from northern and western Europe, the so-called "old immigrants," in contrast to the "new immigrant" populations, those emigrating from southern and eastern Europe, dominant in the East. Finally, Seattle's "old immigrants" did not, by and large, cluster in ethnic neighborhoods. Anglo-Americans scattered throughout the city easily. Germans and Austrians, although they supported a local German-language press, formed no distinct neighborhoods. A specific Scandinavian neighborhood, Ballard, was only beginning to take shape in the 1910s, as a Swedish- and Norwegian-American fishing community evolved. Historian Janice Reiff argues that Seattle Scandinavians' ethnic cultural identity was relatively weak. They were largely "second stage" immigrants who had already learned English and become acculturated in previous settlements in the Midwest. Their interest in the Lutheran church was marginal. Many of the women were scattered throughout the city as live-in servants, dissipating ethnic identification.[7]

From white Seattle's point of view, the most distinct immigrant group was the Japanese. Numbering 6,127 in 1910, Japanese continued to migrate to Seattle in these years. But for them the job market was an experience of severe discrimination, with the vast majority of jobs closed to them altogether. Those who worked for whites found jobs in greatest numbers as domestic servants, both men and women. Japanese-American men also found smaller numbers of jobs as unskilled workers on the railroads, in the building trades, and in saw mills. Others worked as porters, busboys, and dishwashers in white-owned restaurants. A third of Seattle's Japanese-Americans, though, got jobs in a newly thriving Japanese immigrant business sector, in the neighborhood around Jackson Street now known as the International District. In the second decade of the century Japanese-Americans owned and managed a rapidly expanding number of hotels, restaurants, barber shops, bathhouses, and shoe repair shops. Unable to rent or buy housing elsewhere, Japanese-Americans almost all resided downtown in the Japanese business district, with the exception of live-in domestics. Japanese immigrant cultural life blossomed. Railroad, sawmill, and agricultural workers from throughout the region flocked into the neighborhood on the weekends to enjoy noodle restaurants, public bathhouses, and camaraderie. One recalled of the bathhouses:

> Those whose day's work was over relaxed their tired bodies gratefully in the pool. One might feel inclined to start singing a "naniwa-bushi" melody. One after another the usual familiar faces would appear, and people talked about making money, about rumors among neighbors, girls in the Japanese restaurants, and such. The talking rose in pitch and enthusiasm, in a literally naked way.[8]

Fewer than a thousand Chinese-Americans remained in Seattle by this point; most had been driven out by white exclusionary movements in the late nineteenth century. In the immediate pre–World War I years, those who remained almost all lived and worked entirely in what was left of Seattle's old Chinatown downtown, overlapping with the Japanese-American community. There, they ran dozens of small retail businesses, most of them export–import curio shops. Others worked as restaurant laborers, as servants, or in canneries. An illegal sector included gambling houses and houses of prostitution.[9]

Before the war, only 2,296 African-Americans – less than 1 percent of the population – lived in the city. They labored overwhelmingly in service work: half of the men, and four-fifths of the women. The men worked as waiters, servants, porters and laborers in service industries, elevator operators, and janitors; the women as domestics or in laundry work. "Not much they'll let us do," one older African-American Seattle man observed in the 1910s. "Shine shoes, be some rich man's valet. That or work as a common laborer."[10] Before the war a handful of entrepreneurs and professionals, constituting a tiny African-American middle class, enjoyed a certain access to white society only because, along with service workers, they posed little threat. As another African-American resident recalled, "There wasn't an awful lot of prejudice, but there wasn't an awful lot of opportunities either." Housing discrimination restricted African-Americans to two racially mixed neighborhoods: Jackson Street, in the Central District, and Madison Street between 21st and 23rd avenues.[11]

By 1915, 9,000 Seattle workers had joined unions affiliated with the city's Central Labor Council. They were almost all in locals of the American Federation of Labor that represented the most skilled white male workers in the city. Seattle's strongest unions came from the building trades. Others were founded by skilled service workers, such as musicians, butchers, and cooks. The printers' and ironworkers' unions, similarly, represented skilled craft workers. Teamsters and streetcar employees worked in intracity transportation. In the years just before the war new unions of retail clerks from furniture stores, of longshoremen and seamen, and of metal trades workers joined the movement. On the eve of World War I the city's AFL unions had finally established themselves as a presence in the city. They had survived the 1914–15 recession handily and had eyes to expand.[12]

The AFL locals' ethnic character reflected the Anglo- and German-American dominance of the skilled trades from which they emerged. No data on rank-and-file members are available, but a sample of the local AFL leadership in the 1920s reveals that twenty-nine of forty-eight activists were native born. Of the native-born, twenty were of English, Scotch, Irish, or Welsh descent; five were of German. Similarly, of the nineteen identifiably foreign-born unionists, eleven were from the British Isles, three from Germany.[13]

As AFL-affiliated craft unions grew apace in Seattle in the first two decades of the century, so too did their rivals, the Wobblies. The Industrial Workers of the World (IWW) organized themselves on very different structural and ideological lines from those of the AFL. They advocated "one big union" of all workers regardless of skill. They rejected contracts or any "compromise with the ruling class," kept dues low, eschewed long-term bureaucratic trade-union organizations, and advocated revolutionary syndicalism through which workers' industrywide bodies would serve as the seeds of a new society. The general strike was their ultimate weapon. Through it, in theory, the working class would come to power. In the second decade of the century the Wobblies and their philosophies spread like wildfire through the lumber and agricultural camps of the Pacific Northwest. While the AFL grew in the city, the IWW flourished in the country, pressuring through competition the restrictive AFL unions to adapt or be supplanted.[14]

Many in the Seattle AFL movement had since its inception been open to industrial unionism and frustrated by the narrowness of the AFL craft model.[15] Seattle's thriving Socialist Party, moreover, mediated between the AFL and IWW. In 1911, the party received 9 percent of the city's vote for statewide office. Three thousand gathered that year to hear Socialist presidential candidate Eugene V. Debs speak. Statewide, the party counted 4,000 members in 1912 and 1914. More than forty thousand voted for the party's candidate for state attorney general in 1912.[16] The Socialists were able to mediate between conflicting ideological forces in the region's labor movement in part because they placed highest priority on trade-union activity, especially industrial unionism. Unlike the party in other areas of the country, they did not attack the IWW. Nor did their electoral work conflict with the Seattle AFL's political aspirations. Organized labor consistently supported Socialist candidates. Central Labor Council president Hulet Wells ran for mayor on the Socialist Party ticket in 1915, for example. James Duncan, the council's secretary and probably the most highly respected and influential labor figure in the city, was active in the party, as was Harry Ault, editor of the local labor-owned *Seattle Union Record*. Some trade unionists chose to run as independents, but not in opposition to the Socialists' candidates.

By the war's eve, members of Seattle's white working class had established a substantial political presence in the city. In 1915 the Central Labor Council elected its president, T. H. Bolton, to the City Council, and its ex-miner candidate, Robert Bridges, to the city's pivotal Port Commission.[17] In contrast to the years after the war, a relatively harmonious continuity from left to right characterized the Seattle AFL's political spectrum. Relationships between socialists and nonsocialists were not oppositional but, rather, complementary. The center of the movement was prosocialist, and the leaderships of the labor movement and the Socialist Party were in many cases interchangeable.

Yet terms like "conservative" and "radical" assume a single spectrum along which all unionists arrayed themselves, a model that is of limited value in characterizing the Seattle AFL because a fundamental racism cut sharply across socialist–nonsocialist lines. While some Wobblies were actively antiracist, most socialists supported the exclusionary racial practices of the AFL movement. The Seattle labor movement had originated in the 1880s as an anti-Chinese movement. Chinese exclusion was almost the entire program of the Knights of Labor in 1880s Seattle. In the first two decades of the twentieth century the Washington State Federation of Labor, the AFL affiliates' statewide body, lobbied continuously for Japanese exclusion and actively opposed the employment of Asian-Americans in cannery and other employment. All but two of Seattle's AFL locals barred African-Americans on the eve of World War I; none admitted workers of Asian descent, and the local AFL continued to support the legal exclusion of Asian workers from the United States.[18] The 9,000 trade unionists of Seattle were also all male, with the exception of the all-female waitresses' union, with 385 members; the bookbinders', of whom 57 were female, 37 male; the musicians' union, with 200 women; and a smattering of women in the typographers'.[19]

Meanwhile, Japanese-American workers in Seattle built an independent network of workplace organizations completely apart from the white labor movement. Japanese-American shoemakers and barbers formed their own associations in 1907. A *Nihonjin Rodo Kumiai* (Japanese Labor Union) counted 600 members in 1906, though its composition is unclear. By 1918 new organizations included a day workers' association, butchers, and gardeners, and regional unions of timberworkers and railroad laborers. These "unions," sometimes translated as "associations," shaded over into a range of Japanese-American small businessmen's organizations of laundry owners, hotel operators, restaurant owners, and dye workers.[20]

Radical ideas abounded in the Japanese immigrant community in the second decade of the century. Its participants describe a political ferment and thriving radical intellectual culture. Seattle was more politicized, they remember, than its southern counterpart San Francisco. A proliferation of Japanese-language newspapers and magazines produced in Seattle sold briskly. The editor of the local *Taihoku Nippo* (Great Northern Daily News) was a socialist, as were the president of the *Hokubei Jiji* (North American News) and the 1915 president of the Japanese Labor Union. Many of these immigrants were attracted to the ideas of Sen Katayama, the premier Japanese socialist, who came to the United States in 1914. As one recalled, "Obscure Socialists who were influenced by the teaching of Sen Katayama but couldn't live up to their ambitions all came to Seattle from various places, seeking the atmosphere of freedom." "It was a period when men of youthful vigor, giving no thought to money, discussed life and ideals and immigrant political problems lustily," he remembered. "At the very least it was the dream of those 'Meiji bohemians' to orate in the cause of right, becoming statesmen or ministers or attorneys." Japanese-American workers shared many of the intellectual currents and organizational gains of white workers, who appear to have been unaware of the thriving world of Japanese-American radicalism in their midst.[21]

The war boom

World War I transformed the Seattle economy, and that transformation was the key to the upheavals of 1919. The root cause was relatively simple: shipyards. When the war broke out in Europe, U.S. shipping firms lost access to European merchant ships, and profits of both shippers and exporters plummeted. To rescue the U.S. economy, the federal government stepped in to construct hastily an independent U.S. merchant fleet. In 1916 it created the United States Shipping Board and its subsidiary, the Emergency Fleet Corporation, to oversee and finance the actual construction of ships.

They would be owned by the U.S. government but constructed in private shipyards. Lucrative cost-plus contracts sped out to the nation's shipyards.[22]

Seattle's yards were one of the primary beneficiaries of this outflow of federal funds. By August 1918 Seattle firms operated six yards for steel ships and ten for wooden. These yards produced ships at a tremendous rate. In 1918 alone the city's shipyards built sixty-one steel freighters and thirty-five wooden ships. By early summer of that year they launched a ship, on the average, every forty-six hours. All told, by the end of the war Seattle had produced one-fourth of all the tonnage produced for the government during the war.[23]

Most important, the shipyards almost overnight created a mass production sector in Seattle that employed tens of thousands of workers. By October 1918 around 31,500 men were directly employed in the yards, and another 4,000 in subcontracting shops. The financial scale was immense. The yards paid out $4.6 million in payroll a month at their height, all in federal funds.[24]

Nor was the rest of the city left in the economic dust. By 1917 most sectors of the Seattle economy were bustling, as the war heated up the whole U.S. economy. Jobs in local bread baking, flour milling, and brick work doubled or nearly doubled between 1914 and 1919. At the same time the dollars spent by the tens of thousands of shipyard workers rippled through the Seattle economy. The service sector, especially, benefited. Thirty thousand newly arrived shipyard workers patronized restaurants, laundries, barber shops, and boarding houses.[25]

This boom in employment created a tremendous labor shortage in Seattle. For employers, there was a great deal of money to be made during the war, but only if the necessary workers could be hired. Fifteen thousand men, meanwhile, had left the city for the military. This created unprecedented opportunities for working people to find new and better jobs. The War Labor Committee of the Seattle Chamber of Commerce estimated in September 1918 a labor shortage of 14,500 in the city, including 5,000 in the shipyards, 2,000 in metalworking, 4,000 in the building trades, and 500 each in food products, clothing, and lumber.[26]

Tens of thousands of workers flowed into Seattle during the war, looking for jobs in the high-paying shipyards. The population grew to 315,312, an increase of almost 33 percent over that of 1910. Skilled metal trades workers, white and male, from all over the country and recruited by the shipyards and government agents, got the best jobs in the yards. A second group of white male skilled workers transferred out of related trades and into the shipyards. Employers reported an "acute shortage of plumbers and painters," for example, "as they have been attracted to the shipyards by the high labor scale." Other men, trained in completely different trades, learned new skills in order to take advantage of shipyard jobs. The mass of shipyard workers, though, were unskilled white men drawn from the pool of seasonal workers who ordinarily labored in the hinterland but who swelled into the city to capture steady, well-paying jobs in the yards. It was only frosting on the cake that shipyard jobs offered draft exemption.[27]

Throughout the war, white workers continued to swirl about the city from job to job, constantly in search of better employment. Employers complained in 1918 of "an unusual condition of restlessness disturbing to all other industries. The wage scale advanced in one industry after the other; and the men followed that rising scale." This produced what they called "the disturbing question of turnover" as workers realized that if they quit their jobs, often another, better one could be obtained.[28]

White women arrived by the thousands from all over the United States in search of the higher wages and good jobs rumored to be had in Seattle. Once in town, they, too, quit with alacrity. "Women are becoming migratory, and are following the ascending labor scale," the Chamber of Commerce lamented. Yet white women were not able to follow that scale straight up. Despite great shortages, women were not employed in significant numbers in the city's wartime shipyards, metal trades shops, lumber industry, transfer and local cartage, or dock jobs, although there were a few exceptions. Instead, white women found plentiful jobs in the traditional sectors of white women's waged work: sales, clerical, and restaurant work; food processing; and shoe and clothing making. And they quit readily. Laundries, especially, reported a high rate of turnover. An estimated 6,000 women moved into jobs formerly held by men, but these were in areas in which women had already been employed. In restaurants and hotels, for example, women replaced male waiters, clerks, bellboys, and janitors. Slightly more skilled work opened up in baking, printing, and meat cutting. White women could find even more desirable jobs within the white-collar field, in insurance, automobile, and real estate sales, where "women more than ever [were] being employed," the Chamber of Commerce reported. Contrary to the situation for white men, though, employers reported no shortage when it came to women workers.[29]

Japanese-American workers, male and female, still found almost all areas of the Seattle economy closed to them, including all the war-boom industrial work. But the service-sector demands created by the shipyard employees allowed for expansion by the Japanese-American–owned small businesses that serviced those workers. A Japanese-American resident, Monica Sone, recalled in her autobiography that when her father bought a downtown hotel in 1918, "the building fairly burst with war workers and servicemen" who begged to sleep in the hallways. The number of hotels owned by Japanese-Americans grew to 194, retail groceries to 125, restaurants to 64, and shoe repair shops to 57, bringing a degree of measured, though precarious, prosperity to their owners and creating jobs for the Japanese-Americans they employed.[30]

The Japanese-American male owners of these businesses, such as Sone's father, followed a common path. They arrived from Japan in the early 1910s, worked in the region as day laborers for several years, accumulated and borrowed small nest eggs of capital, and then bought restaurants or other small service businesses in Seattle during the war boom. Kamekichi Shibayama, for example, came to Seattle in 1912 and found work as a dishwasher in Tacoma, in Seattle, and on a Bainbridge Island farm. Then he ran a cafe in Seattle and in 1918 bought a cheap 102-room hotel that catered to working men. Most of these Japanese-American men originally emigrated single and then, as they established themselves, sent for wives who had remained in Japan, returned to Japan on brief wife-seeking expeditions, or arranged for "picture brides" to be sent to Seattle. Approximately 200 to 300 Japanese women arrived each year during the war as arranged brides. Depending on the situation of their husbands, Japanese-American wives quickly undertook waged work or joined in family businesses alongside their husbands, intermixing both with child rearing.[31]

African-American workers found employment opportunities just as tightly sealed against them as did Japanese-Americans. No "great migration" brought African-Americans to Seattle during the war. The African-American population increased by only a few hundred. Seattle African-Americans gained access to a few hundred new, better jobs as shipyard laborers, in navy yards and as postal clerks, and on two occasions when employers hired African-Americans as strikebreakers. But Seattle's war-induced labor substitution could also work against African-American employment. In service jobs, the rapidity of turnover in some cases meant that employers substituted white women for African-American women and men. Employers fired African-American male elevator operators and waiters, for example, and replaced them with white women.[32]

With continuing African-American migration to Seattle, however small, the tenor of black–white race relations in the city changed for the worse. Horace Cayton Jr., who would later become a prominent sociologist and co-author of *Black Metropolis*, recalled that "race prejudice was spreading in Seattle at that time, and many restaurants that had previously served Negroes now began to refuse them service." In 1919 police arrested Cayton, who was African-American, for refusing to sit in the segregated gallery of a Seattle theater. The policeman, an old friend of his father's, warned, "[Y]ou know as well as I do that things have changed around town. . . . It's not like it was years ago, when you and I were pioneers in this town." Before the war Cayton's father, Horace Cayton Sr., also African-American, had been a prominent member of the Seattle political scene and editor of a Republican weekly with a widespread white readership. As wartime tensions rose, he began to publish more and more stories opposed to racism. When he ran a front-page story excoriating a lynching, his white patrons scattered, and he was ruined economically. From partial acceptance by the city's white middle class he fell to working as a janitor and living in the back of a hotel that his wife owned.[33]

The war ferment

The wartime labor shortage strengthened the bargaining power of most white working people immensely. They could risk unionization with less fear of reprisal and if fired could find another job. If they went out on strike their employers could not easily replace them. And because the employers probably were making money rapidly during the boom, it was easier for them to meet employees' demands. In this way the war transformed the balance of power between labor and capital in Seattle. The result was a tremendous outburst of activism, a dramatic explosion of working-class consciousness, and an internal transformation of the Seattle labor movement.

The primary, and most important, site of this uprising was the shipyards. Shipyard employers, in consultation with the federal government, capitulated on the closed shop question – granting that all employees would be union members – at the inception of the war. With their contracts on a cost-plus basis, and with labor scarce, the incentive to fight the unions was weak, and shipyard union locals emerged on a gargantuan scale. The most spectacular was Boilermakers' Local #104. In 1916 it had only 80 members; by 1917, 7,000, and by war's end, anywhere from 15,000 to 20,000. It proudly claimed to be the largest local anywhere in the world. Machinists Lodge #79 represented another 3,500 to 4,500 members, up from a hundred or so before the war. The shipyard laborers reported another several thousand. Other craft union locals representing workers in the yards – blacksmiths, shipwrights, ship painters – reported 500 to 1,000.[34] This growth was replicated throughout the country. Everywhere, unions in industries most directly affected by the war grew most rapidly.[35]

The 100 percent union atmosphere in the yards contributed to a highly politicized workplace culture. Among the 35,000 new shipyard workers were thousands, perhaps tens of thousands of IWW- or radical-sympathizing men who had migrated in from jobs in lumber, agriculture, and mining. The effect of their concentration in the yards was electric. Jobs were plentiful, radical ideas equally so, and a sense of celebration and camaraderie was pervasive. One participant remembered:

> What men and what talk! Recall the long, long rows of outdoor toilets with no doors. To sit there for 20 minutes or longer was the usual procedure. (I think of it as the coffee break.) The conversation and the essays on the walls were a commentary on working class spirit. They did not hesitate to express their opinions of the ships, wages, bosses, fellow workers and government.[36]

The line between the AFL and IWW was suddenly permeable. The ship-yard locals were affiliated with AFL internationals, but they achieved quasi-industrial union representation through the city's Metal Trades Council. During the war the council represented 40,000 organized workers, over four times the entire unionized labor force in Seattle in 1915, and well over half all the workers represented in the Central Labor Council in 1918 and 1919. The Seattle AFL movement by 1918 was completely different from what it had been before the war. It had a huge mass production base organized in semi-industrial unions. To the shipyard workers, radical in-dustrial unionism spoke to their interests; the Wobbly concept of the "point of production" where exploitation happened and where militant action could best wound the capitalists made clear sense.[37]

Wartime union fever extended far beyond the metal trades. White work-ers throughout the city, as their bargaining power increased, "saw their opportunities and they took them."[38] This meant both exponential growth in the prewar unions and a mushrooming of new locals in previously unorganized trades. Workers flocked into unions, struck readily, and won significant wage gains. In December 1916, for example, 700 steamboatmen struck for 10 months and won a wage increase. The next month 120 streetcar cleaners walked out and won their raise in 4 days. The issue was not always wages. In October 1917, 400 steelyard laborers walked out to force the reinstatement of a fellow worker. Their employer capitulated in 2 days. By mid-1917 the pace of strikes was feverish. That summer streetcar men, express drivers, candy workers, newsboys, bindery workers, butch-ers, and building trades workers all walked out. Though the gains were uneven – the candy workers, for example, could not get their employers to recognize their union or reinstate their organizers, but they did win a wage increase – the trend was toward union advancement. Each victory, moreover, reinforced the cycle, as more workers seized the chance to better their situation. By early 1919 entire blocs of the Seattle economy were 100 percent organized and had achieved the closed shop – not only white workers in the shipyards, but those in the building trades, transportation, commercial laundries, print shops, tailoring, and thousands of white provision-, amusement-, and service-trade workers.[39]

This explosion of organization produced a dramatic internal trans-formation within the AFL movement as well. Throughout the country, as Louis Lorwin notes, the very rapidity of the gains fed the unions' popu-larity. New members, new to trade-union traditions, brought high expec-tations to their organizations and "were ready for aggressive action. In many locals ... there was a turnover in leadership which brought to the fore new men." In Seattle, leadership turnover in some cases meant radical officers' egging on a relatively less militant rank and file; such was the case in the barbers' and bakers' unions, for example. In other cases cautious leaders fought hard to restrain a barely contained revolutionary fervor in the ranks. This was especially true in the metal trades. Building trades locals, who met in their own Building Trades Council, were less radical, though militants seethed within many locals, including the painters, millmen, and some locals of the carpenters. And across the city, IWW "borers" livened up more staid AFL local meetings.[40]

The wartime upsurge spilled over far beyond the range of workers embraced by trade unionism before the war. Nationwide, "more important than the overall size of the union movement," David Montgomery points out, "was the influx of workers who had previously been on the margins of union organization, at best."[41] This meant, in part, unskilled white men in trades where only the skilled crafts had enjoyed unions before the war. Seattle's white building laborers, for example, gained union recognition during the war. Equally important, the war boom created opportunities for thousands of white women to participate in unions – nearly 400,000 women, nationally, belonged to unions between 1915 and 1920.[42] In Seattle, the number of female trade unionists, all white, grew to approximately 6,000, or 10 percent of the city's total AFL union membership.

Some of this growth came in prewar unions. The waitresses grew to 618; the bookbinders now counted 60 women and 40 men. Other all-new, all-female unions arrived on the scene with the war, like the 1,000-member laundry workers' and the telephone operators' with 900 members. Still other new unions represented large numbers of women in mixed locals: the tailors, with 200 women and 300 men; boot and shoe workers, with 50 women and 175 men; and butter, egg, and produce workers, whose 175 members included 19 women. Two factors converged to produce this boom. First, women appear to have been just as desirous as men of the benefits of unionization, and it was now less risky to obtain. Second, the Central Labor Council, under pressure from women activists, earmarked funds for an organizer specifically for women. In a few cases male workers in a particular industry explicitly fostered the creation of affiliated female locals. The most contested such case was that of the "Lady Barbers." Seattle's AFL-affiliated male barbers defied their international, which explicitly forbade the admittance of women, and helped white women barbers organize their own 100-member local, to which the Central Labor Council granted a charter.[43]

The color bar also fell for the first time. In 1916, waterfront employers broke a strike of the International Longshoremen's Association (ILA) by employing 1,400 scabs. Three hundred of the strikebreakers were African-American men imported from Kansas City, St. Louis, and New Orleans. The white longshoremen concluded that as long as their union excluded people of color, employers could use race against them. When they regained union recognition in 1917 they admitted the African-American longshoremen. Much of the support for letting them in came from IWW sympathizers who had come to work on the docks and joined the ILA.

While African-American longshoremen evidently shied away from IWW membership, with Wobbly support African-Americans gained critical seats on the union's internal committees and actively engaged in the union's policy debates, although they numbered only 300 of the 4,000-member local. In 1919 the ILA sent the first and only African-American delegate to the Central Labor Council from its local. A great deal of white opposition to African-American longshoremen persisted, however. Some white workers, for example, quit rather than work with African-Americans.[44]

The other white unions continued to ban Asian-American members. On a number of occasions during the war years, though, Japanese-American workers extended themselves in support of white unionists. During the 1916 longshoremen's strike the Japanese Labor Association told the Central Labor Council it would not provide Japanese scabs, though all the white unions involved excluded workers of Japanese descent. In other smaller, isolated cases, individuals or small groups of Japanese-American workers refused to scab on strikes by whites. In June 1919 two Japanese-American busboys walked out of a restaurant in solidarity with white workers while a number of white men stayed in. A month later Japanese-American workers sent by an employment agency to break a garden workers' strike similarly refused to scab. These may have been acts of self-protection as well as of solidarity. Given the barely sleeping giant of anti-Asian violence in the Northwest, Japanese-Americans were no doubt well aware of the possible consequences of strikebreaking against powerful white unions.[45]

The Seattle AFL movement was so very expansionary and successful in the war years, then, in part because the wartime labor shortage made strikes and workplace demands less risky for many working people. Inflation lent an immediacy to workers' wage demands as a 70 percent rise in prices between 1914 and the war's end in November 1918 constantly threatened to wipe out any gains. Structural adaptations within the movement – including the admission of unskilled white workers, the willingness to admit African-Americans, the commitment to white women as union members (including funding a special organizer attuned to the concerns of women workers), and the semi-industrial structure of the Metal Trades and Building Trades Councils in part compensating for the fractionary effects of craft unionism – contributed to union growth. Successes snowballed; demands rose; expectations rose still further and political consciousness became newly fluid; the world was changing fast, and for the better. As John Williamson, a shipyard worker in Seattle at the time, recalled, "The workers were astir with a new feeling of strength and with the realization of their own power."[46]

Finally, ideologies celebrating solidarity, working-class power, and the glimmering possibility of a "workers' state" emboldened and inspired working people. There was "a social consciousness, a militancy, a dream of a Good World" abroad, another former shipyard worker remembered.[47]

As his last phrase suggests, a utopian element ran through many workers' philosophies. The idea of some kind of socialism or worker-run society was pervasive in trade-union circles. Many within the Seattle working class had a mounting sense of their collective power as a class – some form of class consciousness.

The range within the movement was vast: from individual rank-and-file workers seeing an opportunity to better themselves through marginal participation in union activity; to the shipyard and dockside radicals who saw everything in terms of class exploitation and believed that the revolution was at hand; to the usually wary business unionist officials of the locals who had to keep up with the spirit of the times if they were to hang on to their jobs in union officialdom but who also themselves got caught up in the excitement of the moment, saw working-class power mounting rapidly, and just as easily as the next person could be found dreaming of a possible workers' society.

All these currents within the AFL movement were negotiated within the Central Labor Council. As the main governing body of the Seattle white working-class movement, the Central Labor Council was the crucial site where delegates debated and implemented overall strategy. The war brought a sudden shift in the council's internal power dynamics. Metal trades delegates now far outnumbered those from other sectors, and they shifted the balance of power far to the left, in part under still further leftward pressure from the IWW sympathizers who disrupted proceedings with hoots and howls from the gallery. Militant, radical stands issued forth. The Central Labor Council heartily endorsed the Bolshevik Revolution in 1917. On May Day 1917 it endorsed a ten-minute national general strike in support of San Francisco radical unionist Tom Mooney, jailed for allegedly throwing a bomb at a 1916 Preparedness Day Parade. Twenty-five thousand Seattle workers observed the work stoppage.[48]

The ferment did not take place in meetings alone. The streets of Seattle seethed with working-class political culture. By 1918 as many as 10,000 workers gathered every Sunday to hear public debates in which nationally known leftist speakers participated. "Hardly a week went by without a meeting at either the Labor Temple or the Longshoremen's Hall," John Williamson remembered. "At such meetings I heard John Reed, William Z. Foster, L[ouise] Bryant, . . . E[lizabeth] G[urley] Flynn, Ralph Chaplin . . . and many others."[49] Hundreds of soap boxers preached on street corners and at plant gates to anyone who would listen. A proliferation of workers' publications flooded the city, from crude leaflets and graffiti on the outhouse walls, to the monthly and weekly newsletters put out by activists of a variety of political stripes, dozens of foreign-language publications, all the way through to the labor movement's own daily newspaper, *The Seattle Union Record*, owned by the Central Labor Council and union locals.[50]

Class, in other words, was quite visible to working people in Seattle. In

1918 50,000 people marched in Seattle's Labor Day parade, one-sixth of the entire 315,312 population of the city.[51] By the war's end in late 1918 the Central Labor Council represented 130 union locals. The total number of workers represented had grown from 9,000 in 1915 to 40,000 in 1917 to 60,000 or 65,000 by early 1919.[52] The AFL movement had emerged as a tightly organized economic force and was a power to be reckoned with.

The same thing was happening all over the country. Workers in Seattle knew that they were part of a national, indeed international uprising of working-class activism. Total union membership in the United States grew from 2,607,000 in 1915 to 5,110,000 by 1920.[53] Seattle workers, like those all over the world, saw the Bolsheviks in Russia not just fantasize or theorize about but actually succeed in a revolution, and they were tremendously inspired by the Bolsheviks' attempt to build a true "workers' state" in which ruling classes would be obsolete. Speakers from workers' movements throughout the world passed through Seattle and spoke of their achievements. The pages of the *Union Record* abounded with international news from a working-class point of view; activists spoke of Ireland, California, Russia, West Virginia, Canada in far-ranging appeals to international class consciousness.[54] Nineteen-eighteen Seattle was one of those moments like 1886 or 1968 when activism and consciousness erupt, when the whole is greater than the sum of its parts, when the world seems to be changing very quickly, and anything seems possible.[55]

The limits to growth

It would be easy, though, to overstate the extent of solidarity. One story is instructive: During the war Horace Cayton Jr. attended his first meeting of the longshoremen's local, to which he had just been admitted. After the main business of the local had been transacted, the secretary announced that he had a letter from the newly formed Lady Barbers' Union. The women were asking for a loan of $200; what action did the longshoremen want to take?

> There was a long silence during which the faces of the men on the platform were just as long. . . .
> Finally a clear, emotionless voice from the back of the room said in slow measured tones, "Fuck the lady barbers."
> The president banged his gavel and said, "So ordered and it shall be done."[56]

The longshoremen, opening their doors, though reluctantly, to African-Americans, were not, on the other hand, necessarily interested in solidarity with their sisters. Solidarity had sharp limits, and we should not underestimate them. Not just local attitudes such as these but the national structure of the American Federation of Labor imposed major limitations on the expansion of Seattle trade unions. One reason the lady barbers had to come begging to the longshoremen was, after all, that the barbers' international did not admit women (the Central Labor Council had issued their charter). A national citizenship clause imposed by the international similarly precluded the admittance of Japanese-American barbers, who were not allowed under U.S. law to become citizens.[57]

Another example, this time from Horace Cayton Sr., is equally instructive. In March 1918, Cayton wrote a page-one editorial on the Tom Mooney case for his African-American community newspaper. Everyone is up in arms about the Mooney case, Cayton wrote; Mooney is perceived as a great martyr to the working class, and hundreds of thousands of workers all over the country are walking out in his support. But what of the hundreds of lynchings taking place yearly in this country? Why doesn't anyone care about them?[58] From a Seattle African-American point of view, in other words, the great advances of the white working-class movement were not necessarily a wonderful thing at all. Indeed, the unions' success could mean an even greater ability of whites to exclude African-Americans from employment. Cayton noted on another occasion unions' agitation for equal pay for equal work for men and women. "Now the colored women who seek employment find that such firms and concerns who will give them work are not inclined to give the colored women the same pay as they do the white women."[59]

Seattle's AFL trade unions often opposed the employment of workers of color and of white women during the war. A Chamber of Commerce survey of labor shortages claimed that trade-union opposition prevented many employers from hiring women.[60] Most AFL internationals had exclusionary racial bars on their rule books and did not lift them with the war. The boilermakers' international, for example, refused to admit African-American workers despite their increasing presence in the industry, while Seattle's shipyard unions "successfully combatted" African-American employment in the yards.[61]

The marginalization of Asian-Americans, African-Americans, and white women was built into the very structure and self-definition of the "labor movement." AFL trade unions had been structured since their inception on the basis of craft exclusion, in which a group of workers restricted the labor supply, controlled apprenticeships, and increased the bargaining power of those on the inside. Industrial unions, by contrast, embraced all workers on the basis of uniting all employees of a given firm. But outside of the brewing industry and mining, they made little headway in the early twentieth century. In Seattle, AFL activists stretched the two models during the war to embrace less-skilled transportation workers and the tens of thousands of unskilled white shipyard workers. But even that left vast areas of the Seattle economy almost completely untouched by trade unionism. No unions represented the city's 3,600 female store clerks, 2,000 female teachers, or 3,000 female domestic servants, nor its 9,000 female clerical workers. For a total of 22,000 women wage earners in Seattle no union was available.[62]

The roots of this structural problem were deep. By the early twentieth century the trade unions' root definitions of "the workers" and "the labor movement" conceptualized work in terms of manufacturing, or at the very least work that involved heavy manual labor. The visual imagery of the movement reinforced this – the heaving chest of the IWW's symbolic worker towering over capital in Wobbly cartoons; or the somewhat more sedate but manly AFL hero, tools in hand, standing nobly at his workbench.[63] These images in some ways accurately represented the movement's strength in manufacturing and the interests of white male workers, but at the same time such a conceptualization of "labor" entrapped it in a limited constituency.

Many other factors kept women out of the labor movement or marginalized them once they were within it. Trade-union men subscribed to the "family wage" ideal, which held that a single male breadwinner should earn enough to support a dependent, domestic wife. The family wage ideal underlay many trade-union men's outright hostility to women's participation in the labor force, just as it ideologically undermined women's full and equal participation in the labor movement. Many men were suspicious of employers' efforts to decrease skilled male workers' power by introducing less-skilled female workers. The culture of male trade unions, at the same time, turned away many women. Meetings might be held in saloons, for example, in which any woman who entered was presumed to be a prostitute. Men dominated local meetings with both a superior mastery of the nuances of Robert's Rules of Order and their own socialization into public speaking. Despite all these barriers, and many others, Seattle's unions did embrace most of the city's female manufacturing employees by early 1919. It was in the new sectors of women' employment in the early twentieth century – service, clerical, and sales work – that the labor movement failed to reach women.[64]

Nor was the AFL movement concerned with domestic service, the single largest area of women's employment for the entire nineteenth century and well into the twentieth. Domestic service was where women of color, especially, labored. On the west coast, Asian- and African-American men worked as domestics as well, along with large numbers of Scandinavian-American women. The AFL unions did not view the home as a workplace, with its own dynamics of employer and employee. Still less did the unions embrace women who worked in the home for no wages at all. In 1919 Seattle, there were 90,000 females over the age of ten not working for pay. We can presume that almost all engaged in housework. Teenagers and older women were by no means exempt from this job. Even those who hired servants still performed a large measure of housework. The AFL movement, in other words, did not conceptualize women's unwaged work of consumption, along with housecleaning and child care, as labor in its own right. This omission would prove crucial to the success with which the Seattle AFL politicized consumption in the postwar decade.[65] It is not preposterous to expect that the labor movement might have embraced all women's concerns as workers on full and equal terms. As Susan Levine has shown, the Knights of Labor, the AFL's predecessor in the 1880s, was structurally flexible enough to include locals of domestic servants and of housewives, and general mixed locals of women of a variety of occupations.[66]

But while facing clearly the limitations imposed by the men who built the Seattle labor movement, it is important not to lose sight of the larger picture. The working-class movement in Seattle, despite its forward march in the war years, was still deeply embattled in its oppositional relationship with the employing class. Furthermore, while the war in Europe had produced the economic boom and strengthened organized labor, it was not an unmixed blessing. The same federal government that poured billions of dollars into the shipyards, ran employment services, and courted skilled workers had other interests too. At all levels, the government was vitally concerned that the new wartime conditions favoring labor not turn into a Bolshevik revolution on American soil, especially because great numbers of working people opposed U.S. entry into the war.[67]

The answer to both problems, for the government, was severe repression. Entire arenas of working-class self-activity were declared illegal during the war and suppressed accordingly as "subversive." Repression in Seattle was especially fierce. Government officials routinely broke up union and leftist street meetings. In January 1919, for example, police used clubs to break up a meeting, co-sponsored by the machinists' union and the Socialist Party, to protest U.S. intervention in Russia. The Socialist Party, because it maintained its antiwar position throughout the conflict, received special attention. By 1919 its leadership, both statewide and local, had been imprisoned under wartime espionage and sedition laws, including Hulet Wells, former Central Labor Council president, and Emil Herman, the state party secretary. The government, though, hated the IWW even more. Wobbly meetings in Seattle were broken up at least once a month. In the summer of 1917 2,000 to 3,000 Minute Men, volunteer vigilantes working with the U.S. Department of Justice, destroyed the Wobblies' printing press. Twenty men dressed like soldiers similarly destroyed the Seattle presses that printed the *Union Record* and Socialist Party *Call*. Repression of the IWW became an obsession. Police officers were ordered, for example, to "make diligent efforts and arrest parties found putting up, or having in their possession," a 2″ × 4″ IWW sticker in support of political prisoners. As they did throughout the country, federal officials in Seattle staged mass arrests and deported at least 150 noncitizens whom they accused of being radicals. Government bodies charged with putting away radicals included the Justice Department, Army Intelligence, Naval Intelligence, and Seattle police, all working hand in glove with the Seattle

Chamber of Commerce and a near-army of thousands of Minute Men, who stationed themselves in hotels and workplaces throughout the city to sniff out subversives. To advocate radical ideas in World War I Seattle was a dangerous act.[68]

The general strike

The Seattle general strike of February 1919 was in some ways the climax of the tremendous growth and political expansiveness of the Seattle working-class movement during the war years. It was the last great moment of defiance before Seattle labor crossed the line into the 1920s and began its long slide downward. But in important ways the strike already took place over that line. Both organized labor and the city's large-scale employers in Seattle knew, by the beginning of 1919, that the tide was turning, that the political–economic context was changing rapidly, and that actions taken in the crucial months ahead would determine the relative powers of each for years to come. World War I had ended in November 1918, but the battle at home raged on. "People who think the war is over are wrong," warned Jimmy Duncan, the secretary of the Central Labor Council. "The war has just begun."[69]

The shipyards had without question crossed over into the postwar era, and it was there that the general strike movement began. During the war, a new federal mediating body known as the Macy Board had controlled labor negotiations in shipyards nationwide. Seattle's shipyard workers, despite closed-shop conditions and a 1917 strike, had been unable to wrest wage gains from the board while the war was on. Inflation, meanwhile, skyrocketed. All sides knew that when the board announced a new wage agreement at the war's end, an explosion would result.[70]

The decision, when it was finally announced in October 1918, incensed Seattle's shipyard workers. It granted only meager wage increases, biased toward the skilled crafts. The mass of unskilled workers got nothing. Shipyard workers felt betrayed both by the yard owners, from whom they were used to a certain complacency and tolerance, and by the federal government, which they had viewed as their ally in pressuring the owners. Neither expectation proved accurate. In any event, the new postwar economic situation was entirely different. The federal government issued no new orders for ships. The city's wooden shipyards closed in January 1919. While the fate of the steel yards was unclear, time was certainly on the employers' side, and a shipyard strike was in some ways in their interest, as they would not have to pay striking workers. Despite all these ominous economic signs, Seattle's 35,000 shipyard workers, in a rage, walked out on January 21, 1919.[71]

It swiftly became clear to both the city's unionized workers and their employers that this was more than just a battle over shipyard wages. The strike became a challenge to the entire strength of organized labor in Seattle. Though the shipyards were completely shut down, at least 40,000 idled workers plus their families had to be fed every day the strike continued. The employers, though, refused to budge or even talk. Within days the Metal Trades Council turned to the Central Labor Council and asked that a general strike of all organized workers in Seattle be called in support of the shipyard strikers. A series of debates on whether to call such a strike commenced.[72]

A. E. Miller first presented the Metal Trades' case to the central council on January 22. Seattle needed a general strike, he argued, "to insure the future existence of the metal trades – and all other Seattle labor organizations." He asked for "a demonstration of power which would convince Northwest management of labor's will to survive," because the city's employers "were attempting to destroy the shipyard unions."[73] This was the core issue. Unionists who voted for the strike shared his view that a mass open shop drive in reaction to labor's gains during the war was imminent and, indeed, inevitable. As Otto Dines of the plasterers argued, "When we plasterers voted unanimously for the general strike ... we did it in self protection. We knew that if the metal trades were forced to their knees our turn would come next."[74] Seattle's unionists, in other words, were groping toward the meaning of solidarity in a context of both unprecedented new powers and heretofore unnavigated dangers. " 'Solidarity of labor' was the slogan reported by speaker after speaker at Wednesday's council meeting in support of the general strike movement," the Seattle *Star* reported.[75] Ed T. Levi of the cooks later recalled: "The propaganda committee of big business was extremely busy trying to show that Labor was losing its solidarity, so the strike was called to show where Labor was at."[76] The barbers' local similarly reported, "We realize that the almost phenomenal growth of our membership and comfortable conditions we have acquired are entirely due to the support of the organized labor movement in this vicinity ... so consequently we felt in duty bound to support those who support us." Again, "solidarity" contained purely practical elements. "It would be suicidal to alienate that support from us," the barbers concluded; just as it would be suicide for the plasterers to wait, passively, for the employers to come after them, too.[77]

Seattle unionists were well aware that theirs was more than a local struggle. "If Seattle gets away with this, the war will be carried further than the confines of Seattle," Jimmy Duncan, among many others, argued. "The eyes of the nation are fixed on Seattle."[78] The city's employers, following with alarm the strike deliberations, viewed the strike equally firmly as a national test case. On January 18, one highly situated manager observed, "As yet no decision as to what they will do has been reached by the shipyard owners. It is anticipated, however, that the yards will be shut down as the present is as good a time as any to see whether our local yards can exist under peace conditions or whether the Unions will run them out of business."[79] On February 1, three days before the imminent strike, he reported, "[It] appears as if the federal government was using Seattle as an experimental station to find out just how much radicalism and unrest there is in labor, and just what to prepare for and expect in the big industrial centers in the East."[80] Horace Cayton Sr., whose basic attitude was "a plague on both your houses," editorialized: "It looks very much like that those precipitating the impending strike are doing so to test the real strength of organized labor and the employers are not much opposed to it because they too are anxious to test out the strength of organized labor."[81]

Not all Seattle trade unionists were eager to take that test. "I want to enter my protest against the mis-called sympathetic strike," dissented Louis Nash of the retail clerks. "I show no sympathy for my starving fellow man by agreeing to starve with him." Rather, he felt, the unions could best serve "brotherly love" by sharing with those less well-off. In any case, he felt, the sanctity of the contract must be upheld or employers would lose confidence in labor's promises.[82] T. H. Bolton, president of the Seattle City Council and delegate from the bakers' union, erupted in anger at labor council delegates who champed voraciously at the bit for a general strike. "We older men don't want to destroy in one day what it has taken us 20 years to build up."[83]

A third, larger group of trade unionists supported the strike but defined solidarity still differently. They argued that it was not right for all the city's unions to sacrifice themselves just for the good of the metal trades. Any general strike decision should include reciprocity demands that would serve all the unions. Members of this camp – which included weaker unions, such as those of the telephone operators and waiters, and radical ones, such as those of the millwrights and longshoremen – pointed out that their own positions were just as precarious, their own demands just as pressing as those of the metal trades. Ultimately they acceded to Duncan's arguments about the necessity of defending the immediate situation of the metal trades and endorsed the strike.[84]

The reciprocity group, though, was aware of what the Seattle AFL movement was doing by calling the general strike. No tactic was neutral. Any choice contained a host of implications for the movement. The Seattle general strike entailed a decision by the Central Labor Council, first, to throw the fullest resources of the AFL movement behind the city's mass production unions in the metal trades; and second, to do so with a tactic based at the point of production, the strike. It also threw female trade unionists' support behind men's; and the local-market sector unionists' support behind the national-market sector. This was solidarity of a particular form.

As the proposed strike date, February 4, approached, the votes of the council's individual affiliated locals rolled in. There was soon little question as to whether the strike would take place. Almost all unions reported either unanimous or strong majority votes in favor. Those very few who did not were the least radical. The musicians, for example, voted 165 to 45 against the strike, but 139 to 34 to participate if the other unions voted yes. The retail clerks said flatly no. The web pressmen reported a split vote and withdrew from the council.[85]

Voting for a general strike was one thing, pulling it off in a city of more than 300,000 another. While the strike was the classic tactic at the point of production, using it successfully in Seattle also meant a brief but large-scale foray into the realm of consumption that would prove important after the strike. By early 1919 at least 30,000 single male workers in Seattle ate all their meals in restaurants. But the restaurants were almost 100 percent organized among white workers, and so if their workers struck, the men would have no food. The Central Labor Council faced an immense logistical challenge. Initially, the waitresses' union asked that it be exempt from the strike for precisely this reason. A second possibility was to open the city's restaurants up under union control. The unions finally decided, though, to run their own kitchens, in union and community halls throughout the city.[86]

When the strike began, the unions commenced their somewhat jerry-rigged system. Members of the cooks' union prepared the food in the kitchens of sympathetic restaurants. Teamsters and other unionists then transported it across the city to twenty-one "eating halls," including the Labor Temple, Longshoremen's and Carpenters' Halls, and the Masonic Temple. For its participants, the success of this system had more than practical importance. Listen to Ed T. Levi of the cooks' union on the eve of the strike:

> This is going to be a big lesson from the culinary workers to the people of Seattle. We are going to show them that with a three hour day for the cooks and waiters, we can feed the people with 35 cent meals and make a big enough profit to supply a big share of all the free meals that may become necessary under the stress of poverty. . . . And if this strike begins to last a while, we will take over regular restaurants and put a little more style into the handling of food.

He continued:

> About this time the big capitalists back east will be sort of worried. We are well enough organized to handle what we need for a short work-day of three or four hours, and quit competing with the Japs and other peoples and keep what we produce to make this spot of the Earth a garden of Eden.[87]

Levi's comments capture wonderfully the tenor of the general strike. Levi represented one of the most skilled, exclusionary craft unions in the city; yet here he was waxing eloquent on the utopian possibilities of labor's acts, looking for ways around racial tensions (if confusedly), and taking pleasure in terrorizing "the big capitalists."

The whole thing was an astonishing feat. The unions served anywhere from 20,000 to 30,000 meals a day in their kitchens. In addition they distributed milk throughout the city at thirty-five neighborhood sites. The results were, though, somewhat uneven. Hostile observers reported that "stew served on paper plates was to be had with dry bread and weak coffee. . . . Later the stew ran out and boiled sausages and dry bread were served with the coffee." Tin spoons "bent double under pressure," and no forks were to be had.[88] Another hostile source reported "a great many people having difficulty in obtaining lunch. The union kitchens . . . were very dirty, the food poor and in every way inadequate, less than 20,000 meals being served."[89] It all depended on one's point of view: Was a "mere" 20,000 meals served "inadequate," or no mean feat?[90]

The same could be asked of the outcome of the general strike. Whether the barrel was half empty or half full depended on whether or not one owned the barrel; whether the strike "failed" or not depended on the class to which the observer belonged. Certainly the strike demonstrated working-class solidarity on a mass scale. At least 65,000 Seattle workers walked out on February 4 and stayed out for the next three days. Tens of thousands of other workers were idled. The strikers included thousands of white women unionists, some of whom were its most eager backers despite their lack of a voice in the central debates over whether to call the strike. Japanese-American unionists, too, walked out and offered their services to the Central Labor Council, which thanked them for their support, "allowed" them to attend meetings, but denied them any votes. African-American members of the longshoremen's union presumably struck, too. The strike, moreover, did not spill over into racial conflict in a year when working-class racial violence tore through eastern and midwestern industrial cities.[91]

The problem, though, was the question of ending the strike. Robert Friedheim, in his book-length study of the general strike, argues that the labor council lacked precise goals, and he blames that vagueness for the strike's "defeat."[92] But the unions had an explicit goal, forcing the yard owners and federal arbitrators to concede on shipyard wages. The problem was that neither budged. A more decisive issue was how to end the strike with dignity if a clear-cut victory was not forthcoming. After all, the movement had been eminently successful in its larger goal of demonstrating solidarity. No exact date had ever been set as to how long the strike would last. After four days had passed, it was unclear what to do next.[93]

The AFL movement's leadership, moreover, appears to have been unprepared for the intensity of the local business elite's reaction. The unions had placed an unwarranted faith in Mayor Ole Hanson's previous sympathy for organized labor. When the strike commenced, the city's upper class panicked. Its daily press fanned the flames, and Hanson announced that he would call in troops if labor did not capitulate immediately. The forces arrayed against continuation of the strike were immense. The owners and federal government remained intransigent, national condemnation intensified, and rumors of impending violence abounded. But the apparently deciding factor in ending the strike came from within labor's own ranks. Most of the officials of the AFL internationals to which Seattle workers belonged were far more conservative, politically, than their Seattle locals and threatened by any rebellion in the ranks that might disrupt their tenure. Many of the striking Seattle locals – including the relatively staid musicians, for example – had walked out without the sanction of their internationals. The internationals' retribution was swift. Emissaries sped to Seattle to revoke charters, uphold the sanctity of the contract, affirm the withholding of strike benefits, and in general reassure the city's employers that the internationals' support was in no way forthcoming. This proved fatal. The Seattle locals could not defy both their own internationals and the city's entire employing class at the same time. By Saturday, February 8, workers were trickling back to work, many of them unwillingly. The dam burst on Sunday. The Labor Council, despite a hurried and chaotic decision to officially end the strike Tuesday, could not stop the flood, and business was almost back to normal Monday.[94]

Back at work, 65,000 Seattle workers were left to reflect on what it had all meant. It had been a daring tactical experiment. And it would remain a legendary radical event for the nation, indeed the world, for the rest of the century. On the eve of the strike, Anna Louise Strong published a famous editorial in the *Union Record* summarizing its purpose. In its most famous line, she concluded: "we are starting on a road that leads – NO ONE KNOWS WHERE."[95] Strong, a flamboyant and self-indulgent middle-class radical, had meant that the general strike might lead to a revolution that would place society in the hands of the workers. At the very least, it would lead to a strengthened position for organized labor in the 1920s. Seattle's businessmen, too, thought the strike meant that they had a revolution on their hands. Only Strong was correct, and only in the most literal sense: No one did know. The Seattle labor movement began the decade at the height of its powers, indeed, the height of any working-class movement in the twentieth-century United States. Its fate remained open.

2

Cooperatives

THE SEATTLE AFL MOVEMENT continued to expand in the months following the general strike. Optimism persisted, energies stayed high, and activists continued to stretch the self-definition of their movement. Organizing spilled over onto multiple fronts, especially a great enthusiasm for institution building. By the late spring of 1919 white Seattle workers had placed cooperatives at the heart of trade-union strategy, plotting vast city- and nationwide cooperative networks. "People are falling over themselves to get into something cooperative," Harry Ault, editor of the *Union Record*, reported in April 1919.[1] A visitor from the East saw the same thing: "Out in Seattle now, they have what they call the 'Big Idea.' This means that the trade unionists do not stop with organizations merely at the point of production. They believe they must use their cooperative power and resources as consumers as well as producers."[2]

In many ways cooperatives were strategically quite different from the wartime labor movement that culminated in the general strike, and distinct from the classic tale of labor history in Seattle. The wartime gains had centered on the point of production, the waged workplace, where employers and workers battled over the production process and over the compensation workers would receive for their labors. Most Seattle cooperatives, by contrast, began "at the point of consumption," to use one of their organizers' phrases, and proposed to organize workers' "purchasing power," rather than their labor power. Rather than a direct frontal engagement with employers, they called for independent instititution building by the working class. Yet as the parallel in cooperative activists' own language between "the point of production" and "the point of consumption" suggests, the two spheres were inseparable. Events in the one sphere precipitated those in the other, just as the same wartime developments that produced the general strike fed what contemporary observers called "cooperative fever."[3] Both the general strike and the cooperatives stemmed from radical impulses to transform U.S. society, both contained a utopian element, and both were possible because the labor movement now embraced a critical mass of the Seattle working class. In many cases the very same people organized on behalf of both militant trade unions and cooperatives.

The differences between the two institutional forms do matter, though. Seattle's "cooperative moment," spanning roughly from late 1918 through 1921, marked the postwar decade's most creative definition of what the "labor movement" would be. Cooperatives stretched the unions' definition of work. By crossing over from production to consumption, they expanded the areas of working-class economic life with which the AFL movement would concern itself. They broadened the definition of solidarity, offering white workers the opportunity to form "one big union of consumers." Finally, the cooperatives created an opening for the politicization of women's unwaged work as part of the working-class movement. Men and women both turned to cooperation. But their visions of the movement and its goals diverged sharply, revealing the very different workplace politics of wage-earning men and of housewives, as well as cooperatives' structural flexibility to embrace both.

Cooperative fever

American workers first began forming producer and consumer cooperatives as early as the 1830s and 1840s. Throughout the rest of the nineteenth century trade unionists repeatedly founded cooperatives, almost all of which failed in times of economic downturn. Cooperatives reached the zenith of their popularity in the 1880s when the Knights of Labor elevated them to equal theoretical status with the strike and boycott.[4] A series of utopian colonies founded at the turn of the century in the Puget Sound region brought especially strong enthusiasm for cooperation to the Pacific Northwest. The Puget Sound Cooperative Colony (founded in 1887), Equality Colony (1897), Freeland (1900), Burley (1898), and Home (1901), all swiftly failing in their attempts to build model "cooperative commonwealths" or socialist enclaves, served as training grounds for later Seattle cooperative activists, including Harry Ault, editor of the *Union Record*. In 1904, workers in Seattle also founded the Labor Union Cooperative Company, one of twenty-two producer and consumer cooperatives in Washington state at the time. That cooperative's fate is unknown, but another cooperative, the Producer and Consumers' Association, appeared in Seattle in 1908. In 1911 farmer members of the Grange operated the Producers and Consumers Cooperative Company. None of these appears to have survived long, but they established a firm tradition of cooperation in the city, to which Swedish immigrant workers contributed their own experiences of cooperation in their homeland.[5]

Rank-and-file enthusiasm for cooperatives in Seattle after World War I moved far beyond any previous experiments, however. At the core of the movement were two large citywide chains, both of which expanded rapidly in 1919. The first, the Seattle Consumers' Cooperative Association

(SCCA), opened in the spring of 1918. Its membership grew to 253 families by the end of that year and to 1,600 by November 1919. Business tripled from $29,897 for the last quarter of 1918 to the same amount in one month in late 1919. The SCCA grew on a neighborhood-by-neighborhood basis until by late 1919 it embraced eight grocery branches that distributed food in all the city's white working-class neighborhoods, including one in Ballard, one known as the "Jewish Branch," and a branch formed by the families of fishermen originally from the Adriatic Sea region. Two producers' cooperatives, formed by tailors and jewelry manufacturing workers, and a cooperative coal and fuel yard joined the chain in 1919.[6]

The second chain, the Cooperative Food Products Association (CFPA), was much more formally integrated with Seattle's AFL locals. It began as a cooperative meat market founded by the butchers' union in early 1918. From that seed it grew in the next two years into a cluster of grocery stalls in the public market, three neighborhood grocery branches, a slaughterhouse and sausage-making plant, bakery, dairy distribution system, and a milk condensary. Members planned, in addition, twenty new grocery stores and a cooperative salmon cannery, a steam trawler, and a $50,000 flour mill. The Food Products Association financed itself through sale of stock to trade unions, farmers, and individual union members, garnering a total of $70,000 by 1922. By the end of 1919 more than a thousand families belonged. The chain employed seventy-eight people and on the economic front was "exceedingly prosperous." At the end of its first year its net profit amounted to $30,000.[7]

Meanwhile, dozens of independent working-class cooperatives proliferated across the city in 1919. City employees and the plumbers' and steamfitters' unions formed their own cooperative groceries. Scandinavian-American workers formed a cooperative bakery, restaurant, and reading room that in mid-1919 employed twenty-five people and averaged $2,500 a week in trade. A "Cooperative Cafe" adjoining the shipyards opened to serve metal trades workers and cater labor-movement picnics. The Equity Print Shop, advertising itself as "Printers to the Proletariat," printed leaflets, journals, and books for radicals. Auto mechanics, barbers, cleaners and dyers, longshoremen, painters, carpenters, and shoe repairers all formed producers' cooperatives. Another thousand people led by Anna Louise Strong joined the "Cooperative Campers" to "make our mountains accessible at low cost."[8]

Activists envisioned a movement larger yet. In March 1919, representatives from trades throughout the city began to plan a working-class, cooperatively owned department store. "THE THING Organized Labor wants in Seattle is a modern Department Store, with its numerous branches and service stations," its promoters declared, "so that we can buy from ourselves, anything we may want, from a paper of pins or a cup of coffee, to a fine suit of clothes, a fine coat for the wife, an automobile or a $2.00 dinner."[9] Others began to organize cooperatively organized dental parlors and a "labor hospital association," to eliminate "profiteering on unfortunates by private institutions."[10] As early as January 1918 Seattle consumer cooperators also started establishing regional and national cooperative wholesale operations. These plans culminated in July 1919 with the launching of the National Cooperative Association, a regional wholesale system based in Seattle.[11]

Much of the impetus for this wave of institution building came from a handful of men who served as the proselytizers, managers, and visionaries of cooperation in Seattle. Their ideas are central to any understanding of the movement. These men, all white, were more middle class in their background than other Seattle cooperative activists and more likely to enter the movement from an intellectual background than out of trade unions. The prominent exception was Carl Lunn, the chief missionary of cooperation in Seattle, who had served as third vice president of the Laundry Workers' International Union. Lunn founded the Seattle Consumers' Cooperative Association in 1918 and spent the next two years speaking all over Washington state in meetings, usually in working-class homes, on behalf of cooperation. Another of this group was John Worswick, manager of the Cooperative Food Products Association. Lunn, Worswick, and others participated in a national network of cooperative activists. They reported on Seattle cooperatives to two national cooperative conventions in 1919 and 1920, for example. National-level activists, in turn, traveled to Seattle to preach cooperation. James Warbasse, president of the Cooperative League of the United States, in April 1919 gave a week-long lecture series at the Seattle Labor Temple. Together, these men wrote the articles on cooperation for the *Union Record* and local cooperative press, most precisely defined "cooperation," and most clearly articulated a long-term strategy and vision for the cooperative movement.[12]

Their theories began with the concept of the "workers' purchasing power," which, if organized collectively, could enhance working-class power. According to their model, the workers would first form consumer distributive branches, which would then unite in a wholesale operation. From these, in turn, producer cooperatives would be formed to produce the products consumed in the consumer cooperatives. From consumption to production, in other words, the movement would build outward to a vast cooperative sector of the economy, which would gradually expand the realm of workers' ownership and, finally, supplant capitalist institutions. As Warbasse argued, "Cooperation penetrates steadily into the business of the capitalistic world and crowds it out."[13] Another advocate explained in the CFPA newsletter: "[T]he thing that it supplants will almost imperceptibly fade away as the new is developed to take the place of the old."[14] The theorists' model, in sum, was one of evolution, even of secession. "Violent revolution not needed," as one promised.[15]

Part of the theorists' package was a precisely codified definition of "cooperation." At its core lay the supremely important Rochdale model. The "Rochdale Pioneers," British cooperators in the 1840s, originated a set of rules known as the Rochdale Principles: one-member, one-vote regardless of the amount of shares held; payment of dividends based on members' patronage; cash only, no credit; and current prices.[16] Based almost religiously on these principles, British working-class cooperatives had grown to an immense scale by World War I, counting 4,131,477 members and a total capital of £66 million. After the war they bought 30,000 acres of tea in India and another 10,000 acres of Canadian wheat fields. This British model was the key to many Seattle cooperators' vision of pure, and therefore successful, cooperation.[17] Many of Seattle's cooperative leaders were themselves British. John Worswick, for example, manager of one chain and board member of the other, was the son of "staunch cooperators" in Manchester, England, and his brother was general secretary of the 30,000-member Cooperative Society of Beswick, England. Dora Hayward, who edited the Food Products Association's newsletter and ran its educational department, had belonged to the Newcastle, England, cooperative society.[18]

Cooperative activists in Seattle were aware of the centrality of cooperation to the working-class movement throughout Europe in the late nineteenth and early twentieth centuries. In Belgium, a federation of cooperatives affiliated with the Socialist Party counted 270,000 members by 1924. Consumer cooperatives called *Maisons du People* ("Houses of the People") used their profits to sustain Socialist Party activities, strike funds, and the radical press, and to provide insurance, maternity aid, and legal and medical advice for their members. French workers similarly organized a variety of cooperatives in the late nineteenth century and by the eve of World War I had established 4,000 cooperative stores. Radicals in all western European countries debated heatedly the importance of consumers' cooperation in relation to their other two strategic fronts, trade unionism and political activity.[19]

The national context for cooperation in the United States, however, differed dramatically. Despite the substantial gains of the Socialist Party in the second decade of the century, there was no powerful working-class party that a nationally coordinated cooperative movement might serve or with which it might dovetail strategically.[20] Even when Seattle workers threw themselves into cooperatives and organized them on a large scale, their movement remained necessarily local. This was true for all the cooperatives that sprang up in working-class communities throughout the United States in the 1918–20 period, from housewives' cooperatives in New Orleans to workers' cooperatives in the Midwest; citywide chains in New York, San Francisco, and Cincinnati; and statewide chains in Nebraska and North Dakota. Washington state alone had workers' cooperatives in at least twenty-three different communities in 1919.[21] Many of these diverse cooperatives communicated with Warbasse's national operation, the Cooperative League of the United States.[22] But they were at sea when it came to uniting with a national thrust for working-class power. In Seattle's context, this meant that the theorists' larger vision, based explicitly on European models of a three-pronged struggle, could be realized only on a truncated, local level.

Men, cooperatives, and the workplace

Thousands of Seattle working people flocked to Warbasse's lecture series in 1919 and attended house meetings to hear Lunn, Worswick, Charles Neiderhauser, and other leaders explain cooperation.[23] But those listeners joined only because cooperatives promised to address their own concerns as working people.[24] Outside of the proselytizers, almost all those involved in Seattle cooperatives fall into two large camps: white male trade unionists and white married working-class women.

The men's interest in cooperation began at the workplace. Many initially developed an interest in consumer cooperatives as a weapon to help win strikes. This was the case most clearly for the metal trades workers whose shipyard strike escalated into the general strike. In late January 1919, members of the city's Retail Grocers' Association cut off all credit to strikers. This placed the shipyard workers, with 40,000 on strike, in a precarious situation. The Cooperative Food Products Association was able to save the day by offering liberal credit to strikers and their families.[25] The Seattle Consumers' Cooperative Association also visibly aided the strike by distributing 10,000 free loaves of bread in a single day.[26] The lesson was not lost on the shipyard unions. Throughout the rest of 1919 metal trades workers organized on behalf of cooperatives, invested money in them, and allocated scarce time at their meetings to cooperative advocates. One speaker summed up the appeal: If labor "has enough food to last him for an indefinite period of time . . . labor will be able to win any fight they undertake for food wins all struggles."[27]

The strongest surge of rank-and-file interest in cooperatives came after the general strike. "The stimulus to cooperative enterprise and the enthusiastic working-together was the most important, permanent and constructive result of the General Strike,"[28] the Central Labor Council's official history of the strike concluded in April 1919. "A month after the strike . . . union after union is talking co-operative stores of various kinds."[29] After the strike, both existing chains increased exponentially in membership and sales. The Consumers' Cooperative Association, for example, expanded its membership by 70 percent, increased its business from $250 to $500 a day before the strike to $2,500 a day a week later, and hired eight new clerks.[30]

We can assume that this growth was in part because union members throughout the city became persuaded, as did the metal trades, of the utility of cooperatives in aiding strikes. Seattle employers also unintentionally contributed further to the popularity of cooperatives. After the CFPA announced that it would extend credit to strikers whose grocers had cut them off, a squad of police from the city's "dry squad," faking a liquor search, raided the cooperative's manager's office and confiscated its files.[31] Designed to shut the chain down, the raid had the exact opposite result. Business at the chain quadrupled the next Saturday.[32] This support may have resulted in part from a heightened sense of class consciousness generated during the general strike, as organized workers made connections between the interlocking spheres of business control of the city. As one cooperative advocate argued, "Strikers supporting antagonistic business men at a time like this really 'kiss the hand that strikes them.'"[33]

Not only did the existing chains mushroom but new cooperatives also sprang up during and after the strike. The plumbers' and steamfitters' unions opened up a "strike relief store" with all-volunteer labor from striking members and sold food at wholesale cost plus overhead. They were so persuaded by the experience that when the strike ended they decided to buy their own store. A month after the strike they were selling $1,800 worth of eggs, potatoes, milk, and meat a day and spreading the gospel of cooperation to pipe trades local up and down the Pacific coast.[34]

An equally important factor behind the popularity of cooperatives was inflation. Despite all of organized labor's wartime gains through strikes and organizing drives, staggering inflation constantly threatened to outstrip wages, both during the war and in the two years following. Nationally, average prices increased from a July 1914 index of 100 to 131 in July 1917, to 165 by November 1918, and peaked in July 1920 at 204 percent of 1914 levels. Seattle food prices, while slightly lower than the national average, increased 110 percent over the same period. One expert estimated that in the nation as a whole, wage rates only barely kept ahead of prices.[35]

Cooperative activists spoke explicitly of their movement as an answer to inflation. The plumbers and steamfitters, for example, talked of their store as "the latest wrinkle in meeting the high cost of living."[36] Theorists argued that the working class had to protect the flanks of both wages and prices. As one article in the CFPA's monthly newsletter, *Co-operator*, put it, "[W]hat labor, organized as producers, *gain* in their great conflict with capital they *lose* in great part through being unorganized as consumers."[37] By eliminating the middleman, cooperative stores would eliminate a layer of profit and therefore be able to offer lower prices.

This was all consumers' cooperation. Another set of trade unionists became convinced of the value of producers' cooperatives, also in order to win strikes. Seattle's butchers, for example, founded the Cooperative Food Products Association's meat market at first so that they could win a 1918 strike. The cooperative "proved the salvation of the Butchers' Union."[38] As one activist reported, "Two weeks after we opened our own slaughter house all meat markets in the city signed with the union." ("We have even organized the cows at $10 a head," he added.)[39] Cleaners and dyers, locked out by their employers in the fall of 1919, bought the Queen Anne Dye Works, the second-largest in the city, and opened it on a cooperative basis, hoping "in that way [to] beat the bosses."[40] Again, the general strike contributed to this process. As employers' hostility rippled through the city's firms after the strike, unionists in many trades turned to producers' cooperation as an alternative to tense and confrontational workplace situations. This was the case for the barbers, for example, some of whom were the most militant supporters of the strike. Many were locked out afterward, and in response, twenty-five came to a mid-February meeting at which they started forming producers' cooperatives and a cooperative wholesale supply house.[41]

Other Seattle trade unionists who formed producers' cooperatives spoke of eliminating employers in their trades altogether. Building trades workers in September 1919 wanted to form a cooperative "leaving the contractors out of any further consideration."[42] The longshoremen's union started a cooperative stevedoring company in April 1919, hired former Port Commissioner Robert Bridges to run it, and by January 1920 had 1,200 members and $20,000. In May the cooperative put out its first bids. "As long as we preach that we can operate industries ourselves we should demonstrate that we can start industries and so conduct them that we will put the bosses out of business," Percy May, chief spokesperson for the cooperative, announced. "Then let them go to work."[43]

The general strike experience fueled these self-management impulses. The Central Labor Council's official history, written three months after the strike, reported that the provision trades gained "a new sense of power to organize and manage activities of their craft or industry." Organized labor in Seattle had "learned a great deal more than they expected to learn. . . . They learned how a city is taken apart and put together again."[44] The tremendous enthusiasm voiced by Ed Levi, the cook quoted earlier, over the ability of Seattle unions to run their city harmoniously and cheaply during the general strike offers further evidence.[45]

The impulse toward workers' ownership inherent in the cooperatives was not the same thing as internal democracy. No available reports on Seattle cooperatives discussed the abolition of hierarchical management structures, though such ideas may have been popular within the more

IWW-inspired institutions. Seattle's cooperatives were not designed to usher in democratic management on the part of their employees. Their democratically elected trustee structure placed overall control in popular hands, but the internal management of the cooperatives shows a traditional business structure. The trustees hired a manager, who in turn was granted power over the cooperative's employees and related to them as would a traditional manager, albeit a pro-union one. The cooperatives recognized their employees' respective AFL craft unions, granted the closed shop, and paid union-scale wages – though not, evidently, above that.

Identifying the exact appeal of cooperation to trade-union men is a difficult task because cooperatives were so many things to so many people. Functions of both production and consumption were intermixed freely. Structurally, both chains included consumer and producer cooperatives. They advertised consumers' cooperatives not just as a way for workers to shop as a class but also as a first step on the road to workers' ownership of production. Many of those who formed producer cooperatives turned around and advocated class-conscious consumption at their enterprise. Trade unionists, similarly, discovered consumers' cooperation as a way to fight back at the point of production. In the Seattle cooperative movement, workers' politics of consumption and of production, in other words, overlapped, reinforced each other, and were ultimately inseparable.

Producer cooperatives were most popular among trades in which the size of firms was small, capital requirements for entry into the field were low, and where a cooperative firm could directly serve a market of working-class consumers – barbers, butchers, auto mechanics, and tailors, for example. For government or railroad workers, by contrast, producer cooperatives were in effect impossible. These workers, though, strongly supported consumers' cooperation. Municipal employees, for example, formed their own store. Streetcar employees, fire fighters, and railroad laborers were among the strongest supporters of the department-store drive.[46]

As with so much else, the metal trades were both an exceptional case and the key to the entire movement. Thousands of Seattle's metal trades workers identified themselves as radicals and were eager to bring about the emancipation of the working class. They grew enthusiastic about cooperation not only because it could help with strikes but also because it meant the immediate formation of autonomous working-class institutions. Many of these men wanted to have nothing to do with employers. Moreover, they constituted the strongest mass base in the city with a vision of a different, worker-run world. That visionary element, however amorphous, was an essential element of "cooperative fever."[47]

Just as important, the metal trades were rich. With somewhere around 40,000 members in late 1918, dues money accumulated rapidly. Looking for class-conscious uses for that money, Seattle's metal trades locals invested thousands in the city's cooperatives. Boilermakers' Local #104 alone bought $12,000 in CFPA stock.[48] "We can go to the labor unions and say, we want five thousand dollars in cash, and they bring it to us," Carl Lunn boasted to a national cooperative conference in late 1918.[49] The institution-building impulse behind Seattle's cooperatives, in sum, was possible in large part because of the combined money and political philosophies of the immense metal trades locals.

Cooperation was extremely popular among many socialists in Seattle outside the metal trades as well, especially those who had been involved with the Socialist Party. This was true of more intellectually inclined, middle-class socialists such as Harry Ault, editor of the *Union Record*, who wrote editorials throughout 1919 and 1920 on behalf of cooperatives; and of Anna Louise Strong, feature editor of the paper, who reported James Warbasse's spring lecture series with almost religious enthusiasm.[50] Socialists more enmeshed in the trade unions embraced cooperation as well. William McNally, a Socialist officer of the janitors' union, for example, was elected vice president of the Seattle Consumers' Cooperative Association in January 1920.[51] Warbasse, when he visited Seattle in April, noted "it is significant that the radical element is promoting Cooperation."[52] Socialist involvement in the Consumers' Cooperative chain was especially strong.[53] While touring its Lake Burien branch Warbasse asked a woman he saw weighing beans whether it was true that the cooperators there were Reds. "Yes," she laughed, "we're Bolshevik clear through, and we don't care who knows it."[54]

This involvement of socialists in the cooperative movement is an important clue to the cooperatives' place in the development of the postwar Seattle labor movement. By early 1919, repression of the city's Socialist Party had taken its toll. While the party retained a few members, it sponsored only a handful of public speeches, had no office, and mounted no political campaigns. Raids and arrests had destroyed its newspaper, the *Call*. Organized socialism in effect did not exist in postwar Seattle. "The Socialist Party vanished as a political factor," recalled Harvey O'Connor, a prominent local socialist intellectual.[55]

Cooperation filled that vacuum. The same people who had previously worked for the party now worked for cooperatives, whether as intellectuals expostulating cooperative theory or as activists building cooperative institutions. No formal channels existed for the explicit advocacy of socialism, but cooperative newsletters flourished, cooperative meetings could be held freely and openly, and the pages of the *Union Record* preached cooperation daily. Cooperation in 1919 Seattle came to serve not as a complement to a thriving Socialist Party, as it did in Europe, but as a substitute.

This helps explain why trade-union men of quite so many political stripes got involved with cooperatives. At one end of the spectrum were radicals such as Socialist barber Phil Pearl; Percy May, the pro-IWW longshoremen's leader; C. E. Stead of the shipyard laborers' union; and Anna Louise Strong. At the other end were men well entrenched in AFL business uniondom, such as Joe Hoffman of the butchers, Ed Levi of the cooks, and even William Short, president of the State Federation of Labor, friend of Samuel Gompers and the leader of the antiradical bloc.[56]

This broad spectrum of interest also explains how thoroughly the cooperatives were integrated with the AFL trade unions in postwar Seattle. Carpenters' Local #131, for example, owned $500 in stock in the Cooperative Food Products Association. Throughout the postwar years it maintained a "cooperative committee" that sent official representatives to stockholders' meetings and tracked the stores' dividend rate. When the CFPA asked for help in attracting new members, Local #131 solicited patronage from among its members and posted notices about the chain on its bulletin board.[57] The musicians' and typographers' minutes, similarly, show a solid, if mild, interest in cooperatives.[58] For other locals the cooperatives were at the center of the union itself. The butchers, for example, depended upon the CFPA's retail meat operation as a wedge against united employers, and its business agent served as one of the chain's trustees.[59]

The drive for a cooperative department store involved the confluence of almost all the concerns Seattle workers brought to the cooperative movement. Of the seventeen locals whose delegates worked on the drive, the most active came, first, from the Retail Clerks' Union. These unionists wanted a department store in order to have a cooperatively owned workplace. Similarly, a second group, the jewelry workers, wanted the store as a producers' cooperative, because they had been locked out after the general strike. Men from the maintenance-of-way (railroad laborers) and fire fighters' unions wanted a department store to expand the range of consumers' cooperation available, because they could not realistically organize producer coops. Metal tradesmen from the sheet-metal workers and machinists contributed the vision and the money. And Carl Lunn, the theorist, provided the expertise.[60]

The cooperative movement expanded outward into farmer–labor alliances popular among Seattle AFL activists. The Cooperative Food Products Association's original board of directors consisted of half trade unionists, half farmers. Its original stock sales were divided fifty-fifty between the two groups. Area farmers invested a total of $30,000, partly as individual investments of $500 and partly in the form of large blocks of stock bought by organizations such as Grange chapters or the King County Dairymen's Association. Both farmers and Seattle AFL unionists were especially interested in the CFPA's milk condensary plant in Tolt, designed to simultaneously process milk produced by the area's radical farmers, guarantee low prices and unadulterated milk to urban workers, and provide union protection for the condensary's employees. The label on each can of milk from the plant featured a farmer and worker shaking hands, the Statue of Liberty shining behind them, and enjoyed no less than three union labels. "Made by Organized Cows," the "Co-operative Brand" milk advertised. These cooperative efforts were the institution-building equivalent of efforts by farmers' organizations and organized labor to establish state-level farmer–labor political alliances in this period. They underscore, again, the structural flexibility of "cooperation."[61]

As with the politics of race, gender, and the labor movement, the usual spectrum of left and right in many ways did not apply to the politics of consumption. Class relations were so polarized, the impulse to build inde-pendent working-class institutions so strong, and the definition of coopera-tion so broad that cooperation appealed to almost all camps. When it came to questions of emphasis, though, distinctions did emerge. The stick-ing point was the strategic importance of cooperation relative to other paths for class advancement. A first position, promulgated by the theorists, depicted cooperatives as an evolutionary road to something akin to social-ism. This position could be called the "primacy of cooperation" – coop-eratives as a sufficient, secessionary model in which capitalism would wither away. Others, following the European model, advocated cooperation as one of three fronts, together with political activity and trade unionism. O. P. Callahan, secretary-treasurer of the shipyard laborers and stock sales-man for the CFPA, for example, spoke of "three great factors in the battle of the laboring class": first, the unions; second, a working-class political party; and third, cooperatives.[62] Carl Lunn referred along these lines to "the foundation already laid" for cooperation: "1- One large union for all the workers. 2- One Big Union of all co-operatives. 3- One political union of all labor."[63] For others, though, cooperation could be used as a weapon against more revolutionary strategies within the Seattle AFL movement. During the third day of the general strike, for example, when radical delegates introduced a resolution to the Central Labor Council advocating that if the shipyard strike were not settled, the "workers seize [the] ma-chinery of production for their own protection," conservatives argued in opposition that if the unions did so, martial law would be imposed, and they passed a measure advocating cooperatives instead.[64]

It seems safe to conclude that many of the men who turned to coopera-tion wanted to fight on a number of fronts. The idea of secession in the aftermath of a general strike must have been quite appealing. Others might have been attracted to the idea of secession, found it unrealistic, and supported cooperatives for more short-term reasons, such as provision of food to strikers, establishing a worker-owned wedge against employer lockouts, or harboring radical organizers. These activists approached co-operation as a secondary weapon, in service to trade unionism as the primary locus of struggle.

Even these distinctions can be misleading. A single individual could easily hold multiple, even mutually exclusive interpretations of the value of cooperation at the same time. Percy May, for example, saw the long-shoremen's cooperative as a hostile "weapon" with which to fight and "beat" employers. "We are going to fight them politically, industrially and by competition." Cooperation, for him, was not a sole weapon to supplant others. He talked about cooperatives as a way to "put the bosses out of existence" by superior competition. "And we won't have to have a revolution to do it," he added. At the same time he was known as an IWW sympathizer and supported his union's refusal, in the fall of 1919, to load arms bound for Aleksandr Kolchak's counterrevolution in Russia.[65]

Women, cooperatives, and the workplace

Cooperatives were as popular among white working-class women in 1919 Seattle as they were among men. No total numbers are available, but it appears that women participated in the cooperative movement at almost as high a rate as did men.[66] Cooperation appealed to a much narrower spectrum of women than men, however. Within the movement, their structural position was almost entirely different. Like men, their interest in cooperation stemmed from their workplace concerns – in this case, as housewives. Yet in part because their workplace was so very different, their definition of cooperation was itself fundamentally different.

Women were involved only in consumer cooperatives, not producer cooperatives. None of the city's all-female unions organized producer co-operatives; nor did mixed-gender locals in which women counted a significant minority, with two partial exceptions: the cleaners and dyers' union, which reported its cooperative enterprise as employing "fifty union men and women," and the tailors, whose cooperative may have included women workers, because the union included many female members (though its advertisements asked fellow workers to buy suits "from your union broth-ers").[67] No female trade-unionist voices were among those advocating producers' cooperation in the *Union Record*, where men's speeches and letters on behalf of cooperatives abounded. Women unionists' overall lack of interest in producer cooperatives is initially somewhat difficult to explain. The great majority of organized women worked in the local-market, consumer-services or products sector, where male unionists were likely to choose producers' cooperation because of the small firm size and low capital entry costs.[68] But other factors would have obviated cooperation. The women's unions were almost all newly formed, their workplace status was always marginal, their dues pool smaller, their access to capital lower, and their members' sense of permanence in the labor force weaker.[69] Some of these factors, especially the financial ones, can also help explain why almost no women's unions bought shares in the city's consumer co-operatives. Of twenty-seven unions listed as owning stock in Seattle cooperatives in early 1919, only the laundry workers and bookbinders represented women, in mixed-gender locals.[70]

The women involved in cooperatives were almost all married. Of more than 150 names of identified women cooperators, only two were single; one of these was an employee. This pattern can be explained more easily. Married working-class women were at the point in their life cycle when they were most responsible for shopping. For them, consumption was their primary job. Single women, by contrast, were most likely to be working in a paid job. Either they still resided at home, where a mother, grand-mother, or aunt did most of the shopping and cooking, or they boarded with a private family, which replicated the situation in their own house-hold. Or they rented a room in a boarding house. It might serve meals or, alternately, a woman might eat a few meals in cheap cafeterias or restaur-ants, fixing other meals in her room if she could get away with doing so. Consumers' cooperation did not, structurally, address her vital concerns as it did those of married working-class women. The distinction should not be made too sharply, however, because many married working-class women also worked for pay, and single women, wage earning or not, contributed housework to their families.[71] In cooperative activities, though, the pre-dominance of married women created a self-reinforcing cycle. Women activists planned their meetings in the middle of the day, for example, when most wage-earning women would be unable to attend.[72]

Married women would have been especially attracted by the coopera-tives' promise to address inflation. In most white working-class families in this period it was the job of the men to earn the wages, sometimes aug-mented by teenage children or more rarely by wage-earning wives. The job of a married woman, by contrast, was to translate those wages into a livelihood for the family by spending the wages wisely and contributing her unwaged work of cooking, cleaning, and child rearing.[73] For her, shopping and consumption were work. A high inflation rate made that work harder. It functioned as the equivalent in housework of the speedup or stretchout in an industrial workplace. Inflation meant that women whose budgets were already marginal had to scour the city for bargains still more assiduously; plan their meals still more carefully; please their families' often finicky preferences still more graciously and within a narrower range of options. In other words, while "protecting the flanks of both wages and prices" was a concern of the Seattle working class as a whole, given the sexual division of labor in the home it was a particularly female issue.

Within the cooperatives, men dominated at the top levels. In the Coopera-tive Food Products Association, all the trustees in 1919 but one were men, as were all the members of its governing committees. Five women served on the board of the Seattle Consumers' Cooperative Association in 1919, but the total number is unclear. In early 1920 its president, vice president, and secretary were all men. All the theorists who proselytized on behalf of cooperation were men, including those from out of town. Three women undertook special organizing work for women in the movement, two of them as employees of the Food Products Association; the third was Lola Lunn, Carl's wife. These women fulfilled many of the same roles the theorist men did, such as organizing house meetings, but they did so always with the particular angle of women's concerns. The only evident occasion on which a woman crossed over to speak of cooperation to men was Anna Louise Strong's series for the *Union Record* on Warbasse's visit.[74]

The chains' employment practices replicated the sexual division in the overall Seattle labor force. Managers at all ranks and those hired to sell stocks in the cooperatives were male, while clerical employees were female. At the Crown Hill cooperative coal yard, for example, Mrs. E. M. Nelson, "in charge of the office," took orders and membership applications, while Mr. J. A. Holman "handle[d] the delivery system."[75] At the level of rank-and-file volunteers, the picture is more varied. All the directors of the Greenlake neighborhood cooperative were men.[76] When 200 attended a March 1919 meeting to organize the Rainier Valley cooperative, the chair and secretary were both men.[77] In the University District that same week, though, three women and two men served on a committee organizing a new SCCA branch; and when workers in the Duwamish Valley a month later organized their cooperative, it was reported that "The women are especially interested."[78]

This rough overall pattern of male leadership and a mixed-gender rank and file meant that men had more formal power within the cooperatives than did women. One telling example suggests that when rank-and-file women in the CFPA attempted to influence overall policy in the chain the men largely ignored their input. In August 1920 women members of the West Seattle Cooperative Club decided that they had amassed enough interested members to warrant the opening of a new store in their neighborhood. They repeatedly visited meetings of the CFPA's board of trustees that fall to ask for a store. The trustees thanked them for their interest in the cooperatives' affairs but did not heed their request. (Perhaps the trustees did so because they had access to information the women did not – information that would have cautioned against expansion. But even that would demonstrate men's superior control of vital information within the organization.)[79]

Such unequal power dynamics echoed informally within the cooperatives. The language with which Dora Hayward, the director of education and women's organizing work for the CFPA, and the highest-ranking woman in the movement, described prominent men in her cooperative, is revealing. First, the manager: "Our Mr. Worswick, whom we dare only approach

about once a week, to be invariably told that this was his very busy day."
Then James Duncan, Central Labor Council secretary and a board member: "whom we at first stood rather in awe of, and now do not mind a bit having for a boss, on account of his fairness and his willingness to help us whenever we ask." Hayward's deference and Worswick's arrogance both suggest informal gender inequalities within the movement.[80]

Over time, though, gender dynamics within the consumers' cooperatives changed. In early and mid-1919, reports in the cooperative and labor press on Seattle cooperatives assumed the target "cooperator" was male and then asked for women's additional participation. A July article advertising a speech by Dalton Clarke on the cooperative wholesale operation, for example, importuned: "Bring your wives and friends."[81] A May 1919 "mass meeting for the benefit of all interested in cooperative stores" similarly added: "women especially being asked to attend the meeting as they do most of the buying."[82] That fall, however, activists increasingly became aware that women members' patronage of the cooperative stores was crucial to the cooperatives' fate, and the balance of power began subtly to shift. A Northwest States Cooperative Convention held in Seattle in late 1919 made it "mandatory that women have equal representation in all offices and committees of the societies represented." The purpose, "for the interest of securing better help from women."[83] Self-interest, in other words, suggested a greater measure of equality. In the winter of 1920–21 the Cooperative Food Products voted four women onto its board of directors, elevating the total number of women in key leadership positions to five of sixteen.[84] By that time, women cooperative enthusiasts outnumbered men at the rank-and-file level to the point that meeting announcements now requested that cooperators bring their husbands. An Interbay branch meeting advertised in April 1921, "It is especially desired that the men come as well as the women."[85] In a movement dependent on a large rank-and-file base of female shoppers, women ultimately held a degree of power. That never fully translated, though, into equality with men within the cooperatives.

From early 1919 on, those involved in Seattle cooperatives understood the activities and meaning of their movement in specifically gendered terms. At the broadest theoretical level, women theorists identified two distinct forms of exploitation, one male, one female. "The labor man fights at the point of production, where he is robbed; the labor woman fights at the point of consumption, where she is robbed," argued Jean Stovel, CFPA organizer for women.[86] While this formulation denied both wage-earning women's situation at the waged workplace and in the labor movement, and union men's interest in consumer cooperation, it nonetheless identified women's unique position in the economy and sought to politicize women's unwaged labors on behalf of a class movement. Women cooperative promoters argued in particular that because women did 90 percent of their families' shopping, the "purchasing power of the workers" was an especially female weapon to be deployed on behalf of the working class.[87]

In 1919 women launched two citywide networks of women's cooperative organizations to match the city's two cooperative chains. Lola Lunn founded the Women's Cooperative Guild, which expanded into several neighborhood-level branches. Dora Hayward and Mary Saunders started in the fall of 1919 a series of neighborhood Women's Cooperative Clubs affiliated with the CFPA. By the end of 1920 the clubs were thriving. "I am happy to say that the end of the year finds us in a wonderful position so far as our Woman's Work is concerned," Hayward reported.[88] "There is not any other movement in the labor world today in which the women are showing such tremendous interest."[89] Lunn, Hayward, and Saunders, in organizing these women's groups, were trying to replicate a British model, the Cooperative Women's Guild, which by 1921 counted 51,000 members in 1,077 branches.[90] The guild was an important site of working-class women's self-education as well as agitation on behalf of cooperation.[91] In Seattle, Hayward proposed the CFPA women's clubs as educational beacons that would attract women to the movement, teach them the principles of cooperation, and, when sufficient numbers in each neighborhood had been drawn in, serve as the seeds of neigborhood buying clubs that would, in turn, become new branch stores.[92]

The women who joined the cooperative clubs had their own ideas about what cooperation meant, however. For the most part these coincided with those of the clubs' founders. But women's activities, ultimately, moved far beyond that. Rank-and-file women's activities began with the social and the educational. This was exactly what Lola Lunn had in mind. In April 1919 she advocated an SCCA "Women's Co-operative Study Club" that would "give information concerning the Rochdale co-operative system, . . . study every phase of the movement, . . . carry into the homes the need and benefit of co-operation, . . . give social entertainments, . . . start classes among children and . . . assist with the general educational activities."[93] A report from the SCCA's Hillman City group in November 1919 showed plans for "vigorous social and educational features," which soon included a Christmas entertainment for children with songs, recitations, and vaudeville skits.[94] Reports of the CFPA women's clubs show a similar content. At most meetings the members heard guest speakers from the trade unions or cooperative movement, such as John Worswick, the store manager. At other meetings members discussed texts from the national cooperative movement, such as E. P. Harris's *Co-operation: The Hope of the Consumer.* Women also organized dances and other social functions for the movement as the whole and for themselves alone, especially tea parties.[95]

The cooperative women's activities were pervaded with an ideal that can be summed up as "homelikeness." Ideally, according to their philosophies, cooperation as a movement and as an ultimate goal would help make the world like a pleasant home. This model began with the clubs' own meetings. Reports spoke of the generosity of so many women offering up their homes for meetings, of the pleasant meals served, and of their gracious settings. One report of a Wallingford district meeting read, for example, "Beautiful flowers and foliage were donated by the members, making the room and tea table very lovely with autumn colors."[96] All the women's clubs' meetings took place in private homes, unlike the mixed-gender functions, which often used labor-owned or public halls.[97] In August 1919, women organized a separate lounge for women in the main Food Products Association branch at 3rd Avenue South and Washington Street. It, too, was designed to be like a home. "The rest room is furnished in wicker and cretonne, and has a huge lounge heavily upholstered. The walls are white enameled, and flowers on the wicker center table give a homelike atmosphere to the place."[98]

Women's use of the home as metaphor for cooperation – and vice versa – extended further to women's role as mothers within the home. In January 1921 women cooperators planned a social club that would sponsor properly chaperoned dances for single girls. "Especially do we desire to reach the lonely ones who dislike to go to the public dance halls and other public places of amusement, and as a result are deprived of the social life which they so much desire," one member explained in a letter to the editor. She concluded, "In co-operation lies our hope for the future, true co-operation that includes not merely the matters of dollars and cents but extends to the social and home life as well."[99]

The women's most independent organizational activity within the CFPA, the Women's Exchange, offers further insight into cooperative women's concerns. Originally, the Women's Exchange began when CFPA women, frustrated with the trustees' lack of movement in establishing a department store, decided to run their own independent dry goods department within the CFPA main store downtown. The exchange soon offered bath towels, wash cloths, thread, silk hosiery, laces, and embroideries for sale. The proceeds went back into buying new stock and to buy china for the Women's Clubs.[100] The exchange quickly evolved, however, into a far more complex operation. In addition to peddling dry goods, women sewed new garments, repaired old ones, or donated used ones to the Women's Exchange, which, in turn, either gave the clothes away or sold them at a minimal markup. The resulting profits went back to the original donor or, alternately, back into the Women's Exchange.[101]

The story of the Women's Exchange suggests many things about the meaning of cooperation to Seattle women. First, it shows working-class married women using the cooperatives to undertake charity work to help those less well off than they. Second, it demonstrates that women, largely cut off from upper-level decision making within the chain, nonetheless initiated and conducted their own independent cooperative activities, separate from the men financially, conceptually, and even literally – they expanded the women's lounge still further to accommodate the exchange and performed much of the labor within their homes.

Third, the Women's Exchange involved an intricate intermixture of waged and unwaged work, market and nonmarket relations. This was true not only of the exchange but also of women's participation in the cooperatives overall. On the one hand, much of the labor women performed on behalf of the cooperatives was volunteer, but nonetheless work. The Ballard cooperative branch, for example, announced a "big social and entertainment at Woog's Hall" to celebrate its opening in June 1919. "Ice cream and cake will be served free of charge," they enticed, "each lady member being requested to bring a cake."[102] The announcement for a Duwamish Valley meeting similarly read, "The ladies will bring boxes of good things to eat and the men will play the part of consumers."[103] Women activists were thus expected to contribute their own labor in order that the movement as a whole might flourish. While women interested in learning about cooperation paid an admission price by cooking up a tasty dish, interested men got to "play the part of consumers." Again, for women, consumption, even "cooperative," could be work. Many men also volunteered their time, however. "A crew of carpenter-members," presumably male, "volunteered to build counters and shelves" for the Ballard cooperative store, for example.[104]

The cooperative women appear to have volunteered for the movement happily. They chose to make quilts, using their own unwaged skills, to bring money into the cooperative. They showed up as volunteers at the stores. They planned dances, for which they would need to decorate and clean halls and prepare still more tasty refreshments.

At the same time, women's words and activities indicate that they understood that their efforts constituted work and that they supported cooperation as a means of alleviating their labors as housewives. The CFPA women first designed their downtown lounge, for example, as "a tastefully decorated public rest room . . . where tired women buyers may find relaxation and comfort."[105] They were interested in cooperation because it promised to lower prices and to alleviate the extra labors created by inflation. The West Seattle Women's club wanted a new branch in their neighborhood so that they could shop closer to home and save time, effort, and carfare. (The cooperatives did deliver groceries, however.)[106] An August 1919 meeting of the SCCA's Women's Cooperative Study Guild included "a demonstration of how to can green beans using the hot water bath method."[107] Finally, women's interest in "homelikeness" can be interpreted as a desire to use cooperation to create a nicer, more pleasant workplace for their labors as consumers.

One more example further illustrates the women's point of view. In April 1921 women of the West Seattle coop club started a day-care center. Members sewed and donated "clothing for the children, and sheets and pillow cases for the little beds," filling up what they described as a "hope chest" for the nursery.[108] Here, the women intermixed their own volunteer work as seamstresses, a concern for wage-earning women's needs for day care, a mothering role toward children, all under the rubric of "cooperation." And again, all this melded together in the "homelikeness" model.

Women also engaged in cooperative activities to earn their own cash. One description of the Women's Exchange noted: "[T]he exchange is a friend in need to the women or woman who wants to sell some garment not needed. Many people who have been well supplied with clothes, now out of a job, find that they need a little cash more than they do the clothes, and the exchange frequently effects the conversion."[109] Married, probably not working in paid jobs, the cooperative women had access to money only through their husbands' paychecks or through such irregular forms of moneymaking as taking boarders or selling garden produce.[110] Sewing garments for sale at the Exchange made it possible for women to earn cash through traditionally unwaged work in the home.

Married women were similarly interested in the dividends on purchases that Seattle cooperatives paid out each quarter. The cooperatives encouraged this. "Be a Cooperator and share the profits," they advertised, or "are you supporting your own store and reaping the profits in dividends?"[111] At a joint meeting of the city's women's cooperative clubs in August, 1920, women pinned their 6 percent dividend checks on the wall proudly to demonstrate how much they had patronized the store. They then called in William Short, president of the State Federation of Labor, to see.[112] As reported, this story represents the women as purely self-sacrificing, shopping cooperatively only to serve the movement. Other evidence suggests more complex motivations. Under the headline "GET YOUR 'DIVIES'" the CFPA's *Co-operator* told the story of a woman who, offered an alternative article, cheaper than the one she had requested, told the clerk, "Oh no, you are not going to cheat me out of my divies."[113] The amount could be significant. One member, for example, Mrs. M. E. Hoffman, spent $127.30 in three months and got an 8 percent dividend check of $10.08.[114]

On the one hand women thus contributed unwaged work to the movement the better to serve it, extending their contributions of sewing, cooking, and weighing beans in a continuum out from their ordinary lives as workers in the home. On the other hand they used cooperatives to address their working conditions in that same workplace context, the labor of consumption. Male workers, we have seen, supported cooperatives as a way to strengthen demands at their own workplaces and, ultimately, to usher in a workers' self-managed world. The women, in the end, were not all that different. They, too, wanted to make their work lives better and change the world at the same time.

Women cooperators' idea of a social movement was nonetheless far away from the world of militant unions and the general strike. They had a very different vision of "the workers' state" and of the "Cooperative Commonwealth" from that of their menfolk. They wanted a working-class movement that would make the world homelike, that would take care of little babies, and that would help women can green beans. They wanted a class movement, in other words, that addressed their concerns as workers in the home. And they wanted an independent space in which to articulate and organize around those concerns. Ultimately, cooperation was flexible enough to allow a flourishing of working-class women's activism, because it could expand to include a great range of economic activities.

Women's power or autonomy within the movement should not be exaggerated, however. Women's sphere within the cooperatives remained a separate and unequal one. Just as important, the cooperatives never addressed the sexual division of labor in the home, limiting their ability to transform the labors of housewives. Nor did they discuss the socialization of housework, a subject much debated on the *Union Record*'s women's pages in these years.[115] Nonetheless, the cooperatives' structural openness, their goal of politicizing both consumption and production, and women's own independent efforts to define them all helped construct working-class institutions that served the workplace concerns of men and women alike.

The question of profits

The cooperatives' approach to the question of profits offers final insight into the definition of "cooperation" and its place in Seattle workers' postwar strategies. For many in the cooperative movement, both male and female, one goal of cooperatives was to abolish profits. Repeatedly, cooperators spoke of their movement as doing away with "profiteering," by which they sometimes meant capitalism, but more often simply the garnering of unjust or excessive profits in distribution. More frequently, though, they attacked not a larger system but individual "profiteers." "How long could the profiteer exist if the workers did not support him?" the *Cooperator* asked.[116] Such remarks were part of a larger, cross-class dialogue about war profiteering taking place in the daily press all over the country during 1918 and 1919.[117]

As we have seen, cooperatives promised to eliminate profiteering by "eliminating the middleman," supplying products "direct from producer to consumer," and thus achieving greater "efficiency" than the "present private profit system."[118] These basic concepts were central to the theoretical "sell" of cooperation, underlying, for example, farmer–labor ties within the movement, the Food Products Association's network carrying cattle from slaughterhouse to butcher shop to working-class table, and the Women's Exchange, of which its promoters spoke as a "direct exchange between producer and consumer, with a minimum expense for distribution."[119]

These propositions underlay a dialogue within the movement about the political economy of consumption. The cooperatives' attack on the profiteer, profiteering, and the middleman involved an implicit debate about what was a fair profit. It embroiled cooperators in discussions about the relationship between wages, prices, and profits. One activist argued on behalf of cooperation, for example: "When you workers get an increase of wages, the employers add just that amount to the cost of production, and prices are increased to you at the counter, and the cost of living goes up."[120]

Such debates were part and parcel of cooperators' discussion of their movement as an answer to the "high cost of living." The entry of the trade-union movement into cooperative institution building required a mastery of the art of running businesses successfully, moreover, with all the knowledge of pricing, wholesaling, and marketing that that entailed. Some of this work was done by professional managers whom the cooperatives hired. But discussion of such questions was broad based among the cooperative rank and file. The committee organizing the cooperative department store, for example, argued that "the profits in general merchandise are much greater than the profit in groceries" – and therefore profiteering so much the fiercer, cooperation so much the more compelling.[121]

All Seattle cooperatives were founded on the common ground that "the present private profit system" was bad, and that "profiteering" should be eliminated. But at the same time all the cooperatives, at least in mid-1919, generated surpluses, raising the thorny question of what to do with them. Here the cooperatives parted ways.

One tidy resolution was the Rochdale system, which prescribed quarterly patronage dividends paid to individual members based on the total amount of their purchases and at a percentage rate determined by the board of trustees. The Seattle Consumers' Cooperative Association followed this system exactly. Lunn, Warbasse, and many other theorists believed in it religiously. We can understand the Rochdale system's popularity not only because it disbursed extra cash to women members but also because its purity rendered further debate unnecessary. It resolved the question in favor of a proven, successful tradition along English lines.[122]

Originally, the Cooperative Food Products Association paid quarterly dividends out to shareholders rather than shoppers, as in the Rochdale plan. In early 1919, for example, it distributed 8 percent dividends.[123] By midyear, though, it too switched to the Rochdale system.[124] While the reasons for this are obscure, the chain's newsletter is replete with elaborate discussions of the profit question. The CFPA's approach can be summarized as "profits to the working class." It did not propose to do away with profits; rather, it offered to redirect them to their proper recipient, the workers. This formulation began with a rough labor theory of value. Cooperation "redistributes the wealth created by labor among the people who create it and does not concentrate it into the hands of a few who do not create it," its promoters argued.[125] An organizing committee for the chain explained that cooperation then "reduces the cost of living by withholding the profits from the capitalist class, and returning them to the purchaser as a consumers' dividend."[126] In sum, when CFPA activists railed at the "present *private* profit system" it was the private part they attacked, not the profitable.[127] One article in the *Co-operator* even depicted "personal profit" as

> a stimulus not wholly bad if held within safe and proper limits – that is, within the limits of public welfare.
> Now, the desire to profit and enjoy in common with others is a worthy motive, while the wish to profit and enjoy at the expense of others is unworthy....[128]

This theoretical finessing led to apparent contradictions with which those leading the CFPA were evidently comfortable. The same page of the *Co-operator* could include two filler inserts, one right above the other, reading "How long could the profiteer exist if the workers did not support him?" and "Be a Co-operator and share the profits."[129] Recanting her enthusiasm for the movement in a 1935 autobiography, Anna Louise Strong captured this tension: "Dr. Warbasse came from New York to tell us that this was the painless, profitable way to workers' ownership."[130]

Many leaders of producer cooperatives in Seattle shared the Food Products Association's perspective on the profit question. "There is no reason why we should not keep the profits as long as there are profits ourselves," Percy May, the longshoremen's business agent, argued.[131] Robert Bridges, manager of their cooperative, agreed. "I want to see an end to the profits on the work of stevedores and truckers going to men who spend their time sitting around the Rainier Club and the Chamber of Commerce." He concluded, "There is no reason in the world why these middle men cannot be illiminated [*sic*] . . . and the truckers and stevedores get the profits."[132]

Sometimes this enthusiasm for working-class profits crossed over into a celebration of workers' small-business aspirations. The *Co-operator*, for example, spoke of the CFPA as "upholding the right of any man or men to go into business for themselves."[133] It even sold the cooperative as a workers' small-business school:

> Each member must look upon our Co-operative venture as an individual entrance into the business world. How often have you as the

father or mother of a family, when trying to think out the future for your family wished that you could save enough to have a little business of your own?[134]

This led the *Co-operator*'s writers onto a theoretical minefield. Small-business owners were also the very same "parasitic middlemen" their movement proposed to liquidate. One article revealed that members were indeed ambivalent about this aspect of cooperation. "It is sometimes asked if it is not unfair for a cooperative to compete with the small dealer who must have his profits to live on," it reported.[135] Many members must have harbored small-business aspirations themselves, sympathized with merchants who supported the trade-union movement (and who often still retained union membership), and felt queasy about the "death to the middleman" program.

Did cooperation de-radicalize the Seattle worker, "conscript his mentality," to borrow a phrase from a 1924 pamphlet attacking cooperatives put out by the national Socialist Labor Party?[136] Not necessarily. Hundreds, perhaps thousands, of Seattle workers were attracted to the "profits to the workers" aspect of the cooperative movement. But this was undoubtedly only one of their many impulses in 1918 and 1919. Working people, male and female, were exploring lucrative possibilities for the present, assessing different strategies through which to advance themselves and their families. Cooperation proferred many benefits: a little extra cash this month, an independent working-class institution at which to spend one's money, and, perhaps, a transformation of one's work. Maybe, even, "the Co-operative Commonwealth." Notice the exact words longshoreman Percy May chose: "There is no reason why we should not keep the profits *as long as there are profits* ourselves."[137] Many cooperatives thrived on precisely that tension: People could both do a little better this year and build for a different future. That was the beauty of it.

A number of Seattle cooperatives, though, did eschew all profits. Their statements could include subtle or not-so-subtle attacks on the big chains' policies. The Co-operative Restaurant and Cafe, for example, in its advertisements needled: "This is not on the Rochdale plan. We do not divide any profit. The profit on our employes toil can only be used by the workers as a class; and on the members decision [*sic*]."[138] The Equity Print Shop, an IWW-sympathizing cooperative antedating the war, described itself as "OWNED BY THE WORKERS CO-OPERATIVELY and where no one receives any profits."[139] The Scandia Cooperative, with bakery, restaurant, and twenty-five employees, kept all profits as "the collective property of the society" and ploughed them back into business expansion "in the interest of working-class education and emancipation."[140] Others waffled. The plumbers and steamfitters at first declared, "[T]here ain't going to be such an animal as profit" in their cooperative store but soon converted to the Rochdale system.[141]

The cooperative movement also came in for outright attacks. Letters to the *Union Record* indicate numerous criticisms of the movement rumbling among the rank and file. DISSATISFIED, for example, who him- or herself supported cooperatives, asked, "Why is it that the working people of this city do not support the co-operative movement? Answer, because they think it is another capitalistic game." He or she reported "talking with some fellows on the job about the co-operative movement." The "fellows" had argued that the cooperative chains' requirement that each member buy $20 in shares in order to join made them "capitalistic."[142] H. G. Mozens, who also supported cooperatives, similarly reported in a June letter, "Recently I have heard quite a lot of argument on Co-operation, both publicly and in more closed circles." Warbasse, he noted, after one of his big lectures "was asked if he didn't think that cooperation would create a sort of bourgeoisie within the working class." Mozens underscored, "This about the petty bourgeoisie is a very common idea among prospective cooperators. People . . . seem to be very much worried about this hitch in cooperation."[143]

These remarks suggest a pool of Seattle workers that rejected cooperatives altogether. Opponents were largely rank and file, at least when it came to public dialogue. In only one available instance did a leadership figure criticize cooperation in a speech or publication. In June 1921 James H. Fischer, a local Marxist intellectual, in a debate with John Worswick argued that "the workers should not waste their energies" on cooperation.[144] Thousands of organized workers and their wives in Seattle voted with their feet and never joined the cooperatives. Some of these included the "fellows on the job" who complained to DISSATISFIED, and the rest of the unquantifiable pool of "left" rank-and-file critics. Others included women union members, approximately 10 percent of the unions' total membership. Few male unionists would have been untouched by cooperation in some form, though. Dozens of union locals, the total membership of which counted in the tens of thousands, dabbled in producers' cooperation.[145] Many of these same locals also owned stock in the big chains. Somewhere around 2,200 families belonged to the chains by the end of 1919. At least another 200 shopped at the other consumer cooperatives, perhaps as many as a thousand, counting the municipal workers' store, the plumbers and steamfitters' outlet, and the Scandia enterprise. Finally, the *Union Record*'s 100,000 readers had at the very least to get irritated or bored by its constant dialogue about cooperation. Cooperation, in sum, while not universally embraced, was ubiquitous.

Conclusion

The Seattle AFL "labor movement" transformed itself in 1919. It was not solely based on trade unions, narrowly defined, anymore. It expanded to embrace a vast range of adjunct working-class, cooperatively organized institutions, designed to serve as additional tools for the transformation of U.S. society. Cooperatives, unlike trade unions – or, better, in tandem with them – spoke to the workplace concerns of both waged workers and women working as housewives. They illustrate the tremendous strategic experimentation taking place in 1919 Seattle. Behind the raging debates – Were cooperatives the answer? Were they backward? How should cooperatives serve trade unions? Could they help achieve socialism? – lay a premise of rapid advancement. Aspirations were high, expansion assumed, and a creative openness to new tactical approaches was pervasive. As Harry Ault put it, "Nearly all of us agree" that "the workers should control the industries." The debate, he said, was merely over how to get to that point.[146]

At the same time, the cooperatives underscore the fundamental tensions in the daily lives and aspirations of working-class people. Even in 1919, at the height of this visionary upsurge, working people still thought in terms of both the short and long run. Just as the general strike called not for a revolution but for solidarity with shipyard workers' immediate wage demands, so too people joined cooperatives because they promised to increase their families' purchasing power, expand the sphere of workers' control, and build a "homelike" world of working-class socializing in the present.

The frame within which Seattle workers built cooperatives was already restricted, moreover. Without a national-level working-class political party or even a nationally coordinated strategic program, the impulse toward institution building among Seattle workers was necessarily a local one. Even locally there was no socialist party with which to ally or into which cooperatives might siphon off surplus funds, as in Europe. That truncated character of the movement then dovetailed with the cooperatives' secessionary appeal to reinforce the least radical side of cooperation, as the question of dispensation of profits revealed. The "workers' profits" could easily glisten more brightly in the present than the Cooperative Commonwealth in a distant future. Cooperation might lead workers not out of the capitalist wilderness, but right back in.[147]

3

Labor capitalism

IN ONE PHOTOGRAPH of a 1920 Seattle parade, nine workers, with union insignia, badges, ribbons, and sashes indicating their respective locals and waving little American flags on sticks, rode by on a float from the Deep Sea Salvage Company. The float's flatbed carried a $9' \times 4'$ diagram of sunken ships lying on the bottom of the Alaska Channel northwest of Seattle. The Deep Sea Salvage Company proposed to recover these ships and with them the "millions" of dollars aboard that had sunk as they returned to Seattle from the turn-of-the-century Alaska gold rush. "Invest a hundred or a few hundred dollars now. Next fall you should be on 'easy street,'" promised the company's daily full-page advertisements in the *Union Record*.[1] The Deep Sea Salvage Company represented itself as "a cooperative corporation created out of the brain of a workingman, financed by workingmen for workingmen and their families. It's going to create a new crop of millionaires. You can be one of them."[2] Moreover, it promised, the money so garnered would not be tainted by exploitation: "[T]hese millions will be clean money – money that need not hang its head in shame over its parentage." Through the Deep Sea Salvage Company, in sum, workers could get rich, and in class-conscious fashion.[3]

The Deep Sea Salvage Company was just one example of a second body of working-class institutions founded in 1919 and early 1920, firms owned and promoted by Seattle unionists as the "workers' own" businesses. They emerged out of many of the same impulses as did the cooperatives but in their internal structure followed the lines of traditional firms. In Seattle, these businesses eventually became known by the label their critics later threw at them, "labor capitalism." They ran the gamut from the *Union Record* with its 120,000 readers, to a union-owned laundry, a union-owned savings and loan, and even "labor's own" stock-brokerage firm. All these labor capitalist enterprises proposed to advance working-class interests, all claimed bona fide trade unionists at their helms, and all described their enterprises in the language of class. Like cooperation, labor capitalism was a mass movement in 1919 and early 1920. As quickly as Seattle workers caught "cooperative fever," so too did capitalism bore from within the ranks of organized labor in the year following the general strike.

What Selig Perlman and Philip Taft called "labor in imitation of business" proved popular throughout the national AFL movement by the mid-1920s, especially at the federation's highest levels.[4] The carpenters' international union constructed a 1,886-acre retirement home in Florida accommodating 400, complete with lake, boats, and fishing poles. The Amalgamated Clothing Workers spent $1.8 million on six union-owned cooperative apartment buildings in New York City. The International Association of Machinists, International Ladies' Garment Workers' Union, and Brotherhood of Locomotive Engineers all founded union-owned banks. Especially popular among high-ranking, often conservative AFL leaders such as Warren Stone of the Locomotive Engineers, the labor capitalist movement came in for vicious criticism from the left. Attacks by the Communist William Z. Foster and others underscored how enmeshed in capitalist entrepreneurial activities the AFL had become by decade's end, if rarely with a lucrative outcome.[5]

Class interest: the workers' money

The origins of the labor capitalist movement lay in the new funds available to the U.S. white working class in the war years. By 1919 many of Seattle's white workers were relatively prosperous in comparison with previous decades. "While the war was at full blast everybody had money," Frank Rust, president of the Trade Union Savings and Loan Association, observed.[6] "All of them had more savings than ever before," agreed Hulet Wells, former Central Labor Council president.[7] This was true both of individual workers, many of whom through trade-union strength had been able to outpace inflation while enjoying year-round employment, and of their organizations, which garnered a regular share of workers' wages through the dues payments of tens of thousands of new members. Throughout the country the coffers of locals and internationals overflowed as organized labor's ranks swelled.[8]

The wartime Liberty Bond drives made this pool of money visible in Seattle. Most Seattle trade unions enthusiastically supported the city's Liberty Loan drives, once the United States had entered the war and opposition had been suppressed. The sums produced were large. The bakers, for example, bought $15,750; the cooks $1,500; the plumbers $3,000; the shipyard laborers $7,000. Topping the list as usual were the boilermakers, who by April 1919 held $54,700 in Liberty Bonds.[9] Reinhold Loewe, who would later become an officer of the machinists' union, recalled that the boilermakers' local had so much money in war bonds that its officials piled them up in wastebaskets around the union office, for lack of any other storage place.[10]

As soon as activists became aware of these sums they began to speculate as to how to employ them. "The way labor bought liberty bonds demonstrated that we can raise the funds for any undertaking," concluded Percy May, the longshoreman.[11] George Listman, who became a prominent local labor capitalist entrepreneur, told a reporter in early 1919 that he had become "more than ever convinced that labor has the financial power to launch its own industries when he recognized the amazing extent to which labor was able to assist in financing the world war."[12] Rank-and-filer E. J. Boyle wrote into the *Union Record* his own scheme for labor's advancement, concluding: "It would be no idle dream, as labor holds millions in bonds and I do believe would furnish the capital."[13] The bond drives not only made the total savings available within the white working class visible; they also provided an example of the use of working-class money for collective, political purposes. War bonds were easily transferred, moreover, as "loans" or investments to workers' enterprises.[14]

In the class-conscious world of 1919 Seattle, the very existence of surplus money raised new political questions. Mrs. C.Y., for example, inquired of the *Record*'s advice columnist Ruth Ridgeway: "Our neighborhood, a typical workingmen's district, is very much divided as to the merits of saving or spending, and your opinion is wanted.... Our opponents say it is a workingman's duty to spend freely in order to give others work and have the good things in life that we create." In her own camp, on the other hand, "[W]e contend that under the present system it is our duty to look ahead and prepare for emergency." Her family's savings, she pointed out, had protected her husband from having to scab during a recent strike.[15] Mrs. C.Y. captures the exact moment of 1919 perfectly. Large numbers of white workers had more money than ever before. They faced two questions: first, whether to spend it or save it (or both); and second, how to do either in the best class-conscious terms. Cooperatives and boycotts offered ways to politicize spending. The question remained as to how to politicize savings.[16]

The question itself was an unprecedented one in U.S. history. Two conditions made it possible: first, the relative prosperity of the white working class, and second, the level of political consciousness and self-organization necessary for the argument that money could be employed to serve collective interests. Labor capitalism evolved out of this exact historical context. It resolved the question of how to use surplus money for political ends by offering a politicized channel for working-class funds.

Seattle workers' own words underscore their political discovery of working-class money. "All of the big financial transactions of the nation are carried on with the money of the workers," declared Jack Mundy, president of both the Central Labor Council and of the United Finance Company.[17] "We are handling working men's money," officials of the Trades Union Savings and Loan announced. Working-class money was a source of power. "Money Power of Workers. What do you do with your savings? . . . The savings of workers when considered separately are small, but when united make millions," pronounced the Seattle Union Theatre Company.[18] Trade-union activist Blanche Johnson argued similarly, "Our meagre savings," if put together in the Trades Union Savings and Loan, "can be used to our advantage and not to our detriment."[19] In other words, once amassed, the workers' money gave another new weapon to the working class. Like both the workers' purchasing power and their labor power, it had to be organized, into labor capitalist enterprises. As the theater company put it, "FORM A UNION OF YOUR SAVINGS" and "ORGANIZE YOUR DOLLARS."[20]

Money at work

Dozens of enterprises called out for workers' dollars in 1919 and 1920, each advertising itself as the best economic niche into which workers' surplus money should ideally flow. They broke down into three broad types. First were enterprises designed to produce propaganda promoting the militant wing of the AFL movement. A good example of these was the Federated Film Corporation. Its promoters plotted labor-owned, labor-produced films that, they argued, would seize the new ideological power of film and employ it as "wonderful propaganda for the cause of labor."[21] J. Arthur Nelson, the company's manager, in a pitch to the Central Labor Council estimated that films could reach an audience of 25 million trade unionists and their friends. In this manner "the non-union man of today . . . can be made the loyal union man of tomorrow."[22] Seattle's metal trades locals were especially enthusiastic about the Federated Film Corporation. Bert Swain, secretary of the Metal Trades Council, served as its main promoter, traveling to the 1921 AFL national convention as a delegate from the project. Overall, though, Seattle unions investing in the film company ran the political gamut, from other left-wing locals such as the millmen and painters all the way through to the butchers. By June 1920 the film company had raised $27,000 and begun to produce its first film.[23]

In contrast to other forms of labor capitalism, the Federated Film Corporation promised not financial but ideological returns on the unions' investments. It evidently paid dividends, in theory at least. Yet those who invested in the project did not, it appears, do so to earn money. The Metal Trades Council, for example, voted in June 1920 to send its anticipated profits from the film company to support striking machinists in the San Francisco Bay area.[24]

Seattle's premier labor-owned propaganda enterprise was the *Union Record*. The *Record* was the ideological linchpin of the postwar Seattle labor movement, and its importance to the solidarity, creativity, and class consciousness of the movement is difficult to overestimate. Its circulation grew from 100,000 in late 1919 to 120,000 by 1920. Through the pages of the *Record* Seattle workers learned of meetings of their locals, of visiting political speakers, and of debates in the Central Labor Council, the State Federation of Labor, and AFL. They read editorials and news stories ranging from the Russian Revolution to Irish strikes to municipal ownership of local traction companies to youthful murderesses, all with a class angle. On its women's pages the *Record* supplied fashion tips, recipes, serialized romances, and reports of dozens of local working-class women's organizations; men could enjoy reading a full-page daily sports section, reports of their own locals, and fishing advice – again, all with a class angle. Rank-and-file workers sent in letters to the editor proposing wild schemes for working-class liberation. Debates on personal and political topics raged in Ruth Ridgeway's class-conscious advice column. The *Union Record*, in sum, was critical both to the ability of a labor movement as complex as Seattle's to communicate with itself swiftly and efficiently, and to its ability to employ a politics of all aspects of daily life.[25]

The *Record* was also a complex financial operation. The paper had first been purchased in 1903 as a weekly, owned and controlled by the Central Labor Council. In 1918 the council decided to turn the *Record* into a daily, necessitating a great deal of capital investment. This meant that the *Record* was constantly selling its stock merely to exist. By 1920 the central council still owned a controlling 51 percent of a total of $100,000 in the paper's stock, the boilermakers owned $15,060, machinists $7,500, carpenters $3,995, shipwrights $2,000, mineworkers $2,000, blacksmiths $1,550, and shipyard laborers, steam engineers, longshoremen, and structural iron workers each around $1,000. More than fifty other locals, along with individual investors, held the remaining stock in smaller amounts. The paper was governed by a board of directors elected by the Central Labor Council. Like the film company, the *Record* never presented itself as a profit-producing enterprise. Indeed, its masthead read "Published for Principle and Not for Profit." *Record* stock paid no dividends. The return here, too, was ideological.[26]

A second, more varied group of labor enterprises supported local AFL trade unions more directly. One type within this group, the labor-owned hall, was by no means new. In the flush times of 1919, Seattle unions expanded their old halls, bought new ones, outfitted them comfortably, and dreamed of still larger palaces. A good example of such halls was the Carpenters' Hall. Local #131 originally incorporated it in 1901 as the "Washington Benevolent Association." Its board of directors was elected from the membership and overlapped with the local's officers. The local paid rent to the association, which in turn paid dividends on the stock back to the union.[27] Seven stories high, the Carpenters' Hall housed a hotel, two stores, "various fraternal halls," a dining hall, offices for both the local and the District Council of Carpenters, and a 40' × 50' meeting room.

In the basement members could use lockers and a grinding room for tools; above, "a reading room with green walls and mission furniture, where games of checkers go on and the world is talked over amid comfortable smoke."[28]

Musicians, west Seattle carpenters, and longshoremen all enjoyed their own halls by the early 1920s, legally incorporated as private businesses but financially interlocked with their locals. The waitresses had their own "rest home," which provided care for infirm members. The largest of Seattle labor halls was the Labor Temple. It housed the offices of dozens of smaller locals and provided an array of halls for their meetings. Its main hall, including a gallery, housed the often-raucous meetings of the Central Labor Council. In 1919 and 1920 the Labor Temple also began to rent space to other labor capitalist enteprises as they emerged. With all these buildings Seattle's AFL locals used their new-found prosperity to expand the services they offered members and to provide physical independence to their organizations, all within the careful context of business unionism.[29]

Other labor-owned enterprises based in the trade unions broke out of that mold. Most prominent of these was the Mutual Laundry. For a number of years Laundry Workers' Local #24 had tried to organize Seattle's laundry industry, only to be rebuffed as the owners relentlessly blacklisted organizers. In 1915, the union decided to start its own labor-owned laundry. Local #24 bought half the stock, and other miscellaneous locals in the city, along with individuals, the rest. Starting the laundry required negotiating a prolonged anti-union obstacle course. To buy the necessary equipment and supplies in the face of hostile employers, organizers had to employ fake names, pay bribes, and engage in a national search for laundry machinery. But after it opened in 1915 the Mutual Laundry surpassed the union's greatest hopes. During a 1917 strike it harbored blacklisted organizers, broke the employers' united front, and opened the door to 100 percent unionization of white laundry workers in Seattle well into the mid-twenties. At the same time it created jobs for more than sixty trade unionists at wages above union scale.[30]

The Mutual Laundry functioned as the cornerstone of the labor capitalist movement in Seattle. It served as the original model of a citywide, cross-trade stock subscription campaign to serve trade-union ends. It worked as a wedge into the industry for the union. Equally important, it was a successful business that paid steady dividends – 10 percent in 1919 – to its investors.[31] Promoters of other, sometimes more dubious "labor" enterprises repeatedly held up the Mutual Laundry in their promotions, promising that labor could "make good" in their particular scheme in the same manner. Equally inspired by the Mutual Laundry were the workers who founded producers' cooperatives in 1918–19, such as the butchers, tailors, auto mechanics, and barbers, all of whom consciously emulated the Mutual Laundry. Unions in other trades used their surplus money to fund noncooperative enterprises outside Seattle with similar goals in mind. Typographers' Local #202, for example, held stock in the Northwest Service Corporation, a print shop designed to uphold union conditions in Walla Walla, on the far side of the state. "This became a regular tactic," Anna Louise Strong recalled of the enthusiasm inspired by the Mutual Laundry in this period; "in any small industry where the bosses opposed trade unions, the unions would start an enterprise which would give jobs to all the agitators who were thrown out of other plants."[32]

Still more ambitious within this second group were Seattle's labor banks. In January 1919 the Central Labor Council launched the Trades Union Savings and Loan Association. The council elected the original directors, who subsequently would be elected by the stockholders. The Savings and Loan then sold stock to union locals and their members only. It opened its doors in March 1919. Deposits climbed to $307,000 by September 30, reaching half a million by the end of the year, with 3,000 accounts. By the end of 1920 the savings and loan grew still further to $884,000. Services to members grew beyond savings accounts to include safety deposit boxes, "trade union checks" in $10 increments, and insurance, issued as a sideline by President Frank Rust. The savings and loan lent its money on improved real estate and kept the reserves in Liberty Bonds.[33]

In its advertisements the Trades Union Savings and Loan cast itself squarely in the midst of the self-management impulses that pervaded the Seattle AFL in 1919. "For the first time in the history of the United States Organized Labor will be in the banking business for itself," the association declared.[34] By depositing with the savings and loan, workers could "show our faith in our own works and our ability to make good in this line as we have in the newspaper, the laundry, the grocery and the meat business."[35] Labor, moreover, should keep its money to itself "instead of giving it to their enemies to be used against them."[36] In the words of a *Record* reporter, "There was more or less obscure feeling that all the money of workers given to local banks was merely adding that much power to the 'enemy.' "[37] As funds grew, though, a new appeal crept into the savings and loan's promotions – high rates of return. "PATRONIZE YOUR OWN INSTITUTION. IT ALWAYS PAYS," ads began to promise.[38] A January 1920 *Record* ad queried, "DIVIDENDS DISTRIBUTED $4,665.17. Did You Get Yours?"[39]

The savings and loan emerged from the AFL movement's new sense of its collective powers in 1919. But the enterprise's general character was quiet, relative to other undertakings that year. Its original directors included almost all the prominent conservatives in the Central Labor Council – Robert Hesketh, city councilman; Charles Doyle, labor council president; and Frank Cotterill, secretary of the Building Trades Council, as well as officers of other labor institutions, including the *Record*'s Harry Ault, the Labor Temple's Frank Rust, and A. G. Dentler, a manager of the Co-operative Food Products Association. These officials were not without their own vision, though. They shared a staid, nonaggressive, non-confrontational model for social change. Frank Rust, the savings and loan's main mover and shaker, summed up this view:

> I am just as radical as any of you, only I use common sense in trying to get certain things. If I wanted to go to Spokane I would take a train to get there.... A wobbly might want to go by airplane or jumping over there. They want to use methods that are not practical at this time.... Just because I believe in only going as far as I can to get results, I am classed as a conservative.... I know we are not ready to do away with the banks so I am contented in trying to develop a bank operated by organized labor.[40]

Yet in the context of 1919, even a self-identified "conservative" like Rust defended himself as "just as radical" as anyone else.[41]

As class relations in Seattle polarized in 1919, the scale of the unions' aspirations expanded to a full-scale bank. The building trades, angered that the city's banks were blackmailing pro-union contractors who agreed to the closed shop, led the campaign. Meanwhile, the *Union Record* had discovered that no Seattle bank would lend to it. Enthusiasm peaked when David Rodgers, manager of the Skinner and Eddy shipyard during the war, tried to raise the guarantee funds to reopen one of Seattle's major shipyards, and the banks, aware that Rodgers sympathized with labor, refused all loans.[42]

Rodgers' rejection, highly publicized by the *Union Record*, galvanized a citywide subscription drive for a proposed Producers' Bank. In May, June, and July of 1920 the paper ran a series of page-one boxed stories in which prominent trade unionists of every political persuasion testified as to just how valuable the bank could be. The arguments largely replicated those on behalf of the savings and loan: Workers should keep their money away from the enemy, support their friends, and build independent working-class institutions. On occasion promoters also discreetly noted that "stock in banks is highly profitable." Throughout the spring of 1920 Seattle AFL locals debated the proposition and pledged substantial sums – $1,250 from the carpenters and $500 from the steamfitters, for example. But the total of $80,000 subscribed by December 1920 fell far short of the $250,000 necessary to launch it, and the money was returned in 1921.[43]

As these examples suggest, the distinction between labor capitalism and cooperatives in 1919 Seattle was not tidy. Some real differences did demarcate the two. Internal structures diverged. Labor capitalist firms were not managed by one member, one vote. Their stock was held by large trade unions, usually, in varying blocks that gave different bodies highly unequal voting powers. Most of the enterprises issued both preferred and regular stock, restricting the voting power of certain stockholders. Equally important, labor capitalism was not part of a gospel like that of the international cooperative movement, with its Rochdale prophets. Labor capitalist enterprises were not trying to transform the nature of the U.S. economy; rather, they were somewhat more instrumentally understood as tools, using the form of a regular capitalist firm to advance working-class interests.[44]

At the same time, though, cooperatives and labor capitalism emerged from many of the same impulses toward workers' ownership, greater leverage on the part of trade unions, and a better life for working people attained through collective projects. Proponents of both appealed as supplicants before union locals, central labor bodies, and individual workers, asking for stock purchases. In the fall of 1919 the Cooperative Food Products Association was as concerned with selling its stock as was the Mutual Laundry, the *Union Record*, or the Producers' Bank. All these enterprises, of whatever form, needed capital if they were to survive and expand. At a basic level, both the cooperatives and labor capitalism offered a way to politicize workers' investments in service to a class-understood agenda.

In the 1919–20 Seattle AFL the two forms of institution building began to overlap and interlock in networks of mutual support. The Federated Film Corporation's first film, *The New Disciple*, for example, completed in 1921, depicted an organizing drive, then a strike, "and at last the employer goes broke because of the strike and the industry is opened up again by the workers under the Cooperative plan."[45] The *Union Record*'s columns abounded with appeals for cooperation. From the other side, cooperative activists joined actively in the campaign for the Producers' Bank because they too wanted access to capital.[46] Advertisements for the Mutual Laundry, Trades Union Savings and Loan, and Deep Sea Salvage covered the back page of the Cooperative Food Products Association's newsletter.[47]

Confusing references to "cooperation," as a result, abounded. The term "cooperative" was not, after all, private property, and labor capitalist promoters' use of it was fast and loose. The savings and loan, for example, described itself as "A Co-operative Savings Institution Established and Operated by Organized Labor." Its ads proclaimed that it was "entirely cooperative," when all that meant was "there being no preferred stock of any character."[48]

Such dubious arguments pervaded the promotions launched by a third and final group of labor capitalist enterprises. These are best categorized as get-rich-quick scams, more capitalist than labor. An especially murky such operation was the Listman Service Company. Its promoters argued that capitalism itself, unreconstructed, could fulfill the workers' wildest dreams, if only it were properly approached. Their seduction began with the simple enough proposition that "the people who produce wealth" should "also enjoy it."[49] Wealth, however, was produced both through production and – here was the key – in investment. Therefore, by entering into the economy as a capitalist, the worker would be able to "derive the fruits from his money as well as labor."[50] "The man who produces the

$ is entitled to what that $ produces," the Listman Service Company's advertisements reasoned.[51] Not only would thus "to the producer belong the production" – the company's other motto – but, indeed, the workers could even "Secure . . . Ownership of the industries in Which they Labor."[52] Therefore, by investing in the Listman Service Company the worker could "own the machine you work and own the machine that works your money." The company concluded by recasting its initials as "Labor's Success Cooperative."[53]

Behind this rhetoric the Listman Service Company was an ordinary stock-brokerage firm, headed by George Listman, a veteran of the printers' union and a man with a finger in many labor capitalist pies. Founded in 1919, a year later the company employed seventy-five people and had branch offices in Spokane, Bremerton, Aberdeen, Tacoma, Bellingham, and Yakima, as well as in Seattle. Its army of salespeople sold stock, in turn, in still another labor capitalist firm, the United Finance Company. That, too, was owned by prominent labor figures and advertised itself as "the salvation of the working people." It bought and sold car loans.[54]

Another enterprise in this category, the Padilla Bay Development Association, offered an alternative dynamic capitalist opportunity, land speculation. Harry Ault, the *Record*'s editor; Saul Haas, its managing editor; and Ben Nauman of the boilermakers' union bought up hundreds of acres of unusable tidelands outside Seattle near the old Equality Colony, formed a reclamation district, and sold lots to individual working-class investors, with the promise that the land would eventually be drained through dikes. Both advertisements and articles in the *Record* promoted the scheme. Saul Haas, under his alias "Paul Harris," the paper's financial-advice columnist, not only wrote it up favorably but personally led tours to the site. Several hundred *Record* readers bought these lots.[55]

The Deep Sea Salvage Company, the enterprise promising to dredge up gold-laden ships from the Alaska channel, belongs in this same final category. Workers could buy stocks in the firm and then get rich quick, all while staying class conscious. As the company's promoters promised, the money was, after all, "clean."

These enrich-the-workers schemes can be understood as part of a broader tactical dialogue within the labor movement in which some voices always advocated an accommodation to capitalism. Labor capitalists of this last stripe advocated not a revolutionary transformation but, rather, a creative approach to successfully using capitalism to serve the working class. Labor and capital were not yet in harmony in their models. The two were distinct groups, often at war. But labor and capitalism, on the other hand, could perhaps get along well.

As murky as was the line between cooperatives and labor capitalism, still more obscure were the actual financial activities of any given labor capitalist enterprise, as opposed to the claims made in its advertisements.

It would take a great deal of research to decipher the Listman Service Company, or to distinguish Paul Harris, the advice columnist, from Saul Haas, the managing editor who owned swamps.

One last example illustrates the obscurity of the actual workings of labor capitalist enterprises. The Seattle Union Theatre Company, founded in 1919, ran almost daily half- or full-page ads in the *Record*. It described itself as another firm "owned and managed by Union Men," through which workers could "Build another Successful Union Owned Enterprise" "without enriching a lot of scheming profiteers," and thus labor would soon "Be Financially Too Powerful for Capital to Treat Lightly."[56] By owning and patronizing their own theater "the 75,000 union men of Seattle" could "pour enormous dividends into their own pockets."[57] In reality the theater was not owned by unions or even particularly workers at all but rather by Harry Ault and Frank Rust, president of the savings and loan. It would be wrong to cast these men as mere scheming interlopers. Ault was a sincere socialist who gave his life to the working-class movement in Seattle. He claimed never personally to have profited from these enterprises. In 1921 he wrote an agent for the company that he "felt it had great possibility as an attribute to the advancement of the organization of the workers by the display of films showing truthfully present conditions. . . . I thought also the project could be made a financial success and bring back to the people who patronize the theatre some of the tremendous profits made by such enterprises."[58]

The line between businessman and union leader dissolved in the enthusiasm for labor capitalism. Harry Ault had his hand not only in the *Record* and the Padilla Bay development, but he was also vice president of the Listman Service Company, a director of the General Distributors Corporation (a labor capitalist car company), and president of the theater company. Jack Mundy was president of both the Central Labor Council and the United Finance Company, and part owner of the Listman Service Company. The list of leaders-turned-businessmen was extensive.[59] In many ways, this was nothing new. Trade-union officialdom had been a path out of the shop and into white-collar positions since the stabilization of the AFL had created hundreds of paid positions in the labor movement at the turn of the century. Many craft unions served as a path upward for their members, helping barbers, butchers, cooks, and carpenters accumulate nest eggs with which to cross over into self-employment. Seattle's cooperatives acknowledged and even encouraged workers' small-business aspirations. The labor capitalist enthusiasm of 1919, though, offered an unprecedented opportunity for union officials to cash in on class consciousness. In the intense context of class conflict that year, labor credentials became a commodity one could peddle with, perhaps, a lucrative outcome.

Labor capitalism, then, was a malleable form into which many widely divergent aspirations might flow. While all the enterprises had in common their basic incorporation as joint-stock firms and shared enthusiasm for using such institutions to benefit "labor" and "the workers," beyond that the range was immense. At one end of the spectrum were the propaganda enterprises that remained hostile to capitalism, eschewing monetary profits. At the other end were those in which the "labor" in "labor capitalism" might be ephemeral indeed. The question of profits, which lurked uneasily around the edges of the cooperative movement, never embraced with entire comfort, lay at center stage for many of the labor capitalist enterprises and sometimes served as the star of the show. Whatever its particular incarnation, labor capitalism had become deeply embedded institutionally into the economic and organizational structures of Seattle's AFL locals and the Central Labor Council. Whether it would enrich that movement remained to be seen.

Whose class interest?

The money that made all these enterprises possible came ultimately from rank-and-file workers and their families. For unions or individual workers trying to figure out how to invest money in class-conscious terms, though, the choice between these potentially rewarding opportunities could be a difficult one. One could buy shares in any number of cooperatives. One could forgo interest and fund labor's ideological weapons. One could put it in labor's savings and loan, or buy stock in a labor bank, pulling dollars away from hostile employers and keeping them within a working-class circuit. Or one could try out one of the many lucrative possibilities for enriching oneself under capitalism.

Potential investors had only a few maps with which to navigate this sea of opportunities. None of the ways in which to inform oneself was sure. Certainly advertisements were suspect. Individuals could look to trade-union endorsements for a perhaps safer recommendation. Some locals created "investigating committees" to look into possible or continuing investments and report as to their viability. But the unions largely depended on the same sources of information as did individual potential investors. An investigating committee's assessment as to the financial status of a particular enterprise could be entangled with political decisions whether to use money for revolutionary propaganda, for get-rich-quick investments, or whether to expect dividends.[60] As a source of information, the *Union Record* retained an unimpeachable reputation up to mid-1920. In 1919 few were aware how deeply enmeshed in labor capitalism its key staff had become.

Most of the AFL locals who chose to invest in labor capitalism had all-male memberships. The overflowing coffers of the metal trades were especially critical. Their money, combined with their radicalism, was particularly important in funding the propaganda forms of labor capitalism. Seattle's more traditional craft locals also proved to be determined supporters of the *Union Record*. Much of the money for the Federated Film Company came from the city's more conservative locals as well as from left-inclined unions. Support for meeting halls cut similarly across left/right, craft/ industrial distinctions between male locals. Both the musicians and longshoremen built halls, for example. The important distinction, in this case, was between prosperous and less prosperous locals. The dozens of smaller unions of the unskilled, newly formed with the war and only barely hanging on afterward, had no halls of their own. Union halls in their very physical presence represented a capital investment only a large, established local with a sense of its own long-term existence and a high dues income could consider making.

Labor capitalism was not, by and large, a tactic chosen by women within the AFL, though no opposition is evident. Two women spoke up on behalf of the bank drive, Alice Lord of the waitresses and Blanche Johnson, who had recently been on the labor council's payroll as its organizer for women. Wives of union members on some occasions organized on behalf of the *Union Record*. Otherwise, labor capitalism was not taken up or even discussed by the great majority of Seattle's working-class women's organizations. When mixed-gender locals such as those of the musicians or typographers debated the disposition of their surplus money, women members had no voice in the process.[61] Most all-women's locals, for their part, were not old, big, or financially secure enough to conceive of buying a hall or getting rich through investments. The one exception, the waitresses' home, had been funded more through donations from wealthy patrons than from dues.[62]

The Mutual Laundry, however, serves as a prominent exception. The cornerstone successful labor capitalist enterprise, it emerged from a largely female union. Most of those who were employed at the Mutual Laundry were female, and white female laundry workers benefited from the closed shop in Seattle's white laundries during the entire 1920s. The Mutual Laundry, though, was entirely managed and promoted by men. Throughout its history it retained the sexual division of labor already established in the city's laundry industry. Men drove trucks and held the most highly skilled jobs; women performed the unskilled, hot, and repetitive jobs. The Mutual Laundry perpetuated the pay differentials between men and women embedded in that division of labor, moreover. In 1926, for example, the laundry paid women workers $17.25 a week, the state minimum wage, and male drivers $30.00 a week.[63]

On closer examination individual white women's relationship to the very "prosperity" of 1919 was often attenuated. One group of women, single wage-earners, obtained better jobs with the war. But that did not necessarily mean decent pay. Single women, living apart from their families, in the best jobs available to white women, still made only just enough to keep from starving. Except in rare cases, they could not save enough money even to consider investing it.[64] For married women the question is more complicated. We do not know who controlled decision making over investments within working-class families in this period. We can assume that patriarchal authority within the household gave men power over how to save money. But because wives were usually responsible for shopping, paying bills, and sometimes overseeing bank accounts, it is not necessarily safe to assume that they had no voice, or even the weaker one, in the matter of their family's economic strategies. Promoters of labor capitalist investments in Seattle, however, did not cast their pitches toward women in any special way that would suggest women's special control over family investments.[65]

White working-class women in Seattle might nonetheless have benefited from labor capitalism. The most prominent source of benefits was the *Union Record*. With a circulation of 120,000, tens of thousands of working-class women in Seattle read the *Record*, which included whole pages of recipes, fashion tips, and a great range of advice to aid women in their labors both as consumers and in keeping their families happy, managing social events, and maneuvering the subtleties of relationships. Regular columns and editorials on the women's pages advocated the collectivization of housework and child care. Indeed, the *Record* served as the strongest, most flexible, and most easily accessible voice of feminism within Seattle's working-class context. On its pages women and men fiercely debated the right of married women to work or talked out the fate of abandoned wives and lovers from a class-conscious perspective. The *Union Record* served as a tool for the achievement of equality within the white working class, and its movement, as well.[66] This helps explain why some wives of AFL members did agitate on behalf of the *Record*, if not other enterprises.[67]

For both women and men of the rank and file and the members of their families, moreover, benefits might accrue indirectly from labor capitalism. By late 1919 the whole of the Seattle AFL movement was much greater than the sum of its parts. A critical mass of money and vision spilled out over the whole city, benefiting far more workers than just those who conceived and funded any given enterprise. The Federated Film Company, for example, in its propaganda efforts, was designed to help press the cause of unionists from every trade. Similarly, and with far more immediate effectiveness, all white workers belonging to the AFL who could read English could potentially benefit from the *Record*. Any of the unions could advertise meetings in its pages and benefit, in multiple indirect ways, from the class consciousness and solidarity it fostered. So too the Producers' Bank was designed to support friendly employers of any sector of the Seattle economy. The *Record*, the laundry workers, the cooperatives – each of these had problems with which they believed the bank could help. The scope of the bank drive was so large that even Seattle's mass production sector, the metal trades industry, could benefit, not just the small-scale sector in which producer cooperatives and labor capitalist businesses like the Mutual Laundry emerged. Opening a shipyard was an immense capital investment possible only through the amassing of working-class money from all sectors of the movement. Seattle's trade-union leaders were well aware, along with the city's employers, of the importance of a mass base of organized shipyard workers to the whole white working-class movement.

Which "workers'" money?

Still deeper structural factors begin to explain why all those involved in both the cooperative and labor capitalist movements were white. No Japanese- or African-Americans appear to have participated in Seattle's labor capitalist or cooperative enterprises, except insofar as businesses owned by Japanese-Americans advertised in the *Union Record* and the paper on rare occasions reported on Japanese-American unions or black–white relations.[68] In other U.S. contexts in this period, however, workers from both groups formed cooperatives. Japanese immigrant shoemakers in San Francisco formed cooperative buying societies. African-American packinghouse workers in Chicago formed a union-sponsored cooperative store in 1919, as did African-Americans in St. Louis.[69]

The explanation for the all-white character of Seattle's labor institutions begins at the point of production. In part because of the actions of AFL unionists, Japanese- and African-American workers were excluded from most of the jobs in which AFL unions were present. White unionists then barred Japanese- and African-American workers from AFL membership, as we have seen. Therefore, at a very basic level Japanese- and African-American workers were excluded both organizationally and conceptually from the AFL movement's definition of the "workers." So if the "workers" and "labor" were all-white, then "the workers' money," "the workers' purchasing power," and "labor's own businesses" were by implicit definition white. In other words, the same white workers who built cooperatives and labor-owned businesses participated in the construction of racial walls around those institutions as well.

Just as the AFL movement's racial barriers extended from organizing at the point of production to that of consumption, so too African-, Chinese-, and Japanese-American residents of Seattle experienced racial discrimination in consumption as well as production. In this most northern of cities, whites enforced segregation of restaurants, theaters, and housing.[70] Monica Sone's family, for example, tried to rent a house near Alki Beach for the summer when she was a young girl. Through repeated failures they learned that Japanese-Americans were barred not only from the beach but from the entire neighborhood as well; the Ballard beach was "whites-only," too.[71] In renting or buying housing African- and Asian-Americans were restricted to a handful of central-city neighborhoods. Both groups consistently paid a larger portion of their family budgets for housing than did whites, in exchange for inferior housing stock.[72]

These patterns of discrimination in consumption helped forge forms of ethnic consciousness in the Japanese immigrant and African-American communities that in many ways echoed white workers' impulse toward labor capitalism. In their ability to realize such aspirations in concrete form, however, the Japanese- and African-American communities diverged sharply. By 1919 Seattle's Japanese-Americans had built a network of ethnic enterprises in many ways paralleling those of the AFL. They owned dozens of hotels, stores, laundries, and bathhouses and their own newspapers, five banks, and even a chain Japanese-import emporium, Furuya's, that approximated a department store of Japanese products.[73] These enterprises were built by an immigrant Japanese entrepreneurial class, many of whose members had entered the United States with capital in hand. As Sylvia Junko Yanagisako has shown, most Japanese immigrants to Seattle came from regions "where the market economy was most developed." Once in the United States, they could participate in tight-knit prefectural associations (*kenjin-kai*) that recruited and trained fellow members into the same line of trade, whether it be horticultural nurseries, restaurants, or hotels. Through their *kenjin-kai*, moreover, Japanese immigrants had access to rotating credit associations, expanding their access to capital for small businesses. Even those Japanese immigrants who came from peasant families, worked in menial jobs, and came to the United States without savings could gain access to this thriving network of mutual technical and financial support, if only to hear of an undervalued hotel for sale or obtain a job at which it might be possible to save money.[74]

For Seattle's African-Americans, the situation was quite different. With a population of only 2,894, the community could support financially only a tiny entrepreneurial sector. Most successful were two transfer and local cartage companies, a real estate agency, a cleaning and dyeing establishment, and a catering firm. Seattle African-Americans also published at least three weekly or monthly newspapers. Despite a strong sense of community identity built through churches, benevolent associations, charity work, and a host of other undertakings, however, African-Americans in Seattle did not have the access to credit available to Japanese immigrants. African-Americans had no independently owned financial institutions or credit pools in Seattle on which to draw. Unlike white male workers and many Japanese-Americans, African-American workers did not experience wartime prosperity that might have produced new funds. Therefore, for Seattle's African-American community, the question of how to invest the surplus fruits of prosperity never even came up.[75]

The question of how to spend money from an ethnically conscious point of view nonetheless arose within the African-American community during the period. Horace Cayton in his weekly paper repeatedly chastised African-Americans for failing to support African-American–owned businesses with their patronage.[76] But given the economic and demographic numbers of the situation, there was only so much to be done. Seattle's prosperous Japanese-American businesses had all gotten their start by serving the city's 8,000-strong Japanese-American community. Often barred from patronizing white-owned concerns, Japanese immigrants sought out products and services replicating those available in Japan, thus creating a local market for Japanese-owned firms, augmented by thousands of Japanese-American workers in the hinterland. Only after they had established themselves serving immigrants from their homeland did Japanese-American entrepreneurs cross over to serve white patrons. By 1919 Japanese-American businesses interlocked in tight webs of mutual support, in part to help counter white opposition. Japanese-American farmers from throughout Washington state traveled to Seattle to shop for specialty products and thus support local Japanese-American entrepreneurs who, in turn, bought the farmers' agricultural products. Japanese-American hotel owners sent their sheets and towels to laundries owned by Japanese-Americans. The Japanese-American community, in sum, had its own critical mass of ethnically conscious capitalism, while the African-American community did not. While African-American leaders advocated a "black money" policy that in many ways paralleled that of "the workers' money," its effectiveness was sharply restricted.[77]

Conclusion

Class-conscious prosperity, then, was limited. Not all were part of the imagined "class" whose money power was about to be mobilized. The AFL movement's question of how to politicize surplus money was really an appropriate question only for white male trade unionists.

Through labor capitalism members of the AFL were groping toward how to use their own money collectively, for what they perceived as their class interests. As they did in the cooperative movement, workers pursued strategies that might either serve individual advancement under capitalism through enterprises such as the Deep Sea Salvage Company, or, alternately, use collective power to overthrow it. Rank-and-file workers, leaders, their organizations, all were trying to figure out how best, strategically, to use their newly invented "money power." Some voices wanted to use this new tool to deploy revolutionary propaganda; others opened the door gladly for capitalism to bore from within. In the process seeds of accommodation and class harmony received a new and different form of nurturance, right within the middle of the class-conscious upsurge of 1919.

Labor capitalism, in sum, in all its chimerical forms, embodied the full contradictions rapidly emerging within the postwar Seattle labor movement. The question of how to march forward, with newly acquired dollars in a clenched, maybe even upraised fist, was not an easily answered one, and it could be asked only by a subsection of the working class, at a rare moment in U.S. history. Whatever the reply, labor capitalism symbolized still further the creativity, expansiveness, and vision of the Seattle AFL as it peaked after the war. Here was yet another sphere in which Seattle's white working class discovered new powers, tried new tricks with them, and expanded, still further, its sense of the possible.

Part II

Revision

4

Counterattack

THE SEATTLE AFL'S EXPERIMENTS in institution building during 1919 were predicated upon trade-union strength at the waged workplace, where workers confronted employers over both control of the work process and the hours and terms of their labor. Both cooperatives and labor capitalism depended directly upon money obtained through the unions' wage demands. They were designed to serve as a second front, developed in tandem with trade unions to enhance and complement workplace demands. Without the trade unions, in other words, there was no "labor" in "labor capitalism," no primary organizations to look to cooperation as an appealing adjunct strategy. The Seattle labor movement began, and could end, at the point of production.

In 1919 Seattle's employers had their eyes on precisely that bedrock of organized labor's strength. They were profoundly threatened economically, as individuals, and collectively, as a class, by the city's trade-union movement as it climaxed with the February general strike. They had their own vision of expansion and creativity. Over the course of 1919, the two visions of postwar Seattle – organized labor's and organized capital's – clashed like great stones grinding together. For all the ostensible independence of the institutions that Seattle workers built during that year, labor still existed in relation to capital. In the fall, just as the cooperative and labor capitalist movements reached their peaks, the city's employers brought that reality home abruptly, and the context of the trade union movement in Seattle changed dramatically. The party, for labor, was most definitely over.

On borrowed time

Seattle trade unionists knew in early 1919 that an axe was hanging over their heads. Their awareness that Seattle's employers would soon try to roll back the unions' wartime gains had been a primary reason why they chose the general strike, in order to take the offensive while their strength was at its greatest rather than wait passively for the employers' counterattack. When the strike was over, some unions found themselves in immediate difficulty. Skirmishes broke out over reinstatement of workers who had walked out. Most returning members of the building service workers' union, for example, reclaimed their jobs "without discrimination," but Central Labor Council officers had to intervene to ensure the jobs, and members who had worked at Rhodes department store and the Greater Theatre Companies found themselves locked out.[1] The State Federation of Labor reported in late spring that the teamsters and other unions were "still paying benefits to workers who were pulled out during the General Strike and whom they were unable to replace in their former positions."[2] Carpenters' Local #131 sponsored a benefit on April 18 to raise funds for a "General Strike Victims Defense Fund."[3]

But by and large Seattle's AFL unions continued to move forward in the spring and summer of 1919. The axe did not yet fall. Most locals not only reinstated their members but put still greater demands to their employers and usually won them. By June, the butchers raised their rates and gained recognition at ten new shops. The white male barbers, "faced by a rapid growth," hired a new assistant financial secretary. By August, the retail clerks had gained an increase of $10 a week and reported their membership to be "gaining rapidly."[4] That same month both the musicians and teamsters successfully raised their rates. In the two largest-scale confrontations of the period, the unions also emerged victorious. In May, Seattle's carpenters, arguing that they had not received a wage increase in two years, gained an increase to $7.50 a day and successfully imposed the five-day week by proclamation, with only one small brief strike of 200 workers. With somewhat more apprehension 3,800 culinary workers prepared for a May 1 strike to gain their own demands for a $1-per-day increase. They won all their demands on the eve of the strike.[5] Overall, Seattle unionists did not just slip back to work, demoralized, after the general strike but raised their sights still further. "Labor has confidence in itself," one visitor in April observed.[6]

Organized women workers benefited especially from this spring and summer upsurge. More new female locals were founded – of cloth, hat, and cap makers in June, and of 300 factory workers in September. Fifty garment workers at the Seattle Custom Garment Makers factory used a one-day walkout to demand Saturdays off and won forty-eight hours' pay for a new forty-four-hour week. In part the labors of special women organizers produced these gains. Blanche Johnson still served as the Central Labor Council's organizer for women, while Myrtle Howarth served on the payroll of the AFL. Charles Doyle, the central council's business agent, also gave aid to women's unions in this period. In addition, Seattle's male unions bankrolled the female unions directly. The machinists, for example, advanced $2,500 to striking telephone operators in June. More typical but nonetheless useful was a $100 gift from the carpenters to striking candy workers. (The longshoremen's earlier pithy response to the lady barbers' financial request turned out to be more the exception than the rule.) Equally important, women trade unionists united in support of one another. The laundry workers, for example, tutored the candy workers in how best to solicit funds from the city's other unions. Aided by the wives of male trade unionists, union women in May formed the first local branch of the Women's Trade Union League.[7]

The density of Seattle trade unionism that had been crucial to the growth of women's unions during the war years continued to support female trade unionists afterwards. Almost all Seattle women's unions emerged in lines of work that produced either goods or services for a local working-class market. They were able to benefit from the politicized consumption choices of many of the city's organized male workers. White male workers' support had long been one of the key factors behind the success of the waitresses' union, for example, accelerating during the war. As Dorothy Sue Cobble has shown, the growth of kitchenless rooming houses for single workers in the second and third decades of the twentieth century created a large category of people who ate all their meals in restaurants, in turn creating a restaurant boom.[8] In Seattle, men who lived in hotels often brought class consciousness to their meals out, boycotting non-union restaurants, loyally patronizing those friendly to labor and displaying the union shop card, and participating in creative job actions in support of union waitresses. During one successful Seattle waitress strike, for example, "at a quarter of noon, the seats of the big restaurants suddenly filled up with men who said 'Give me a cup of coffee' and sat there drinking it till half past one," thus costing the owners the lucrative lunchtime trade.[9] The same clientele also came to the aid of the hotel maids. Organizers of their new local asked that unionists try and persuade both the maids at their residences to join the union and the hotels' proprietors to recognize it.[10] Such support could be strikingly effective. The new, female, candy workers' union owed its existence in part to unionists' pressures. As the local industrial-unionist *Forge* reported, "The union was originally formed during the period of war-time prosperity, and the manager of the Nut House took kindly to the idea because it meant the gaining of union trade from the shipyards."[11]

That same critical mass of organized workers also made it possible for female trade unionists to hold union men responsible for the behavior of female members of their families. "The wives of some card-carrying unionists of other industries are . . . scabbing," the candy workers detected during a May strike at the Nut House.[12] Furious, they named names in the *Union Record* and asked "all unions to check up any member of theirs who has a daughter or wife acting as a strikebreaker."[13] "Watch your wife and daughter, Mr. Union Man," an article on the strike warned.[14]

In June, unionized telephone operators brought the same message home still more forcefully. Blanche Johnson, reporting to the Central Labor

Council, "asked that unionists having relatives or friends among the 'hello girls' use their influence with the girls in persuading them to join the union."[15] The next month, when 800 telephone operators struck for higher wages, the female unionists charged that wives of union men were scabbing on their strike and that it was the men's job to stop them. The Central Labor Council endorsed this approach. "All local unions are to appoint special committees to investigate cases in which the wives or close relatives of members are known to be acting as strikebreakers, all unionists to report such cases as fall under their observation among their neighbors or acquaintances."[16] Male unions did respond by disciplining their members. When a committee of telephone operators visited the musicians' union to complain of a scabbing musician's wife, for example, the local's board of directors voted that "the Pres[ident] use his influence to have Whitney to stop his wife scabbing during the trouble."[17] The painters' union "instructed its business agent to 'pull from the job' any man known to be harboring strikebreakers in his home or family." Through such pressures women workers and their allies were attempting both to institutionalize class consciousness and to harness men's patriarchal authority within the family in service to female trade unionism. Only a high density of unionization of male workers throughout the city, politicized with an ethos of solidarity extending across gender lines, could made such a strategy possible.[18]

Despite the wartime repression and the elimination of the Socialist Party, left-wing ideas and activists flourished in Seattle in the spring and summer of 1919, along with the cooperatives and labor-owned businesses. During this period the Seattle left reached its greatest strength. Especially in the early summer, leftists mobilized a number of radical campaigns that, while not always sucessful, illustrate the grassroots energy and mass support for radical ideas very much alive in Seattle. Rallies and street meetings continued unabated, including those sponsored by the IWW and drawing several thousand. In April radicals in the city's left-leaning AFL locals spearheaded an unsuccessful drive for the Seattle movement to adopt May 1, International Workers' Day, rather than the traditional U.S. Labor Day – the first Monday in September – as Labor Day. More successfully, when Seattle's longshoremen refused to load arms from the U.S. government bound for Aleksandr Kolchak's counterrevolutionary forces in Russia throughout the summer and fall, the Central Labor Council endorsed them unanimously.[19]

The most deeply felt issue was the "framing" of Tom Mooney. Throughout 1919 Seattle trade unionists debated how best to show their support for Mooney, imprisoned in San Quentin for allegedly throwing a bomb during a 1916 Preparedness Day Parade in San Francisco. An estimated 25,000 Seattle unionists participated in a ten-minute strike to "Free Tom Mooney" in 1917. In February 1919 many of the city's prominent union leaders attended a nationwide conference of unionists in Chicago planning actions to secure Mooney's freedom. Plans for two mass strikes on July 4 and October 8, 1919, precipitated hotly contested referendum campaigns as to their observance, keeping solidarity with Mooney constantly before Seattle unionists, and keeping the more radically inclined unions needling the more cautious as to the measure of their true solidarity. Neither referendum carried a majority of Seattle locals, but the strong support they received underscores the continuing willingness of tens of thousands of Seattle unionists to contemplate two subsequent general strikes in 1919.[20]

As leftist ideas grew in popularity and trade unions continued to gain in both numbers and workplace demands, Seattle's trade-union radicals and progressives began to strain against the institutional limits of the AFL and experiment with structural innovations with which to break out of the strictures of craft unionism. These were organized by unionists who chose not to throw over the AFL for the IWW, the other choice for those advocating industrial unionism, but instead to reform the AFL from within. One out-of-town sympathizer wryly described their efforts that spring as "the fight to make the AFL safe for the workers."[21]

One such attempt was the shop stewards' movement. It was first developed in England during World War I as a means of transcending skill divisions and the constraints of craft unionism, while at the same time laying the seeds of a workers' revolution.[22] In the spring and summer of 1919 at least five Seattle unions adopted some form of shop-level representation, explicitly trying to replicate the English example. The machinists, for example, in April adopted a structure in which union representatives were elected plant by plant rather than at large, as they had been before. "The system," they affirmed, "is patterned after the now well-known shop committee plan of the English workers."[23] Blacksmiths, tailors, and boilermakers similarly adopted the system, as did the shipyard laborers, riggers, and fasteners who devised a monthly meeting of stewards as a "clearing house and training school."[24] More than just a program for workplace control, these shop steward systems were consciously designed, as in England, as the basis of a syndicalist model of working-class action, in which factory committees would serve as the embryonic governing bodies of a post-revolutionary society.[25]

A second, more controversial campaign sought to supplant the AFL's control over the structure of local solidarity. In May, the longshoremen invited delegates from all locals to a "mass meeting" to create a new local cross-city organization to be called the "Federated Unions." Archie Robertson, chair of the publicity committee, explained that organizers hoped it would "operate as a central labor body, taking over work now done by the Central Labor Council, leaving it a sort of semi-political clearing-house for oratory and debate, the 'Federated Unions assuming authority over economic and industrial questions.' "[26] One goal would be to arrange for all contracts to expire on the same day; another would be the adoption of the shop steward system throughout the city. Not surprisingly, the moderate and conservative leaders of the Central Labor Council were immediately up in arms, and they mobilized a campaign in which numerous locals denounced the Federated Unions as "dual unionism." A vote in the Central Labor Council condemning the plan carried by 100 to 43. But the tally revealed that at least a third of the council's delegates wanted to replace the council with a body more amenable to radical structural innovations.[27]

The largest battle was over the reorganization of the American Federation of Labor itself. Here was where the greatest support for structural change emerged among Seattle AFL unions. In early March 1919, the Central Labor Council's Committee on Resolutions endorsed a proposal for reorganization of the AFL that became known as the "Duncan Plan," after Seattle's labor council secretary, James Duncan. The proposal called for the AFL's restructuring into twelve new industrial units in lieu of the craft unions, a universally recognized transfer card, a system allowing members to accrue benefits from any local within the AFL, and "blanket agreements to cover all crafts in a given plant," with uniformity of wages within skill groups. The plan called for a referendum on all these issues. If it passed, a committee would be authorized to devise measures for their enactment. Unlike the IWW, the Duncan Plan did not set up a rival federation. But it certainly promised a radical restructuring of the AFL from within, one that would eliminate the craft internationals and create instead a set of entirely new national-level bodies with entirely new rules.[28]

The Duncan Plan paralleled a larger movement known as the One Big Union (OBU) that emerged in the U.S. Pacific Northwest and western Canada in 1919. Although AFL loyalists equated the OBU with the IWW, the two movements were in fact quite distinct, often in conflict, and each disavowed any connection with the other. In Canada, the One Big Union movement spread rapidly among skilled workers affiliated with the AFL. They were drawn by the OBU's revolutionary syndicalist model as well as its promise to erase craft divisions. By January 1920, 50,000 to 70,000 had joined it, along with the British Columbia Federation of Labor, Vancouver Trades Council, Winnipeg Trades Council, and two districts of the mine, mill, and smelter workers and the United Mine Workers. For these Canadian advocates, the OBU meant outright secession from the AFL. Heady with a sense of possibility, they carried their ideas to Washington state in the months following the general strike. But in Seattle the Duncan Plan proved more popular. It offered the same potential for industrial unionism, without the risk of secession, and with the added potential of persuading AFL loyalists.[29]

Support for the Duncan Plan in Seattle that spring and summer of 1919 proved enormous. More than 3,000 attended a July 5 mass meeting in support of One Big Union ideas sponsored by both the Metal Trades and Central Labor councils. Numerous locals forwarded to the councils their endorsements of the Duncan Plan. Seattle unionists then moved the industrial-union plan through the State Federation of Labor's June convention, where they helped vote in a referendum of all locals statewide, resolving

> That the State Federation of Labor, in convention assembled, recommend that each local affiliated vote upon the advisibility [sic] of forming one big union along industrial lines, and that should the majority of the numerical vote of the rank and file vote in favor of industrial unionism, that the State Federation of Labor issue a call for a special conference to be held in the city of Seattle not less than 60 days after the final count of votes to outline the form of organization.[30]

At the same time, the Seattle Central Labor Council wrote to locals, central labor councils, and state federations throughout the country calling for debate on the proposal and requesting endorsement. Tacoma delegates spearheaded a drive for Duncan Plan supporters to meet the week before the national AFL convention in June and plot its adoption. Things were moving quickly; many hoped that craft unionism would finally be transcended.[31]

Industrial unionists would have to wait another sixteen years for the CIO to achieve that emancipation. Nonetheless, during the spring and summer of 1919 tensions within the AFL were heightening. Activists were aware that the federation's loyalists would not long tolerate such direct threats. In mid-February, an employers' spy asked Frank Turco, an IWW sympathizer from the blacksmiths' union, "if he thought the radicals would be ousted from their locals." Yes, he replied, "because they [i.e., his opponents] outnumber us two to one." But what would result if Turco and friends were thrown out? "Do you suppose we will fall asleep like whipped dogs!" roared Turco. No, thousands would "follow those leaders anywhere. . . . If we organized a seperate [sic] organization on the lines of Industrial Unionism with these leaders as its sponsors we would have one third of the workers of Seattle as members the first month. And if we did we would break the A.F. of L. in this town inside of six months."[32]

Many local AFL loyalists did want to purge Turco and others who shared his views. On February 26, a week after this interview, the produce workers' union introduced a resolution to the Central Labor Council "urging that unions having delegates to Council known to hold membership in dual organizations be requested to replace them with delegates whose allegiance is undivided."[33] In March, after a ninety-minute debate, the council voted the resolution down only because it would look as if they were following Mayor Ole Hanson's command that labor "clean house." Then, in April, the federal employees' local announced it was withdrawing from the Central Labor Council as "a protest against the radical control in the labor temple."[34] The biggest, and by far most sobering, defeat was that of the Duncan Plan. In August, Frank Morrison, secretary of the American Federation of Labor, acting as Samuel Gompers's messenger, threatened to revoke the Washington State Federation of Labor's charter if it did not call off the referendum. When the state executive board acquiesced, the Seattle movement was left out on a limb, and the proposal died a swift death.[35]

Still more ominous clues suggested trouble on the industrial front. On March 11, in a clear-cut defeat, Seattle's shipyard and metal trades workers returned to work under the Macy Award, the offending October 1918 decision granting only meager wage increases. A week later Machinists' Local #79 reported that the open shop had been established in at least six shops. Employers had increased the hours of returning workers from forty-four to forty-eight and reduced their wages from ninety to eighty cents an hour. By mid-April a prominent employer reported that "t[he] shipyards, which have been the center of everything disturbing the last two years, are running with full crews and the men are very quiet and apparently satisfied."[36] The men were not, in fact, satisfied. At the beginning of May the Metal Trades Council voted to demand the six-hour day and forty-hour week and to fine any member working more than four hours a week of overtime. But the metal trades locals were unwilling to strike again, and their powers to enforce such demands were weak. As the same employer commented, "A number of . . . demands are being made by the shipyard men, but just at present they are all very anxious for work."[37]

Another kind of solidarity

Abruptly, the context in which the Seattle AFL had flourished changed altogether. In September 1919, Seattle's employers unleashed a tightly co-ordinated counterattack on the city's labor movement and within six weeks had transformed the entire map of labor and capital in postwar Seattle.

While the change came swiftly, those watching the sky could have read the signals. Immediately following the general strike Seattle's employers had launched a new wave of repression against organized labor and the left. Their use of the government against labor was quite open. As one employer reported, "The 'demonstration' was really on the part of the city, county, state and national authorities, which were solidly arrayed against the general strike and the promised disorder which terrorized the citizens."[38] He had no problem acknowledging the interests behind this "cooperation of authorities." "Law abiding citizens led by business men vitally interested in the larger commercial interests of Seattle backed up the movement to destroy Bolshevism. . . ."[39] A week later he calmly noted the "very satisfactory" results: "The Government apparently is going to deport most of the strike leaders as alien enemies and has already made a good start by arresting between fifty and a hundred to date."[40]

While most Seattle AFL leaders were native born and therefore immune to deportation, authorities arrested and tried to deport hundreds of non-citizen radicals in 1919, including more than 30 Italians and 316 Russians. The day after the general strike, police raided the Seattle Socialist Party's headquarters and arrested the party's candidate for City Council. Others raided the pro-IWW Equity Print Shop, arrested its managers, and closed the plant. A third raid swept down on Seattle's IWW headquarters, where officers seized the Wobblies' papers and their officers, then posted a policeman at the entrance to arrest those who walked in the door as they arrived to pay their dues. Meanwhile, the police, the federal government, and employers planted additional spies within labor's ranks, ferreting into the very heart of the labor movement. One agent reported daily to Broussais C. Beck, manager of the Bon Marche department store, and got far enough into the IWW's Northwest Defense Committee for political prisoners to audit its financial reports. Another, who appears to have spent his days loitering at the Labor Temple and attending union meetings, claimed that "Chas. Doyle, Business Agent of the Central Labor Council considers me one of his best friends."[41]

But it took time for Seattle's employers to fully gather their forces and to react to labor's new audacity. The general strike had been their worst nightmare come true. By March 15 the shipyard and general strikes had cost the city an estimated $44 million. More important, one manager stressed, "the setback to Seattle cannot be measured in money."[42] Rather than mourn, the employers organized. Within days of the general strike they formed a new employers' association, the Associated Industries, that by May claimed 191 members; by October, 700. The new Associated Industries amalgamated all the city's prewar employers' organizations, including the Waterfront Employers' Association, the Master Builders' Association, and the Metal Trades Association, into a single body. Its membership represented all sectors of the local business community, under-scoring how very tightly interlocked those sectors were. Frank Water-house, a reputed millionaire with interests in banking, metalworking, and the Bon Marche department store, presided. Active members included O. D. Fisher, manager of the Fisher Flour Mills Company and president of the Merchants' Exchange; J. H. Bloedel, president of the Bloedel-Donovan Lumber Mills and vice president of the National City Bank; and J. H. Fox, president of the Seattle Astoria Iron Works.[43]

The Associated Industries symbolized the larger political consolidation of business interests in postwar Seattle. Employers' associations had at-tempted open shop drives in Seattle as early as 1905. Until the war, though, the city's large employers and financiers had been counterbalanced by a group of middle-class Progressives joined together in the Seattle Municipal

League. Identifying themselves as a distinct class in the middle between entrenched financial elites, on the one hand, and the "masses," on the other, for pragmatic reasons the Municipal League had allied with organized labor on a variety of campaigns, such as those for municipal ownership of utilities or for the initiative, referendum, and recall. As historian Lee Pendergrass argues, before the war members of the Municipal League "had looked at municipal life and seen evil personified in vice, immorality, machine politics and monopoly by private traction companies and other special interests." The war, though, forced the Municipal League off the middle ground and split it apart. One group sided with the elite to combat the newly ascendent evils of "traitors, pacifists, radicals, boycotts and strikes." By war's end Bolshevism was their great enemy, to be repressed even at the cost of civil liberties. Symbolic of the alliance between the middle and upper classes that resulted was the Chamber of Commerce's merger with the Associated Industries. Another group of Municipal League members recoiled at the wartime and postwar repression of civil liberties but found themselves isolated and relatively ineffective, dwarfed by the polarized conflict between large employers and organized labor.[44]

In the spring the newly consolidated Associated Industries began to test how best to strike back at labor. For its first target it chose the *Union Record*, knowing full well both the importance of the *Record* as the linchpin of the local AFL movement and that the paper, always on the brink of financial collapse, was its Achilles' heel. In March, the Associated Industries announced a boycott by its members of all display advertising in the *Record*. Thirteen months later the paper reported "we have not carried since the general strike an advertisement from a bank, a department store, a dairy or a large moving picture theatre."[45] Like big-city dailies today, the *Record* was especially dependent on department-store advertisements for its revenues, and income plummeted. Nonetheless, the paper rallied and even prospered over the following summer and fall, calling its readers' attention to the association's boycott, raising needed capital through stock subscription drives, and by the end of the year increasing its circulation another 20,000, to 120,000.[46]

The employers' advertising boycott illustrates the complexity of the developing contest between labor and capital, and how enmeshed it was in both production and consumption. By pulling their advertisements from the *Record*, Seattle employers in part hurt themselves. They were, after all, interested in working-class patronage or they would not have advertised in the paper in the first place. Yet they were choosing to forgo such patronage and incur the wrath of politicized shoppers for perhaps some time to come, in service to a broader agenda of business-class power.

Not all Seattle merchants and businesses went along with this program happily. The Associated Industries evidently coerced many smaller business owners into withdrawing their advertisements by threatening to cut off supplies and, especially, bank loans to noncooperating businesses. Those that joined the association pledged themselves to pay $100 to every other member firm if they broke ranks, a price that would amount to $7,000 per transgression by the fall.[47]

The employers waited until the fall, though, to strike directly at the trade unions. As Jimmy Duncan properly surmised at the time, "They wanted the winter months ahead," when unemployment would rise.[48] Finally, in September, the axe fell. The Associated Industries launched an open shop drive that within two months had wiped out the closed shop in almost all Seattle industries. First a lockout destroyed the relatively small cereal and flour mill workers' union.[49] Then, when the city's tailors, printers, and cleaners and dyers walked out in September strikes, the employers in each trade refused to budge, quickly turning each strike into a successful lockout and, ultimately, a rout of the unions. The most crushing blow was to the building trades. On September 9 all the city's building trades workers walked out to demand wage increases of $1 to $2.50 per day. Rather than negotiate, much less give in, as they had in the past, the city's contractors stayed firm. Gas workers, iron molders, carpet workers, and bookbinders also found themselves locked out or losing strikes by the end of the year. All in all, between August 1919 and March 1920 the Associated Industries fought a total of seventeen lockouts and strikes.[50]

In October the Associated Industries backed up this assault with a citywide propaganda campaign, named the "American Plan," on behalf of the open shop drive. According to the employers' proclamation, the "open shop" meant a workplace that did not discriminate against non-union workers. In practice, it meant a union-free shop. Anti-union placards appeared in more than 600 Seattle streetcars. A succession of 15 full-page advertisements in each of the city's three pro-employer daily newspapers trumpeted endorsements by the Kiwanis Club, Rotary Club, and Chamber of Commerce.[51] The papers' owners contributed anti-union editorials, glowing news stories on the American Plan campaign, and scathing denunciations of labor's allegedly seditious activities. Speakers from the Associated Industries permeated the city.[52]

This propaganda campaign was designed to serve multiple purposes. First, it reinforced solidarity within the ranks of employers, in precisely the period when they would be most tempted to break ranks and settle with the unions as the strikes and lockouts drew into their second and third months. Second, it legitimated the antilabor activities of the city's largest employers and financial interests to the city's middle class, some members of which were still critical of the repressive methods undertaken during and after the war. Third, the campaign sought to encourage anti-union sentiments among rank-and-file workers. The Associated Industries placed some of its full-page advertisements in the *Record* itself, arguing for the benevolence of the American Plan, which would give workers a "square deal." Its streetcar signs spoke explicitly to workers, seeking to drive a wedge between individuals and their unions. "THINK IT OVER," one sign began. "When you think you are being 'fair' to a principle, during a strike, are you 'fair' to the wife and babies? While listening to the 'leader' consider the home."[53] While the trade unions sought to pull working-class family members into the labor movement, the city's employers were trying to use family commitments to pull workers away from their unions.[54]

For all the brash self-confidence evinced in their assaults on the unions in the fall of 1919, Seattle's employers were still running scared. They were trying to grasp the immensity of the problem on their hands and to formulate an effective response. They had already lost a great deal of money during the early 1919 strikes, whether as industrial employers, as merchants, or as bankers. Seattle's reputation as the hotbed of American radicalism, they knew, threatened to eliminate their current investments and eliminate any future growth from which they hoped to profit. They watched as the AFL movement's institutional network of unions, cooperatives, banks, theaters, and buildings grew over the course of the year. They looked on as the movement's insurgents experimented with restructuring the AFL to increase its power and grew more militant in their demands over the course of the late spring and summer.

By the fall of 1919 Seattle employers' two main concerns converged: the trade unions' increasing economic power and ability to wrest gains that cut into the employers' immediate profits; and the larger threat of a socialist revolution, which the employers saw as an immediate danger. Edwin G. Ames, manager of the Puget Mill Company, one of the area's larger lumber companies, for example, read obsessively about the Bolshevik Revolution that year and believed that the Seattle general strike "was organized more along the lines of a revolutionary activity than to do anything for labor."[55] He believed that the strike had failed but that its leaders had merely gone underground to continue their plotting. At the same time Ames had his eye on more immediate labor relations. While he could rest easy in the summer of 1919 because a lumber boom and shipyard layoffs produced a labor surplus in the lumber industry, much to the employers' benefit, he was on the lookout lest a reversal of those conditions bring a return of militant unions to the industry. His approach, in other words, as Robert Ficken has aptly phrased it, was "part hysteria and part calculation."[56]

Mark Allison Matthews offers another example of the thinking of Seattle's larger employers, financiers, and their allies. Rev. Matthews was the minister of Seattle's First Presbyterian Church, which, with 10,000 members, was reputed to have the largest Presbyterian congregation in the world. Tall, thin, and silver-haired, with a sharp nose like an eagle's beak, Matthews thought highly of himself and envisioned a national-level career as an anti-Bolshevik. In Seattle, he allied himself with elite businessmen while corresponding with national-level business leaders. The tone of his correspondence that fall of 1919 was alternately brash, confident, and terrified. On October 8, Matthews wrote George W. Baker Jr., of the First National Bank in New York, of the situation in Seattle:

> I am on the committee of fifteen that has been handling the situation here. We have nine strikes we are going to win. We must win. We are working day and night. . . . If we can swing this great Northwest section into the open shop program . . . [along with California] . . . it will help the Eastern situation very much and will prevent the Reds from carrying out their political program.[57]

A letter dated November 5 carried the same combination of breathlessness, excitement, and an edge of fear.

> I have been detained. The labor situation has engaged my entire time. . . . We are going to emancipate this city from unionism. We have been able to unite all the business forces and we are trying to emancipate labor, to establish the open shop, and put the industrial and business world upon an American foundation. . . . My plan of personal attack and contact is the plan that will save the situation. . . . We must fight incessantly.[58]

Events throughout the United States in 1919 continued to reinforce Seattle elites' worst fears. More than 4 million workers, nationally, joined in 3,500 strikes by the end of 1919 in the greatest strike wave until then in U.S. history. Three particular strikes in the fall especially frightened employers. First, on September 9, Boston policemen walked out, their strike broken only when the state police intervened, replacing the strikers. Then on September 22 a national steel strike began that eventually involved 350,000 workers. Not only was this the largest single strike in U.S. history, but it struck at one of the nation's most basic, and unorganized, industries and threatened to transcend the limits of AFL craft unionism in mass production. In response, the national press spewed forth a mass anti-Bolshevik campaign, further fanning anti-Red hysteria. Then, on November 1, 425,000 coal miners walked out against the command of United Mine Workers President John L. Lewis.[59]

Just as the Seattle general strike had been the vanguard of this 1919 national strike wave, so too was Seattle employers' response the cutting edge of a national open shop drive unleashed by employers' associations across the country in late 1919 and 1920, under the name "American Plan." While it is unclear who coined the phrase, Seattle's Associated Industries borrowed their declaration of principles from employers in Toledo, Ohio. Seattle's was the first coordinated citywide campaign. In San Antonio, Dallas, Louisville, San Diego, and Minneapolis employers formed other early open shop committees during the spring and summer. Throughout late 1919 open shop drives grew in local popularity, galvanized into a national movement by the November steel strike. By late 1920, 240 cities boasted open shop associations. Their activities were largely coordinated at the local level, though, as in the case of Toledo, employers' associations enthusiastically shared information horizontally with groups in other cities. In one year the Associated Employers of Indianapolis alone distributed 1.5 million pieces of literature promoting the open shop. By the late spring of 1920 the National Association of Manufacturers jumped on the bandwagon and began to coordinate national-level activities.[60]

Seattle employers' answer to their plight that fall involved a sophisticated analysis of the roots of labor's advances. First, the Associated Industries' members understood the political importance of the cost of living. One particular missive in Mark Matthews' files underscores Seattle employers' consciousness on this question. On September 13, 1919, Matthews sent a telegram to President Woodrow Wilson to present the concerns of "the most prominent citizens of the city" who had "met in representative capacity" to deal with the labor situation. At the top of their list was a plea that Wilson "defeat the high cost of living." Other Associated Industries members formed a committee to curb "profiteering."[61] For its second front the association turned to wages. Six of the city's most prominent employers sat on a committee that investigated wage rates throughout the Pacific coast region in order to regulate Seattle wages in accordance with regional scales. At the same time all Associated Industries member firms pledged not to lower wages as long as the cost of living stayed at its current level. The employers, in other words, decided not to assault Seattle workers' wage rates. Accordingly, at Christmastime the Master Builders' Association, which had just finished breaking the closed shop in the building trades, announced a fifty-cent-per-day wage increase for the city's carpenters.[62] The third and primary front was organized labor's institutionalized power at the workplace. Here the employers sought to destroy the unions altogether, and with them workers' collective control over the work process and their growing sense of power. That was the core of the open shop drive. In sum, the Associated Industries' members planned to address some of the needs unions sought to meet for their members, specifically the financial erosion of working-class living standards after the war. But they would not tolerate unions. Finally, the employers advocated employee representation plans – a.k.a. company unions – to create a smokescreen of employee input into the shop floor.[63]

Their strategizing paid off handsomely. Over the course of that fall the employers' fears gradually dissipated. By November a certain victorious glee began to supplant their former panic. The tide, indeed, turned. Reports sent by A. L. Kempster, a manager of Seattle's largest utility, to his superiors at the Stone and Webster conglomerate on the east coast trace this process: "The labor situation in Seattle, in the opinion of the writer, is improving," he judged on October 4. "In spite of the fact that we are having more strikes and more trouble than ever, the fact that many trades are going open shop and succeeding indicates that labor is more plentiful and less independent."[64] Seattle's tailor shops, he noted, "are being run on an open shop basis at the old scale and the men are slowly going back to work."[65] The same was true of the printers. All eyes, though, were on the building trades. Men gradually trickled back to work. By November 8 the building tradesmen called off their strike and returned to work at their old scale and under the open shop, completely defeated. That same week Rev. Matthews concluded, "It is a big task, but we are winning."[66] Kempster reported in January: "The labor situation is improving, there being plenty of men in all the skilled crafts who are willing to work." "A slight improvement in output by man is evident," he added.[67]

By early 1920 the Associated Industries had won all its seventeen strikes. Organized gas workers, printers, tailors, cleaning and dye workers, carpet workers, bookbinders, and workers throughout the building trades industry lost the closed shop. Metal trades workers had already lost it the previous spring; they were shaky enough by the fall to eschew even a defensive strike. When the Skinner and Eddy shipyards cut the wages of 1,200 workers in September, Kempster noted: "This is the only instance in Seattle in nearly four years that a reduction in wages has not resulted in a strike at once."[68] The Chamber of Commerce estimated that 85 percent of firms belonging to the Associated Industries had closed shops in April 1919; in October 1920, the Associated Industries claimed the numbers nearly reversed: 75 percent had liberated themselves from unions. A tiny 9 percent of Seattle workers labored in union shops. The giant of the Seattle AFL had been brought to its knees.[69]

The success of the open shop drive can be attributed to a convergence of factors. First, the employers discovered solidarity. They maintained a united front among the different employers within each single industry, and citywide across different economic sectors. Then, as the weeks progressed, they held ranks. Such unity was possible in part because the Associated Industries created a financial pool which supported individual firms that might otherwise have been tempted to negotiate. Its coercion of member firms helped hold the line, too. Any firm that broke ranks would face potential materiel embargos, bank harassment, and for some a loss of valued customers.[70] Second, the Associated Industries' propaganda campaign marshaled the support of the city's middle class, leaving the labor movement without many of its former valuable allies.[71] Third, the employers' drive caught the unions off guard. Poised for institution building, expansion, and internal restructuring, Seattle's union locals were simply not prepared, strategically, for the months-long citywide strike in self-defense in which they suddenly found themselves. And finally, and perhaps most important, by waiting until the fall the employers had both time and the Seattle economy on their side. Beginning in the summer, metal trades employment in the city began to plummet. The tenor of the city's economy subtly began to shift, creating a growing pool of unemployed workers more willing to strikebreak than during the war years. Many of those who scabbed on the fall building trades' strike were reported to be unemployed former shipyard workers.[72] Other Seattle workers, sensing that times were beginning to change, must have been less willing than before to stay on strike indefinitely. Subtly, they knew, times were changing, and risk taking was dangerous once again.

What was to be done?

For Seattle trade unionists, the change was both sudden and overwhelming. One day the locals were rich with dues money, planning movie theaters, joining cooperatives, and dreaming of bigger and better union halls and overthrowing the AFL. The next they were fighting for their movement's life.

At first, the unions lagged in their response. During September, as the open shop strikes commenced, the movement's earlier priorities persisted. Judging by the *Union Record*, for example, the cost of living stood as the unions' greatest concern well into early October.[73] By mid-month, though, the scale of the employers' assault became clear. "Labor is today facing critical times in Seattle," one *Record* reporter observed on October 16. "We have five big strikes and [it] looks bad."[74] L. W. Buck, a socialist from the barbers' union, grasped the situation thoroughly: "Labor has got to act and act quickly if we are going to save the situation. We are passing the most critical period labor has ever had right now and something must be done at once."[75] The entire program of the Seattle AFL changed almost overnight from expansion to survival.

Unionists soon pivoted inward to attack one another. Conservatives blamed radicals for the situation. "I know and every other right thinking man knows that the labor movement of Seattle is shot to pieces and the worst of the matter is that the labor movement in Seattle is to blame," complained John Dallager of the teamsters. He continued:

> We have too many in our labor movement that are doing nothing but blowing bubbles. The radicals succeeded in inducing the building trades, the tailors and the printers to go out on strike and ask for an exorbitant increase in wages and shorter hours, but they don't do anything then to get them out of the scrape after they get them in. It takes the conservative heads to pull them out. . . .[76]

Radicals, in turn, blamed conservatives. As the pro-OBU *Forge* reported, "Radicals point to the fact that this strike was handled almost entirely by the conservative officials of the building trades."[77]

The spring and summer's earlier debates over restructuring the AFL took on a new cast in the fall's defensive context. "Just such [a] thing as the associated industries [was] necessary to bring us together and I hope that the Associated Industries will keep in their fight long enough to organize us into [the] O.B.U.," argued John McKelvey, an officer of the boilermakers. "That's the only way we can convince our conservatives of the necessary [*sic*] of one big union. . . ."[78] Others suggested that if the Associated Industries wiped out the AFL altogether, then the OBU could start from scratch. "The employers would be doing us a great favor if they break the grip of the A.F. of L. on labor," one worker argued.[79] Another group of socialist supporters of industrial unionism was appalled at that suggestion. "This is [a] time for real constructive action and not for experimenting with new social ideas," the barbers' Phil Pearl countered. "Labor in Seattle is losing ground and we must do everything possible to save ourselves."[80] His colleague L. W. Buck, who had recently been elected by the radicals to the State Federation of Labor's vice presidency, agreed: "[W]e can't afford to let them break the building trades strike and establish open shop in that industry for [if] they do that then you can look for open shop in all industries in Seattle."[81]

By mid-October the AFL locals began to formulate their collective response to the open shop drive. Their most formal act was the creation of a Committee of Fifteen, charged with coordinating the unions' defense, within the Central Labor Council. Even the formation of the committee aroused fierce contention, as different factions fought to have their representatives included. The committee began strategy meetings, raised a benefit pool from the locals to fund the different strikers, placed advertisements in the *Union Record* to counter the Associated Industries' propaganda, and tried to talk any more unions out of demanding wage increases or striking. To no avail they proposed to the Associated Industries a mediation board to arbitrate the multiple disputes. In this first stage of defending itself, the Seattle AFL underwent an internal consolidation. A more elite body, the Committee of Fifteen, insulated from the contentious democracy of delegate debates on the council floor, would govern during the crisis. And not all locals that wanted to press their demands would be supported with the full solidarity of the citywide movement.[82]

With that consolidation, portions of the Seattle AFL began for the first time to be thrown to the wolves. In the first instance it was women who lost. The process was subtle. In initiating their fall strikes, the tailors, cleaners and dyers, and bookbinders had all included equal pay for equal work and a disproportionate increase for lower-paid women workers among their demands. Their strikes began as offensive actions for feminist concerns. As the employers announced they would settle only for the absolute open shop, however, the strikes turned into defensive battles for mere union survival. Then, when the male leaders of the Central Labor Council consolidated their power, debated how to respond to the employers, and then formulated the unions' collective defense, these locals' original feminist concerns dropped out of the conversation altogether. Attention focused, instead, on the all-male building trades, and after them the largely male printing industry. In that initial defensive turn, women's concerns fell by the wayside.[83]

More concretely, the AFL jettisoned married women. A general animus toward the employment of married women had been present in the movement earlier in the year, as tensions mounted over their increased labor-force participation during the war and the question of its continuance afterward. But the issue came to a head in the Seattle Central Labor Council at exactly the moment when panic over how to respond to the employers' offensive peaked. At its October 25 meeting the immediate issue was the election of a new organizer for women workers. In a vicious two-hour debate delegates successfully barred Myrtle Howarth from candidacy because she was married. Married women, the delegates voted, should not be employed by the council and therefore, implicitly, had no place as trade-union members in the labor movement.[84]

An immense debate erupted in the pages of the *Union Record* that fall over the right of married women to work, and male and female trade unionists, wives of unionists, and married working women all took part in it. Feminist unionists argued that women had the right to work both as independent individuals and out of need to support their families. Their opponents responded that the labor movement should fight for the "family wage" – that is, one salary for a male head of household that would be enough to support a non–wage-earning spouse. The issue was deceptively complicated: Some of the female trade unionists who chose to criticize married women's employment did so because they were still furious at the wives who had scabbed during the candy workers' and telephone operators' strikes in the fall. It also turned out that Myrtle Howarth, around whom the council's debate had so heatedly revolved, was also the candidate of the pro-IWW left. Many of those who attacked her as married also wanted to defeat the far left's agenda. At the broadest level, though, the attack on married women symbolized the AFL movement's response to the open shop drive: It would turn away from expansion, from building a movement creative and confident enough to embrace a wider and wider range of workers under its rubric. Instead, it would close ranks. That, at some level, was the beginning of its decline.[85]

An injury to some

Then the climax came: the Centralia Massacre. Centralia was the most dramatic and fundamental turning point in postwar Seattle labor history. On November 11, 1919, in the town of Centralia, Washington, eighty miles from Seattle, members of the American Legion capped their Armistice Day parade with an armed mob attack on an IWW meeting. In the ensuing chaos, four legionnaires were shot and killed. Vigilante raids rounded up dozens of Wobblies. That night they dragged Wesley Everest, an IWW organizer, from his jail cell, castrated him, and then hanged him from a railroad bridge.[86]

In the days that followed, anti-Wobbly hysteria swept the Pacific Northwest. Officials launched yet another wave of repression in Seattle, arresting still more in what one approving observer spoke of as "a concerted drive against I.W.W.'s by the city, state and federal authorities."[87] The Centralia Massacre fanned the flames of anti-Red sentiment once again, bringing the Wobblies back to center stage in the employers' dramatic imagination.[88]

Seattle's employers were quick to tar the Seattle AFL with the same brush. Anticipating this, the day after the massacre the *Union Record* published an editorial entitled "Don't Shoot in the Dark," cautioning all camps against further violence in the massacre's aftermath. Seattle's district attorney immediately raided the *Record*'s offices, occupied the plant, and seized all the paper's files on the patently absurd grounds that the *Record* had incited violence. He threw Harry Ault, its editor; George Listman, president of its board of directors; and Frank Rust, its treasurer, into jail for violation of the Espionage Act. When they were released on bond, officials promptly rearrested Ault for defaming the character of the arrested legionnaires. The *Record* stayed shut down for six days. Finally, on November 21 the U.S. Justice Department released the *Record*'s premises. As a last stab a grand jury then indicted Ault, Listman, Rust and Anna Louise Strong on espionage charges.[89]

The *Union Record* survived. The sympathetic owner of a neighborhood paper offered his presses, and after a day's delay the *Record* was able to put out a small edition. It lost a great deal of advertising income as a result of the raid, especially since the attack frightened away many of the advertisers who still remained. But the paper's supporters stayed loyal. Circulation even increased in sympathy after the raid.[90]

The Seattle AFL movement, though, cracked under the strain, splitting over the issue of its identification with the IWW. In the aftermath of the Centralia Massacre, the AFL locals faced the choice of either defending the IWW or dissociating themselves from it. The musicians promptly announced "we denounce and repudiate the I.W.W. and demand that all officers charged with law enforcement do their duty to punish the guilty."[91] Electrical Workers Local #46 sent to the Central Labor Council a resolution commanding all locals to expel Wobblies from their ranks and to bar reporters from the pro-OBU *Forge* and Wobbly *International Weekly* from AFL meetings.[92] On November 19 the council relented and reactivated an old resolution purging all IWW members from its meetings thereafter. Most significant about this event was the support the resolution received. Predictably, the council's more conservative delegates introduced and backed it. But a solid block of the council's radical delegates also turned on the far left and attacked their former comrades. Phil Pearl of the barbers, Frank Clifford of the shipyard laborers, and Percy May of the longshoremen all joined in the purge.[93]

That split was exactly what the employers wanted. All year they had sought to drive a wedge between the local AFL's business unionists and its more radical wing. All year they had deliberately encouraged the unions' conservatives in order to undermine the left. Right after the general strike the *Times* had editorialized, "These radicals must go and it is the business of employers TO SEE THAT THEY DO GO by cooperating with conservative labor in the reconstruction."[94] In July they greeted with joy the election of Gompersite conservative William Short to the presidency of the State Federation of Labor, observing, "The best thing done at the convention was the re-election of Mr. Short as president, his record in the past having been excellent, safe and sane."[95] Short reciprocated the feelings, meeting secretly with representatives of employers' associations across the state. He conferred, for example, with lumber baron Mark Reed on how best to nurture "a community of interest" between labor and business. Louis Nash, a conservative leader from the Retail Clerks' union, similarly spoke at employers' functions in Seattle that fall.[96] He was the favorite of a new pro-employer, virulently anti-left weekly paper called the *American Union*, which it seems safe to assume was bankrolled by employer dollars.[97]

Leftist power within the overall Seattle labor movement slipped on other fronts as well. In a series of internal elections that fall radicals lost their positions in the boilermakers', electrical workers', machinists', and some building trades' locals.[98] Those losses, in turn, undermined the radicals' voting power at the Central Labor Council. Their power at council meetings also depended on their control of the meeting process. As one spy observed in April:

> The men that stay at the meetings until ten and eleven o'clock are usually the radicals and they are the ones that pull this eleventh hour stuff and have radical delegates appointed to fill the vacancies. Few members stay at the meetings at this hour and the result is our Central Labor Council in this city is largely radical.[99]

By the fall the other side had mastered that device. As the *American Union* reported in late October: "With its usual filibustering tactics the Red element strung the meeting along until past midnight, but the conservatives stuck to their posts for once and learned a lesson."[100]

The left was still very much alive in the city's AFL movement, however. This was not a question of elimination. Pro-IWW "disruptionists" still whooped it up in the gallery.[101] Radical resolutions still came to the floor. The big radical metal trades locals still had plenty of delegates, as did the more radical craft union locals. And even the purge of the IWW did not mean utter lack of sympathy for the Centralia Wobblies' plight. In mid-January council delegates unanimously approved a resolution "asking the council to appoint a committee to see that the I.W.W. on trial . . . get a fair trial and also act as a labor jury."[102] But the tide, for the left, had turned.[103]

Conclusion

The time from January to December 1919 was a long and tough one, unprecedented in the history of Seattle and, indeed, the entire nation. The city's employers moved from horror to terror to a tentative self-confidence, the city's organized workers from audacity to visionary experimentation to a rout. At the beginning of the year Seattle AFL unions were in a position of tremendous power that seemed only to flourish as the months passed. By the end of the year they were completely knocked off their feet and fighting one another for mere survival.

It was a period of overt, if not armed, class conflict. The general strike, the open shop drive, state repression – both sides understood these in terms of explicit class power and within a context of open antagonism. That war, though, was not fought only at the point of production. While the trade unions and employers fought tooth and nail over workplace power all year, in the same period the AFL movement also constructed its whole world of cooperatives and labor capitalist enterprises. Unionists designed their consumer tactics to serve the struggle at the point of production, to transform the political economy of consumption as well, and to change the very system of producing and consuming. Organized employers, too, politicized consumption. During the shipyard strikes the employers cut off credit at the city's grocers. Immediately afterward they boycotted advertisments in the *Union Record*, undermining labor's key labor capitalist propaganda tool. When that failed they brought in the state to crush the *Record*. They understood the politicizing effect of inflation, trying to develop their own analysis of the cost of living.

By the end of 1919 the first glimmers of a new postwar order could be detected. As the employers gained the upper hand, the AFL movement began its decade-long downward spiral. In the year's first half, the unions had opened the door for more and more white women to join; in the second half, they began to throw them out. In the year's first half, left and right had stood together. The question had been not whether the working class was moving forward and changing the world, but how it would do so. In the second half, a cycle of ever-more vicious denunciations had begun. The solidarity of the February general strike, in sum, was shattered.

5

Boycotts

IN ITS AUGUST 1920 NEWSLETTER, the Associated Industries continued to lament the power that Seattle's radical labor bosses held over the rank-and-file union member. Not only did union strictures dictate where, whether, and how "he" would work and for how much, but

> [h]e is forbidden to spend his money as he likes, but must refrain from buying anything in certain places pointed out to him by his masters. He is not even free in his amusements; he must not patronize certain amusement places which are in disfavor with the bosses. The bosses tell him the places where he must not buy the clothing for his family, the food they eat, the articles of luxury they buy, the places of amusements they must not attend and the like.[1]

Seattle's organized workers, in other words, had begun to pressure the city's employers through their shopping habits. By late 1920 the AFL movement had shifted the arena of class conflict in Seattle from the waged workplace to a new confrontational politics of consumption. At the center of its tactical approach was a citywide boycott in the spring of 1920 of Seattle's largest department store, the Bon Marche. With that boycott the Seattle AFL's politicization of consumption expanded beyond institution building to deploy a consumer tactic in the direct fight against organized employers. The politics of consumption would determine, in part, the outcome of the postwar contest between the employers and the unions.

Choosing to employ a boycott, though, presented the AFL movement with a new set of challenges. It gave the trade unions an additional, potentially powerful weapon with which to defend themselves. It opened possibilities for broad forms of solidarity across lines of skill, trade, race, and gender, potentially mobilizing the economic power of the entire working class as consumers as well as producers. But it also highlighted fault lines across such solidarity. Politicized shopping depended, above all, on the enthusiastic support of female members of the working class. The battle between labor and capital would depend, ultimately, on the movement's gender relations. Even the solidarity a boycott embodied at the waged workplace could prove a precarious construction. Especially in so defensive a context, craft unionism could easily widen still further cracks in the edifice of united labor.

Why a boycott?

By December 1919 the leaders of the Seattle AFL knew their movement was in trouble and that their traditional primary weapon, the strike, no longer worked. "People are getting tired of strikes and then the labor market is so overflooded with unemployed that chances for winning strikes are very slim," noted Charles Doyle, business agent for the Central Labor Council.[2] Phil Pearl, the barber, agreed: "Labor has got to change its tactics if it wants to save itself. Not one strike has been won since the armistice was signed, and there is no reason to believe that any other strike will be won if we keep on striking as we have in the past."[3] Doyle and Pearl represented majority thinking among the AFL leadership that winter, though some activists retained their faith in the strike while arguing that its use be modified. Daniel Georges of the tailors, for example, concluded, "It is time that we quit these individual strikes and save our energy for a strike of the whole labor movement. . . . Mass strikes, not craft strikes."[4]

As soon as the open shop drive hit home in October 1919, Seattle unionists began experimenting with tactics other than the strike. The boot and shoe repairers announced that, rather than walk out as the Associated Industries hoped they would, they were "striking on the job," though exactly what they meant by that is unclear. By February 1920 they had won closed shop agreements with a number of former Associated Industries members.[5] Other locals began to adapt the year's earlier structural experiments to the new defensive context. The Metal Trades Council converted to the shop stewards' system in order to retain union organization under open shop conditions. Tailors, shoe repairers, and cleaning and dye workers founded or promoted their producer cooperatives in this period as a defensive wedge against the open shop in their industries.[6] The building trades, angered by the Associated Industries' ability to blackmail pro-union contractors, began their drive for the Producers' Bank.

In late November the local AFL leadership first began to experiment with consumer campaigns as a lever against the city's employers. To retaliate for the post–Centralia Massacre raids and arrests, the Central Labor Council and the *Union Record* called for a boycott by unionists and their families of all Christmas presents, especially those purchased at the city's department stores. "The department stores['] heads are in the vanguard of the movement to crush labor," charged Harry Ault, the *Union Record*'s editor.[7] The paper gave front-page coverage to the boycott, and a council committee visited all Seattle's locals. In their arguments they evinced a sharp business acumen, asking, "Do you know that 60 percent of the business done by the department stores is done in the 6 weeks before

Christmas?"[8] Longshoreman Percy May, visiting the boilermakers' union on behalf of the boycott, pointed out to members that they would be "able to secure toys ninety percent lower a day or two after Christmas."[9] This boycott foreshadowed the next year's attack on the Bon Marche: It identified the department stores with the Associated Industries, sought to mold working-class shopping habits in service to the trade unions, and involved a careful understanding of the political economy of consumption.[10]

As strikes dropped off the movement's list of tactics, politics rose to its top. Before the war Seattle AFL activists had run for and often gained places on the city council and such local offices as school board and port commissioner, sometimes with the endorsement of the Socialist Party, of the Central Labor Council, or of both. Seattle trade unionists had also mounted campaigns for state-level offices, albeit less successfully. During the war years, though, political action dropped in priority for the movement. Strikes, collective bargaining, and civil-liberties issues moved to the foreground, as labor shortages strengthened the unions' bargaining power at the waged workplace. As many as four labor-endorsed candidates retained places on the city council, and Anna Louis Strong gained election to the school board; but she was recalled in 1917 on an anti-Red platform.[11]

Immediately following the February general strike both unions and business interests again turned their eyes to the ballot box. Seattle's employers feared that the strike's display of solidarity would translate into a seizure of political power in the March city council elections. But none of labor's candidates won, despite a great deal of publicity in the *Union Record*. And in terms of the unions' organizational priorities, political action still remained on the back burner.[12]

Over the summer and fall of 1919 interest in politics grew steadily within the Seattle and entire Washington state AFL. At its June convention the State Federation of Labor entered into a new "Triple Alliance" for political action with the Washington State Grange and the Railroad Brotherhoods. Under the "Triple Alliance" rubric Seattle AFL unionists began to build toward local-level political power in the fall. They tested their strength by entering three strongly pro-labor candidates in the fall elections for school board and port commissioner. In the middle of the campaign, though, the Centralia Massacre added a note of antilabor hysteria. The *Union Record* officers arrested on sedition charges in its aftermath included George Listman, one of the alliance's school board candidates. Some believed that Listman had been arrested deliberately to discredit his candidacy. All of the unions' candidates lost, though one, Lorene Wiswell Wilson, came in a respectable third for the school board.[13]

Those committed to political work were undaunted. They concluded from the campaign that it would take merely more organizing with greater thoroughness to vote in labor's candidates, and they began gearing up for Seattle's nonpartisan mayoral and city council elections in February, 1920. By January the nonpartisan mayoral campaign had become the chief priority of the Central Labor Council. James Duncan, the charismatic industrial unionist at the head of the Seattle AFL, agreed to run. Registering voters and building a get-out-the-vote system that tried to identify the voting attitudes of every member of every union and then help sympathetic voters get to their polling places, the Seattle AFL briefly transformed itself into a political-campaign operation. "At the present time it looks like we are going to change our industrial organizations into political organizations," one activist observed. "All you can hear in any labor organization is who they are going to put over on the political field."[14]

At the broadest level this political enthusiasm emerged from the Seattle labor movement's still-strong aspirations for expanded power. Many unionists had learned specific lessons from the previous year about the importance of controlling the government. Ben Nauman, for example, a left-leaning labor activist who also served as a city boiler inspector, argued on January 21:

> Since the war ended we had several great industrial struggles, and we might say that each of those struggles was partially lost. Why? Not because Labor was lacking organization, but because we had political power against us. They had all the advantage. They had the government behind them. That fact demonstrated to the workers that before they can accomplish anything ... they must first acquire political control.[15]

Other unionists shifted their sights from the waged workplace to the ballot box only as the futility of strikes became clear. The growing unemployment situation encouraged their strategic realignment. "We tried industrial action and failed," Charles Doyle argued. "From now on we are going after political action with all fours. Labor cannot afford to go out on strike now, there being too many unemployed, but they can all put up a good fight on the political field."[16] Some scattered criticism of the movement's growing emphasis on politics emerged in the IWW-leaning ranks. The Wobblies had long opposed political action of any sort. Many of their sympathizers in Seattle argued that political work only distracted the workers from industrial action. Pointing to the cases of Anna Louise Strong and Congressman Victor Berger, a Milwaukee Socialist, they argued that even if elected, radical representatives would never be allowed to serve in office. But they did not oppose the mayoral campaign, in part to prove that political action was pointless.[17]

James Duncan, labor's candidate, received more votes than the incumbent, Ole Hanson, and trailed the winner by only 2,000 votes in the February 17 primary. Hopes surged. Many observers believed that labor would, in fact, seize the mayor's office. But in the runoff Hugh Caldwell beat Duncan handily. The vote was not even close – 50,873 to 33,777. In the election's aftermath, political work lost its appeal for many in the Seattle AFL. To have worked so hard and still lose was startling. For those who remained committed to political action, it would be eight months before the next election, in the fall for statewide offices.[18]

The Seattle AFL was in a difficult situation. Both strikes and electoral politics had failed to serve the unions' interests, and the Associated Industries was still on the offensive. In this exact context the leadership turned to the boycott. On March 3 and 10, 1920, the Central Labor Council voted to concentrate the Seattle movement's full resources on a boycott of the Bon Marche department store. Its advocates hoped that Seattle's working class would use this boycott to dispatch the Associated Industries once and for all. After the Bon Marche the association's members would fall one by one like dominoes.[19]

The Bon Marche was in the process of constructing a new adjunct building, the McDermott Building, using largely non-union building trades labor. The carpenters on the site did have a union contract, but on election day in February the store refused to grant the half-day holiday it guaranteed. Using that incident as a trigger, the labor council declared both the main Bon Marche store and the McDermott Building, including a number of merchant-tenants beginning to occupy its first floor, "unfair" (that is, non-union). The council's leadership, aware that the city's department stores were among the leaders of the Associated Industries, hoped that the Bon Marche could serve as a lightning rod with which to attract rank-and-file hostility to the open shop drive.[20]

The *Union Record* had a strong hand in the decision to boycott the Bon Marche. For a year the *Record* had gone without department-store advertisements, as a result of the Associated Industries' continuing boycott on advertising in the *Union Record*. Before the boycott department-store advertising had been a major source of revenue. Harry Ault, the *Record*'s editor, wanted the unions to force the Bon Marche to bring those advertising dollars back to the *Record*; otherwise, he feared, the paper might fail.

It also appears that the Bon Marche received more working-class patronage than did Seattle's other department stores. One unionist claimed that 95 percent of the store's patronage came from the working class. Frank Cotterill, secretary of the Building Trades Council, asserted that "labor made the Bon Marche what it is today" – both in the sense that its business had been built up with working-class dollars and in the sense that union workers had literally constructed the building.[21] This made it all the more egregious that the Bon's management was spurning organized labor by not recognizing the building trades. Given the Bon Marche's dependence on working-class patronage, a boycott might prove highly effective.[22]

Historians have noted that trade unions usually turn to boycotts either when strikes are especially prolonged or when they fail.[23] The latter certainly fits the case of the Seattle AFL in March 1920. Second, they argue that unions choose boycotts because they appear cheaper for workers than strikes, because they do not involve a loss of pay for workers out on strike.[24] Seattle unionists who advocated the Bon Marche boycott shared this point of view. James Duncan, for example, argued on April 23 that the boycott "will be just as effective as a strike and it would not cost the workers anything."[25] Third, historians argue that boycotts are safer, because the workers do not have to worry about losing their jobs.[26] Pro-boycott Seattle unionists apparently echoed this sentiment as well. "The Bon Marche fight is the most important fight that organized labor has ever waged in this city," William Kennedy of the janitors asserted, "and [we] don't have to strike to win."[27]

Finally, a boycott allowed the Seattle movement to draw upon one of the strongest if least tangible resources it still retained in early 1920: class consciousness. Despite the devastating open shop drive the previous fall and the immense membership losses it entailed, Seattle's rank-and-file unionists had only recently been severed from their unions. The city's tens of thousands of metal trades workers, while beginning to experience layoffs, still remained in town and were still attracted to confrontation with the city's employers. The *Union Record* still published every day, expanding now to four editions. Both leaders and rank-and-filers within the movement still spoke of "the working class" and its collective interests.[28] Historian Norman Ware has argued that the success of late-nineteenth-century labor boycotts depended on just such "a condition of labor solidarity and class consciousness."[29]

Seattle workers had also developed through the cooperative movement a sophisticated dialogue about the political economy of consumption. The concept of the "workers' purchasing power" was widespread in the labor and cooperative press. Through the labor capitalist movement the idea of "the workers' money" had become equally current. Seattle AFL members were conscious of themselves as people with money to spend and whose money could be spent to promote collective interests. Seattle merchants who sold to working-class patrons, moreover, were dependent on that money. The "workers' purchasing power" was not a fiction.

Solidarity as consumers?

Once the boycott was declared in March 1920, the task for the Central Labor Council was actually to mobilize Seattle workers as politicized shoppers, so that they would achieve solidarity as consumers as well as at the waged workplace. Publicity was the key, its leadership learned from the Associated Industries. "Discovering that propaganda when used by them for any purpose is always successful we decided to use that method for combatting the Associated Industries," announced Frank Cotterill, secretary of the Building Trades Council.[30] "Now we have learned that trick," concurred Jack Mundy, Central Labor Council president.[31] The council instituted its own saturation campaign on behalf of the boycott. A committee of three coordinating the campaign – Doyle of the painters, Cotterill of the plumbers, and Kennedy of the janitors – printed leaflets, sent letters to all the city's locals, and paid visits to their meetings to promote the boycott. Individual locals in turn communicated internally with their members. The butchers, for example, pledged that none of their members nor their relatives would shop at the Bon Marche and asked that all other unions take the same pledge. The typographers answered the pledge and in turn sent delegates to the council's publicity committee. Anti–Bon Marche posters appeared at the Labor Temple and at labor halls throughout the city. The boycott's promoters also took their campaign to the labor movement statewide. They wrote letters to all central labor bodies in the state, erected billboards, asked out-of-towners to avoid the store when visiting Seattle, and exhorted workers to forgo purchases from the Bon's mail-order catalogue.[32]

The *Record*, thirsting after the Bon's advertising dollars, served as the unions' premier propaganda organ. In both daily news stories and editorials, the paper's writers constructed a political and moral critique of the Bon Marche that asserted, first, the store's exploitation of its workers: It had long opposed unions; it refused to sign contracts with its engineers, laborers, lathers, plasterers, and bricklayers; and above all its managers were intimate with the Associated Industries. The Bon accorded especially cruel treatment to its female clerks, the *Record* charged. The women's pay was so low they were just one step away from "the street" (i.e., prostitution). The store monitored clerks' budgets in order to lobby against a raise in the state minimum wage, laid them off just before they were scheduled to receive bonuses, refused to provide chairs for the women to rest in when not actually waiting on customers, and forced them to toil in "foul smelling basements." One especially lurid story was headlined "WIDOW MAIMED IN BON MARCHE IS IMPROVING." A clerk had fallen down an elevator shaft, and the Bon was being "secretive" about her condition.[33]

A second set of stories argued that the Bon Marche also exploited Seattle workers as consumers. The store's prices were too high, went this argument, exceeding those at comparable stores. The store also derived "excess profits," that is, engaged in profiteering. It employed misleading sales practices. The *Record* charged that the store lured shoppers into a special basement with ostensible "bargains," and then, when the unsuspecting customer discovered only off-sizes available, sold him or her the same article upstairs at a high markup. Unionists, here, not only were aware of such bait-and-switch tactics but could also criticize them in service to a political program.[34] One irresistible *Record* headline summed up the unions' campaign: "Bible in Window of Bon Marche Condemns Owners." A Bible placed in a window display had inadvertently fallen open to Ezekiel 28:17: "By the multitude of thy merchandise they have filled the midst of thee with violence, and thou hast sinned; therefore I will cast thee as profane out of the mountain of God; and I will destroy thee." Even God, in other words, boycotted the Bon Marche.[35]

In mobilizing this campaign, Seattle unionists drew on a long tradition of trade-union–based consumer boycotts that had begun in the nineteenth century. These boycotts had built habits of politicized shopping that by 1920 were deeply ingrained in working-class life. Trade unions first employed boycotts in 1806. During the 1880s boycotts flourished under the rubric of the Knights of Labor, who sustained an array of local boycott campaigns, published extensive national "unfair" lists of boycotted firms, and most important, fostered a deeply moral politics that extended workers' political identities into the spheres of both consumption and production. The emerging craft unions of the American Federation of Labor similarly learned to use the boycott in the late nineteenth century. By the turn of the century the AFL had published its own massive national "We Don't Patronize" list.[36]

Employers nationwide noticed. In the first decade of the 1900s they formed the American Anti-Boycott Association, which mobilized legal action against AFL boycotts, culminating in two major U.S. Supreme Court rulings that sharply restricted the unions' use of the boycott. In *Loewe* v. *Lawlor* (1908) the Court held officers of the Danbury, Connecticut, hat workers' union financially responsible for $250,000 in damages to a boycotted hat firm, concluding that the boycott had involved restraint of trade, which was forbidden under the Sherman Anti-Trust Act. Five years later in *Buck's Stove and Range* v. *American Federation of Labor et al.* the Court upheld an injunction against the AFL's national unfair list. Samuel Gompers and other top AFL officers defied the injunction, were found guilty of contempt, and narrowly avoided jail over the case.[37]

The Court's assault produced a measure of restraint on the part of the national AFL office thereafter in publicizing its "We Don't Patronize" list. But U.S. trade unions appear to have continued to call and promote boycotts unabated, merely shifting the site of their publicity from the national to the local. In the early twenties the internationals continued to send to Seattle union locals a stream of letters asking that trade unionists observe boycotts.[38]

The most important centers of boycott promotion were the central labor councils. They had long been the locus of solidarity on the local level, structuring and mobilizing cross-trade assistance while trying to ameliorate the jurisdictional fratricide built into craft unionism. As Gompers knew, the central labor councils embodied a serious threat to his centralized power over the AFL. Throughout the early twentieth century he steadily worked to undermine their power relative to the AFL national office and the internationals. But in western U.S. cities in particular, central councils successfully resisted Gompers's aggrandizement and remained strong bases from which to mount local boycott campaigns.[39]

In 1920 the Seattle Central Labor Council possessed a complex machinery through which it sought to regulate boycotts. Individual locals, after exhausting negotiations with a given employer, could present their cases to the council's Executive Board, which was charged with adjudicating boycotts. Elected by Central Labor Council delegates, the Executive Board controlled a council "unfair" list that it updated monthly, distributed to the city's locals, and published erratically in the *Record*. Most often the board agreed with the petitioning local and proclaimed the firm unfair, adding it to the list.[40] This system produced a lengthy and always fluid "unfair" list. In 1923, for example, the list included seventeen restaurants, fifteen manufacturers, eleven markets and groceries, and fourteen places of amusement. When combined with the boycotts announced by the internationals, the list identified a dense web of boycotts requiring constant vigilance and hard work for any Seattle worker who chose completely to observe trade-union shopping principles.[41]

Yet as the council's leadership was aware, the rank and file's loyalty to boycotts had always been incomplete. "Places have been placed on the unfair list before and [this] did not bring results," the building trades' Cotterill acknowledged in February 1920.[42] In 1919 Seattle locals repeatedly charged other unionists with failing to observe boycotts. In July, for example, a representative of the cooks complained, "We certainly feel peeved after going 100 percent union to find that two of the eating houses that remained open during the general strike are feeding union people." Although both were still unfair, their owners were "boasting of the patronage given them by organized labor."[43] Alice Lord of the waitresses' union, more than "peeved" herself, told the Central Labor Council that an employer had informed her that he did not need to recognize her union because he already had union patronage. Disbelieving, she had visited the establishment and discovered that the story was true. She announced to the council that she was getting a photographer to "take some pictures of some of the gentlemen with union buttons that patronize scab restaurants."[44] Joe Hoffman of the butchers similarly swore "that several dozen union people are patronizing the unfair Schuman's market at Hillman City." He vowed to get a list of the names . . . "and then will come the fireworks."[45]

As these examples suggest, though, unions had more than moral exhortations at their disposal in promoting boycotts. Many Seattle locals employed coercive measures to guarantee their members' boycott observance. A shipwright from Carpenters' Local #1184 announced to the Central Labor Council in May 1919, for example: "Have committee watching Sunset Market and placed $10.00 fine on any member caught buying meat in unfair markets."[46] The next month the laundry drivers instituted a $25 fine on any member "caught buying scab bread."[47] Disciplining members with fines was integral to the functioning of craft unionism.[48] What was unique here was its application to the politics of consumption.

The woman question

The big task for the Central Labor Council, though, was to win women over to the boycott cause. Both male and female activists agreed that women did 80 to 90 percent of the shopping in working-class families. Therefore women's support was crucial to the success of the Bon Marche boycott, in particular the support of those who worked full-time in the home.[49] Women's labors as consumers mattered directly, now, to the power of the unions in postwar Seattle. The problem, though, was that women, from trade unionists to the wives of the leadership to the family members of the rank and file, had their own perspectives on the question of politicizing their shopping. They were not enthusiastic about boycotts; nor, in a movement in which men controlled decision-making processes, were they part of the choice to call one in the first place. Here male unionists' chickens came home to roost. They needed women's full support; but just as in the cooperatives, women's priorities for the movement did not match their own.

The Central Labor Council's male leaders, aware that they had to secure women's support, shaped their campaign from its inception in order to better reach women. "It would be impossible to convince the people not to patronize any of the large department stores for the women will buy in these stores," Charles Doyle, the council's business agent, argued. "But it is a very easy matter to convince them not to patronize any one store in particular."[50] Doyle believed that women would be especially persuaded by arguments that the store's prices were too high. "This publicity will be the greatest aid in our campaign because the women knowing that if a store is liable to overcharge them they will stay away from it."[51] Because they believed it was the best way to reach women the boycott's promoters focused their promotional efforts especially on the *Union Record*.[52]

But wanting to reach women and actually convincing them were two different matters. Women's response to the boycott call was embedded in the broader relations between men and women and the Seattle AFL movement, and in particular the way male trade unionists saw their wives fitting into the movement. Both limited the full involvement of women in boycott support.

Although they recognized women's importance to the boycott, most men conceptualized non–wage-earning women's role as fundamentally subservient. "Put Women in Second Line of Labor Defense," read the headline of a November 1919 *Record* article reporting on the decision of the State Federation of Labor to mobilize working-class wives.[53] Women's job was to serve the trade-union movement by shaping their shopping choices according to union dictates and generally offering their services to the movement. Men assumed that it was in women's interest to do so, because then the working class as a whole could advance. This perspective cut across lines of ideology within the movement. The pro-OBU *Forge*, speaking of "the wives and sisters of the workingman," proposed that they "help in the distribution of literature and in the education of others."[54]

Male trade unionists even at times expressed outright contempt toward working-class wives. Max Eastman recounted in *The Liberator* of April 1919 that he had heard "some of the men who lead the left wing of the American Federation of Labor talk about their wives" during a meeting of the Seattle general strike committee:

> "I want to ask the brothers here," said one of them, "if any of them thinks that, aside from what he might have done, his wife would have held out for another day even if we could have won our demands?"
> "Naw!" was the answer. "Ask 'em what the women are good for anyway" was another, which brought a derisive laugh, and settled the matter finally for a good many of those present.[55]

Other trade unionists, while they endorsed the idea of involving wives in the union movement, nonetheless preferred barriers keeping them out of its central workings. A correspondent to the *Record* who signed himself "union man," for example, disagreed with a previous letter that had advocated women's attendance at their menfolk's union meetings. "I think if a woman is enough interested in her husband she can find out enough about their welfare by them telling her."[56]

A common point of view held that housewives were politically backward and therefore a hindrance to the working-class movement. One activist, for example, proposed organizing wives so that women could "help instead of clog [impede] their men."[57] Those within the Seattle labor movement who were most progressive on "the woman question" shared this perspective, albeit from a different angle. They argued that the increasing entry of women into the labor force would gradually lead them to identify with the trade-union movement and thus integrate them as full participants in the class struggle. The *Forge* cautioned in a long, supportive article on bringing women into the movement: "The process in some cases may be long and tedious, but we must remember that women have not been in industry very long and that their education has been all wrong."[58] Advice columnist Ruth Ridgeway argued that the socialization of housework would free women to be full and equal wage workers and thus equal partners in the class movement.[59]

Women who worked in the home full-time had their own outlook on trade unions. Their job was to spend money creatively, mixing their unwaged labors with clever buying habits to manage an always-skimpy family budget. As did inflation, boycotts made that work harder. A given boycott could be successful, after all, only if working-class women had patronized a given establishment or purchased a given product before the boycott was called. Otherwise there was no threat involved, no "purchasing power" to withdraw and in so doing injure a firm. Yet there was a reason why women had patronized that firm in the first place. Price might be only one of the possible reasons. Others might be quality, convenience, service, fashion, or familiarity. It might simply have been more fun to shop at the Bon Marche. The Bon Marche might have provided rest areas for tired feet, or a nicer bathroom. Women also shaped their shopping choices to satisfy their family members, in order to decrease their emotional labors. For a housewife, to observe a boycott was to speed up her own labor in contribution to the trade unionists' efforts to change the terms of labor at the waged workplace. From many working-class women's position, the boycott was not "cheaper" at all.[60]

With a boycott such as that of the Bon Marche, men's and women's interests as waged versus unwaged workers clashed directly. By resolving those opposing interests in favor of largely male trade unionists, the boycott institutionalized the subservience of non–wage-earning women within the movement. Because the only progressive point of view on housewives available was that all women should gradually become wage earners, Seattle unionists had no theoretical ability to grasp what they were asking of women. They then felt stymied or angry when housewives responded negatively to their exhortations.

The *Record* did in small part recognize this contradiction and seek to resolve it when it argued that the Bon Marche's prices were higher than those of other stores. More representative, though, was a 1918 speech by John Manning, secretary of the AFL's Label Trades Department, to the barbers' national convention reprinted in their monthly journal. Haranguing the assembled barbers to observe the union label and shop card, he pointed to the "crime of ignorance" committed by union men's wives who did not look for the label. Had the men "taught the principles of trades unionism to their women folks?" he asked. Capturing exactly the opposing interests involved, he queried, "Have you pointed out to them the danger of bargain rates?" For women, though, bargain rates meant more cash.[61]

To ensure wives' support of boycotts, male trade unionists sought to institutionalize the subservience of women by employing the coercive mechanisms of craft unions. Just as they used internal discipline to force rank-and-file union members to observe unionized shopping, they also tried to force those same men to control their wives. The musicians' union, for example, fined Elmer Wells $25 after his wife was seen entering a boycotted theater. The minutes of the local's internal trials indicate that men could not control the consumption patterns of their wives and also suggest the possibility that men used their supposed lack of control over their wives to escape punishment for their own transgressions. Elmer Wells "expressed himself as being a good union man and in sympathy with all that was done to win the fight. He stated that he had heard his wife attended the show and brought it to her attention but she denied ever going there."[62] Joe Barosso, accused by the musicians' union of patronizing an unfair cab, admitted he had done so but pleaded, according to the minutes, that "He was late for rehearsal and that his wife called for a cab . . . he being ignorant of the fact that it was unfair patronized same."[63] Like earlier efforts to stop the wives of trade unionists from scabbing, these measures assumed patriarchal control within the family and sought to manage it in service to the labor movement; the effort foundered on the rocks of both women's resistance to patriarchal control and of rank-and-file men's resistance to coercion.

Scattered but consistent evidence indicates that many wives of the rank and file were alienated from their husbands' trade-union activities. Their reaction to the boycott call constituted only the tip of an immense iceberg of estrangement from the trade-union movement altogether. Few women attended the mass street meetings of the immediate postwar years. One participant estimated that of those attending two protest meetings in late 1919, the male–female ratio was approximately forty to one.[64] While the same observer speculated that child-care responsibilities may have kept women home, other evidence suggests that housewives were simply not engaged by the Seattle labor movement. The *Forge*'s piece on reaching women reported that "A man may put up an unassailable argument and be able to convince the most conservative man but he *cannot* convince a woman. If you doubt this statement, get acquainted with the wives and sisters of some of our most well known radicals." Only a woman could – maybe – reach other women, the author concluded.[65] Men's hostility to women's equality within the movement contributed to such resistance. A week after the Central Labor Council's October vote against married women Mary Nauman observed, "I heard one man say of the vote, 'Good; let her stay at home where she belongs.' I tell you it's the wives of just such men" who were the "hardest to interest in supporting unions."[66] A writer for the *Record*'s women's page noted "in many cases the [woman's] only thought about the union to which her man belonged has been one of hatred in time of strike."[67] Indeed, women could hate a strike for the same reason as a boycott: Both intensified women's work by calling for the substitution of wages, earned by men, with greater unwaged work by women. The male unionists who spoke of their womenfolk as "clogs" to the movement were not completely inaccurate: Wives did not, in many cases, want to help the movement; they had their own point of view on the efficacy of sacrifice on behalf of the "class" movement.[68]

One group of Seattle working-class housewives, the Women's Card and Label League, did choose to organize in support of the trade-union movement. Originally founded in 1905, the group at first languished, until the Central Labor Council founded a new league in 1911. By the eve of the war it had grown to 500 members. In these years the AFL founded similar card and label leagues in hundreds of cities throughout the country.[69] Seattle's Card and Label League, in its 1919–20 incarnation, counted about 100 members. They were all full-time housewives, many of them wives of the labor movement's male leadership. All of them, evidently, were white. They met once a month for luncheon, a business meeting, and, often, a card party. In part, their activities paralleled those of a handful of ladies' auxiliaries to trade unions in Seattle, albeit on a citywide, cross-trade level.[70]

These women in many ways embraced the role men prescribed for them. Addressing the Central Labor Council in June 1919, Minnie K. Ault, wife of the *Record*'s editor, endorsed male unionists' attempts to persuade their wives to serve the movement: "If you men have any influence at all with your wives, and you certainly should have ... why is it that so many of them have never joined the league and helped with the work we are doing?"[71] Members of the ladies' auxiliary to the boilermakers' union, on the first day of the general strike, similarly announced that they were "standing by their husbands" and called on the boilermakers' members to "use their influence to induce their wives to join the auxiliary."[72] The core of the Label League's organizing agenda, as its name indicated, was support work on behalf of the union label and shop card and union-sponsored boycotts.[73]

Women's choice to accept this role made sense on a number of levels. First, assuming responsibility for boycott and label promotion gave housewives, otherwise marginalized, their own place in the working-class movement. It gave them an organizational base from which to assert their own opinions about the nature of the movement. It even gave them representation, and sometimes votes, at the Central Labor Council.[74] Second, the Card and Label League recognized and dignified women's unpaid labors in the home. While it conceptualized their work in subservient terms, nonetheless it acknowledged that women's work as consumers mattered to the labor movement as a whole and, therefore, however partially, could empower housewives within the movement.

Third, it was in many ways in working-class housewives' interest to support the trade-union movement. At the level of the family women could identify direct benefits from their husbands' trade-union activities. Higher wages meant more money to spend. Shorter hours meant more time for men to help with child care, with housework, or in simple companionship. Job security meant less fear of layoffs, fewer periods of frightened penny-pinching while husbands were unemployed, or the possibility of saving money. Safer working conditions meant fewer days home sick, fewer disabling injuries, and a longer life span. All these trade-union demands at the point of production were directly in women's interest. Once they accepted the sexual division of labor and the family wage system, housewives could see how it might make sense to throw their support behind the trade-union movement.[75]

In the spring of 1920 the members of the Card and Label League offered their support to the Bon Marche boycott. On May 13 they presented a resolution to the Central Labor Council asking for the formation of additional propaganda committees to publish the facts about the Associated Industries and to agitate against the Bon Marche. A week later they sent a letter to all the city's locals enclosing pledge cards with which, they requested, each local's members should vow not to shop at the Bon.[76]

But the Card and Label League's support for the Bon boycott was less than completely enthusiastic. The members of the Card and Label League engaged in boycott support work only late in the game, and then only in a perfunctory fashion. While the Central Labor Council announced the boycott in mid-March and mounted its campaign most forcefully in late March and April, the Card and Label League at its April 20 meeting took up entirely different issues.[77] Its members did not send out their pledge cards until mid-May. Another campaign later that year suggests a similar response. In early August, Jean Stovel, the State Federation of Labor's organizer for women, in conjunction with the Label League called a "mass meeting" of Seattle women in support of "massing their purchasing power behind *Union Record* advertisers." The *Record* gave the event front-page advance publicity. Yet evidently only a handful of stalwarts showed up.[78] Both campaigns suggest that the members of the Card and Label League were aware of their official role as mobilizers of trade-union families' shopping habits. In both instances they performed some solid organizing work. But they did not mobilize themselves on behalf of either campaign in any great numbers, let alone energize the female "masses" to join the fight.

A close examination of the league's activities in 1919 shows why: Its members had other priorities at the time that expanded well beyond the "subservient shoppers" model. While some of their activities involved support work for male trade unionists – such as supplementing picket lines, agitating on behalf of the butchers' shop card, or organizing for the movement as a whole social functions such as dances or card parties – often their political priorities diverged from or even contradicted those of the Central Labor Council majority. For example, in 1919 and 1920 members of the Card and Label League worked on behalf of Tom Mooney, for the release of political prisoners, against capital punishment, and for the reduction of judges' salaries.[79]

Members of the Card and Label League also actively allied themselves with women trade-union members. They introduced a resolution at the 1919 State Federation of Labor convention calling for an organizing campaign for women workers. They lobbied assiduously for a raise in the state minimum wage for women. In 1919 the league came to the aid of the telephone operators, pressured the city hospital to establish a separate ward with female doctors and nurses for the treatment of women with sexual diseases, and affiliated with the national Women's Trade Union League.[80] In their support for wage-earning women's concerns they did not shy from conflict with trade-union men. They battled both the Central Labor Council and the State Federation over the right of married women to work and the woman organizer question.[81] The Women's Card and Label League, in sum, was a broad-ranging, feminist, citywide political organization. While it might have begun from the role of submission, its actual activities expanded far beyond that.

The Card and Label League was just one of a large number of white working-class women's organizations loosely associated with the AFL in immediate postwar Seattle. The Women's Modern Study Club, a study group in political and economic theory, included many of the most prominent trade-union women and activist wives in the city. The Business Women's Civic Club, a discussion and debating group, admitted wage-earning women only. Union members and wives together formed a chapter of the Women's Trade Union League in 1919. Other groups included active women's clubs of the Workers', Soldiers' and Sailors' Council, a radical postwar veterans' organization, and of the nascent Farmer–Labor Party. To this list we can add the dozens of women's clubs of the Cooperative Food Products Association and the Seattle Consumers' Cooperative Association and, finally, a handful of ladies' auxiliaries, which shaded over into sewing clubs.[82] The membership of all these groups overlapped a great deal. Mabel Clothier, for example, was a leader of the active auxiliary to Boilermakers' Local #104, an agitator on behalf of *Union Record* advertisers, and a member of the boards of directors of the Cooperative Food Products Association and Lake Burien Cooperative Women's Club.[83] Such overlaps in personnel should not, however, diminish our assessment of the rank-and-file enthusiasm that was necessary to sustain so many groups.[84]

This proliferation of organizations, when added to the Card and Label League, underscores the fact that when women chose their own priorities and organizations, political activism among Seattle's white working-class housewives flourished. Three elements distinguish these activities: first, organizational independence from men;[85] second, a mixture of concerns; and third (though not always) a degree of feminism, in part necessary to make women's independent activism possible at all, because so many of the men believed women's place was in the home only.

Several thousand Seattle women participated in the AFL movement as union members themselves. Their position within the movement was distinct both from that of male trade unionists and that of their wives. And they had their own perspective on the Bon Marche boycott.

On many occasions female trade unionists worked in tandem with activist wives, especially when wives engaged in support work on their behalf. At one point the waitresses' Alice Lord in return expressed solidarity with wives in their unwaged labors. Speaking on behalf of the six-hour day and six-day week for women at the 1919 State Federation convention, she added, "Housewives also should be included in this happy arrangement." But this was not a widely held position. More commonly trade-union women appear to have agreed with their union brothers about the place of non–wage-earning wives in the movement. Mrs. Laura Judah, president of the Garment Workers' local, followed Lord by arguing that "organization of housewives" was "a necessity if the union label was to receive the proper amount of attention." Non–wage-earning wives should organize, in other words, not to agitate on behalf of the conditions of their own work but in service to wage-earning women.[86] Trade-union women also at times expressed hostility to the wives of trade unionists. The debate over married women's right to work, in particular, brought out tensions over the job rights of single women versus the rights of those with employed husbands.[87]

Almost all the city's organized women workers labored in sectors of the Seattle economy in which consumer tactics could work effectively. Women unionists fell into two categories. The first consisted of workers in manufacturing plants that produced commodities for a working-class market: the candy makers, cigar makers, ladies' garment workers, typographers, press assistants, and bakery workers. The second group, which accounted for the overwhelming majority of organized women in 1920, consisted of workers in the service sector: waitresses, laundry workers, musicians, janitors, cooks, cleaning and dye workers, retail clerks, tailors, and boot and shoe repairers. Given this distribution it would be in women unionists' interest to encourage wives' observance of unionized shopping.[88] Yet Seattle's female trade unionists never came forward in support of the Bon Marche boycott. No women served on the publicity committees. No trade-union women, apparently, agitated or spoke out on behalf of the boycott at all.

If we trace the activities of Seattle's most active trade-union women it becomes clear what they were doing instead. In the spring of 1920 the female leadership figures, along with activist wives, were deeply involved in a campaign to increase the state minimum wage for women. Alice Lord, Jean Stovel, and Sophie Pugsley (the Central Labor Council's woman organizer), and members of the Card and Label League traveled weekly to the state capital in Olympia to lobby for the minimum wage at a series of special state hearings. Sometimes as many as twenty-five women attended. For these women, a raise in the minimum wage was a higher priority than the Bon Marche boycott. As Alice Kessler-Harris has shown, in the 1910s and '20s women throughout the country turned to protective labor legislation such as the minimum wage because they were frustrated by men's lack of support for women workers. Male unionists even encouraged this orientation because it meant that they did not have to integrate fully into their movement the concerns of women. Seattle's women trade unionists, then, chose a political agenda in the spring of 1920 quite different from that of their male counterparts.[89]

As in the AFL nationwide, Seattle's female trade unionists had little power to shape a labor movement that would serve wage-earning men and women equally. Despite the solid presence of women in the city's unions (approximately 10 percent), the Seattle AFL remained under male control. All the council's officers, almost all the members of its governing committees, and all the members of the inner-circle Committee of Fifteen formed in response to the open shop drive were men.[90] The one perennial exception was the waitresses' Alice Lord. At the level of the locals, women held major offices only in all-female locals. In locals with a minority of men, such as the laundry workers, men assumed leadership. In locals with a strong minority of women, such as those of the typographers or the musicians, women held no substantial offices.[91]

Male trade unionists' tendency to speak of both the female members of trade-union men's families and female trade-union members as "women," when they meant only housewives, further marginalized unionized women within the movement. "Put Women in Second Line of Labor Defense" implicitly put all women in a subservient category. Concrete policies, moreover, institutionalized this conceptualization. The Central Labor Council required women who attended its meetings, whatever their role in the movement, to sit in a segregated section next to the left side entrance. More informal patterns of sexual harassment kept women subordinated as well. Theresa Schmid McMahon, an economics professor at the University of Washington, recalled of her visits to the council: "The gallery was always crowded with men and I not being exactly timid would not have ventured alone to sit there without expecting unfavorable comments."[92]

The sexual division of labor of the Seattle trade union movement at the broadest level adds further perspective to the role of trade union women. Overall, men controlled the movement's leadership, policies, and strategic agenda. Not only did they control the Central Labor Council, Building Trades Council, Metal Trades Council, and almost all of the city's locals, but they also served as the movement's candidates for political office, with the exception of the school board, for which both of labor's candidates in this period were women. Women, on the other hand, performed the day-to-day labor of the larger movement. They organized socials, planned dances, circulated petitions, and carried out most of the work of fund raising outside of dues collection, which remained the terrain of the largely male paid staff members. This division of labor spanned the entire range of the AFL movement. Women members of the Farmer–Labor Party, for example, collected signatures on petitions to ensure that a new primary election law did not outlaw the party.[93] Activists discussed this division of labor, moreover, in specifically gendered terms. One *Union Record* advertisement read, for example, "WANTED 100 LADIES. To Assist on Tag Day, Saturday next, for the relief of discharged Soldiers and Sailors." By asking for women rather than for volunteers, such requests both assumed and re-created the movement's sexual division of labor.[94]

In part these distinctions demarcated male trade unionists from their wives. Within the movement's larger division of labor, though, female trade unionists often took on the same roles within the movement as did wives who were not themselves members. In some cases this meant that a female union as a body performed support services for the citywide movement. In March 1919, for example, the waitresses' union undertook the sale of tickets for a dance to benefit the Soldiers' and Sailors' Council.[95] In other cases women unionists took on "female" roles within a mixed-gender local. Three of the four women serving as "committeemen" for the Typographers' Local in 1920–21 (of a total of forty-seven) served on the Relief Committee.[96] The role of trade-union women overlapped with that of activist housewives; both performed the "housework" of the movement. Both were perceived as "women" by male trade unionists. While female trade unionists could directly benefit from the unions' demands at the waged workplace, thus finding themselves in a different structural position from that of wives, that did not mean they were accepted as equals within the trade-union movement.

The appeal to pro-union shopping, then, assumed a cross-gender class unity that did not exist. The decision to boycott the Bon Marche emerged from a male-defined agenda for the labor movement that the Central Labor Council's leadership presented to the women of the movement as a *fait accompli*. Women did not participate in the choice to boycott the Bon; nor did they greet the boycott's promotion with great enthusiasm. The root of the problem was a fundamental tension within the Seattle AFL movement: Male trade unionists needed women's support, but the movement's agenda had been defined without women's input. The boycott centered on the politics of consumption; it sought to politicize women's unwaged work. But in contrast to the cooperatives, it was not designed to improve the conditions of that work or address the workplace concerns of those who performed it. Quite the contrary, it made their work harder. Wives conceptualized their role within the working-class movement in broad terms, spanning a range of issues and tactics. Men conceptualized wives' role in narrow terms, restricting women's work to subservience, socials, and loyal shopping. As these two visions clashed, women and men contested and negotiated the nature of the working-class movement. The Seattle AFL's ability to achieve solidarity as consumers foundered upon the unequal nature of those negotiations.

Whose boycott?

The Bon Marche boycott also depended on another kind of solidarity within the Seattle working class, the traditional kind between workers of different trades. As the Bon Marche boycott progressed it quickly became clear that Seattle workers in the "American Separation of Labor," as the Wobblies liked to call it, could not for long transcend the fragmenting effects of craft unionism, even in the name of a united front against the Associated Industries. In 1920 solidarity among organized workers proved just as elusive as that between male wage earners and housewives.

A boycott such as that of the Bon Marche required resolution of two key questions. First, if many different trades worked for the same firm, and the unions representing those workers reached different agreements with that employer, when should the firm be declared "fair" or "unfair"? In June 1919 the Central Labor Council had decided this question in favor of the greatest solidarity: Once a firm was placed on the "unfair" list, it could not be removed until all its employees were organized. Otherwise, as the janitors complained in pressing for this resolution, "as soon as a certain one of the crafts get organized they want that establishment placed on the fair list regardless of the other craft[s] in the establishment."[97] Second, since the fewer the boycotts, the greater the effectiveness of a given boycott, which boycotts should receive priority?

Resolving both questions depended upon power dynamics within the citywide labor movement. If a particular union could lay claim to the solidarity of the labor movement as a whole, then it would be empowered vis-à-vis employers more than other unions that did not receive such support. The outcome of struggles over which boycotts to pursue and when to terminate them therefore mattered vitally both to the outcome of the struggle between unions and employers and to the nature of the labor movement that would survive that battle. Formally, the Executive Board of the Central Labor Council adjudicated these questions. But it was only a creature of the council itself and its internal power relations, and of the broader, more informally resolved power dynamics within the movement. The development of the Bon Marche boycott over the course of 1920 soon illuminated where such power did and did not lie.

Power lay with the building trades. It was the building trades that originally wanted the Bon Marche boycott and the building trades that had the power within the council to throw the movement's energies behind it. As William Kennedy of the janitors pointed out, the Bon Marche had been unfair to his own union for a long time: "We tried to get the Central Labor Council to take some action on the matter but could not get any results until finally the Bon Marche had a couple of buildings built by scab contractors. . . . This got the building trades to working."[98] "The building trades were able to set machinery in motion, where we couldn't," he noted on another occasion.[99]

The building trades not only got their boycott, but they also got a commitment from the Central Labor Council to drop all other boycotts and concentrate the movement's energies on the Bon Marche. Charles Doyle, the council's business agent and a representative from the painters' union, now started talking about how the best "unfair" list was the shortest, with his trade's boycott at the top. "The C.L.C. will devote its interests to the Bon Marche exclusively. The whole trouble with us in the past was that our unfair lists were not effective enough.... If we are going to use the unfair list we must make it effective, and we decided to make it effective with the Bon Marche first."[100] Unionists from other trades greeted this arrangement less happily. As a delegate from the furniture salesmen's union protested in April, the Standard Furniture Company had been unfair for six months, but the Labor Temple did not even have a sign saying so. If the council was going to fight the Bon, it should include the Standard Furniture Company too. "They are both unfair to organized labor, and one is no better than the other."[101]

Once the Central Labor Council decided to focus all energies on boycotting the Bon Marche, still thornier questions of inter-trade solidarity emerged. The Bon Marche was a large and complex firm employing hundreds of workers other than building tradesmen. The janitors, retail clerks, candy workers, lady barbers, and waitresses all represented workers at the Bon Marche and would presumably be part of any negotiations with its management. It was not even easy to determine who did and did not work at the Bon Marche, or what solidarity with the boycott exactly meant. At the first meeting of the Central Labor Council after the boycott was declared, delegate Fink of the electrical workers asked, "[S]hould their men be sent to the Bon Marche to repair a company wire, the company being fair and under contract to the local, would they be classified as scabs?"[102] Delegate Anderson of the machinists similarly queried whether a repairman sent in to fix the Bon's elevators would be considered a scab.[103] The chair initially tried to avoid answering the questions. The delegates, though, demanded a resolution, and a two-hour discussion ensued, never quite settling the issue.[104] As debates over the nuances of boycott observance continued, solidarity between the different locals representing workers at the Bon Marche swiftly evaporated. Already broken up into separate craft unions, each union had its own interests in the matter and began to pursue them.

When Central Labor Council delegates arrived at the same March 20 meeting they found leaflets on their seats announcing that the Bon Marche was *fair* to the Candy Workers' Union. "This resulted in a regular stampede in denouncing the candy workers," one observer recorded. James Duncan finally quelled the uproar but only by dismissing the candy workers.

"We should leave them out of this fight, as they will cut no figure one way or the other," he argued. "We are not fighting the Candy Workers right now. We are fighting the Bon Marche. Don't let them get you to fighting each other. Forget the insignificant Candy Workers." As he had in the debates over whether to call the general strike, Duncan appealed to an overarching solidarity within the labor movement. The unions should not fight one another; they should jointly fight the Bon Marche. The candy workers' point of view should therefore be not only overridden but ignored.[105]

The members of the candy workers' union, on the other hand, did not agree that "we" should fight the Bon Marche. No evidence suggests they were ever consulted as part of the decision to initiate the boycott. Nor were they considered in the Executive Board's discussions with the Bon Marche's management over union conditions at the store, although the waitresses, janitors, and retail clerks were.[106] In distributing their heretical leaflets the candy workers may have been reacting to their marginalization within the movement or out of fear that the boycott would lead to layoffs. A number of prominent delegates charged at the time that the Associated Industries had paid them to put out the leaflets.[107] Presumably this was not true; but even if it were, the question then arises why these workers chose to ally with the employers' association rather than with the Central Labor Council. The incident illustrates both the extremely divergent interests unions brought to the boycott and the power dynamics within the movement. Internal power, again, was gendered. The candy workers were 85 percent female; the leadership's reaction to their concerns was dismissal.[108] This was the kind of situation that prompted Seattle's trade-union women, like those in other cities, to turn to protective legislation like the minimum wage rather than rely on aid from the AFL.

The situation of the Bon Marche's salesclerks illustrates still further how complex were the interests different unions brought to the boycott and how embedded in gender dynamics they were. From the largely female clerks' position, the big problem was that if the boycott were successful at all it would lead to layoffs. The *Union Record* acknowledged this dynamic, only to celebrate it as evidence of the boycott's effectiveness. In mid-March the paper reported that one-fourth of the Bon Marche's staff had been laid off or placed on part-time status. In May a salesclerk told a *Record* reporter that more than fifty clerks had been let go. The *Record* tried to give an anti–Bon Marche angle to these stories, pointing out that the women had been laid off just before they were to receive bonuses. But in general, its line was that the layoffs were happy evidence of labor's strength.[109] From the clerks' point of view, though, the boycott was a disaster. Unemployment in Seattle continued to increase in the spring of 1920, coming on the heels of seasonal post-holiday layoffs in January. The unions' boycott only exacerbated their situation.[110] Just as the boycott turned out not to be "cheaper" for women, neither, for the retail clerks, was it "safer." Male building trades workers, in alliance with the overall male leadership of the council, had chosen a tactic that benefited largely male workers at women workers' expense.

A careful look at the history of the retail clerks' union in the previous year explains why its leaders did not object. Twice the year before – first in response to a proposed boycott of all firms that refused to advertise in the *Record*, and second in response to the Christmas presents boycott – the local had protested to the Central Labor Council that such boycotts would produce layoffs of retail clerks.[111] By March 1920, however, the union's attitude had changed dramatically. Its members were almost all male, as were its officers; and the local largely represented workers at smaller stores, many of which were 100 percent union in mid-1919. Well aware of the all-important bloc of unorganized women workers at the city's department stores, the union had launched a major organizing drive at the stores in late 1919. It enlisted Sophie Pugsley, the new organizer for women, full-time on its behalf. But by January 1920 the union had abandoned its campaign. In explaining why the drive failed to make headway among the clerks, both Pugsley and business agent Sam Wiesfield fell back on the assumptions about white-collar women workers' supposed lack of interest in unions that undermined organizing drives throughout the early twentieth century. Women were working only temporarily. Too many of them were married. They were working only for pin money. Women did not know anything about unions. "I would much sooner organize the men," concluded Pugsley.[112]

Frustrated, by March the union fell back on an approach to organizing that had worked effectively before in the city's smaller stores: using consumer pressure to force employers to recognize the union. As Wiesfield explained this approach in early 1919: Because "the women clerks do not want to join . . . the only thing left for labor to do is to make the women join."[113] "If labor withdrew its patronage from the unorganized stores the managers would come to us and beg us to take their clerks into our organization."[114] Note the relationship to the actual clerks this tactic called for. The employer would "force" the women to join, "compel their clerks to organize."[115] The retail clerks' union, in other words, welcomed the Bon Marche boycott's potential ability to force the store's management to recognize the union. They wanted to build the union from the top down. A boycott, like other consumer tactics, could obviate the need for the active, enthusiastic involvement of rank-and-file workers in their union, because it displaced the locus of struggle from employer and employee to customers and employer. It gave a new form of strength to the movement, but it could also enervate it at the roots. Like so much else it was also caught up in the gender dynamics of the movement.

By the third week of April further inter-trade tensions over the Bon Marche boycott had emerged, bringing power dynamics within the movement to a head. This time the dissenting voices came from the janitors' union. "I am disgusted with the labor movement of Seattle," raged William Kennedy, an active member of the local.

> They start a thing with great enthusiasm, and they forget all about it. When the Bon Marche was first placed on the unfair list, there was great enthusiasm. They weren't going to leave a stone unturned in making the boycott a success. But since then we don't seem to get any action. The janitors and the watchmen are the only ones who are keeping the fight up.[116]

The building trades' support for the Bon boycott, in other words, had largely evaporated. The janitors were now left to go it alone.

It is not difficult to explain the building trades' lack of interest. Once the Bon's McDermott Building had been completed, the unions were protesting a fait accompli. Victory through a boycott would not create new union jobs. The Associated Industries alleged that once the non-union work on the building was done, union workers under "strictly closed shop conditions" had performed the building's plumbing, electrical work, and most of its finishing work.[117] Whatever the Bon Marche situation, by late spring Seattle's building trades unions had evidently reestablished the closed shop on an informal basis.[118] Structurally empowered by their position as skilled workers, when the seasonal construction industry picked up in the spring Seattle's building crafts were able to make a separate peace with the Associated Industries. In February and March, they had needed solidarity. Now they did not. The janitors could push the Bon Marche all they wanted, but the building trades did not have to care. In this instance internal power dynamics demarcated the skilled and the unskilled, the building trades versus the janitors, clerks, and waitresses, with women in the unskilled camp.

The building trades' waning enthusiasm suggests the final reef on which boycott solidarity shattered: ending the boycott. Boycotts, as Norman Ware put it, are "more easily imposed than lifted."[119] How could the Central Labor Council gracefully admit it no longer cared? Declare victory? Concede defeat? The building trades' apathy indicates how rapidly actual practice might diverge from official Central Labor Council commitments. So did the actions of the musician's union. In July, it decided that because other unionized crafts were already working at the Bon Marche, it would allow its members to work there, too, although the store was still on the official "unfair" list.[120]

Internal differences over whether to keep a firm on the "unfair" list or not could go on indefinitely without formal resolution. In May and June of 1920 infighting over the list intensified among Central Labor Council delegates. One fight involved the culinary workers. The highly skilled cooks had decided in March to demand a raise for themselves, which they subsequently obtained at all union restaurants except the Panama Cafeteria. Their delegates then announced to the Central Labor Council that the Panama Cafeteria was unfair. The waiters and waitresses, though, charged that the cooks were interested in higher wages only for themselves and should instead support higher wages for lower-paid culinary workers, especially women. They announced the Panama Cafeteria to be fair. This conflict produced a "regular ritual" at council meetings in May and June, with the chair each week confirming that the cafeteria was not in fact on the council's "unfair" list. Meanwhile, the cooks distributed leaflets at the restaurant and, as management put it, made "every effort . . . to ruin the restaurant."[121]

The Bon Marche boycott went on indefinitely, too. Over the course of the summer and fall agitation for the boycott continued to wane; in part, it was eclipsed by another boycott, of the Von Herberg theater chain.[122] A mid-November victory in the theater boycott produced renewed enthusiasm for the anti–Bon Marche fight, and negotiations with the Bon Marche's management continued. By early 1921 interest in the campaign plummeted once again. In June a debate erupted within the building trades over whether to officially revoke the boycott. By August, the boycott's opponents had triumphed within the Building Trades Council, and its officers asked the Central Labor Council to rescind the Bon Marche boycott. The central council, though, refused; it would not remove the Bon from the "unfair" list until gains had been won for the store's non–building trades workers as well. The Building Trades tried again in September. The council again said no, calling for another mass campaign against the Bon. By late November 1921 only fourteen locals, of more than a hundred affiliates, had pledged their support. Accepting the reality of the situation, the Executive Board officially removed the Bon Marche from the "unfair" list in February 1922.[123]

The protracted demise of the Bon Marche boycott shows, first, the continued support of a number of Seattle trades for the boycott. Long-term supporters included radical unions such as the shipyard laborers' and many other locals that did not themselves represent workers at the Bon Marche. Second, it demonstrates how the building trades nonetheless called the shots, eventually getting what they wanted. Third, it shows that the Central Labor Council could, at least in 1920 and 1921, still check the power of the building trades in behalf of less skilled workers. But unless widespread support for continuing the boycott could be mobilized, the building trades would eventually win out.

The Bon Marche boycott both grew out of and shaped the internal power dynamics within the Seattle labor movement. Ostensibly it united all the store's workers into a united block across lines of trade, skill, and gender and then in turn united all the city's AFL unions behind those workers at the Bon. Such solidarity swiftly proved illusory. The spectre of craft unionism still haunted the movement. Lines of skill and gender could then further rend any solidarity the labor movement might muster. Nineteen-twenty brought not deeper solidarity to Seattle's unions but new ways in which to abandon it.

The solidarity of the Associated Industries

The thorny issue of ending the Bon Marche boycott points, finally, to the question of its effectiveness. No "objective" polls or financial data are available to answer this all-important question. The *Union Record*, certainly, proclaimed the great effectiveness of the Bon boycott. It claimed that the Bon Marche's crowds of shoppers had thinned and its profits plummeted. The Bon, it asserted, had stepped up out-of-town advertising to compensate for its loss of local sales. According to the *Record*, a department head had confided to a friend that the store's business was down 50 percent from that of the previous year. When a *Record* reporter counted customers as they entered three downtown department stores, 712 people went into McDougall-Southwick's, 662 into Fraser-Patterson, but only 316 into the Bon Marche. The *Record*'s stories alone, however, cannot be considered a reliable source. It would have been in the paper's interest to exaggerate its claims, and in other, more verifiable instances the *Record*'s editors had few compunctions about lying.[124] Part of the psychological warfare involved in any boycott campaign would induce the labor movement to claim that the boycott was completely effective and the boycotted firm simultaneously to announce it to be a complete failure.[125]

Seattle employers' internal literature makes it clear, however, that the boycott hurt the Bon Marche and put the Associated Industries on the defensive. In a pamphlet published in the early fall the Associated Industries acknowledged that "there is little question but that it [the Bon Marche] is being injured."[126] The association spoke of firms' being selected for boycotts on the basis of "vulnerability," implicitly granting that firms were, in fact, vulnerable to boycotts. A bulletin to members alerting them to the boycott quoted the tenants in the McDermott Building to the effect that "their business was being wrecked by this unjust and unwarranted attack."[127]

Organized labor's subsequent boycotts of non-union bakeries in the summer and Von Herberg theaters in the fall further frightened the Associated Industries. One contemporary pro-employer article noted that in its first eighteen months the Associated Industries lost only two battles, those against the bakers and against the theater musicians.[128] Speeches, organizing priorities, and literature of the Associated Industries in the fall indicate that one of their highest priorities became defense against boycotts. In a pamphlet published in August 1920 entitled *Revolution, Wholesale Strikes, Boycotts*, for example, the employers identified three successive postwar attacks by organized labor: first, the general strike; second, the nineteen separate strikes of late 1919 and early 1920; and third, boycotts, not just the Bon Marche boycott, but also those that followed of the Von Herberg theaters and non-union bakeries.[129] Seattle's businesses, it noted with alarm, were now "confronted with the poison gas of a constantly-growing list of venomous boycotts." The association's newsletter summarized on August 14: "The boycott is the most effective weapon in the hands of the red radicals who control the local unions."[130]

The employers' protests offer persuasive evidence that thousands, perhaps tens of thousands, of Seattle workers observed the Bon Marche boycott. The totals are impossible to gauge or break down by gender. But given women's control of working-class shopping, many of the boycott observers must have been women, despite the evidence demonstrating women's lack of enthusiasm for the campaign. The contradiction here is not as large as it might seem. Lackluster involvement in the boycott campaign and a preference for alternative tactics did not necessarily mean that female union members and the female family members of male unionists would actually have shopped at the Bon Marche. Given the heightened level of class tensions in the city and the pervasiveness of publicity against the store, it seems likely that when it came time to shop, women and men active in the AFL movement would have supported the campaign. As the *Record* reporter posted at the door and the vehement denunciations of those patronizing non-union restaurants suggest, moreover, shopping at the Bon Marche was a visible act. Activists in the movement certainly must have wanted to avoid being seen entering the store. The shopping choices of less active members and their families remain unknown, along with those of the middle class. It would have taken more than just boycott observance by the AFL leadership, though, to cause the Associated Industries to admit that the boycott was effective.

Some members of Seattle's working class, though, might have ignored the boycott or even deliberately shopped at the Bon Marche. Given the layoffs the boycott precipitated, female retail clerks at the Bon Marche and other nearby department stores may have been hostile to the entire campaign. Other unorganized workers may have been untouched by unions and simply lacked interest in the matter. Wobblies may have shopped at the Bon to spite the AFL, though it seems likely they would have been still more hostile to the Associated Industries. More importantly, once the AFL locals had barred Japanese- and African-American workers from membership (with the exception of the longshoremen), they could not then turn around and ask them to observe the "workers'" campaign for politicized shopping. The Seattle AFL's movement's institutionalized racism, combined with its earlier failure to organize the full range of the city's waged workers, restricted the range of the city's working class who would want to shop in service to the AFL program.

For the Associated Industries, the challenge was how to combat boycotts. The Associated Industries conceded that "the difficulty of obtaining convictions makes appeal to the courts an unattractive means of securing adequate relief," even though both county and state courts had declared boycotts illegal.[131] Thwarted on that front, organized employers chose to copy the unions' strategy and mobilize their own purchasing power to counter the workers'. At an August 14 meeting employers discussed "the solidarity of the Associated Industries and the massing of the purchasing power of its members in combatting boycotts."[132] *Revolution, Wholesale Strikes, Boycotts* concluded that the "best alternative" to the courts was the "use of the same weapon employed by those attempting to destroy those businesses – our buying power. . . . Where there is a concerted effort to destroy a business by the boycott, we will make a concerted effort to build and conserve that business by our patronage."[133] The Associated Industries began to engage in estimates as to the superiority of the business class's organized purchasing power over labor's. One article in their newsletter, entitled "MASS BUYING AS FOIL TO BOYCOTT," concluded that the 5,000 families represented by the association could act as a "complete and satisfactory counter" to labor.[134] The association then duplicated the unions' consumer organizing tools: It circulated its own list of union and non-union firms; published an "honor roll" in its newsletter of boycotted firms; drew up pamphlets during the bakers' strike enumerating fair and unfair bread bakers; and printed cards identifying anti-union print shops.[135]

Just like the leaders of organized labor, the men who led the Associated Industries realized that women of their class controlled its "purchasing power." "The boycotts instituted cannot be combatted except by enlisting the cooperation of the homes," one pamphlet concluded.[136] The employers designed their own outreach tactics the better to reach women. When they printed lists of unfair bread firms, for example, activists in the Associated Industries requested of the association's membership: "We are anxious to have these slips reach the lady of the house who does all of the bread buying."[137] While no evidence is available as to the response of employers' wives and female family members to the anti-boycott call, one article in the Associated Industries' newsletter, the *Square Deal*, suggests gender dynamics similar to those within the AFL movement. "A great share of the family purchasing is done by women," it noted. Therefore, "The women of this city have the duty of breaking down all attempts at boycotting."[138] This reference to women's anti-boycott observance as a "duty" suggests an acknowledgment of both women's possible lack of immediate enthusiasm for the task and of men's expectation that women should subserviently promote their movement.

Final evidence of the boycott's success and the Associated Industries'
response lay in the employers' overall behavior vis-à-vis organized labor.
While the reasons given are multiple, all observers agreed that the Associated Industries backed off from its frontal assault on organized labor
beginning in the summer of 1920 and gradually let up over the next year
and a half. After May 1920 the Associated Industries initiated no new
lockouts or anti-union drives. In its internal literature the association continued to espouse the open shop. But in the fall the Industrial Relations
Committee of the Seattle Chamber of Commerce issued a report that
seemed to signal an about-face in the employers' strategies. Entitled
"Profitism, Slackism, and You," the report advocated scientific management,
employee representation plans, bonus systems, and, in general, a less confrontational approach to the problem of trade unions.[139]

The *Union Record* gave prominent coverage to the report, presenting it
as a direct repudiation by the Chamber of Commerce of the Associated
Industries, revealing, it charged, a fatal split in the ranks of organized
capital and the failure of the association's hostile stance toward unions.
James Duncan, discussing the employers' association in December, argued
that as small businesses had felt the crunch of the city's contracting economy,
"This reacted on the morale of the Associated Industries and many refused
to pay more dues."[140] Both sides in the split immediately denied the *Record*'s
interpretation, praised each other profusely, and reiterated their united
goals.[141]

While the employers' internal documents suggest real disagreements,
the split was less fundamental than it appeared. Employee involvement
measures such as company unions represented not so much an opposing
strategy to union busting as the carrot to the open shop drive's stick.
In previous years a variety of Seattle employers had already experimented
with these tactics. Both the Bon Marche and Standard Furniture Company
had instituted employee associations before the war.[142] The Seattle Taxicab
and Transit Company and the Nut House similarly experimented with
profit-sharing schemes in 1919.[143] In the fall of 1920 employers' literature
proudly celebrated successful employee representation plans at two prominent firms, the Bloedel-Donovan lumber mills and the Pacific Steamship
Company.[144]

Company unions and profit sharing, these employers hoped, would in-
oculate their firms against the reinstatement of militant trade unions. The
American Plan had served its purpose – eliminating the union shop; by late
1920 the next task was to make the open shop permanent. The fiercest
anti-union employers in the city could now agree amicably with more
liberal professionals such as those represented in the Municipal League,
who in 1919 had similarly advocated profit sharing as a vaccine against
strikes, turnover, inefficiency, and socialism.[145]

The changing national context helped make such a shift in strategy possible. Open shop drives had swept through U.S. cities in late 1919 and 1920, by the fall of 1920 pushing back the labor movement throughout the country. National-level political repression likewise accelerated. In the winter of 1919–20 the new Bureau of Investigation (later to become the FBI) launched its infamous Palmer Raids against radicals, soon replicated in hundreds of cities with local-level sweeps and anti-Red witchhunts such as that by New York state's Lusk Committee. All this took its toll on working-class militance. No mass strikes followed the monumental coal and steel strikes of late 1919. By the fall of 1920 Seattle employers could breathe far more easily than a year before. Both locally and nationally, labor had been pushed far back; business interests now had the upper hand, and they knew it.[146]

That did not translate into unrestrained power. While the Seattle AFL might be disintegrating into opposing crafts, each making its separate peace, the movement still retained powerful institutions such as the *Union Record* and the Building Trades Council, and with its boycotts it could still put the Associated Industries on the defensive. The employers, for their part, had cracks in their own solidarity as well. Different sectors of capital, such as building trades employers, could make their own separate peaces, just as labor had done. Further outright attacks on organized labor, moreover, could possibly backfire. It was, after all, only a year and a half since the general strike. Viciousness was not necessarily desirable or necessary. The result, by the end of the year, was a stalemate. Neither side was in the mood for aggressive posturing.

Conclusion

With the Bon Marche boycott the AFL unions brought consumption directly into the center of class conflict in postwar Seattle. The boycott pitched organized labor and organized employers into a new kind of battle in which the outcome would be decided not on the picket line but in the dress department. In this war over shopping both sides turned immediately to the women of their class. Women controlled the "purchasing power" of both labor and capital. But women were also workers. The "working-class movement" had been defined by men in ways that did not acknowledge the conditions of women's labors. Some women did join in serving that movement, whether actively as members of the Card and Label League or more quietly in their daily shopping habits. Others, though, looked to advance their own work lives. If wage earners, they chose protective legislation over the minimal "protection" offered by a Central Labor Council that largely ignored them. If workers in the home, they kept their distance from the movement altogether, aided, in part, by the many men who preferred that they stay at just such a distance.

The earlier failure of Seattle's AFL unions to achieve industrial unionism during 1919 took its toll on workers' solidarity at the waged workplace just as surely. While the Central Labor Council still struggled to achieve unity, craft unionism and the differential powers of each trade at the point of production set the labor movement up for still deeper fragmentation than the initial betrayals of late 1919.

Yet all was not lost by any means. The AFL movement's call to Seattle workers to shop as a class did not fall on entirely deaf ears. Despite all the reasons a union member or the members of his or her family might be alienated from organized labor's strategic agenda, thousands of white workers still chose to bring class consciousness to their shopping habits. Collectively, those choices paid off. Labor's "venomous" boycotts of 1920 indeed scared off the Associated Industries. The trade unions' continued tactical creativity, commitment to collective advancement understood in class-conscious terms, and institutionalized power set limits on the ability of the city's employers to use the unions' internal weaknesses to utterly fragment the movement. Soon, though, the depression of 1921–22 would change the character of class relations and the labor movement so thoroughly as to make that stalemate of late 1920 irrelevant.

Mayor Ole Hanson and a wartime shipyard worker shake hands.
Courtesy Pemco, Webster, Stevens Collection, Museum of History and Industry, Seattle, Washington, Photograph #83.10.7236.2.

Striking workers serving and consuming food at one of the labor-managed
dining halls during the February 1919 general strike.
Courtesy Pemco, Webster, Stevens Collection, Museum of History and Industry, Seattle,
Washington, Photograph #83.10.1736.

Workers and employers at the Japanese-American–owned Bush Hotel,
Jackson Street, 1928.
Courtesy University of Washington Libraries, Special Collections, Negative #14043.

Unionists serving meals at a labor-managed dining hall during the February
1919 general strike.
Courtesy Pemco, Webster, Stevens Collection, Museum of History and Industry, Seattle, Washington,
Photograph #83.10.1735.

(*Opposite, top*) Outside the Co-operative Food Products Association's main store.
Courtesy Pemco, Webster, Stevens Collection, Museum of History and Industry, Seattle, Washington, Photograph #83.10.1376.

(*Opposite, bottom*) Inside a branch store of the Seattle Consumers' Co-operative Association.
Courtesy Pemco, Webster, Stevens Collection, Museum of History and Industry, Seattle, Washington, Photograph #83.10.1377.

The union-owned Carpenters' Hall.
Courtesy University of Washington Libraries, Special Collections, Photograph #14042.

Float, Deep Sea Salvage Company, with union members aboard, 1920.
Courtesy Pemco, Webster, Stevens Collection, Museum of History and Industry, Seattle,
Washington, Photograph #83.10.8579.2.

The Bon Marche at night in its 1911–29 main location downtown at Second
and Pike.
Courtesy Museum of History and Industry, Seattle, Washington, Photograph #10.787.

Inside the Labor Temple.
Courtesy University of Washington Libraries, Special Collections, Photograph #28727.

A Japanese-American–owned cleaning and dye shop.
Courtesy University of Washington Libraries, Special Collections, Photograph #11548.

(*Above*) Lady barbers.
Courtesy Pemco, Webster, Stevens Collection, Museum of History and Industry, Seattle, Washington, Photograph #83.10.8533.

(*Left*) Dave Beck.
Courtesy University of Washington Libraries, Special Collections, Photograph #860.

(*Opposite*) Members of the retail clerks' union at work. Note the "union store" shop card in the center of the shoe display.
Courtesy University of Washington Libraries, Special Collections, Negative #423.

Garment workers eating in the Black Manufacturing Company cafeteria.
Courtesy Pemco, Webster, Stevens Collection, Museum of History and Industry, Photograph
#83.10.3803.2.

6

Depression

THE OPEN SHOP DRIVE OF LATE 1919 had wounded the Seattle AFL movement, but not fatally. In 1920 organized labor had proven itself still capable of concerted, effective pressure on the city's employers through boycotts. Meanwhile, labor capitalism and cooperation continued to grow during late 1919 and 1920. But in order to have trade unions at all, people had to have jobs. In order to buy shares in a cooperative, a newspaper, or a swamp, they had to have incomes. In 1920 and 1921 mass unemployment slowly ate away at that taproot of the experimental working-class movement.

Since 1917, Seattle's war-boom economy had been essential to the AFL movement's success. When the Seattle economy collapsed in 1920–21, strategies formulated within that expansionary context suddenly fell apart. The cooperatives and labor-owned enterprises tumbled down one after another, their leaders and ideals alike cursed roundly. Devastating unemployment left the union locals vulnerable to still further depredations by the city's employers. While the Associated Industries remained cautious in its demands, the labor movement was in no mood for renewing its visionary march forward. It was no longer a time for dreaming but, rather, for resignation and bitterness. Working people went home and stayed there, by and large, for the rest of the decade. It was not just that the party was over, but, far more tragically, that few thought it appropriate to plan another one.

The depression

The story began, yet again, with the shipyards. Shipyard production remained steady through the spring of 1919. But by the end of the year it had dried up altogether. The city's yards launched their last ship with symbolic tidiness on December 31, 1919. Industry analysts agreed that without the federal government's subsidized cost-plus contracts, steel freight costs were too high for west coast yards to compete with Atlantic producers. Seattle's shipyard financiers and forward-looking manufacturers were not entirely unhappy, moreover, to see the shipyards go. The yards, after all, were the hotbed of radical unionism fueling much that they preferred absent from their city's future.[1]

Tens of thousands of workers lost their jobs when the yards shut down. Of 31,500 working in the yards in late 1918, only 3,400 were still employed in June 1920, largely on repair work.[2] The layoffs swiftly devastated Seattle's metal trade unions. Machinists' Local #79, which had once counted 4,000 members, reported in January 1920 that its members were dropping out rapidly because of the layoffs. By April only a third of those members who remained had jobs.[3] During the year after the November 1918 armistice the shipyard laborers' union membership fell from 500 to 200. Its officials reported in November 1920 that "not 6 have had a day's work in the last month."[4] The largest-scale devastation was of the boilermakers' union. In late 1918 it had claimed 10,000 to 15,000 members; by March 1920, 90 percent of its members were unemployed, and by May 1921 there were only 30 employed boilermakers in the entire city.[5] For Seattle, unlike most of the United States, the postwar depression began in late 1919 and was well underway in 1920, only exacerbated by thousands of servicemen's return to the city after their release from nearby Camp Lewis.[6]

In late 1920 the rest of the nation caught up. When the federal government shrank the money supply in the summer of 1920, the war-boom inflationary spiral, extended after the war by deferred spending, collapsed. First prices and then production plummeted nationwide. By June 1921, 4 million workers were unemployed, and another several million were working only part-time. In Seattle, unemployment rates reached 10 percent and stayed there throughout 1921. Sectors of the city's economy that had been unaffected by the shipyard layoffs slid into depression in 1921 along with the country as a whole. As labor lawyer Mark Litchman observed in December 1921, "General depression has hit the town with tremendous effect, business is dull, unemployment is on the increase."[7] While month-to-month figures are not available, several contemporary estimates indicate just how severe the situation was for Seattle workers. In February 1921, the Chamber of Commerce spoke of 9,000 unemployed families in the city. In May the Central Labor Council estimated 3,000 unemployed married men, with more than 10,000 dependents. A city employment survey that same month reported 12,000 to 15,000 unemployed men in Seattle. These numbers suggest that at the very least 10 percent of the city's wage earners in 1921 lacked jobs. Each of the statistics, moreover, disguises the full effects of the depression, because the assessments omit unemployed wage-earning women.[8]

Seattle's employers were aware of the potential volatility of the situation and fearful that mass unemployment would detonate simmering class resentments. In December 1920 members of the Associated Industries' Industrial Council agreed not to lower wages and to hire as many men as possible in "small and part-time jobs," presumably to keep the unemployed from becoming restless.[9] A week later the Chamber of Commerce set up a committee "to study the question of care for homeless men."[10] As the depression waxed, Seattle's city government tried to address the question, appointing an investigating committee, establishing a wood yard to employ out-of-work men, expending a million dollars on public works, and encouraging industries to increase their total employees by staggering work hours.[11] These efforts presumed that male heads of household were the only "deserving" unemployed and also, implicitly, that unemployed men were more dangerous than women.

The employers' caution proved unnecessary. Unemployed workers' main response was to leave town. In March 1920 alone the boilermakers' secretary reported that his union had issued in the previous week 2,000 cards authorizing members' transfers out of town, with another 2,000 members awaiting clearance.[12] A representative from Shipwrights Local #1184 reported that same month that men from his local were "leaving by the hundreds."[13] The *Union Record* estimated that during the first two months of 1920, 5,000 workers left the city.[14] Rental agencies reported growing vacancies, especially in working-class neighborhoods.[15]

John Williamson provides an individual's story of this exodus in his autobiography, *Dangerous Scot*. Williamson, at the time an apprentice patternmaker, recalled that in 1920 "the process of closing down the shipyards finally reached my yard." He left Seattle for a new job in Vancouver, Washington, to which he commuted from Portland (across the Columbia River) for five or six months until that shop, too, closed. Eventually he returned to Seattle and, after he had "tramped the streets and scanned the want ads," finally found a job at a neighborhood cleaners. Williamson's story is unusual in that he came back to town, unlike the tens of thousands of other workers who returned to the midwestern and eastern cities from which they had originally migrated during the war.[16]

Seattle's AFL locals, already prostrated by the open shop drive, struggled feebly to serve their members in the face of this overwhelming situation. The bakers decided that they would neither admit new members nor accept inter-city transfers for the duration of the depression, and they restructured their workloads to guarantee each member two days' work or two days' pay every week.[17] But the larger, more devastated metal trades locals faced a Sisyphean task. The scale of the crisis was immense beyond their resources. Dozens of members wrote to the boilermakers or pleaded at their meetings, crying that there was no food in their houses or that eviction was imminent. Many unionists attempted to turn the exodus of unemployed workers into a virtue. One carpenter reflected, for example, "Conditions are getting worse right now in Seattle, and the best thing that many of us can do is get out of this town and go where organized labor has some say."[18] Harry Ault argued similarly in April 1920, "[T]he associated industries depend on the oversupply of labor, in order to successfully create [the] open shop," but if the workers left for other parts of the country where labor was scarce and wages therefore were high, the employers would be thwarted.[19] Following this same logic, Seattle's metal trades unionists hired special trains to transport their members to prearranged jobs in the East.[20]

The Central Labor Council groped toward a solution to the crisis. In January 1921, the council initiated a relief committee to aid the unemployed and held on January 23 a mass protest meeting that was attended by 3,000, an estimated 75 percent of them unemployed. The committee also opened a restaurant in mid-February that on its first day served 500. All that spring a newly formed Association of the Unemployed solicited donations and distributed food to unemployed workers. Need, though, far outstripped supply. Organizers turned to a strict gender division to try to mobilize adequate aid. In late February, the "central committee" of the Association of the Unemployed "found need among Seattle women and children to be so desperate and so widespread that it . . . decided to ask the organized women of the labor movement who are not hungry [to] take over this phase of the work of relief." Jean Stovel, speaking for the committee, noted "many single women needing care" along with eleven widows with their thirty-two children. The committee, whose gender composition is unknown, asked the Card and Label League, Women's Trade Union League, cooperative clubs, and Women's Modern Study Club to attend a special meeting to organize aid for women and children. It also asked that "all unions having women members" send representatives – presumably paid staffers, because they scheduled the meeting for 2:00 P.M.[21] While the committee's request indicates a willingness to acknowledge women's unemployment as well as men's, it also suggests a possible unwillingness on the part of men to mobilize in behalf of women. The Association's activities in any case were short-lived. In July the Central Labor Council found it to be supplying workers to employers at non-union wages, revoked its credentials, and evicted it from the Labor Temple.[22]

The city's employers did not wait long to take advantage of the possibilities for concessions from organized labor opened up by the depression. Since the fall of 1919 one of the Associated Industries' key committees had studied wages throughout the Pacific coast region, the better to assess the possibilities for wage reductions in Seattle. Metal trades employers cashed in on that research in February 1921 by slashing wages citywide to make Seattle's match those of the rest of the coast. One manager foresaw this as the bellwether of a lowering of wages throughout the Seattle economy, because it represented the "first reduction affecting a large group of workers in this district."[23] Throughout 1921 the Associated Industries continued to notify its members as to the declining cost of living so that they could more effectively demand cutbacks.[24]

Over the course of 1921 increasing numbers of Seattle's employers pressed for concessions from the city's unions. The unions only partially fought back. The plumbers and steamfitters accepted a two-year contract that cut their wages from $9 to $8 a day. John Belanger, their representative, admitted that given the present depression, he could not see fighting the cuts successfully and saw "no alternative."[25] When the Master Builders' Association demanded a 20 percent decrease in rates from the carpenters, the union acquiesced to $12^{1}/_{2}$ percent.[26] The reports of other unions indicate a similar pattern of partial resistance, partial concessions, though the forms of resistance are unclear. The electrical workers, for example, thanked the Central Labor Council for its help "in preventing bigger wage cuts for their members working for the city."[27] While these locals granted concessions, they nonetheless also won contracts.[28]

Some did go down fighting. The culinary workers fought back, hard. In the fall, Seattle's restaurant owners, in their own words "depressed and discouraged with the lowest business tide known to Seattle in a decade," announced that they would reduce wages at all union establishments beginning October 11, 1921. The culinary unions that day initiated a series of rolling strikes that struck the city's leading restaurants randomly and with no notice. On October 18 at 11:30, workers at Meve's Cafeteria, for example, one of the largest restaurants on the west coast, walked out right before lunch. The owners, though, apparently experienced few problems obtaining strikebreakers and kept their restaurants open, drawing easily on the city's 10,000 unemployed. By November 8 the unions had accepted wage cuts and changes in working conditions, and they stayed out only to retain the union shop. In February 1922, the employers claimed to still be operating with the open shop. By the June 1922 State Federation of Labor convention, though, the unions reported that "a complete victory was registered" and the locals were as strong as or stronger than ever.[29]

Many locals did not survive. Most of the twenty-seven locals that disappeared altogether during the depression fell into two categories. The first consisted of unions in the metal trades and shipyard-related trades: the shipyard laborers, foundry employees, stove mounters and fitters, ship caulkers, ship painters, and an auxiliary local of the iron, tin, and steel workers. A second group to go under comprised locals of all-female workers that had been founded in 1918 or 1919 but fell apart in 1921–22: the bookbinders, candy workers, bakery "salesgirls," hotel maids, broommakers, theater cashiers, and an AFL-chartered local of miscellaneous factory workers. Among the other failed locals were those of the cleaning and dye workers and of the tailors, the two mixed-gender locals that had fought for equal pay in 1919. Thus the depression eliminated many of the unskilled and semi-skilled female workers who had joined the movement during the boom years.[30]

The arguments union workers marshaled to defend themselves against the employers' incursions reveal further how far the Seattle labor movement fell. In 1919, workers of many political stripes had participated in discussions about the relationship between prices and wages, their attention paralleling employers' investigations into regional wage rates. In May 1919, a *Record* editorial had warned, for example, "Beware the 'Old Wage' Fraud," cautioning returning soldiers against accepting prewar wage rates. The crucial factor, it argued, was the "relative wage," a concept that embraced not only maintaining real wages (i.e., the matching of wages with prices) but also the "American standard of living" (keeping real wages high relative to those of other countries).[31] Further debates took on the question of whether wage increases only led inexorably to price increases. The cycle was endless until the system was changed, argued Ed Levi, the cook, in a letter to the editor.[32] The *Forge*, by contrast, countered that because "the raised prices are distributed over the whole community, including the non-producers," therefore "a net gain can be recorded for those workers who receive the advance."[33] In other debates workers contested the wage–price link altogether. A milk wagon driver, for example, denied that milk prices had gone up because of a wage increase gained by his union; instead, he blamed bulk purchases by the government. The spring 1920 struggles over the minimum wage for women can be seen as part of this same dialogue, depending, as they did, upon correlations drawn between women's wages and the cost of living.[34]

These arguments had been marshaled in 1919 and 1920 to justify the unions' aggressive wage demands. In 1921 workers reversed the discussion, debating the relation between wages and prices from a defensive position. When members of Boilermakers' Local #104 gathered at a special meeting in January 1921 to assess employers' demands for wage cuts, they focused on the current relationship between wages and prices only to conclude that they would not allow a wage reduction until the cost of living went down.[35] That April, the *Record* ran a long editorial arguing that while employers were demanding huge wage cuts, statistics showed that the cost of living was not dropping at a rate by any means comparable; therefore, workers should resist wage cuts.[36] Both discussions granted an important a priori concession to the employers. In contrast to the 1919 debates, which concerned how workers might get ahead in the wage–price matchup, they now granted that wage fluctuations should only match price shifts, not keep ahead of them. This concession symbolized the difficult, defensive position in which the Seattle labor movement found itself by 1921. The unions were not even trying to advance workers' position vis-à-vis the employers. They were only trying to hold their own against further slippage.[37]

That task was too large for the Seattle AFL movement to pull off alone. Throughout the country the labor movement lost ground in 1921 and 1922, as the open shop drives, postwar repression, and deepening depression left unions in an ever-weaker position. In 1922 employers' demands produced mass strikes once again. More workers struck, nationwide, in 1922 than had in 1916, though not more than had in 1919. "But the mood surrounding the two strike waves could hardly have been more different," David Montgomery notes. The 1916 strikes had been based on labor shortages, high hopes, and a mood of infectious enthusiasm. Nineteen-twenty-two, by contrast, "was a year of grimly determined defensive warfare . . . in defense of wages, hours, and union rights that employers were stamping out." Textile workers, their unions devastated, fell back to the fifty-four-hour week in Rhode Island and New Hampshire. Three hundred thousand coal miners, the largest number ever, walked out in both the anthracite and bituminous fields, eventually winning a reasonable contract but only by sacrificing tens of thousands of unorganized miners who had walked out in solidarity. In one of the most spectacular and devastating strikes of the decade, 400,000 railroad shopmen nationwide walked out in protest against wage cuts and the abolition of overtime, only to be defeated by a sweeping federal injunction. Nationally, the rate of strikes plummeted thereafter and remained low for the rest of the decade. The great uprising of organized workers spanning 1916–22 was over. And the Seattle labor movement was not an exception, but the rule.[38]

The withering away of cooperation

One of the principle casualties of Seattle's postwar depression was the cooperative movement. Many cooperatives, such as the proposed hospital, department store, and barbershop, never got off the ground. Others, such as the boilermakers' cafe, lost their patronage as early as the summer of 1919. Still others such as the plumbers', Scandia, and longshoremen's cooperatives were never mentioned in the labor press or the minutes of labor organizations after mid-1920 and can be presumed to have failed. Of the two large chains, the Seattle Consumers' Cooperative Association liquidated itself in mid-1920. The Cooperative Food Products Association (CFPA), its patronage dropping 12 percent in the first quarter of 1920 and another 35 percent by August of that year, straggled through 1921 and into 1922 and was finally sold to a chain of warehouses owned by the Grange. By August 1922, Harry Ault wrote a friend, all the city's co-operatives had "gone out of business entirely."[39]

Seattle labor's "cooperative moment" proved to be brief. Part of the reason the cooperatives failed so quickly and so completely lay in the nature of the project. Because workers had brought so many different expectations to the movement, fulfilling those expectations and sustaining further growth proved to be difficult tasks. Far more important, the entire context in which cooperatives had boomed in 1919 disappeared in 1920 and 1921. Almost as quickly as workers founded cooperatives, the economic and ideological conditions sustaining their growth vanished. The cooperatives were left an empty shell that, by 1921, no longer made strategic sense.

Many of the factors behind the cooperatives' failure were economic. A large part of the cooperatives' problem lay in their original task. As the *Co-operator* summed up the challenge of cooperation: "If you can do business cheaper and better, then go to it, and pretty soon there will not be a profiteer or exploiter in existence."[40] Olive Johnson, a theorist for the Socialist Labor Party, objected in a 1920s pamphlet criticizing the cooperative movement nationally, "The only and great problem with this kind of 'socialism' is that its very heartbeats depend on . . . successful competition in the marketplace."[41] Seattle labor, ultimately, could not beat capital at its own game.

Inadequate management and unfortunate business decisions plagued Seattle's cooperatives. The CFPA's slaughterhouse lost money every month of its operation. After accounting reviews failed to identify financial "leakages," the cooperative sold it in January 1920 at a loss of $2,000. Although both chains consistently reported revamping their accounting systems, an indication of consistent problems, a reporter for the national journal *Co-operation* noted in January 1920 that "the importance of efficient bookkeeping and accounting has not been adequately realized" among Seattle cooperators. Part of the problem was inadequate expertise. The CFPA's milk condensary in Tolt, after losing money every month of its operation, failed because of construction errors, erroneous estimations of milk supplies, and marketing problems. The CFPA sold the plant to the King County Dairymen's Association at a loss of $30,000. As this example indicates, the cooperatives' most fatal mistake may well have been overexpansion. When the condensary failed, the CFPA was left with worthless property in south Seattle that it had bought in order to expand the milk operation. That land, too, had to be sold at a loss. More drastically, the Consumers' Cooperative Association drained its retail store chain of liquid assets to launch a wholesaling cooperative, leaving both wholesale and retail operations on shaky ground and leading swiftly to the collapse of both.[42]

Seattle's postwar business depression signaled disaster for all the city's small businesses, not just for workers' cooperatives. Failure rates for such businesses were always high, even in the best of times, and the cooperatives were especially at risk. Historians have noted that workers throughout U.S. history have tended to establish cooperatives in the riskiest sectors of the economy – those in which entry costs are lowest, competition is fiercest, and in which failure rates are therefore the highest. Seattle's co-operatives fit this pattern exactly. The ease with which workers started small businesses in this sector was matched by the rapidity with which their enterprises failed. In a hostile political environment such as that of postwar Seattle, moreover, the trade-union–based cooperatives' access to lifesaving credit would have been especially restricted.[43]

Postwar unemployment began to undermine Seattle's cooperatives almost as quickly as they had been founded. Trustees of the Cooperative Food Products Association spoke as early as May 1920 of "the lack of employment, and general uncertainty that prevails in the industrial world" producing a slowdown in their membership drive. In August they again complained that organizational work was being "handicapped by the present industrial depression." By February 1921 the trustees reported that it was "next to impossible to secure new members" because of the present "period of unusual depression, many workers being idle and many more expecting to be laid off." By May they attributed a further decrease in sales to the depression.[44]

Equally injurious to the cooperatives, inflation halted in early 1920. After June, prices fell in one of the most precipitous drops in U.S. history. By June 1921, the cost of living had fallen to barely half of early-1920 levels. Seattle food prices dropped from an index level of 102.3 in June 1920 to 30.5 in December 1921. However welcome such price cuts must have been to Seattle workers, they spelled trouble for the cooperatives, because fighting inflation had been one of the fundamental imperatives behind the whole movement.[45]

In both the inflationary and deflationary periods, Seattle's cooperatives evidently failed to offer prices below those of other merchants, although they advertised themselves precisely on the basis of lower prices.[46] Gradually, cooperative promoters argued that union shoppers should place alternative political values over price considerations, in the process acknowledging that prices were, indeed, higher at the cooperatives. Delegates from the Food Products Association complained to the Central Labor Council in one such plea that unionists were buying "scab" milk at $^{1}/_{2}$ cent less than the cooperative brand, although the "scab" milk concerns paid their workers 35 cents an hour, the cooperative 65 cents.[47] Seeking a way out of their promotional bind, cooperative promoters argued that their concerns had lowered prices overall in the city by undercutting the regular firms and thus initiating price wars redounding to the benefit of all workers.[48] The CFPA meat industries had suceeded in bringing down prices by 15 to 20 percent all over the city, Carl Lunn claimed along these lines in 1919.[49] In another set of arguments cooperators heralded the superior quality of cooperative merchandise and condemned the deceptive nature of other merchants' ostensible "deals."[50] In a *Co-operator* article entitled "Our Prices are Not High" the CFPA granted that many of the members of our association have been fooled into believing that they can buy groceries and meat at lower prices in private stores than in their own institution. This condition has been due almost entirely to the fact that they are *uneducated* as to the questionable methods and trickery used by the private dealer.

Such alleged trickery included selling damaged or reconditioned goods at ultra-discounts, explaining "the *seeming* high prices of the co-op stores and the *seeming* low prices of the private dealers."[51]

More than prices could lure shoppers away from the cooperatives. The Food Products Association acknowledged in April 1920 that, even with its three branches, it was "not as convenient as the corner store."[52] It appears that the Consumers' Cooperative Chain did not give credit, while the CFPA granted credit only on a limited basis. This policy must have sharply limited the cooperatives' appeal, because working-class families in this period relied heavily on grocery-store credit.[53] A woman cooperative supporter writing to Ruth Ridgeway's *Union Record* column in August 1919 confirmed the credit concerns of Seattle working-class shoppers: "After enjoying a co-operative meeting the other evening, I determined to get at least two other members, and find out why some of their members did not trade at THEIR store. I find that most of them run grocery bills [i.e., buy on credit]."[54]

The economic effects of the depression on the cooperatives were, then, multiple. Thousands of class-conscious workers left town each month, cutting into the cooperatives' potential membership base. Those workers who remained – unemployed, underemployed, or fearing layoffs – had to scrimp and save with special care. But the cooperatives, themselves scrambling to survive in a fiercely competitive marketplace, could not offer the lower prices on which their appeal had in part always rested. At the same time, Seattle worker's precarious financial situation meant that they were unable to buy stock in the cooperatives, and this inability, in turn, cut into the cooperatives' pool of capital, crucial now in times of retrenchment. It was a fatal downward spiral.

Yet the reasons for the cooperatives' demise were not wholly economic. Perhaps the cooperatives could have survived if the families of organized labor had been sufficiently loyal to the movement as to countenance inconvenience, narrower product selection, and higher prices. The unions' counterweight to the employers' power had always been rank-and-file support. Throughout the depression the city's unions managed to come up with money to donate to handicapped children, striking miners, or the starving unemployed.[55] Part of the problem for the cooperatives was that they lost the rank-and-file enthusiasm that had been crucial to their initial success.

From the first issue of their newsletter in April 1920, leaders of the Cooperative Food Products Association complained about members' apathy. The June issue featured a long article complaining that "the growth, character and work of the societies do not receive that intelligent interest by the great body of the members that they should." The article went on to charge that members ignored public lectures about cooperation, never inquired as to the growth or decline of the cooperative's membership, and took "no active steps to augment its numbers and increase its power."[56] Reviewing the causes of the CFPA's failure a few years later, former director U. G. Moore noted that the members had become "lazy, inert, indifferent, and easily diverted."[57] Part of the problem, the leadership concluded, lay with unionists who joined the CFPA, bought shares, but rarely if ever shopped there. Combing the records in February 1921, CFPA trustees found that only 20 percent of the coop's members shopped at their own stores.[58]

The economic reasons for members' failure to patronize the cooperatives must have contributed to this pattern of avoidance and apathy. Unresolved issues of internal democracy may have also thwarted the full involvement of rank-and-file members in "their own institutions" and undercut the cooperatives' ability to expand as a grassroots movement. Over the course of 1920 and 1921, as the Cooperative Food Products Association lost its glow of success, its rank-and-file members became increasingly critical of their cooperative's leadership. CFPA leaders began to defend themselves against members who, they countered, tended to criticize the coop's management without themselves getting involved in its decision making. The *Co-operator*, in exhorting members to attend stockholders' meetings, complained that "it is unfair to those who give so much of their valuable time to the welfare of the society, to criticize their actions if we do not exert ourselves enough to be present and help them reach a decision."[59] Former trustee Moore observed that "'Satan finds mischief for idle hands' is certainly true in a co-operative and it is a hard fact that if the Board does not enlist the members in constructive work for co-operation they will soon be busily engaged in tearing the Board and the organization to pieces."[60]

The touchiness with which the *Co-operator* and the CFPA's trustees reacted to their critics suggests that the CFPA leaders ostensibly wanted rank-and-file involvement, but not if that meant disagreement with their leadership. "*Remember, Patronize first, criticize second*, then if you don't get results, ostracize us," summed up the trustees in February 1921.[61] The trustees' indifference to and rejection of the West Side women's request for a branch store further indicates the limits of their commitment to internal democracy.[62] Yet precisely such democracy was necessary if the rank-and-file members were to feel a long-term commitment to the project sufficient to sustain, let alone expand, the cooperative movement.[63]

Rank-and-file apathy was deeply embedded in the difficult position in which the Seattle working-class movement found itself by 1920. The problem lay in the premises on which "cooperative fever" had so rapidly spread. As the Associated Industries' open shop drive burned through the trade-union movement, as the shipyard shutdowns dismantled the city's employment base, food did not, in fact, "win all struggles." The consumer cooperatives had been useless against the employers' Shermanlike march through the unions. A few of the producer cooperatives had briefly sheltered locked-out tailors and printers, but most of the envisioned producer cooperatives, designed to protect organizers and offer a wedge against the complete open shop, had never materialized, tumbled down in the economic crash, or survived as minuscule exceptions to the otherwise drastic humbling of the unions. The cooperatives might have been strategically useful in a context of organizational expansion and forward movement, but in the new, defensive context they had little to offer.[64]

Still more basically, the labor movement had to stand on its feet before it could run. Activists had always envisioned cooperatives as a complement to the trade unions, as a way of advancing beyond, while serving, successful trade-union activity as it was traditionally conceived. Cooperation, in theory, would protect the second flank, that of consumption. It would help the workers move beyond supplication to employers to the construction of a worker-owned, worker-managed "cooperative commonwealth." But without healthy, stable trade unions, such dreamy advancement now became unthinkable. If Seattle's trade unions were fighting for their lives in 1920 and 1921, how could the cooperative commonwealth even be on the agenda? Cooperation became a luxury the labor movement could not afford. Its wildfire spread in 1919 had rested fundamentally on an explosive sense of the possible that by 1921 had largely disappeared.

The cooperatives' response to the unemployment crisis underscored how inappropriate were 1919 strategies to the 1921 context. In January, February, and March 1921, the Cooperative Food Products Association sponsored a series of meetings to address the unemployment situation. Forty locals sent delegates. At those gatherings CFPA activists proposed a scheme echoing the classic institution-building impulses of 1919: If 8,000 union families brought their purchasing power of $40 a month to the CFPA, that would produce a business of $320,000 per month. At a 5 percent profit rate, that patronage, in turn, would generate $16,000 a month that could support 8,000 needy families at $20 a month. The answer to unemployment, in other words, was to create a profitable business. Here again was the "profits to the workers" idea, this time reincarnated to serve depression-era needs. But in the depression, businesses were not profitable. And creation of the cooperatives' all-important profits depended, once again, on convincing workers to shop at the cooperatives, which they apparently did not want to do. Despite considerable enthusiasm, the CFPA's plan was never implemented. Most unions evidently agreed with Carpenters Local #131 that it was "impractical."[65]

In this context of both economic and spiritual decline the cooperatives' prestige plummeted. The greatest blow came in May 1920, when the Seattle Consumers' Cooperative Association (SCCA) and its affiliated North-western Cooperative Wholesale failed.[66] Its demise produced immediate skepticism about the other chain, the Cooperative Food Products Association, producing "an atmosphere of distrust with anything and everything that claims to [be] co-operative," as John Worswick, the CFPA's manager, lamented.[67] U. G. Moore, assessing the factors that led to the CFPA's downfall, agreed that the SCCA's failure damaged the cooperative movement throughout the Pacific Northwest.[68]

The SCCA's failure triggered a flurry of recriminations and personal attacks. "Everybody who has ever been connected with it has been cursed up one side and down the other," Harry Ault wrote in August 1920.[69] Carl Lunn, the former great apostle of cooperation, came in for his share of attacks, "and perhaps a little bit more," in part because he was absent from the city at the time, and his absence made him a convenient scapegoat.[70] For his part, Lunn attacked Worswick and other "experts" who, once the movement was successful, had wanted to be "Dictators."[71] The biggest demon of Seattle cooperation became E.O.F. Ames, a veteran cooperative activist whom the SCCA had imported from San Francisco to "straighten out" the chain. When the SCCA nonetheless went under, critics cast Ames as a scheming interloper who was "swindling organized labor" and had left town with the SCCA thousands of dollars short.[72] While the vehemence of these attacks suggests that Seattle workers saw the problem to be one of personalities rather than of structure, the sniping degeneration of the former prestigious leaders cast aspersions on all the remaining vestiges of the movement. Worswick, writing in September, believed it would take "some considerable time and hard work to regain the confidence that [had] been betrayed."[73]

Its membership dropping, its integrity challenged, and opportunities for expansion unlikely, in early 1921 the Cooperative Food Products Association made one last spectacularly bad business decision. The trustees chose to take out a twenty-three-year lease on a huge building in the downtown market area, in theory to make the CFPA both more convenient and grandly appealing. Launching a new store with an open-house gala in April 1921, the CFPA returned to the rank and file with a local-by-local organizing drive. But the anticipated patronage that would have made the new store a success never materialized. The cooperative lost customers when it closed down for the move, while also losing the local trade from its previous South End location. Adapting the new building cost the CFPA between $10,000 and $20,000, exhausting the chain's reserves. And the new store, it turned out, was located next to "three of the worst price cutters in town." As creditors circled for the kill, the Associated Grange Warehouse Company, a local marketing branch of the Washington State

Progressive Grange, stepped in and assumed ownership. The store's ultimate fate remains a mystery. It may have survived as a branch of the statewide grange system through part of the 1920s.[74]

With the loss of the CFPA, cooperation lost its last hold on Seattle workers. Musicians organized a spate of informal "cooperative" dances in 1922, but their local quickly banned them because they undercut the union scale. Theatrical workers reportedly organized a cooperative that same year, but the company never materialized. Sporadic, small efforts to "eliminate the middleman" through direct marketing with local farmers cropped up occasionally in the Central Labor Council's minutes, and educational programs within the local AFL included cooperation among their topics of discussion a few times. But in 1920s Seattle, cooperation was in great part dead.

Caught between the pitfalls of the marketplace and a rapidly contracting labor movement, the cooperative movement in Seattle never lived to usher in a new workers' world or even to enrich the workers in the present one. Its success ultimately depended on what can be called a "logic of cooperative expansion." Both the political appeal of cooperatives as a vehicle for social change and their promise of profits for working-class members depended upon institutional expansion. Without such growth, and, equally important, without a widespread faith in its imminent arrival, the movement lost much of its appeal. The cooperatives' failure, in the rapidly changing political context of 1920–21, both contributed to and symbolized the loss of the Seattle labor movement's impulse toward fundamental social change. The cooperatives had represented vision – the will to experiment. Rejecting cooperation, the Seattle labor movement crossed that tactic off its collective list of strategic avenues to working-class power.

The labor capitalism debacle

Labor capitalism fared no better. The same economic pressures that brought down the cooperatives spelled doom for the "workers' businesses" as well. Labor capitalism's intermixture of celebrating capitalism and taking advantage of it for often radical ends had been possible only because Seattle's white working class had been relatively prosperous, and because its affluence had allowed for a harmonious outpouring of many schemes and projects. If those projects conflicted one with another, few objected, so long as the workers' movement still had money and the urge to experiment. But the deepening depression, again, undermined all that.

Labor capitalism was more directly and deeply embedded in the city's trade unions themselves than were the cooperatives, so when it went down, it carried with it many of the institutions, political agendas, and leaders that had held together the citywide AFL movement. Still more tragically, that debacle alienated thousands of rank-and-file workers from the entire movement.

The depression wiped out the locals' finances as surely as it did those of individuals. In January 1921 the Scandinavian-American Bank of Tacoma, in which many of the city's unions had deposited their money, failed. Eventually the bank paid 67 percent of its claims, but smaller depositors got the short end of the settlement stick, unionists claimed. Losses from the bank failure placed many of Seattle's locals in precarious financial straits. Others, whose money had been deposited elsewhere, nonetheless suffered from a declining pool of dues money as membership levels dropped, unemployed members failed to pay, and reserves were scraped to help needy members.[75]

The ever-increasing financial difficulties of both individual workers and their unions at the very least meant that few were interested in investing new monies in labor enterprises. "The workers are hard pressed for cash, so the chances of selling *Record* stock do not look good," Mark Litchman, the labor lawyer, told a friend.[76] Not only was expansion cut off, but as unions and their members met with hard times they began to fall back on their financial reserves, to the money they had invested in 1919–20 for just such perennial "hard times." Reporting on the unemployment situation in September 1920, the *Record* noted working-class families "living by selling from time to time the few Liberty bonds they accumulated while work was plentiful in the shipyards. . . . [T]he carefully hoarded bonds finally disappear at $10 to $15 below the prices originally paid."[77]

The immediate cash value of postwar investments became a pressing issue for the city's rank-and-file workers. O. B. Clausen wrote to the *Record*:

> Last week several young men called at the YMCA asking me to take them to a bank or to any trust company where they could sell or borrow some money on bonds which they had bought from different companies. As you know it is pretty difficult to get work nowadays even for skilled laborers, and some are in urgent need of money.

He soon discovered that "some of these bonds were not only of doubtful character, but some were altogether valueless."[78] Investors who similarly sought to sell their stock in labor enterprises soon discovered, to their shock, that much of it, too, was valueless. A Mr. Guise, the elderly father of a union member, had invested all his $500 savings in United Finance Company stock in early 1920. When, a year later, he sought to withdraw his money, the company's president, Jack Mundy, told him, "[T]he stock hasn't any market value as yet." "I believed that the stock was an investment and not a speculation," Mr. Guise lamented.[79] His experience was replicated all over the city. "The great rank and file was suffering from unemployment and disillusionment," Earl Shimmons recalled of early 1921.

"When they had tried to raise money . . . by selling some Listman Service or Deep Sea Salvage Stock, they found there was something the matter with it. . . . [I]t would not sell."[80] That discovery of the false pretenses of labor capitalism combined in late 1920 with the failure of the Deep Sea Salvage Company to cast the whole labor capitalist program into profound doubt.[81]

Labor capitalism had always had its critics. The most formal attacks had been leveled at the Seattle Union Theatre. In July 1919 the Central Labor Council turned down its request for endorsement, replying that the enterprise was "strictly an individual undertaking."[82] The longshoremen's union simultaneously condemned the firm, charging it was "organized for personal profits and with the intention of exploiting labor" and that the Union Theatre's promoters "misrepresented themselves when they claimed they had the support of organized labor."[83] The most explicit early theoretical attacks on labor capitalism came from the industrial unionist *Forge*. A June 1919 article deplored "*The Get Into Business Element*" who were "going to lead us out of bondage by embarking in business." It charged that "[T]hese ignorant men are so many barnacles on the labor movement." Not only would workers never have enough money to beat the capitalists at their own game, but an economic collapse was impending; and, in any case, what would become of workers who lacked the money to invest in such schemes? "These schemes," it concluded, "furnish a lot of ex-business agents . . . with a chance to make a living from the working class and still wear white collars."[84]

Such "rumblings of discontent," in the words of one observer, "crystallized" in March 1921 when a seemingly routine committee, charged by the Central Labor Council in the wake of the theater company criticisms with investigating all the city's labor-affiliated enterprises, returned with its report.[85] The report scathingly attacked Seattle's labor capitalist enterprises, especially the personal involvement of the movement's leaders in them. Rallying around the report's findings, the left wing of the city's AFL consolidated its forces and used the issue to raise questions about the overall direction and goals of the Seattle AFL movement. A newly formed "Committee of One Hundred" spearheaded the drive, leafleting rank-and-file union members throughout the state, taking their concerns to meetings of the locals, and leading the charge through the Central Labor Council.[86]

The critics leveled four accusations. First, many of the so-called labor enterprises had not been the workers' vanguard at all but, rather, ordinary capitalist businesses, designed to enrich their promoters. The Trades Union Savings and Loan, for example, was "a savings enterprise precisely like all others." Harry Ault, they charged, had shared in $65,000 profits from the Padilla Bay Development Association, reaped dividends from the Class A Theater, and now luxuriated in "The House That Profit Built," in the pricey neighborhood of Capitol Hill. "Out of the coinage of Labor's hopes [they] are lining their nests with the easy comfort of new-found wealth."[87]

Second, they charged, the labor capitalists were employers and therefore had no business leading the labor movement. J. C. Mundy, they pointed out, was president of the United Finance Company, which employed members of the same union of which he was president (the office employees), and he signed contracts between the two. Ault controlled dozens of jobs at the *Record*. "No one can serve both labor and mammon, and since these men have signified a greater interest in mammon, they should step out of labor and serve mammon."[88]

Third, the critics made visible the complex web of interlocking directorates through which the same handful of men controlled almost all the city's labor enterprises. They produced a chart entitled "CHARACTERS: Showing intertwining and interlocking control of the Union Record and Organized Labor with Capitalist Corporations and Companies for private gain." George Listman, for example, simultaneously served as president of the Union Record Publishing Company, the Listman Service Company, and the Trades Union Savings and Loan and was "principal owner of Controlling Stock" in the United Finance Company.[89]

Finally, the labor capitalists had allegedly used their prestige in the trade unions to beguile unwitting workers into investing in their enterprises. "Labor reputations are peddled in wild-cat stock schemes."[90] This was particularly heinous because the very strength and authority of the post-war Seattle labor movement, they charged, had been compromised in the process. "Names that we have honored so long that they are things of the household are appearing at the head of beautifully printed prospecti."[91] When the leaders and their scams became undistinguishable, "'Whom Can We Trust?' is becoming a common expression."[92]

From the critics' point of view the worst betrayal was of the *Union Record* itself. Through Ault's involvement in stock schemes, shoddy advertisements for labor capitalist enterprises, and shady financial dealings, the labor capitalists had corrupted the paper, twisted it to their own purposes, and nearly destroyed its usefulness. For the critics one particular scandal illustrated this corruption exactly. In a series of front-page stories written by Anna Louise Strong in October 1920, the *Record* had ostensibly presented to readers a remarkable opportunity to "eliminate the middleman," to "unite the producer and consumer" by snatching up a special batch of salmon available for sale at the paper's office. It turned out that the salmon company had been about to default on a loan from the United Finance Company. Salmon prices had recently fallen, and the firm had been unable to sell its fish. The United Finance Company then thought up the "bunk of getting the producer and consumer together. Thanks to free advertisements in the *Record* and the readership's naive faith in the *Record*'s political exhortations, the United Finance Company got almost all its loan paid back."[93] The critics presented themselves as the *Record*'s redeemers. They named their bulletin *Save the Record*, with the slogan "Really 'Published for Principle and Not for Profit.'" Inside, the editors warned:

"Workers: The Union Record may be lost to you. There is a chance for its recovery. That chance lies in as early as possible driving out the money-changers who have befouled it."[94]

The critics represented a coalition of three camps. At their core was a group of former Socialist Party left-wing activists that included David Levine of the jewelry workers, Jean Stovel and William McNally of the office employees, William Kennedy of the janitors, Phil Pearl of the barbers, and Frank Clifford of the shipyard laborers. These activists had long advocated industrial unionism, political action, and fealty to the AFL. They were joined by the handful who had joined the nascent Communist Party in Seattle. At this point the Communists had little organizational presence, existing mainly as a discussion group in political theory. A third group was composed of disgruntled former and present *Record* employees, critical of both the paper's managerial inadequacies and its recent drift rightward politically. The critics' spring offensive was at root a political contestation of the nature of the Seattle labor movement, understood by all camps as more than just a fight over a few businesses.[95]

Even after they had mounted their attack in March 1921, the critics distinguished between "union card workers conducting private enterprises, exploiting labor" and "real co-operative enterprises." They would still support "true" labor enterprises that served a militant, radical labor movement. That was why the *Union Record* mattered so much.[96] As the radical millmen's local proclaimed, "It must be obvious to the most superficial observer that a strong, vigorous, fearless, truthful and incorruptive daily newspaper would be a tower of strength, a flaming sword in our battle for the legitimate rights and ideals of Labor."[97]

At first, this coalition of the left achieved success on the Central Labor Council floor. On March 24, it passed a resolution 100 to 94 asserting

> [t]hat when one of our fellow unionists engages actively in private business, employing labor for profit, or allows the use of his name for promotion purposes, or receives the major portion of his income from profit, interest, rent or commissions derived from the labor of others, he shall be barred from all Executive Offices or Boards of Control within the Control of the Council.[98]

Then the sparks flew. Ault fired a critic from the *Record*'s staff, the labor council reinstated him, and Ault physically assaulted another critic on the council floor. For the next two months the council's meetings degenerated into a morass of personal recriminations, political machinations, and vicious attacks. One socialist who participated in the whole debacle sighed months later, "There may be beauty in every soul who attends central labor council meetings, but why in hell has it not manifested [itself?]."[99]

Those on defense bided their time before mounting a counterattack. They, too, came from three camps. First were the key labor capitalists themselves, Ault, Listman, Mundy, and Frank Rust, plus those sufficiently entrenched in the enterprises to know that their names would come up next. Second were the diehard conservatives who would oppose anything the left advocated and who expressed few criticisms of capitalism in most of its forms, especially the lucrative kind. These included delegates from the building, teaming, and culinary trades. A third group included delegates who had consistently supported radical stands in the past but who, in this case, would not support the investigating committee. These included Frank Turco of the blacksmiths, who leaned toward the IWW and was always of an independent mind; James Duncan, ever the swing vote in the middle, building coalitions and smoothing over conflicts; and Harvey O'Connor, evidently personally loyal to Ault and wanting to keep his job at the *Record* – eventually he swung over to the critics' side. Anna Louise Strong, who had always identified herself with the left, got implicated over the fish story. She claims in her autobiography that she left Seattle in the spring of 1921 out of disillusionment, but it was also because she got caught with her hands dirty. Rather than take sides, she ran.[100]

On the whole, the labor capitalist entrepreneurs denied the charges, though they did capitulate on the traffic-in-reputations issue, promising to keep their names off promotional literature in the future.[101] But their defense was based more on practical political intrigue than on explanations of their activities. They went into the local unions and persuaded the members to change their Central Labor Council delegations to those favoring the labor capitalists. The office employees' union, for example, recalled leftist delegates Joseph Havel and William McNally. As a result, the council's fights began to focus as much on the seating of delegates as on the actual charges. Conservative locals that had previously been lax in sending representatives began to send full delegations, swelling the defendants' voting power. The critics attempted to counter these tactics. When Machinists' Local #79 recalled Duncan as its delegate, he reported the next week from Local #289, the auto mechanics; and when the blacksmiths recalled Frank Turco, he too, reappeared, from the mine workers.[102]

But over the course of April and May the labor capitalists' strategy began to pay off. Despite the initial passage of the investigating committee's resolution banning from council offices those who made money off labor enterprises, the left could not enforce it. A new resolution calling for Ault and Mundy's resignation failed. Ultimately council president Mundy went so far as to declare the initial resolution unconstitutional. AFL President Samuel Gompers, even, stepped in to reinstate Mundy, whose eligibility as a delegate from the office employees' union had been challenged.[103] The fight was over.

By the fall of 1921 the winners and losers in this seedy fray began to sort themselves out. On the one hand the critics had won their point. The affair between labor capitalism and the labor movement had been largely discredited and formally condemned by a majority vote in the council. The city's radicals "rose in this issue to the zenith of their power" in the Seattle AFL, Paul Mohr, a veteran from the bakers' union and a Communist, told an interviewer in 1926.[104] On the other hand, those attacked as labor capitalists had subsequently gained a majority in the council and initially remained as firmly entrenched as ever in their positions of power. "Only a moral victory was gained," dissident delegates soon concluded.[105] Overall, then, the critics lost.

From a more subtle perspective the rank and file lost, too. The fight over labor capitalism had been largely between upper-level activists. But the whole edifice of labor capitalism had been built on the dollars and faith of the rank and file, and it was their votes within the locals that controlled the councils' delegates. Over the course of the spring and summer of 1921 letters and resolutions from the city's locals poured into the council alternately condemning or supporting the investigating committee's report. When, in further retaliation against the critics' attacks, Ault launched a major stock subscription drive in the summer and fall of 1921, the locals' replies to his pleas proved a litmus test of the rank and file's response to the labor capitalism fight. The iron and steel workers' reply spoke for many: They could "be depended upon to support the Union Record whenever the paper is properly operated in the interests of labor," which it was not.[106] Letters from the sheet-metal workers, bakery salesmen, and shipwrights reiterated that they would not approve an assessment for the membership to support the *Record* "under present management." As the machinists put it, "Hope Lodge [Local 79] has in the past supported the Union Record as a liberal Press and will again support the Record when it again becomes a liberal Press."[107]

This rank-and-file defection from the *Record* stemmed first from disillusionment with the *Record*'s links with labor capitalism. As one supporter wrote Ault in 1928 upon learning of the paper's demise that year,

> I cannot help but feel that its not altogether lack of capital that was the primary cause of its downfall, altho probably the main cause. Your own connection with, and the boosting of the Listman Service created a suspicion in the minds of hundreds down here that you were not wholly desirous in keeping the masses from being exploited if perchance you were interest yourselve in the spoils.[108]

Ault's involvement in other schemes had further contributed to a "spirit of distrust." When individual workers lost their savings, the loss fed their suspicions of and anger against Ault and his cohort. "Lots got stung," observed Bruce Rodgers, a socialist and former *Record* staffer. "They naturally blamed the Record for wiping out their lifetime savings."[109] One reader wrote to Ault: "I think your roping in Suckers for Dawson Salvage Co Sparks & Dye and United Finance has had a bad influence among your supporters. I am one of the victims."[110] Another, Mrs. A. W. Blumenroth, first wrote to Ault to inquire why her Federation Film Company stocks were worth only half as much as she had thought. She wrote again in 1922 that she had learned from her lawyer that her Seattle Union Theatre Company stock was worthless, and the firm bankrupt. "I consider you are to blame for me loosing [*sic*] the money. I would not have minded it so awful. Only as I told you I need the money so bad. I hope the day will come when you will need money as much as I do tonight, and you won't be able to get it."[111]

Many locals did remain loyal to the *Record*, if only temporarily. Several conservative locals used the stock drive to assert their support for Ault. The culinary crafts stayed the course, grateful for the help the paper had given their 1921 strike. But as the depression deepened, even those who believed in Ault often lacked funds to support him. The laundry workers, for example, explained that, much as they wanted to, they had no funds to give the paper.[112] The railway clerks apologized, "While our organization is small and our salaries have recently been reduced to a point barely sufficient to sustain life . . . we are glad to help out in this emergency in our small way."[113] The effects of this evaporation of support for the *Record* would soon become clear.

If the left lost, and the rank and file pulled away, neither did the labor capitalists win. During 1921 and 1922, as the economy continued to decline, their enterprises continued to fail. "The depression of 1921 removed the issue of labor capitalism as a cause of dissension by removing, through insolvency, labor's capitalistic enterprises," Harvey O'Connor recalled.[114] Down the proverbial tubes went the Listman Service Company, United Finance Company, Padilla Bay Development Company, Class A Theatre, and Seattle Union Theatre Company, to lurk at the bottom of the sea along with the Deep Sea Salvage from the year before. The only survivors were those projects most directly tied into the locals. The Mutual Laundry met with hard times but pulled through, surviving until 1932. The Trades Union Savings and Loan Association lapsed into "unsound" condition in mid-1920, couldn't pay its expenses in 1922, but lived to complete the decade. Of the survivors the Labor Temple had the roughest time. In a complicated internecine fight the cleaners and dyers' union sued the Labor Temple Association in the fall of 1921 for failing to protect their monies against a false-check signer. The Temple's finances began to falter; several unions lost their funds; even very conservative locals began to balk at the resulting higher rents.[115]

As their projects fell into disrepute, the labor capitalist leaders began, as one observer put it, to follow the left "off the stage."[116] "The Labor Caps [capitalists] have lost out," another wrote, but not because they were being pushed out. "It is not necessary," for as their enterprises collapsed, "Rust, Listman and the others are being more and more repudiated by their own Unions."[117] Listman and Rust soon lost their seats on the *Record*'s board.

Rust, blamed for the Labor Temple's troubles, was repeatedly denounced at the labor council and retreated to the Savings and Loan for the rest of the decade. By 1924 Jack Mundy was unemployed, had lost his home, and had his car repossessed by the Inland Finance Company, a Listman Service Company affiliate.

The ultimate winners came from neither camp. They were the staid, conservative, anti-experimental, loyalist business unionists who had shifted their sights to the left a bit in the postwar uproar, but who, lacking much of a radical commitment of their own, shifted back to complacency in the face of the postwar barrage of defeats and disappointments. Melvin DeShazo, who interviewed several men prominent in the Seattle movement in the mid-1920s, concluded that the "disclosures that resulted from the investigation of 'union' enterprises and the experience of the Council with the *Union Record* added to a dissatisfaction with activities beyond the scope of trade union bargaining and confirmed in the eyes of labor the conservative, opportunistic policy of the A.F.L."[118]

Contemporary observers agreed that late 1921 and 1922 was a time of disillusion and disaffection within the Seattle AFL movement, not just with labor capitalism. The two had become so intertwined that once labor capitalism had been discredited, little was left to inspire and lead. "The demoralization is complete," observed Bruce Rodgers late in 1921. "Faith is destroyed. What was the splendid Seattle labor movement is gone."[119] Describing the *Record*'s fourth-birthday party in 1922, Earl Shimmons concluded dispiritedly, "There was not much new to be seen. The rank and file was apathetic, and suffering from spiritual letdown."[120]

Even the Central Labor Council itself spoke for a smaller portion of the city's labor movement. After its right wing in September 1921 voted permanent "executive session" – banning all nondelegates except those admitted by a two-thirds vote, guests not to exceed 10 percent of the delegates – a succession of locals in protest withdrew their affiliation with the council. Jurisdictional fights led to the expulsion of more locals. "The Central Labor Council meetings that used to have such fine speeches from workers all over the world have turned into nasty wrangles between carpenters and plumbers for control of little jobs," Anna Louise Strong recalled.[121] Nineteen-twenty-two brought still more withdrawals, most prominently those of Machinists' Local #79 and Teamsters' Local #174, evidently for political reasons. By the end of the year attendance of even the delegates who remained had declined to such an extent as to become an issue for debate.[122]

With fewer locals affiliated, and an overall decline in union membership cutting into per capita tax funds, the council's finances collapsed. The leadership's response was to lay off Sophie Pugsley, the organizer for women. In part, it was an act of retrenchment. Those advocating her dismissal pleaded a lack of funds. But Pugsley had sided with the left in the labor capitalism fight and been repudiated as a result by her own union, the musicians. While some locals protested her layoff, arguing that other council staff positions could be consolidated to retain her, or a special per capita tax raised, it was to no avail. Wage-earning women were therefore caught in the crossfire. Without their special organizer, their presence in the labor movement would be still more precarious.[123]

Little militancy evinced itself in late 1921 and 1922. The Seattle AFL movement engaged in fewer strikes than in any other year since the United States had entered the war. The only issues that galvanized the locals at all were relief work for a long-drawn-out Washington state coal miners' strike in the winter of 1921–22, and for the equally disastrous railroad shop workers' strike the next summer. Otherwise, little happened. The council's minutes show the delegates going home early, hanging on to a precarious organizational toehold in their trades, and repeatedly thanking one another cordially for aid in narrowly defined minor defensive battles with their employers.[124]

Conclusion

The postwar depression proved as fatal as the open shop drive. Unemployment rippled unrelentingly through the Seattle working class, wiping out the financial security of individuals, families, and their organizations alike. As the tide of white working-class prosperity receded in 1920, 1921, and 1922, the institutional structures of cooperation and labor capitalism were left empty. They were no longer appropriate in the new economic and ideological context.

Perhaps most striking was how fast it all happened. One moment white workers set their sights as high as they would at any point in the whole century, daring to dream of an independent workers' state achieved maybe through secession, maybe through profit, maybe through seizure of the state. The next moment it was over. The sense of the possible, so high in 1919, plummeted. In part because they had achieved so much in 1919, Seattle workers had further to fall in the years that followed. The depression of 1921–22 was not, after all, an unprecedented experience for organized labor. Cyclical depressions had been the bane of the labor movement since its inception. Chastened by the 1920 boycott wars, Seattle's employers did not use the occasion to go after the labor movement's jugular as much as they might have. The problem for Seattle's AFL movement was deeper than that. Experiments had been tried, and they had failed. So many tactics had been creatively mustered to gain so little. The disillusionment was not so much with any particular approach such as cooperation, but with experimentation altogether.

Nineteen-twenty-two was fundamentally different from 1915, when the whole cycle had begun. Before the war, socialism had been very much on the labor movement's agenda. The unions had seethed with untried plans, secret dreams, an itchy impatience for a try at something greater than just demands on individual employers. By the end of the depression, that vision was more or less dead. J.B.S. Hardman, reflecting in 1928 upon the aspirations of the war years nationwide, captured with chilling echoes of our own time the fundamental difference between 1919 and the postdepression 1920s:

> We seem to be generations away from the age of missions and large enterprise.... The winged hopes of those days, the first blushes of an incipient radicalism, have long been duly deflated and their dried shells tucked away in the filing-cabinets of the unmade makers of the revolution which failed to come.[125]

In Seattle, many still held the torch. But their days at the center of the movement were numbered.

7

Accommodations

ON APRIL 10, 1923, the Executive Council of the American Federation of Labor demanded that the Seattle Central Labor Council either toe the AFL line once and for all, or it would revoke the council's charter – in effect eliminating it, because the international unions to which its constituent locals belonged would not permit them to participate in an unsanctioned body. AFL President Samuel Gompers and the Executive Council were fed up with the Seattle council's progressive stands, egged on in their hostility by Washington State Federation of Labor President William Short, who sought to eliminate his own opposition in the state. In its 1923 ultimatum the AFL Executive Council accused Seattle of treating communications from it with "indifference and contempt," openly defying the state federation of labor, "needlessly arousing and antagonizing" the citizens of Seattle, turning the council into an arm of Soviet Russia, and, worst of all, taking an independent political stand in support of the Washington Farmer–Labor Party. Moreover, it charged, the Seattle council insisted on chartering and recognizing locals of shipyard laborers, blacksmiths, and lady barbers against the explicit wishes of their respective internationals. Enough was enough, the AFL leadership pronounced.[1]

The AFL's ultimatum, well after the economic depredations of 1921, revealed that progressive activism was by no means dead in 1923 Seattle. If it had been, the Executive Council would not have had to protest so much. The Seattle AFL movement still had enough fight in it to be a thorn in the side of the more conservative AFL national officers. Nonetheless, the Executive Council's charges and the Central Labor Council's self-defense highlighted the tensions within the immediate postdepression Seattle AFL. The Seattle unions' answer would signal what was left of the movement after the depression-era smoke had cleared. In 1922, 1923, and 1924 a round of debates took place in which the nature of the Seattle AFL movement was contested for the last time that decade. The 1919–20 movement had perished, but the self-definition and program of the labor movement that would emerge in its place were still up in the air.

At the core of the transition that emerged from those debates was a series of accommodations to the dramatically different economic context in which organized labor now found itself. The period 1922–23 was marked above all by adjustment – to the city's economic development, to new occupational configurations of race and gender in the labor force, and to the national evolution of the AFL movement. No longer would the Seattle AFL be out of step with Gompers or, indeed, with capitalist development. Those who still envisioned a more oppositional movement passed from the stage, less likely to walk off than to be shoved.

Power shift

A fundamental shift underlay the transformation of the Seattle AFL movement in the 1920s. It is best understood by dividing the city's AFL into two broad sectors that correspond to two broad spheres of the economy. The fate of each in postwar Seattle proved dramatically different.

In a first large sector lay the metalworking industry trades and the waterfront. Here the unions' plight changed from bad to worse. Seattle's metal trades industry and its corresponding union locals of machinists, boilermakers, ironworkers, and blacksmiths never recovered from their immediate postwar devastation. In June 1921 officials from the three largest locals described metal trades employment as "so negligible as to be almost inconsequential."[2] Five years later, in 1926, Reinhold Loewe reported for the machinists, "The entire metal trades industry since the war days has taken a tremendous slump, from which it has not recovered as far as this vicinity is concerned." The only exception was automobile repair work.[3]

The longshoremen's union in Seattle met with an equally ruinous fate, though by a more contested path. Like the metal trades unions, Local #38–12 of the International Longshoremen's Association (ILA) had depended for its success on the special circumstances of wartime. Strengthened by labor shortages and federal pressure to ensure uninterrupted shipping, the union struck in 1917 and again in April 1919 to force Seattle's waterfront employers to hire exclusively from the union hall rather than through the infamous "shape-up" – at which employers chose workers on a daily basis – or through employer-controlled halls. In August 1919 the union won a wage increase and a contract specifying hiring preference for union members through an ILA-controlled list.[4]

But when the favorable wartime context evaporated, the union met its maker in the form of a united front of waterfront employers. In 1919, when labor shortage turned to glut, the longshoremen were highly vulnerable to Seattle's newly resolute Waterfront Employers' Association, which, in turn, felt emboldened by the Associated Industries. In December 1919 employers announced that they were abrogating the August agreement. In January 1920 they declared that henceforth they would operate Seattle's docks under the open shop, ignoring the ILA's list system and hiring workers on an entirely casual basis or through their own hall.[5]

The members of ILA Local #38–12 did not want to be goaded into a losing strike in response. On May 6, 1920, believing they had no choice, they finally called a strike to reinstate the list system. But the president of their international, T. V. O'Connor, refused to sanction the strike and instead revoked Local #38–12's charter. Without the international's support the strike was hopeless. Several factions within the local refused to walk out, and by May 14 the leaders of #38–12 conceded defeat.[6]

Waterfront employers assumed that the cycle of alternating defeats and victories by the longshoremen's union would continue. The Waterfront Employers' Association was well aware that the union would soon regroup. "Under the open shop condition we have been living more or less on a volcano . . . and if we can judge anything by past history, we should be prepared to face that same situation again," its November 1920 minutes admitted.[7] To break the cycle it turned to a new labor-relations scheme known as the Foisie Plan (named after its author, University of Washington professor Frank P. Foisie), which its members unilaterally imposed on Seattle's docks in March 1921.[8]

The Foisie Plan represented the first large-scale imposition of company unionism in postwar Seattle. Where other firms had merely investigated the possibility or experimented timidly, the waterfront employers' scheme included both a full system of employee representation committees and a restructuring of the hiring process itself. Employers allowed only workers from a drastically reduced list of approved longshoremen to work on the docks. To those, they guaranteed steady employment and respectable wages. All others were banned from the docks. For Seattle's waterfront employers the plan proved to be a dream come true. The ILA, once one of the largest and most explosively radical unions in the city, almost vanished. It regrouped in the mid- and late twenties to cause a bit of trouble through occasional job actions. But the employers by and large had their way.[9]

This counterrevolution on the docks had mixed consequences for the 300 African-American longshoremen who had been admitted to the ILA in 1918. In 1919, as postwar unemployment on the docks grew, African-American workers' situation became increasingly precarious. The overall decline of dockside employment cut into their total numbers and reduced the amount of work available for those who remained. As competition for scarce work increased between all longshoremen, white union officials began increasingly to discriminate against African-Americans in dispatching workers, often on the pretext of union seniority. Horace Cayton Jr. recalled:

> When work was slack, colored longshoremen were frozen out. Soon I lost my job and was then more convinced than ever that I'd been right:

however desirable a mixed union was, you just couldn't trust any white man.[10]

African-American workers' decreasing ability to obtain work in turn cut into their ability to pay dues, leading to lapsed memberships. By the end of 1920 fewer than one hundred African-American longshoremen remained on the Seattle waterfront.[11]

The Foisie Plan reduced their numbers still further. The employers did place African-American workers on employee committees, including the top-level Executive Committee, and African-American longshoremen apparently shared in the economic security the plan brought many of those who were still employed. By the end of the decade 40 percent of African-American longshoremen owned their homes. But the Foisie Plan's drastic reduction of the total number of approved dock workers shrank the actual number of African-American workers to a mere forty. Whatever the intentions of upper-level management, moreover, individual dispatchers continued to discriminate against African-American workers. Employers placed African-American and white workers in separate gangs and then played the two groups off against each other to speed up the work pace. They sent African-American gangs to perform the most dangerous tasks where they could be blamed for damaged goods or accidents. Many white workers refused to work alongside African-American workers, and if enough stood firm they could send African-American longshoremen back to the hall. In the long run the postwar transition diminished the position of African-American longshoremen almost as thoroughly as that of the ILA.[12]

On the waterfront and in the metal trades, then, the first half of the decade brought both a dramatic reduction in total employment and a still more dramatic reduction in union membership – from a combined total of 35,000 to 40,000 metal trades and dock workers in 1919 to fewer than a thousand skilled metal trades unionists in 1924. The unions' fate could not have been starker.[13]

Unions in a second large sector of the Seattle economy, on the other hand, drew a different lot. In this sector we can place workers in the building trades, local transportation, printing, and service work, including the musicians and theater workers, those in the culinary trades, and those in other skilled service trades, such as the barbers and the butchers. In a context in which persistence meant victory, unions in this sector survived the postwar transformation intact, if in a weakened condition. The building trades regrouped as early as 1920, and as work picked up in 1923 and 1924 the locals built steadily in the mid-decade years toward consolidated job control and wage gains, if modest ones. The teamsters grew by leaps and bounds, never wounded by the depression. The printers, musicians, and service workers all fought hard battles in the 1919–22 period, but by the mid-1920s their total memberships were larger than their prewar numbers.[14]

Unions in the two different sectors can be distinguished not only by their divergent economic and organizational fates but by their political orientations as well. In the first sector, the metal trades' and longshoremen's unions had housed the city's mass base of radicals since the war's start. From the machinists, boilermakers, and blacksmiths issued the pro-OBU agitation for the reconstitution of the American Federation of Labor. Delegates from the Metal Trades Council almost always initiated the radical measures raised for debate in the 1918 and 1919 Central Labor Council.[15] Delegates from both the docks and the metal trades consistently sided with the council's left wing in key Central Labor Council votes.[16]

The second sector, by contrast, produced the city's business unionist conservatives. The first sector was not without its officialdom, and many of the most radical activists in the city hailed from unions – such as those of the barbers, painters, bakers, and millmen – in the second sector.[17] But the diehard conservatives represented locals in the second sector, and it was here where the votes could be counted to oppose the left. First and foremost were the building trades. Despite the solid presence of many socialists and progressives in the city's three locals of the carpenters, William Short could write Gompers's secretary R. Lee Guard in July 1919 that "[T]he one solid rock in the whole labor movement of our State against which all appeals of the O.B.U. always break is the Carpenters. . . . [T]he least danger in the whole situation will come from their Organizations."[18] Such a possibility became even more remote when the Building Trades Council swept all radicals from its offices in a reaction against the losing strikes that fall.[19] Nor did Short have reason to fear radicalism in the ranks of the teamsters. Along with the streetcar employees, their delegates always voted with the council's right wing, as did the printers and musicians, the remaining large unions in this sector. The culinary unions similarly fell in line behind the building trades. Alice Lord, the waitresses' business agent, approvingly described her local as "conservative" in a 1919 *Union Record* interview.[20] E. Teasdale, a radical in the cooks' union, described his local as "the most reactionary union in town." ("I am really ashamed to belong to it but I have to," he moaned.)[21] A few scattered service unions elected prominent radicals as their labor council delegates, but, those same delegates observed, the unions could not be described as radical themselves. Phil Pearl, the Socialist barber, for example, described members of his union as "naturally from their mode of operation of a bourgeois mind."[22] Paul Mohr, a veteran Seattle labor activist and Communist by the early twenties, spoke of his own local, that of the bakers, as "rather conservative."[23]

When combined with the unions' divergent economic fates, these political differences produced a profound transformation of the Seattle AFL in the postwar years. As Harvey O'Connor recalled, "The closing of the shipyards and the subsequent decline in membership of the metal trades caused a shift in the Central Labor Council. The older building, teaming and service trades resumed their previous importance while the militant radical delegates found their ranks dwindling."[24] A local Wobbly lamented in May 1920, "With the dying of the industrial business here in Seattle, the activities of the labor movement died. The active workers went to places where active industry prevails, and Seattle is once more left in the hands of the real reactionary movement."[25] This shift in power took place gradually over the course of 1919, 1920, and 1921 and was not complete until 1925. Certainly it never went uncontested. But its significance for the nature of the Seattle labor movement in the 1920s was profound.[26]

This sectoral shift was not only the key to the transition from radical programs to conservative retrenchment over the course of the decade. It was also the key to the place of consumer tactics in the evolution of the postwar Seattle AFL movement, because the same bifurcation of trades and politics marked a distinction between unions whose primary organizational concerns lay at the point of production and those who placed consumer organizing consistently high on their list of organizational strategies. The Seattle AFL movement's new power alignment thus marked a departure of those who articulated radical solutions centered at the paid workplace, and an accession of those who gave highest priority to consumer organizing.

Those divergent priorities, in turn, stemmed from the economic structures of the different trades. The sectoral line distinguished between parts of the economy that catered to a local market of working-class consumers and those that did not. Locally based consumer pressures could most easily aid unions in the local-market sector. Consumer organizing therefore made sense to workers in local-market industries while it did not to workers in the metal trades, for example. Seattle's working class could not easily boycott warships. It would have been similarly difficult for longshoremen to pressure faraway purchasers of commodities that passed through Seattle's docks. Workers in the printing, teaming, service, and building trades, on the other hand, could all gain leverage over their employers through consumer organizing because their trades involved working-class patronage. Thus Seattle's postwar economy, as it undermined one sector of organized labor more than another, led to a fundamental realignment within the city's labor movement, and therefore in the strategic priorities of the Central Labor Council.[27]

The transitional process reinforced these dynamics. As the Bon Marche boycott illustrated, control of strategic resources contributed to a snowballing process in which those who were weakened were soon out, as they could no longer compete for the distribution of solidarity within the citywide movement and were left to hang alone. Another look at the major resource-distribution decisions the Seattle Central Labor Council made over the course of the postwar years reveals their critical importance and illustrates the AFL movement's changing balance of power and priorities.

The general strike of February 1919 had placed the movement's full resources behind the metal trades. Next, during the winter of 1919–20, the Committee of Fifteen directing the Central Labor Council's response to the open shop drive chose how to distribute the financial resources garnered from the locals to support embattled unions. A close look at the committee's finances shows that its $9,000 in total funds flowed in from the blacksmiths', painters', and boilermakers' unions, and flowed out to support striking tailors, printers, gas workers, and cleaners and dyers – redistributing the movement's funds from unions in the first sector to unions in the second.[28] The council's choice in March 1920 to center its resources on the Bon Marche boycott threw the AFL movement's resources first behind a consumer organizing strategy and second behind the building trades. While the building trades had not exactly captured the labor council in March 1920, they had gained enough influence that they could divert precious resources to their cause. The Bon Marche boycott symbolized just as it contributed to the postwar ascendance of the consumer trades and, again, of the movement's right wing.

By late 1921, the transition was well underway. As their per capita count declined, Seattle's metal trades and dock unions no longer had the right to send mass delegations. The tide turned gradually as it became increasingly difficult for radicals from other locals to hold their own, especially in the aftermath of the labor capitalism fight. The death of the longshoremen's union was both a cause and an effect of the long-term power shift. On the one hand, the devastation of the ILA contributed to the decline of radical voices and programs within the Seattle labor movement citywide. On the other hand, by the time the local came under assault from the waterfront employers in early 1921 the increasingly isolated radical longshoremen did not have the power within the citywide movement to save themselves. It was too late. The Central Labor Council did officially support Local #38–12 in its dispute with the longshoremen's international over the May 1921 unsanctioned strike. But the council's increasingly conservative power brokers did not extend more than verbal support.[29]

The Seattle AFL's internal transformation was part of a national trend in the 1920s. While only a few case studies are available, it appears that across the United States, unions in the local-market sector thrived while unions in mass production industries or trades serving a national market languished. Irving Bernstein, in his national study of the labor movement in the 1920s, notes that economic crises in the coal, garment, brewing, and textile industries undermined the more industrially structured international unions. Total membership in both the building and printing trades, by contrast, grew from 789,500 to 919,000 and 150,900 to 162,500, respectively, between 1923 and 1929.[30] In a 1929 study of Chicago, C. L. Christenson found that in the late 1920s unions grew especially well in the local-market sector, in particular the building trades, the teamsters, the printers, and the musicians.[31] In San Francisco, Michael Kazin found, the building trades lost the closed shop during the 1920s, but otherwise the city's pattern echoed Seattle's: Iron molders and seamen met with the open shop, while laundry workers, musicians, teamsters, and culinary workers successfully resisted it.[32] The Los Angeles labor movement replicated San Francisco's. It remained the classic open shop town in the building trades and most manufacturing work, but teamsters, musicians, and printers made solid gains.[33]

By 1923 and 1924 the winners and losers in the 1920s Seattle labor movement were beginning to emerge, as in the labor movement nationwide. The death of the radical industrial unions and the concomitant rise of local-market craft unionism underlay all that would follow: the self-definition of the labor movement, the strategies it would employ, and even those who would be counted as union members.

Lining up the Japanese by taking them in

The sectoral transformation of the Seattle labor movement brought to the fore a question most white activists would have preferred to have ignored: the issue of organizing Japanese-American workers. In the postwar years, Seattle AFL unionists became increasingly dependent upon strength in the service sector and in the local-market economy. Success there would make or break the movement. But locals in the service sector had long held firm on racial exclusion. By 1921 and 1922 their chickens had again come home to roost, forcing many in the AFL finally to question the wisdom of exclusion.

In late 1919 postwar tensions produced a fierce new wave of anti-Japanese agitation in Seattle. As layoffs multiplied and returning servicemen worried about finding jobs, white business owners grew more and more anxious about their economic futures. The new, war-boom sector of flourishing Japanese-American small businesses offered an easy scapegoat. Encouraged by a series of incendiary anti-Japanese articles in the daily *Seattle Star*, whites formed a new Anti-Japanese League, the members of which came from sectors of the middle class most challenged by the growth of Japanese-American businesses, especially owners of hotels, apartment houses, grocery stores, and laundries. In mid-1919 the league launched a vicious legal and political attack on Seattle's Japanese-American community. By late 1919 it had successfully pressured the city of Seattle to refuse to give licenses for Japanese-Americans to operate pawn shops, employment agencies, billiard halls, junk shops, dance halls, or detective agencies. In December the Anti-Japanese League obtained a ban on the importation of "picture brides" from Japan, cutting off many Japanese immigrant men from their traditional mode of forming families. Anti-Japanese agitation peaked triumphantly in March 1921 when Washington state enacted a law prohibiting noncitizens (e.g., Japanese immigrants, already barred from citizenship) from owning land.[34]

Seattle's Japanese-American community mobilized quickly in response to this assault. Constrained on the legal and political front by their noncitizen status, Japanese-Americans nonetheless managed to roll back the city's licensing restrictions. Their primary defense was on the cultural front. In 1919 community leaders formed a new "Americanization Association" that drew together a broad cross-class alliance within the Japanese-American community, including representatives of churches, newspapers, business owners' associations, the Japanese Association of North America, and Japanese-American unions such as the shoemakers and day laborers. In November the Americanization Association issued a formal statement declaring its goals:

> As Japanese in America we will respect the establishment of the United States of America and the customs and way of life, and cultivate the intention of permanent residence. . . .
>
> We will promote the self-awareness and the moral and educational development of Japanese in America. We will do our best to improve the living situation and actively cooperate to preserve and enhance the economic system of the United States in order to become perfectly integrated in the society. . . .[35]

Or, as one representative of the Japanese-American business community summarized the association's goals more bluntly in a speech to Japanese-American sawmill workers, "You have to be Americanized in order to avoid exclusion."[36] As part of this campaign community leaders launched a de-Japanification program in Seattle's Japanese-American business district. Americanization proponents tore down electric signs and other prominent billboards that featured Japanese lettering. At least one proprietor of a Japanese-American business, a Mrs. Umida, wept as the signs disappeared. "We sadly resigned ourselves to the Americanization program," another resident recalled.[37]

Although anti-Japanese activism in large part shifted from the working class to the middle class after the war,[38] the postwar depression nonetheless strained Japanese–white relations within the working class as well. As employment contracted, Japanese-American workers became caught in the same scapegoating vise as white women workers who, in turn, at times blamed Japanese immigrants for their plight. One correspondent to the *Union Record*'s Ruth Ridgeway who signed herself "A married woman who works" excoriated "wealthy families who employ Japs when so many ex–service men can do this work better," and asked "why all the hotels keep the Japs on elevators, also doing the chamber work keeping girls out of a job."[39] Many within the AFL movement continued to promote Asian exclusion in the postwar era. The janitors' union objected loudly when the metal trades unions in May 1920 advocated the organization of Japanese-American workers.[40] The musicians ran a continuous series of anti-Japanese, anti-Chinese, and anti–African-American jokes and remarks in their newsletter, such as one long poem in 1923 condemning the "Japanese invasion" of the United States.[41] Exclusionary attitudes extended to the top levels of the Central Labor Council. Charles Doyle, its secretary, in a 1921 interview told the Japanese-American *Great Northern Daily News* that "[w]hile not bitter toward the Japanese," he regarded them as "a menace because of their willingness to work long hours and also because of their morals." In 1919 the council's Executive Committee came to the aid of local white salmon-cannery workers in their efforts to force an employer to stop hiring Asian-Americans and hire only union – that is, white – workers in the future.[42]

Less exclusionary views were growing within the Seattle AFL movement, however. When in 1923 the University of Washington Sociology Department asked the Central Labor Council for a speaker on Asian workers and the labor movement, the council replied that "a speaker could only express his personal views as the Council was divided on the question."[43] The *Union Record*'s evolving treatment of the Japanese question both reflected and influenced this trend. In 1919 *Record* editors produced reportage of the "yellow peril" genre. "JAPANESE MONEY IS BUYING SEATTLE," read one April 1919 page-one headline. The story began: "Japanese capital is quietly and insidiously gaining financial control of the city of Seattle."[44] Another story, reporting on the growth of Japanese-American vegetable merchants at the public market, referred to "little brown men" and "invaders."[45] But more positive signals began to appear as well. The paper noted approvingly that Japanese-American businesses had donated money to striking metal trades workers.[46] In 1921 the *Record* printed two statements indicating growing ambivalence: A January editorial criticizing the bill prohibiting alien land ownership equivocated: "We are not attacking Mr. Tindall [the bill's author], nor are we defending the cause of the Japanese," but anti-Japanese agitation at that moment would "cause mischief."[47] A month later the paper replied to a letter to the editor: "The Union Record does not favor Oriental immigration. It believes, however, that at a time when race antipathies are in the ascendancy is the time for reasonable beings to step slowly and carefully."[48]

The *Record* had its own unique reasons for downplaying anti-Asian sentiments. Steadily over 1919, 1920, and 1921 it had built up a base of Japanese-American small-business advertisers that in the face of a steadily contracting base of white-owned firms represented a valuable source of revenue. One January 1921 issue ran a two-column, almost full-length strip of advertisements from Japanese-American businesses, including banks, hotels, a photography studio, a dry goods establishment, a watch repairer, and a tire dealer.[49] The relationship between the *Record* and

Japanese-American businesses grew into an ongoing one of mutual support. In July 1921, when Ault was reelected editor in the wake of the labor capitalism fight, the Japanese Labor Association wrote to congratulate him.[50] A year later Ault wrote to the Japanese Hotel Keepers' Association soliciting subscribers: "We believe that the fair attitude of the Union Record toward the Japanese is worthy of recognition by the display of the Union Record in the Japanese hotels and rooming houses."[51] The only slightly veiled hint in Ault's solicitation, however, suggesting that the Japanese-Americans owed Ault for his restraint on the exclusion question, underscores how unequal the relationship nonetheless remained.

Not all pressures to transcend anti-Japanese racism came from self-serving motives. A strong current of more ideologically rooted antiracism emerged in postwar Seattle as well, suggesting still further cracks in the exclusionary edifice of Seattle's AFL unions. Ault himself, long a socialist, was influenced by these more leftward sentiments while hemmed in by his official position as servant of the overall more exclusionary Central Labor Council.[52] Anti-exclusionary, explicitly antiracist voices came overwhelmingly from the IWW/OBU/metal trades sector of the Seattle labor movement. Seattle's Wobblies, in an October 1919 "Appeal to Japanese Workers in America," exhorted Japanese-American workers not to waste their time on the AFL, whose doors were closed to them, but rather to join the IWW, and they invited Japanese-Americans into their Seattle reading room and hall.[53] The independent *Forge* in May 1919 reported approvingly the positive effect of Japanese-American workers' observance of the general strike and noted that the radical Workers', Soldiers', and Sailors' Council had admitted Japanese-American and Filipino-American delegates from its inception. The *Forge* hoped that body would be "the means whereby existing race prejudice among the workers may be eliminated."[54] Rank-and-file worker Otto Jahn echoed the *Forge*'s perspective in a letter to the *Record*: "Teaching race hatred has been the foundation rock on which the capitalists have been able to induce the workers to sanction and enlist in wars. If we would allow every Jap worker in our unions that would solve the question. . . ." Though Jahn's use of the term "Jap" suggests limits to his analysis, he signed off, "Yours for a one big union, with nobody that works barred, no matter what his or her color, race or creed."[55] Other unionists held back from such a firm stance but nonetheless opposed exclusion. James Duncan, for example, told the *Great Northern Daily News* rather weakly in January 1921, "The Japanese in this country, as a group, do work, and do produce much more than they consume; therefore, in spite of problems which are bound to arise, labor has no particular quarrel with them."[56]

Gradually a handful of Seattle AFL locals came forward in support of admitting Japanese-American workers. In February 1919 the Photographers' Protective Union voted unanimously to admit Japanese-Americans.[57]

In May 1920 the Pacific Coast Metal Trades Federation announced to the Central Labor Council that it had "abolished the color line," whereupon the longshoremen declared that they already admitted members "regardless of race," though it remains unclear whether their local actually admitted any members of Asian descent.[58] Seattle AFL locals in which Communist workers were active sustained these pro-Japanese attitudes into the mid-1920s. In 1923 the machinists' and painters' unions, for example, both donated money to earthquake victims in Japan.[59]

Most of the openly pro-Japanese, anti-exclusionary sentiment in the Seattle AFL movement came from workers and unions in the metal trades/dock workers sector of the Seattle economy, where IWW and inclusionary industrial-unionist ideas were strongest. But locals in that sector were rapidly disappearing. What makes the story of race relations in postwar Seattle so fascinating is that Japanese-American workers made their largest gains within the opposite sector of the AFL movement, among those unions least ideologically inclined to oppose racial barriers. In a significant number of Seattle's service-sector unions, white workers made startling new accommodations to Japanese-American workers in the 1920–22 period.

The roots of those accommodations lay in the sectoral transformation of the Seattle labor movement, along with the changing Seattle economy. By 1921–22, Seattle's service-sector unions were at the center of the AFL movement. If the citywide movement were to prosper, it would have to prosper there. Yet it was precisely in that service sector that Japanese-American businesses had been thriving since the early war years. As the depression undermined white unions and businesses alike, several, though not all, of Seattle's white service-sector locals realized that if they were to survive, let alone grow, they would have to come to terms with Japanese-American firms.

Japanese immigrants had built up their business community in large part because of the exclusionary dynamics established by those same white unions. Japanese-American workers, excluded from vast reaches of the Seattle economy by white workers' and white employers' discriminatory practices, had sought entrepreneurial niches in which to employ and, they hoped, improve themselves. In the service sector capital entry costs were low. Not only could Japanese immigrant entrepreneurs avoid discrimination by employing themselves in an independent business sector, but they could also profit by serving a guaranteed base of Japanese-American customers, who, in turn, depended upon Japanese-American providers because white establishments refused to serve them or because they sought culturally specific goods and services. When the war boom brought tens of thousands of single white workers to Seattle, Japanese-American firms were poised to expand their clientele and multiply in total numbers. The postwar depression damaged many of the Japanese-American–owned service-sector firms just as it did white firms. But their overall numbers continued steadily to grow.[60]

Seattle's AFL locals in the service sector devised three responses to this challenge. One was to continue to exclude, only work still harder at it. So chose the culinary unions. Another strategy, more unusual, was to pressure Japanese-American firms to observe the union's wage scale and working conditions but never actually unionize Japanese-American workers at those firms. Following this model the jewelers' union announced in 1921, "Have had several raises in the recent past and find Japanese always follow suit."[61] A year later the sign painters reported similarly, "Had trouble with the Japanese until five years ago, when a conference was held with them and price list submitted. Since that there has been no trouble with that source."[62]

The third approach led to the first large-scale participation of Japanese-American workers in the Seattle AFL labor movement: the admittance of Japanese-American workers from Japanese-American firms, but on a separate-and-unequal basis. The premier example here was the barbers. Japanese-American barbers had formed their own local in 1908, affiliated with Seattle's Japanese Labor Association, and promptly applied for membership in the white barbers' union. Ritsu Sato, a Japanese-American barber, recalled, "Spending both time and money, we made much effort to join the Barbers' Union in order to slacken the anti-Japanese movement."[63] The whites refused. But with the war boom the number of Japanese-American barbers in Seattle increased, their customers now including thousands of white men as well as Japanese-Americans. After the war, the white barbers' union felt increasingly threatened by Japanese-American barbers, while at the same time its position among its own constituency slipped. "During the depression," Sato recalled, "the Union lost control over its members because many members violated the Union regulations regarding length of work-day and prices charged."[64] Suddenly, as a result, the tables turned. "Then, contrary to their former attitude, the Union asked us: 'Would you Japanese cooperate with us in disciplining the violators?' "[65]

By 1921 an evidently amicable, formalized cooperation between the white male and Japanese-American barbers' unions had evolved, building on cooperative arrangements begun in 1919.[66] According to its terms, Seattle's 150 Japanese-American barbers remained formally affiliated with their own local, because the white barbers' international continued to bar noncitizens. Both locals observed the same price list, working hours, holidays, and working conditions as determined by the white local.[67] Every year the Japanese-American barbers' union hosted a banquet at which its guests included the white male barbers, those white officials of the Central Labor Council who could swallow cooperation with Japanese-Americans, and prominent representatives of the Japanese-American community. In 1921 the vice president of the Barbers' Union of Japan attended, in 1925 the Japanese consul.[68] Phil Pearl of the white barbers' local gave a speech at the 1921 banquet that captured the agreement's elements: the white barbers' recognition of economic reality, the Japanese-American barbers' desire to allay discrimination, and a rhetoric of transracial solidarity bridging the two. Seattle barbers, Pearl celebrated, enjoyed the best conditions of any in the United States, and those conditions "can only be maintained by our getting together and understanding each other's hopes as workingmen." As a leftist within a service-sector trade Pearl himself served as a key bridge between inclusionary philosophies and the competitive realities of the local-market craft unions.[69]

The barbers' agreement served as the model for a similar arrangement between members of Seattle's Japanese-American and white shoe repairers' unions. "Japanese competition in the shoe repair business of the city has assumed considerable proportions," the white shoe workers' local noted with distress in April 1919. They reported that Japanese-American workers, laboring in a total of fifty-seven shops, had requested admittance to the white union, which was "seriously considering admitting them."[70] But it did not do so. Again in January 1921, the shoe repairers considered lifting their racial bars, "as a means of meeting the situation now confronting" their members. Delegates complained to the Central Labor Council that "many Japanese shoe repair shops are being established in the city and ... almost universally, these shops are cutting prices...." The wages of workers in Japanese-owned shops had plummeted to 20 cents an hour, while hours had climbed to fifteen a day. Citing their own amicable arrangements, the barbers and sign painters advised the whites to sign up the Japanese-Americans.[71] But the shoe repairers still did not relent. Finally in March 1922 the union announced it was "lining up the Japanese by taking them in," in part through the cooperation of the Japanese Association of North America.[72]

In the case of the butchers the complex negotiations that made such resolutions possible become clearer. Like the barbers and shoe repairers, the butchers were hurting after the war. In 1923 they reported, "Depression of last two years has struck a hard blow at [the union's] minimum scale."[73] Joe Hoffman, Local #81's business agent, reported with Sisyphean resignation, "[W]e lost a bunch of shops and slowly but surely get them back."[74] By April 1921 Hoffman had reached the same conclusion as the barbers and shoe repairers. "Unorganized Japanese are a menace to conditions in the meat industry ... so long as their wages are on a level far below that of white butcher workmen."[75] His local, #81, initiated the admission of Japanese-American butchers carried out through the Japanese Association of North America as intermediary. Correspondence between Hoffman and the association reveals that Seattle's Japanese-American butchers were well aware of the pitfalls of the situation. They informed Hoffman that they would enter into an agreement only if two concerns were addressed: First, would the white union guarantee protection for the Japanese-American firms against non-union shops in their neighborhoods? Second, could the Japanese-American butchers be admitted into a separate branch within #81, but with all the full rights and privileges of the regular, white local? Yes, and yes, Hoffman replied, adding that he was eager to close the agreement so that it could be presented to the butcher workmen's international convention in time for prompt endorsement (and therefore in time for his local to accrue prompt economic benefits from the arrangement). For Joe Hoffman, admitting Japanese-American butchers was a pure business proposition untainted by antiracist principles. Immediately after concluding the agreement he reported gleefully that Japanese-American restaurants as well as retail meat shops were now boycotting Barton's, a wholesaler against which the white local was struggling. "If Americans gave the support to white unions that the Japanese people are giving to their organized workers," he concluded admiringly, "our troubles in the labor movement would be half over."[76]

A curious mixture of forces thus produced the numerical gains obtained by Japanese-American workers within the Seattle AFL movement in the early 1920s. Ideologies advocating transracial class unity resulted in the first admission of workers of Asian descent to Seattle AFL unions in 1919 and 1920, that is, to the metal trades and dock unions. But the largest numerical gains came later in the service sector, where craft unionists read the economic handwriting on the wall and bargained for survival in the worst of times. When Seattle's AFL locals admitted Japanese-Americans they did so only on a carefully codified subservient basis. No Japanese-surnamed delegate ever attended the Central Labor Council as a voting member in the decade.[77] No evidence suggests that Japanese-American workers ever served as officers in any mixed-race local. Whites admitted Japanese-Americans only because they were threatened economically by the growth of Japanese-American–owned, Japanese-American–employing firms. Many whites undoubtedly retained their stereotyped and racist images of Japanese-Americans. Seattle AFL locals, in sum, lowered their exclusionary walls for the first time less to welcome Japanese-American workers than to contain them.[78]

Japanese-Americans and whites reached those accommodations in part because the Japanese-Americans now had something with which to bargain. Japanese-American business owners had clout as employers of large numbers of workers. Japanese-American workers, meanwhile, were in a position, once organized, to make collective demands of white unions. Finally, Japanese-American workers and employers together identified common interests within the Japanese immigrant community as a whole and formed cross-class alliances with which to pressure the white unions. The often gray line between employer and employee in small-shop, entrepreneurial trades like shoe repairing, retail meat sales, or barbering made such partnerships, often negotiated through the cross-class Japanese Association, still more possible. The admission of Japanese-American workers to white unions was not a question of white workers' choosing, out of noble principle, to recognize victimized Japanese-Americans. Rather, whites had to recognize the countervailing power of Japanese-Americans. Thus did white workers, dependent now on success in the local-market sector, learn how to adapt to the new realities and rules of its game.

Capitulation

Adaptation proved a still greater challenge when it came to the Seattle trade unions' relationship to the national AFL. The AFL Executive Council's April 1923 ultimatum to the Seattle Central Labor Council placed the movement in a tight place. It would either have to adapt or face expulsion. Each of the AFL's charges, in particular those that objected to the Seattle council's stands on organizing women workers, on independent political action, and on recognition of the Soviet Union, demonstrated the Seattle AFL movement's last vestiges of progressive independence, even radicalism. But each of the Seattle council's responses to those charges by late 1923 demonstrated that the overall Seattle AFL movement had finally surrendered to the realities of life within the mid-1920s national AFL. Those capitulations underscored the effects of the power shift within the Seattle movement long underway, just as they marked the conservative forces' final triumph.

Revoke the lady barbers' charter, Gompers demanded in 1923.[79] That ultimatum, and the central council's response, highlighted the fate of white women wage earners within the new context of Seattle AFL unionism. Since 1920 women unionists' position within the Seattle movement had declined precipitously. In 1921, as part of its depression-era retrenchment, the Central Labor Council laid off its organizer for women, despite protests from left-inclined locals. Without the female organizer's special efforts women unionists were then unable to stay the disappearance during the depression of more than a dozen all-female and mixed-gender locals. The growth and survival of women's unions had always depended upon an expansionary labor movement, and by 1921 that context had evaporated.[80]

Women unionists labored overwhelmingly in the local-market sector of the economy, and this fact had two consequences in 1921–23. Many of the city's all-female locals, such as the waitresses, hotel maids, and candy workers, depended upon a mass base of pro-union male patrons. Tens of thousands of those men disappeared after 1920, drastically reducing the women's bargaining power. With potentially more salutary effect, almost all organized women workers inhabited the local-market sphere, on which the male AFL unionists' fate now depended. If male craft unions were to prosper in the service sector, it would be in their interest to question gender as well as racial exclusion. The controversy over the lady barbers symbolized that challenge.[81]

The all-white "lady barbers'" union had begun with a tremendously successful organizing drive in August 1918 that by mid-1919 had garnered 160 members and signed up 40 shops. The white male barbers' union, Local #195, extended its enthusiastic support to the new local, as did thousands of pro-union patrons who observed an informal boycott of non-union female barbers. The women were able to achieve swift and significant gains in their wages and working conditions. They changed their method of payment from 60 percent of earnings from each customer, to a guarantee of $18 a week plus 65 percent of all business over $26.50. While they were unable to obtain the 8-hour day, which they acknowledged was "impractical because of the spasmodic nature of the work," they succeeded in bringing more regularity to their work schedules.[82]

The lady barbers also used their union to address issues specific to women workers. Women barbers were particularly concerned that their trade not be associated with prostitution. In 1919 Blanche Johnson, the Central Labor Council's organizer for women, expressed her hopes that as the lady barbers achieved gains in their conditions, the craft would, "as nearly as possible, be made clear of any temptations. Then the stigma will be removed from the name of the lady barber."[83] Johnson's reference to "temptations" suggests that female barbering did shade over into prostitution, as do the observations of a University of Washington student who investigated the migrant-worker neighborhood of Pioneer Square in 1923. "There are lady barbers to trim his hair and shave him and there are lady dancers in the basements and upper floors, and courtesans in the hotels who will 'trim' him as handily as the ladies who operate the clippers and razor."[84] Blanche Johnson noted that the lady barbers' piecework payment system encouraged the countenancing of sexual harassment. "This basis of compensation has a tendency to affect the morals of the woman worker. She must let pass, apparently unnoticed, offensive remarks which she would ordinarily resent."[85] The lady barbers sought to deal with this problem by changing their method of payment to abolish piecework and by regulating the type of shop at which they would allow their union shop card to be hung, excluding those they associated with prostitution. Members were not allowed to work in such shops. In April 1919 the local threatened to suspend a member when she continued to work in a shop "of doubtful reputation" in defiance of the union's designation of the shop as such.[86]

By April 1921 the lady barbers' union spoke of the city's female shops as "100 percent" union.[87] That claim, however, masked multiple exclusions. While the local claimed 100 members in 1919, the 1920 census counted 321 women as "barbers, hairdressers, and manicurists."[88] In part the disparity can be accounted for by the lady barbers' exclusion of women working in shops of alleged ill repute. The union also excluded beauticians – that is, women who served female customers – evidently considering them outside of the sphere of the "barbering" trade, which served male customers.[89] But the lady barbers also excluded the city's 43 Asian-American and 23 African-American barbers and beauticians.[90] Some, perhaps most, of those women may have served female customers and been excluded along with white beauticians. But Japanese-American women, at least, did serve male customers in Seattle.[91] Like the male "barbers'" local, which admitted no women but omitted "male" from its name, the female "lady barbers'" local admitted only white female barbers, while it named itself, and spoke in the name of, all female barbers.

Whether Japanese-American women found union protection in the "Japanese barbers'" union remains uncertain. Sources on the Japanese-American union never mention female barbers as union members. All the spokepersons for the local were male. But the Japanese-American local's announced total of 150 members in this case suggests the inclusion of women, as the census counted a total of only 124 Asian barbers and hairdressers – 81 of them male, 43 of them female. The tight level of organization within occupational groups in Seattle's Japanese-American community further suggests that the Japanese-American barbers' union counted women among its members.[92]

Within a male-dominated local, though, Japanese-American female barbers would most likely have lacked the ability to use the union to address their special concerns as women, and still more particularly their concerns as Japanese-American women serving both white and Japanese-American male customers. One story confirms that Japanese-American women barbers experienced sexual harassment, and it also suggests the degree to which their concerns were taken seriously within the Japanese immigrant community. Izo Kojima, who worked in a Seattle laundry during World War I, recalled how one day a twenty-six-year-old Japanese-American woman barber came in and complained, "A certain white customer who was here just now is a nasty guy. He touched and rubbed my hips while have his hair cut." Kojima's boss, presumably Japanese, responded, "Why, don't get mad! It'll be good for you to let someone touch you sometimes." "We all burst into laughter," Kojima recalled.[93] This incident, perhaps isolated, does not suggest support in the Japanese-American community for Japanese women barbers' concerns.

When originally founded, Local #195, the white male barbers' local, had admitted an African-American man who served as corresponding secretary. He was the only African-American member, however, and by 1920 none of the city's thirty-nine African-American male and twenty-three African-American female barbers and hairdressers evidently belonged to the white unions. African-American barbers and beauticians, though, could still make a living serving African-American customers. White beauticians similarly enjoyed guaranteed markets, because only female beauticians served female customers.[94]

The constitution of the Journeyman Barbers' International Union (JBIU) contained a clause limiting its membership to "any male journeyman barber other than an Oriental," barring both the Japanese-American and lady barbers' unions.[95] Seattle's white men in Local #195 challenged that clause to force the admittance of white women, although they evidently never raised the issue of Asian exclusion within the international.[96] Throughout the first half of the 1920s Local #195 fought hard to obtain white women's legal admission to the Journeyman Barbers' international. In 1918, when the JBIU rejected the lady barbers' request for a charter, Local #195 then tried unsuccessfully to get a separate federal charter from the AFL. As a last resort the local obtained a charter from the Seattle Central Labor Council. The JBIU promptly asked the council to revoke it. In 1919 and again in 1921 the Seattle barbers tried to change their international's policies at its annual convention, only to meet with defeat. In 1923 the international, furious, brought in Gompers and the AFL Executive Council to force the Seattle council to revoke the women's charter. In trying to organize the women the Seattle AFL ran head on into the constrictive, exclusionary, and increasingly aggressive AFL. In the spring of 1923 the council and Local #195 put up a brave fight, sustained by letters of support from locals across the spectrum of Seattle unions and across the country. On June 6 they capitulated. "With feelings mingled with shame and humiliation," the council replied to the AFL, "we must disassociate [*sic*] them [the lady barbers] from this Central Labor Council and cast them into the slough of despond with other unorganized [workers]."[97]

After that capitulation the members of the lady barbers' union were left for a time in limbo. Their worst moment came in August 1924, when Local #195, acquiescing to the international, requested that the lady barbers' shops be put on the council's "unfair" list. A month later the JBIU finally agreed to admit (white) women. Seattle's Local #195 promptly initiated fifty women barbers. Through the rest of the decade the joint local sent both female and male delegates to the Central Labor Council, usually in equal numbers. Whether the local served women's interests as well as had the separate female local remains unclear. One clue suggests that after the admittance of women Local #195's leaders continued to conceptualize their union in male terms. Asking members of all unions to observe the barbers' shop card in September 1926, a representative from #195 argued that such aid "enable[d] the journey*man* to support *his* family properly."[98]

The lady barbers' 1923 expulsion exemplifed the fate of wage-earning women in the Seattle AFL, as the movement completed its internal transformation. AFL unionists who tried to fight for the right of white women to union representation found that they had only a tight space in which

to maneuver. The logic of intra-class solidarity across gender and racial
lines pressured locals in the service sector to adapt or face diminished
economic clout. But still greater pressure from the AFL and craft union
internationals forced their acquiescence to still stricter dictates from on
high: exclude, or be expunged.[99]

For the AFL Executive Council, the Seattle Central Labor Council's second
transgression in 1923 was in the realm of political action. "The Seattle
central body not only ignored the Non-Partisan Political program of
the A.F. of L. . . . but worked in direct opposition to that program," it
charged.[100] Such had in fact been briefly the case. In mid-1920, a statewide
coalition of the Washington State Federation of Labor, the Grange, the
Railroad Brotherhoods, the Socialist Party, Nonpartisan League, and
Triple Alliance joined to form an organization of all the state's "producers"
that they named the Farmer–Labor Party. The party's constituents agreed
on a broad-ranging reform platform that included planks of interest to the
labor movement, such as the eight-hour day and workers' compensation;
planks designed to address the concerns of farmers, such as publicly owned
grain elevators, flour mills, and markets; and general reform measures such
as nationalization of the telephone and telegraph industries, release of all
political prisoners, and democratic electoral reforms.[101] Despite considerable chaos at the local level, the new party succeeded in winning 30
percent of the state's votes for its gubernatorial candidate, to the Republicans' winning 52 percent and the Democrats' diminished 17 percent.
Although it was not victorious, with that election the Farmer–Labor Party
burst triumphantly onto the state political map. Employers watched the
Farmer–Labor Party grow with mounting apprehension, as both workers
and farmers spoke in terms of the "producing classes" and imagined new-
found collective political power. Like the workplace and consumer battles
of 1919–20, the Farmer–Labor Party symbolized the Seattle AFL movement's aspirations to class power – this time pursued through a third
sphere, the ballot box. Like the other experiments of those years it grew
out of the movement's broad vision, as unionists dared to think big on the
political front with an eye for a long-term reconstruction of U.S. society.[102]

As the Farmer–Labor Party stood poised for advancement after the fall
1920 elections, Washington's Republican legislators immediately threw a
rock in its path by passing two laws designed to quell the nascent movement.
One required that any party on the state ballot have been in existence for
two years; the other reduced public ownership of utilities. In April and
May 1921 the Farmer–Labor Party focused all its energies on blocking the
two measures, gathering the signatures necessary to call for a referendum
on the two measures in the 1922 state election. In the interim, the two
laws would be on hold. The drive succeeded; but larger forces at work in
the meantime soon shattered the fragile coalition that had briefly held the

party together. As statewide politics shifted rightward, the party's adherents pulled out one by one. In 1921 William Short gained control of the State Federation of Labor. Long an opponent of independent political action, he withdrew the federation from the Farmer–Labor Party in favor of non-partisan political pressure. Meanwhile, the 1921 labor capitalism fight discredited the Seattle forces that were at the core of the statewide Farmer–Labor movement, just as it split apart the Seattle progressive–left alliance from within. At the same time the state Grange fractured over the issue of working with the labor movement, and only a partial organization centered in western Washington, the Western Progressive Grange, remained within the Farmer–Labor Party. By mid-1922 the Farmer–Labor Party was left to a coalition of leftists centered in the Puget Sound area: the Western Progressive Grange, the tiny Socialist Party, the still tinier Socialist Labor Party, the Workers' (soon to be Communist) Party, independent progressives such as Harry Ault and James Duncan, and progressive unionists in nearby Tacoma. The party got nowhere in the 1922 elections and finally fell apart in 1923 when the Socialists, too, pulled out.[103]

Meanwhile, national farmer–labor politics developed along a similar if more convoluted trajectory. In early 1922 officials of the Railroad Brotherhoods, Nonpartisan League, Minnesota Farmer–Labor Party, International Association of Machinists, and a number of other progressive international unions together formed the Conference for Progressive Political Action (CPPA). CPPA leaders specifically eschewed formation of a third party, choosing instead to launch a combined political initiative to elect pro-labor and pro-farmer candidates to Congress in 1922. The CPPA effort was a great success, electing 23 of 27 endorsed candidates for U.S. Senate and 170 U.S. representatives, while defeating a number of antilabor incumbents.[104] The new body completely eschewed the new Workers' (Communist) Party, which, together with the dissenting Minnesota Farmer–Labor Party and a range of nationally active trade unionists, advocated instead an independent third party. In July 1923 this second grouping formed a national Farmer–Labor Party. The AFL reacted with hostility. It forced the all-important Chicago Federation of Labor to withdraw from the Farmer–Labor Party, leaving the party in the hands of the Communists, who alienated the remaining members.[105]

In Washington state, William Short aspired to bring statewide farmer–labor politics into line with the national AFL program. After a series of secret meetings with the Railwaymen's Political Club, Nonpartisan League, and Grange over the summer of 1922, Short announced the formation of the Washington Conference for Progressive Political Action. It would pursue a purely nonpartisan approach, Short affirmed. Its program consisted only of support for C. C. Dill, liberal Democratic candidate for U.S. Senate, a far cry from the broad platform of the 1920 Farmer–Labor party, two years before. The coalition's biggest goal was the defeat of antilabor

Republican Senator Miles Poindexter. That it achieved, electing Democrat C. C. Dill by a narrow 5,000-vote margin.[106]

The rise and fall of third-party farmer–labor politics in Washington paralleled exactly the sectoral shift underway within the Seattle AFL movement. Hamilton Cravens, the party's historian, notes that as early as January 1921, Farmer–Labor activists admitted that their party's proposed advancement "would be a difficult task, for the unions which gave the party its heaviest support were those which had been hurt the most by economic recession."[107] Shipyard unionists and the *Union Record* along with progressives such as James Duncan and Phil Pearl were at the heart of the third-party movement. Seattle's building trades, amusement, culinary, and teaming unions, by contrast, allied to rescind the Central Labor Council's endorsement of the Farmer–Labor Party.[108] By 1921 the mass base of support for the Farmer–Labor party present in 1919–20 was gone, and AFL craft unionists who had long advocated the classic "pure and simple unionist" approach of rewarding friends and punishing enemies had their way in politics as in the Seattle AFL movement as a whole. The Farmer–Labor Party was left another empty shell, symbolizing like so much else the Seattle AFL's loss of vision, its retrenchment from a self-conscious movement for class advancement to a narrow pressure group pursuing limited goals. The Seattle AFL's involvement in city politics had long since retracted similarly. A contemporary student of labor and municipal politics concluded that after the 1920 mayoralty campaign, labor's political stance became "very much like the conservative business interest." The demands he cited did, though, suggest a measure of specifically pro-labor concern: shorter hours and higher wages, combined with less-class-specific calls for a municipal market and public ownership of utilities.[109]

By the time the AFL commanded in 1923 the Seattle Central Labor Council to renounce independent politics, the real contest was long over. In 1920, the city's locals had defiantly challenged the AFL's longstanding ban on third-party politics. But by 1923 the internal transformation of the Seattle AFL movement had made such defiance largely symbolic. In its reply to the AFL that summer the council repeatedly and proudly asserted its right, in theory, to take stands independent of the state federation or AFL. But it no longer had the desire to do so.[110]

Tragically, the Farmer–Labor Party pulled the *Union Record* down in its wake. The *Record* endorsed the party enthusiastically in 1922 and continued to support it well after the Central Labor Council, the paper's major owner, withdrew its own endorsement. The *Record* was soon caught between the pro- and anti–Farmer–Labor Party camps, satisfying neither. As one labor activist wrote a friend:

> The upshot of the whole thing is that the *Union Record* from being a prosperous, aggressive, live-wire paper has been brought down to the

status that it hardly dares open its mouth for fear of offending one group or the other, and it has lost almost all of its advertising patronage because neither side makes any effort to get support for it as long as it doesn't give them exclusive support.[111]

This stranglehold followed sharply on the heels of the labor capitalist controversy, in response to which thousands of subscribers lost faith in both Ault and the paper and canceled their subscriptions. Circulation, as a result, sank lower and lower, from a 1920 peak of 120,000 to 39,000 by late 1922.[112]

Subscribers' defections only exacerbated the downward financial spiral in which the *Record* had long been caught. From 1921 on Ault engaged in a constant search for new stock sales, loans, and outright grants with which to rescue his dying newspaper. Sometimes his search succeeded, garnering, for example, a $5,000 loan from the New York–based Garland Fund and another loan from the Brotherhood of Locomotive Engineers' Bank in Cleveland. But those infusions were not sufficient. In 1922 and 1923 circulation and advertising income continued to fall. In an effort to free the paper from the editorial constrictions of the Central Labor Council, in 1924 Ault and managing editor Saul Haas created a new corporation, the American Free Press, and bought the paper from its stockholders for $60,000 in 6 percent bonds, secured by the *Record*'s plant. In Harvey O'Connor's words, the paper by then had become a "respectable bourgeois hybrid that even so could not survive."[113] The paper ran a column of labor news but other than that largely hid its left and labor origins, dropping "Published for Principle, Not for Profit" from its masthead and even shrinking the paper's name to read "SEATTLE Union RECORD," with "Union" set in tiny type. To hasten the *Record*'s demise and supplant it ideologically, William Short in 1924 started his own Seattle-based weekly paper, the *Washington State Labor News*. The next year in a highly symbolic act the Central Labor Council voted to employ the *Labor News* for its annual Labor Day Edition, rather than the *Record* as customary, depriving the latter of vital advertising. The *Record* managed to struggle through 1926 and 1927 but on February 18, 1928, published its last issue.[114]

Mary Joan O'Connell, in a 1964 history of the *Union Record*, identified a number of reasons for the paper's failure. The paper began with a "ridiculously small base of capital," $20,000 where a million would have been more appropriate. The government's seizure of the paper in November 1919 in the aftermath of Centralia cost the paper $25,000, a loss it could not afford. The paper expanded too hastily when it bought a new press in 1920 and its own building in 1921. The postwar business depression and shipyard closures cut into the paper's advertising revenue, its potential circulation, and its pool of funds from local unions all at once. Finally, the cresting wave of labor strength on which the paper had ridden was long gone. The conditions that had originally sustained it no longer existed. Like the other institution-building experiments of 1919 the *Record* was yet another empty form, its original base of support gone. The *Union Record*'s sale in 1924 symbolized all too tidily the demise of Seattle's progressive AFL movement by the end of 1923.[115]

The AFL Executive Council's attack on the Seattle Central Labor Council contained a final charge, this one cutting at the heart of the long-term purpose of the labor movement. "Despite the declarations of the conventions of the A.F. of L. the central body declares for the recognition by the United States government of the Soviet government of Russia." Worse, "the efforts of those who control and direct the policy of the Seattle Central Labor Union are directed along lines the object of which is to mold the Seattle labor movement to conform to the policies and principles enunciated by Soviet Russia."[116] On this count the Seattle council stood its ground somewhat. While assuring the AFL that it had never contemplated making the Seattle labor movement over into little Soviets, it affirmed,

> [W]e do believe that a government which recognized and had no compunctions about doing business with the governments of the Czars need have no scruples about recognizing the present government of Russia. Indeed, we believe that such a course would be distinctly beneficial to the interests of the workers of Russia and the United States alike.[117]

The left–right conflict within the Central Labor Council symbolized by the 1923 AFL controversy unleashed, however, a chain of expulsions and forced withdrawals that would soon make such pro-Soviet attitudes unmentionable. First to go was the progressive leader of the postwar Seattle labor movement, James Duncan, who was largely driven out. In January 1923 he announced that he would not run again for the all-important secretaryship of the Central Labor Council. In July he officially resigned, stating that he wanting to "provide better for his family at this expensive stage."[118] He retreated to activism solely within the auto mechanics' local, where he remained for the rest of the decade. Duncan's resignation meant the end of progressive–left independent radicalism within the Seattle AFL trade unions. The center that had bridged so much for so long did not hold.

Still less did the ascendant craft union conservatives tolerate the left within their movement's ranks for long. The AFL's 1923 charge that the Soviets had captured the Central Labor Council could not have been further from the truth, but Communists maintained a small but important presence in the mid-1920s Seattle AFL. The local Communist Party originated with veterans of the Socialist Party. Its core was a group of labor intellectuals the most prominent of which, John C. Kennedy, served as state secretary of the Farmer–Labor Party in 1922 and went on to teach at Brookwood

Labor College in the 1930s. In 1920 and 1921 Seattle's Communists were largely a discussion group, with a few members underground in justified fear of police repression. By 1922 and 1923 they counted thirty or forty members. Their activities included support for the Soviet Union, including recognition of the Soviets by the U.S. government, resumption of trade relations, and financial support for the Soviets from U.S. workers. More centrally, Communists sought to "bore from within" the AFL trade unions. In these early years Communists became actively involved in the city's AFL machinists', painters', shipwrights', bakers', office employees', and mill-wrights' unions. Activists in Local #79 of the machinists carried radical planks to their international convention opposing the Baltimore & Ohio Railroad's plan for labor–management cooperation, attacked the International Association of Machinists' (IAM) leadership for supporting World War I, and advocated the amalgamation of all metal trades internationals into one industrial union.[119]

With Duncan out of the way, in 1924 conservative delegates from the local-market sector came fully to power in the Seattle Central Labor Council. One of their first goals was to expel the Communists. In February 1925 delegates from the Building Trades Council introduced a resolution banning all Communist delegates from the Central Labor Council. On March 25 delegates voted seventy-eight to seventy-one to expel all members they could identify as Communists. The closeness of the vote was surprising. Many delegates were evidently reluctant to exclude members on the basis of political views, although precedents in purging Wobblies abounded. The locals that the Communist delegates represented – the machinists, painters, bakers, shipwrights, and office employees – protested vehemently, but to no avail. To spite the council they continued to send back the same banished delegates for years and years, only to have their credentials perpetually rejected. The locals did not withdraw from the council, however, apparently by mutual agreement.[120]

Communists remained active in the Seattle labor movement throughout the rest of the decade, as the dissenting locals' ongoing loyalty demonstrates. William Short's equally continual diatribes against Communists in his *Washington State Labor News* offer additional evidence of the Communists' continuing viable presence within the Seattle AFL movement.[121] The best window on Communist activism in late-1920s Seattle, if a clouded one, is an October 1930 hearing of a U.S. congressional committee investigating "Communist Activities in the United States." Both Communist activists and police officers from Seattle who testified agreed that the Seattle Communist Party counted twenty-five to forty active members in the last years of the 1920s. Of the October 1930 membership, 50 to 70 percent were foreign-born. Judging by those arrested at Communist demonstrations that year, they came from at least a dozen different countries. While none of the committee's informants mentioned Communists of Asian descent, Japanese-American Communists were also active in Seattle in the late 1920s and produced a newspaper targeted at Japanese-American sawmill and cannery workers.[122]

All such activities took place outside of the sphere of the Central Labor Council and most of its constituent locals, which conducted their own purges in conjunction with the council's. By mid-1925, with the Communists, Duncan, and Ault out of the picture, the only remaining dissident leadership in the council came from longtime Socialist activist Phil Pearl of the barbers. Pearl voted against purging the Communists and immediately paid the price.[123] He had long been a thorn in the side of his international union. In 1925 its president, James O'Shaughnessy, struck back, charging that Pearl had improperly accepted an advertisement from the non-union Koken Barber Supply Company while editing the *Pacific Coast Barber*. In 1925 O'Shaughnessy and William Short joined to expel Pearl from the convention of the Washington State Federation of Labor on the grounds that Pearl had attended the previous year's convention with fraudulent credentials. In October Pearl resigned from his posts as secretary and business agent of Local #195. His swift and summary fate underscored how sharp indeed would be the limits to dissent in the late-1920s Seattle AFL.[124]

For every activist drummed out of the movement, a dozen others left town in a long exodus stretching from 1920 to 1925. Anna Louise Strong recalled that once the shipyards shut down, "The young, the daring, the best fighters went." As the unions' bargaining power decreased, many left-inclined workers once again became vulnerable to blacklisting and were forced to leave in search of jobs. Strong herself, embroiled in the labor capitalism controversy as an editor at the *Record*, in 1921 asked herself, "What was there to hold me in Seattle? . . . My job was now a disillusion" and fled to the Soviet Union.[125] Thousands of Seattle activists took up union activities in other U.S. cities rather than remain in increasingly depressed and depressing Seattle. One former *Record* staff member, in a 1928 letter to Harry Ault from his new home in Los Angeles, mentioned two additional former *Record* employees living in San Francisco along with a man who had been active in Seattle cooperatives. In Los Angeles he knew of two Seattle women working for the garment workers' union, another who was now secretary of the waitresses' union, and a machinist who had been a member of the metal trades' strike committee during the Seattle general strike and now served as business agent for the Los Angeles machinists' local and as president of the Central Labor Council. Another former Seattle man had become business agent of the hod carriers. "And they tell me of other Seattle Labor Folks here," he added.[126]

The Seattle Central Labor Council's ultimate response to the AFL, despite a degree of rhetorical instransigence, proved to be largely one of capitulation. Out went the lady barbers. Out went the Communists, Socialists, and progressives. The Farmer–Labor Party did not even live long enough to be purged, though its supporters, Duncan, Ault, and Pearl, were soon cast out. For all the prideful independence with which the Seattle council replied to the Executive Council's charges in April and June 1923, the controversy underscored the extent to which the national-level AFL held power over the Seattle movement, if in no other way than in its ability to consume the greater part of the Seattle AFL's energies that year. AFL international officers had opposed and restrained the activities of Seattle locals since the movement had first erupted in 1919. Representatives of a number of internationals had rushed to Seattle to quell the general strike. Their opposition had proved key to the strike's untimely end. Many Seattle locals, battling against the Associated Industries that fall, did so without the support of their internationals. The next spring the longshoremen's local lost their strike in part because the ILA revoked their charter. The white male barbers' local had to fight the JBIU tooth and nail over the right to admit women. The city's employers, moreover, were aware that Seattle's AFL locals frequently lacked the support of their internationals, and they used that knowledge during the early years of the decade to push for greater concessions.[127]

In 1923 those diverse international officials, long plagued by Seattle dissidents, finally allied with Gompers, the AFL Executive Council, and William Short to close in for the kill, sensing that their prey had stumbled. The long-term structural transformation of the Seattle labor movement had made defiance increasingly difficult. However much the progressives and leftists in the Central Labor Council and in the locals might want to stand their ground, once the mass base for dissent was gone, that ground had long since been eroded from under them. In October 1923 the Seattle Central Labor Council and the Executive Council finally reached an informal, by and large agreeable rapprochement. By that point the two sides were not all that different any more.[128]

Conclusion

By early 1924 the Seattle AFL movement was on the far side of a great divide. The transformation that had begun with the open shop drive was now complete. Industrial unionists advocating radical solutions had been wiped off the economic and political map, along with so many projects their visions had sustained and their dollars bankrolled. By 1924 a third party uniting Washington state's "producing classes" was as unthinkable an option as were the institution-building experiments of labor capitalism and cooperation. Even the all-embracing *Union Record*, which had once served all sectors of the movement, had no place in the new order. After 1924 the scope of the Seattle AFL movement would be narrow indeed. Within that scope, service-sector craft unionists still faced the challenge of constructing solidarity that could unite a racially and sexually divided labor force. There might be a place, if a small, segregated, subservient one, for white women and Japanese-Americans in the new model labor movement. But its adherents declared in no uncertain terms that there would henceforth be none for union activists who advocated a labor movement that extended beyond trade unionism, narrowly defined, or who dared to ask whether the whole system in which those trade unions operated might be at fault.

Part III

Contraction

8

Harmony

"THIS WAVE OF RED RADICALISM will soon have spent itself and then real trades unionism will again come into its own," prophesized Louis Nash of Seattle's retail clerks' union in October 1919.[1] His prediction proved on the mark. In 1924 and 1925 business unionists from the local-market sector of the Seattle AFL came fully to power. They defined the labor movement in its narrowest sense, eschewing larger goals of social change in favor of delivering services to union members.[2] With the left opposition out of the way, these new leaders – including Nash himself – were at last in a position to implement their own vision of an ideal labor movement. At its center lay a final consumer organizing strategy: promotion of the union label and shop card.

This time Seattle's AFL unions wielded "the workers' purchasing power" in a dramatically different context from that of the immediate postwar years. The business unionists who ran the locals by mid-decade, like the unionists who had turned to boycotts and cooperatives in earlier years, found consumer tactics appealing because their unions could benefit from pressures exerted by local consumers. At the same time they had made their peace with capitalism. Increasingly they greeted the city's employing class with respect rather than with hostility and promulgated ideals of harmony between labor and capital. Union label promotion provided a perfect merger of the two impulses. The structural imperatives of craft unionism in the local-market sector, meanwhile, dovetailed neatly with label unionism. Union label promotion in the late 1920s proved intimately interwoven with a new politics of class, as the AFL unions sought one final time to bring politics to the shopping cart.

Button, card, label

The trade union label originated in the 1870s with the consolidation of national trade unions in the United States. White union cigarmakers in San Francisco first employed it to mark their products with a white label, signaling that the cigars had been manufactured by white, not Chinese, workers – who, because the whites excluded them from their union, were by definition unfair. During the 1880s and '90s the label spread in popularity among AFL internationals as a weapon against recalcitrant employers. By 1908 sixty-eight internationals issued the union label, shop card, or button.[3]

Before World War I a number of Seattle AFL unions, most prominently those of the butchers, restaurant workers, and bakers, employed union label and card promotion. Their tactical dependence upon it was limited, however. Like AFL unions nationwide, they struck a balance between boycotts and union label promotion, while combining both with political action and strikes. Label promotion nonetheless occupied a solid enough strategic position to prompt the Central Labor Council's male leadership to form the Women's Card and Label League in 1905, and to call upon loyal unionists to look for the union label and card with ritualistic regularly.[4]

With the war, union label promotion dropped in popularity. "Union men are losing interest in the boosting of the union label as a means of gaining their desires," a charter member of the Card and Label League sighed. "When you say 'union label' to them they answer back 'direct action.' "[5] Strikes and other tactics at the point of production supplanted the union label as labor shortages increased and Wobbly-influenced philosophies gained in popularity. Label and shop-card promotion never completely disappeared. But when the unions considered consumer tactics once again after the war, they were more likely to select boycotts or cooperatives over the union label and card.

By 1924, though, the woman would have received just the opposite reply. If asked about direct action the average union leader would not only have immediately replied "union label" but also would have purged the offending questioner as a Wobbly sympathizer. During the mid- and late 1920s promotion of the union label rose to the top of the Seattle AFL movement's collective list of tactics. Two mutually reinforcing trends fueled its rise: the increasing usage of union label and shop-card promotion by individual trades, and the concomitant prosperity and rise to power of trades that employed it. By 1925 label promotion was so entrenched as to be inseparable from the Seattle trade union movement itself.

The general category of "label promotion" in practice broke down into three distinct but related tactics: the union button, union shop card, and union label. Of these, the button was the least prominent. While many of Seattle's AFL locals issued union buttons to their members, it remained largely marginal as a tactic. The button was most often employed in trades with shifting workforces and worksites, such as the building trades, for which union strength depended in part upon union members' refusal to work next to non-union workers.[6] These unions issued monthly or quarterly buttons to their members.

The streetcar employees' union illustrates the union button's employment as an adjunct, but not central, strategy. The local issued new buttons monthly and asked pro-union patrons of the city's streetcars to demand a union button of railway employees as they boarded the car. The union prospered in the 1920s. It signed up 95 percent of eligible workers, gained one day off in eight in 1923, and obtained a small wage increase the next year. The union's advances, though, stemmed more from the transfer of the streetcar lines to city ownership in 1919, which eliminated strong employer resistance, and from its relative insulation from the depression, than from button promotion. The button served best to bring the fifty or so "stragglers" who resisted union membership into line.[7]

Unions that employed the shop card, by contrast, relied centrally upon the tactic. Seattle's white butchers serve as a prime example. Their dependence on the shop card grew out of the nature of the retail meat trade. As David Brody has shown, most butchers in this period worked in shops with only one or two employees other than the owner. It was ineffectual for those isolated workers to withdraw their labor because the employer could easily cover the shop's operations himself. At the same time retail butchers' neighborhood-level markets made working-class consumer pressure a viable option. These factors converged to prompt Seattle's butchers' union to employ shop-card promotion as its primary tactic. Joe Hoffman, its business agent, even stated bluntly at one point, "The *only* way that we can compel any butcher to organize his shop is by withdrawing labor support."[8] This strategy apparently worked. Seattle's local was one of the strongest in the country. In 1923, after it admitted Japanese-American butchers, it began to thrive again. By 1925 the local was doing its "best ever" with 470 members, a gain of 200 over 1919.[9]

That growth, however, came with a price. As shop-card promotion grew in the butchers' strategic approach, it led the union into firmer and firmer alliances with those employers who recognized it. During the 1920s Local #81 and the master (employing) butchers began with increasing frequency to engage in joint political campaigns – for meat inspections, for example, or credit guarantees. One such campaign, for early closing laws, allied union butcher workers and the shop owners, both of whom wanted to go home at six, against working-class patrons who wanted to shop after work. The ideological and practical lines between unionists and employers narrowed. "Mutual interest cemented labor–management unity," Brody found.[10] He describes the butcher workmen as "incipient capitalists" who expected to become proprietors themselves one day in a matter not unlike that of eighteenth-century journeymen craftsmen who identified as much with their masters as with one another.[11]

Seattle's white barbers, too, depended upon the shop card. Like the butchers, the barbers worked in a trade with low capital-entry costs and a proliferation of small firms, in which employees looked forward to eventual ownership of their own shops. Like the butchers as well, the barbers engaged in joint campaigns with their employers for early closing and sanitary conditions.[12]

The retail clerks' use of the shop card was more complex. Like the street-car employees, the clerks issued monthly buttons to their members and asked union patrons to encourage buttonless clerks to join up. The union also placed the retail clerks' shop card in the window or behind the counter of union establishments. The presence of the card could mean either that all the store's clerks were union members or merely that the employer observed the union scale and working conditions. Complicating this ambiguous situation still further, the clerks also functioned as potential guides for the selection of union-labeled goods in their stores. This produced multiple confusions. Were all goods sold in stores displaying the clerks' shop card therefore label goods? bewildered rank-and-file workers asked. If they were not, why were they on display in a store with a union card? The clerks' location as guide in this bottleneck in the distribution of goods placed them in a position to exercise solidarity, but only at risk to themselves. "While the clerks, like other trades are interested in promoting the welfare of sister organizations," one reporter noted in 1927, "they are primarily interested in promoting their own conditions. . . . The clerk is . . . in no position to tell the owner of the store that he must stock his shelves and counters with union made products."[13] In the hands of white men with no commitment to the white women of their trade, still less to clerks working for African-American– or Japanese-owned firms, the clerks' union consistently provided conservative leaders such as Leo Ledwich and Louis Nash to the citywide AFL movement in the decade's second half. The depression nearly wiped out the local's wartime gains, but the union grew steadily in the next three years, reporting "great progress" by 1926, with a strong presence in men's furnishings, shoe, and hat stores.[14]

The culinary unions similarly combined use of both the union button and shop card, along with regular consumer boycotts. They, too, could hope to influence working-class patrons to seek out or eschew a given restaurant on the basis of its union affiliation or lack thereof. Like the butchers', the culinary unions' reliance on the card grew out of their relative weakness in strikes. Dorothy Sue Cobble, who has studied waitresses' unions nationally, notes that culinary employees could replace striking workers with family members or scabs. Just walking out carried little force.[15]

Between the immediate postwar years and the mid-1920s the culinary unions' selection of tactics shifted gradually from the boycott to the shop card. They continued to employ both, moving a given firm on or off the "unfair" list and alternately picketing or endorsing it. But overall, waitresses nationwide "re-evaluated their early reliance on strikes and pickets," Cobble found. "While organizers did not wholly abandon adversarial tactics . . . they increasngly replaced strong-arm tactics with rational persuasion and an appeal to the employers' savvy."[16] This last proved key. As the union's approach gradually shifted, culinary employers recognized business advantages to union recognition, Cobble notes. In a field notorious for business failures, unions offered a guaranteed, skilled labor supply, standardized labor costs across a cutthroat industry, and a wealth of free advertising.[17] The culinary unions, for their part, consciously embraced the task of promoting fair employers. The Los Angeles waitresses' local, for example, asked new members to pledge to "interest themselves individually and collectively in protecting the trade, and the business of the employers."[18] Applicants to other locals pledged service to the "efficiency and profitability" of their employers.[19]

Seattle's culinary unions fit exactly this model of growing labor–management cooperation. After the adversarial period of 1921–22, the culinary locals and Caterers' Association appear to have reached a peaceful accord. The unions settled into an exclusively card-dependent organizing style and evidently struck up friendlier relations with most employers, of whom they made few demands. As with the butchers and barbers, the line between the two was often indeterminate in small firms. The cooks' union, in the words of its business agent in 1926, made "ample provisions for the owners . . . to become members of the organization."[20] After 1923–24 the cooks were able to regain and then surpass 1919 levels of strength. In 1925 they reported "more houses 100 percent [organized] than ever before in the history of the organization." The waitresses never completely regained 1919 levels but nonetheless obtained a 50-cent wage increase in 1925.[21]

The total number of workers in Seattle AFL unions employing the union label itself was relatively small, though the label's ideological presence was great. Seattle's printing unions, with 1,000 combined members, were the only large body of workers using it. The Allied Printing Trades Council issued a single label, jointly negotiated between local representatives of the eight different internationals in the printing trades.[22] Their internationals, as in most trades, left jurisdiction over the printers' label largely up to the discretion of individual locals. In Seattle the largest and by far the dominant printing union was the International Typographers' Union (ITU) Local #202. Highly skilled, cautious, and, like the other unions in the local-market sector, relatively conservative, the typographers had long relied heavily on the boycott in newspaper work. A strike and accompanying boycott of the daily Seattle *Post-Intelligencer* in 1925 sealed the closed shop in the city's daily newspapers for the rest of the decade.[23]

The typographers deployed the union label to line up Seattle's job shops. Here the union's strategic trajectory mirrored the citywide trend. After its 1919 lockout by the Associated Industries, Local #202 participated in a second, nationwide strike in 1921 for the forty-four-hour week. Thereafter it turned away from the strike to heavy emphasis on label promotion. "The mutations of time have left labor but one weapon of aggression, the union label," the local resolved in 1923.[24] During 1924, 1925, and 1926 Local #202 embarked on a major drive to promote the Allied Printing Trades' label. Members competed to see who could accumulate the largest amount of printed matter lacking the union label. Union officials then confronted offending merchants who had purchased the printing services, to "pound these leeches until something happens."[25]

As in the shop-card trades, this approach subtly turned the union's attention toward amicable relationships with cooperating print shops and their customers, despite the latter's sometimes characterization as "leeches." Label promotion activities illustrate this evolution. At the peak of Local #202's label drive the union ran a promotional booth in the 1925 state fair at which union printers passed out 5,000 hand mirrors with union labels affixed. Reporting on the exhibit's success, Local #202's officials concluded, "The members of the committee made numerous friends among the merchants present. These associations, we believe, are worth a great deal to the Allied Printing Trades and will be the means of placing the Union Label on a much larger amount of their printing for the next year."[26] In 1927, with their traded 97 percent organized, the typographers concluded that label promotion worked quite effectively, though only if the union exerted continual pressure.[27]

The original and most symbolic union label in the United States had always been the cigarmakers'. Despite the minuscule and rapidly diminishing membership of Seattle's cigarmakers' local in the 1920s (down to seven in 1923 from seventy in 1919) union label cigars still occupied an important place in the political imagination of the Seattle AFL movement. Unlike the products of the previously examined trades, union label cigars served a national market. Promotional materials issued from the Cigar Makers' International Union (CMIU) rather than from the locals. Patricia Cooper has shown that by the early twentieth century the cigarmakers' international had become so dependent upon the label that its national organizers had become merely label promoters. They only rarely organized the unorganized; instead, they asked other unionists to look for the label. The cigar- and cigarette-label promoters who passed through Seattle in the 1920s demonstrate, moreover, that such international representatives could at the same time be employed as manufacturers' agents, the interests of the two had become so identical. George Downs of the Clown Tobacco Co. and A. J. Helck of the Axton-Fisher Tobacco Company traveled regularly to Seattle as part of a regional circuit. They spoke on behalf of both the tobacco unions and their employers, exhorted unionists to look for the label, and (guaranteeing their entrance to union meetings) passed out free samples.[28]

Seattle's garment workers forged a merger between employer and employee interests even more actively. The garment workers' label, like that of the cigarmakers, carried a symbolic meaning far larger than the Seattle local's 300 to 400 members would seem to warrant, both because of the presence of tens of thousands of organized garment workers in other cities and because of the visibility, commonality, and relative availability of union label clothing. Seattle's local of the United Garment Workers used label promotion as almost its exclusive strategy. Dependence on the label meshed with identification with employers to the extent that the local became, in essence, a company union. Paternalism permeated labor–management relations. Not coincidentally, employees at the two unionized firms were almost all female. When George Black, one of the two owners, died in 1927, the *Washington State Labor News* reported approvingly: "His employes at the plant ... resemble a great family, all happy and contented."[29] The employers provided paternalistic amenities such as holiday dinners and picnics planned jointly with the local, in exchange for which members of the union pleaded to other Seattle unionists that their job security depended upon their employers' prosperity, which, in turn, rested upon purchase of the firms' products. "Every girl employed is an ardent booster for what they call 'Our Boss,'" the *Labor News* noted later that same year.[30] The rewards of this deference, however, were not mighty. After a third of the unionized firms shut down during the depression, the union's members remained dependent upon the vicissitudes of its two patron firms for a marginal existence.[31]

Unions in Seattle's service- and consumer-products trades thus moved gradually toward greater dependence upon union label and shop-card promotion over the course of the decade. Their "look for the union label" approach grew out of the nature of their different industries, in the appeal of consumer tactics where employers sought to engage a local market, the limited efficacy of strikes, and the permeable line, in many cases, between employer and employee. At the same time the locals' choice of tactic locked them in ever-tighter identification with the interests of their employers.

Let's make a deal

Not all AFL unions in mid- and late-1920s Seattle depended so fully on the union label and shop card, but they developed relations with their employers that melded harmoniously with evolving relations in the label trades. In part, the similarities were those of ideology; in part, of structural position in the local market. Most importantly, both groups were moving rapidly toward their own institutionalized harmony between labor and capital.

Building trades unions represented almost two out of every five organized Seattle AFL workers in the second half of the decade, counting for

7,000 out of a total of 18,000 unionists affiliated with the Central Labor Council in 1927. The strategic approach of the building trades, therefore, was crucial to the tenor of the late-1920s Seattle labor movement as a whole. After the concessions of 1921, Seattle's construction unions began to rebuild their position as building activity picked up. Workers in the skilled construction trades moved from steady employment to a surfeit of available jobs. Beginning in 1923 unions in individual trades began to assert and win new demands. The carpenters gained a $1-per-day increase in April that year; the plasterers a raise from $10 to $12 a day. Pressures built as each year's total volume of construction surpassed the previous year's.[32]

By mid-decade labor relations centered on annual spring negotiations between the Building Trades Council (BTC) and the Associated General Contractors (AGC). In 1924 the two were ready to put in writing a sixteen-month-old oral agreement recognizing the unions and holding conditions at the present state. While the agreement, in the opinion of the *Seattle Times*, represented a concession by organized labor because it contained no wage gains, "outside pressure" on the contractors' association stopped the agreement.[33] For another two years the same informal resolution held. Meanwhile individual trades gained another round of wage increases. In the spring of 1926 the Building Trades Council and Associated General Contractors finally signed a blanket contract calling for unchanged conditions until the next year. "The industrial sky is cloudless," the *Seattle Times* reported with pleasure.[34]

In 1927, though, as the construction industry still boomed, the unions were ready to fight for more. They had two key demands, the five-day week and recognition of the building laborers' union. A strike loomed. In stepped the "outsiders" who had mysteriously stopped the 1924 agreement. They turned out to be the ghost of the Associated Industries, re-incarnated as the Citizens Industrial Adjustment Board, which revealed itself at the Chamber of Commerce and was led by none other than former Associated Industries president Frank Waterhouse. Its members represented the array of employers and business owners' associations that had come forward eight years earlier to try to obliterate the labor movement, including the Waterfront Employers' Association, the Real Estate Board, Retail Trade Bureau, and Chamber of Commerce. They held back the unions from striking by calling for arbitration. Eventually they convinced the building trades unions to give in on the question of recognizing the building laborers but informally granted the five-day week for skilled workers during the summer months. The next year, 1928, the Adjustment Board negotiated an unprecedented three-year contract for peace in the building trades. The laborers still went unrecognized – the employers refused to budge on that question because to do so would mean the complete closed shop – but the five-day week for skilled work would be official every summer.[35]

The breadth of this agreement documented the new terms of union–management relations in the Seattle building trades. Each side marshaled considerable countervailing powers. The unions achieved the closed shop for all but unskilled workers on all projects costing more than $5,000, and many under that. They gained the five-day week and guaranteed steady incomes, if not continuing wage gains. Their gains were possible in part because each trade was tightly organized in seventeen separate locals and then negotiated collectively through the highly disciplined Building Trades Council. Yet the building trades unions rarely looked outside that circle, beyond their immediate concerns and interests as skilled craft unionists. They got what they wanted in part because they asked for so little.[36]

The employers, for their part, got what they wanted because they knew what mattered most: uninterrupted production. In the fast-paced world of construction finance, a strike could prove devastating. On the other hand, in boom times they could afford to pay their workers well and still turn a handsome profit. Concessions on wages and hours could prove a healthy investment if they came as part of a package that averted strikes. Like the culinary employers, moreover, building contractors could achieve benefits from the standardization of wages and conditions through unionization. In construction, as in food service, a multiplication of small and large firms all jockeyed to undercut one another. By erasing competition, union standards made guaranteed profits possible. The AGC–BTC 1928 contract symbolized much: The unions had solid power but did not seek to use it; the employers had organized a united front but needed the unions to avoid their own cannibalization. The two found peace by recognizing each other's concerns. The achievement of peace through the intervention of citywide organized capital symbolized the stakes involved. In a boom sector of the economy, white male skilled craft unions could now achieve an immense separate peace. In many ways their three-year contract presaged the longer and longer contracts of the CIO mass production unions in auto and steel in the late 1940s and 1950s, as organized labor settled for a contained but guaranteed slice of a pie it assumed would last forever.[37]

The building trades employed the union label, if sparingly. Their work often involved sites such as the Bon Marche, whose owners would ultimately seek working-class patronage. Construction unions asked unionists to inquire as to the status of painting done on hotels, or of remodeling work on restaurants. In 1925–26 the building trades mounted an "own your own home" campaign that called on unionized workers to employ only union laborers when having homes built. Such label use was common enough to prompt Carpenters' Local #131 to establish a new committee in August 1921 to oversee the issuance of its label. Seattle's building trades also issued the union label on production work. Electrical Workers' Local #944, for example, called for union label observance in the purchase of electrical fixtures. The building trades, then, used the label enough to sympathize with the label concerns of other trades. The Building Trades Council's minutes regularly carried at the bottom of each page a slogan alerting readers to a specific label or boycott campaign underway or generically promoting the label, such as "*NOTICE: BUY ONLY UNION LABEL GOODS WHEN MAKING YOUR PURCHASES.*" Still more important, the building trades harmonized politically with the label-promoting trades.[38]

The second largest group of organized workers in late-1920s Seattle, the teamsters, developed into almost a caricature of twentieth-century business unionism. Seattle's teamster locals grew in membership in the decade to surpass even immediate postwar levels. The bakery salesmen expanded from 175 members in 1920 to 315 in 1929, the milk wagon drivers from 325 to 400, the laundry drivers from 300 to 400, and the citywide general local from 1,350 to 1,450 members. The biggest growth came at mid-decade, when the locals won the closed shop and a series of wage gains. By 1929 Seattle's teamsters totaled 5,000 members and counted for 28 percent of all AFL unionists in the city.[39]

The secret to that success was Dave Beck. The man who would go on to achieve infamy as president of the International Brotherhood of Teamsters in 1952 started his career in 1917 as a truck driver for Seattle's laundries, among them the labor-owned Mutual Laundry. The laundry drivers' union elected him their business agent in 1924. The next year, when the International's convention met in Seattle, an eager, ambitious, and attentive Beck, in charge of local arrangements, ingratiated himself with international president Dan Tobin and got himself appointed northwest district organizer for the teamsters' international in 1926. He also ruled as secretary of the Seattle Joint Council of Teamsters, in addition to the laundry drivers' local.[40]

In Seattle Beck pioneered the style of labor unionism that would in later decades bring him mastery over much of the western U.S. trucking industry. Like the cooperative activists in 1919–20 and the unionists who had sought to allay concessionary bargaining in 1921, Beck began with a theory about the relationship between wages, prices, profits, and trade unions. He carried out a meticulous study of the exact profit structure of firms in the industries he sought to organize. "That fellow knew everything about my place," one proprietor exclaimed when he saw the results of one of Beck's surveys.[41] Beck's appropriation of the bakery industry serves as a good example of his methods. When he commenced his campaign, the owners claimed that they could not raise wages and still turn a profit. Beck responded by calculating the total number of bakeries in the city, their total potential market, the cost of flour and other materials, and current wages. "Pretty soon . . . Dave knew more about coffee cake and hard rolls and Boston cream pie than the owners themselves," one observer noted admiringly.[42] The next step, for Beck, was to grant that employers had a right to make a profit. "We recognize that labor cannot receive a fair wage from business unless business receives a just profit on its investment," he told a 1938 interviewer.[43] One Seattle industrialist confirmed, "Beck is the only [union] official who ever showed any sympathy with the difficulties faced by the businessmen."[44] Beck saw the union's role as participant in that profit-making process. "I run this office just like a business – just like an oil company or a railroad," he announced proudly. "Our business is selling labor. We use businesslike methods."[45]

The final step was to propose an industrywide deal to employers in a given industry. The package had three elements: first, a reduction or limitation of the number of firms; second, stabilization of prices and wages; and third – the catch – the closed shop. To the baking industry Beck promised that if the employers signed with the teamsters' union, he "would see to it that neither price cutters nor immediate new competition obtained men to drive their trucks."[46] Within a year of Beck's tenure as an official in the Seattle teamsters not only had Seattle's bakeries said yes to that offer, but so had all its local trucking firms, laundries (except one), dairies, and taxi firms. Nineteen twenty-five proved the turning point in labor–capital relations in local transportation. Strikes disappeared. Arbitration and negotiation served instead. In 1927 the teamsters got a three-year contract, too, that granted the closed shop and left open the possibility of future wage increases. To serve as go-between in the negotiations arose another ghost from the Associated Industries, Rev. Mark Allison Matthews. But the man running the shop this time was Dave Beck. "Dave Beck runs this town," Mayor John F. Dore would admit by 1938, "and it's a good thing that he does."[47]

Why did all those employers say yes to Beck, who must have been a rather unsavory figure in their eyes? As in the building trades, the key was stability. Beck offered to bring peace to the industries he organized. And he kept his promises. "Dave Beck sees to it that union contracts are inviolate," praised John Boettiger, publisher of the *Seattle Post-Intelligencer*. "When he signs a contract, he keeps it. Employers know that, and they have confidence in him."[48] Beck offered two kinds of stability. The first was respite from cutthroat competition. With a cap on the total number of firms, and wages and prices stable, employers could expect to ensure a safe, steady profit. Investors, too, knew what they were getting. The second respite was from strikes. Beck's ability to sell stability depended fundamentally on the threat of instability. This not-at-all-veiled threat emerges clearly in the tales of his successful negotiations. In the bakery case, when he promised to "see to it" that no new competitors entered the field, he also observed that such competitors would need teamsters if they were to move their products. No teamsters, no bakery. Describing his efforts to organize the city's gas stations, Beck commented frankly, "First, I advise promoters against starting new stations. If that doesn't work, the Teamsters' Union simply will refuse to serve them. They won't last very long."[49]

Beck's threats rested on very real examples before the employers. The teamsters were not unafraid to apply a little thuggery, carefully selected. As Carl Westine, who studied the Seattle teamsters in a 1937 thesis, put it, teaming work was "mainly physical labor and attracts hardy men. Naturally a militant personality is developed."[50] He described the teamsters' methods as "pragmatic and violent."[51] In a late 1920s campaign against the Golden Rule Bakery teamsters allegedly overturned trucks, bombed bakeries, and employed physical persuasion. Examples of strikes, too, lay before the employers. The teamsters struck Seattle citywide in 1917 and showed no lack of commitment to repeating the act at key junctures in management negotiations in mid-decade. Finally, labor had its own ghost looming over mid- and late-1920s employer–union negotiations. The 1919 general strike was still only a few years past. While Seattle's employers had largely locked up their active fears by 1921, it seems safe to assume that in 1925 or 1927 "stability" was still quite precious.[52]

Seattle's teamsters, then, proved an almost exaggerated model of the new relations of labor and capital forged by the unions in the mid-1920s. Dave Beck was the quintessential business unionist. He bargained hard for his constituents and looked no further than the power of his own union. "Their belief is in immediate gains," Westine summed up the Seattle teamsters.[53] The key to "success" was embracing the employers' agenda of profit making but locking that embrace tightly in closed shop contracts enforced by a few rocks and sticks.

The teamsters did not employ the union label, button, or shop card much. The taxi drivers issued union buttons and tried to enforce observance of them by unionized consumers. The bakery salesmen and milk wagon drivers asked housewives not to patronize non-union firms. But in the second half of the decade such firms were few and far between. The teamsters didn't use the label because they didn't have to. But their philosophies and approach to management, like those of the building trades unions, meshed perfectly with those of label unionism.

Cooperation and collaboration

The union label rode to strategic prominence in the Seattle AFL atop two converging waves. One was the increasing tactical preference for label and shop-card promotion on the part of unions in the service and printing trades. The other was the prosperity of that sector of the labor movement, along with unions in two other sectors – construction and local transportation – the evolving strategic approach of which echoed those of the label trades. As those trends reinforced each other, the Central Labor Council's "label trades department" gradually became synonymous with the "labor movement."

We can trace the label's rise to prominence equally clearly within the Washington State Federation of Labor, which by this period worked hand-in-glove with the new conservative leadership of the Central Labor Council. State federation president William Short first proposed the formation of a new standing committee on the union label in 1921. In 1924 the federation launched its first statewide label campaign. The federation's Executive Council in its 1927 report unwittingly summed up its increasing dependence on, and lack of vision beyond, label promotion: "[A] good share of our time and effort could be put to no better purpose than to work for the union label."[54] Its report the next year went so far as to conclude that "widespread demand" for labeled goods and services "would solve practically every labor problem confronting our movement."[55]

In enshrining label promotion so thoroughly the Seattle and statewide AFL brought a fundamental shift to the politics of their consumer organizing campaigns. Unlike the boycott, which embodied an oppositional relationship to employers, the union label represented collaboration. It shifted the locus of consumer pressure subtly from confrontation to cooperation. Seattle labor conservatives explicitly celebrated its nonconfrontational nature. The June 1922 issue of *Musicland*, for example, explained:

The Union Label Means
Peaceful collective bargaining.
The avoidance of both strikes and lockouts.
Steady employment and skilled workmanship.
Prompt deliveries to dealers and public.
Peace and success to workers and employers.
Prosperity of the local community in which union label products
  are produced and consumed.[56]

Three years later the *Washington State Labor News* concurred: "The strike and boycott invite retaliatory measures. Even in victory it is difficult to estimate the cost or measure the gain. The Union Label scores gains but inspires no revenge."[57] "Wage Earners are Satisfied with Few Strikes," another article began.[58] As these examples suggest, the label's star rose in proportion to the strike's fall, as strike rates fell both locally and nationally.[59] Label promoters specifically contrasted the desirable label with the distasteful strike. President John Hayes of the AFL's national Union Label Trades Department, for example, told the barbers' international convention that if 50 percent of workers' incomes were spent on label goods, "you would have no need for strikes or boycotts or lockouts."[60]

While the boycott called on unionists to spurn a given employer, the label, by contrast, asked them to flock toward selected employers. At root, label promotion began with the idea that good employers could, in a real sense, be the workers' friends. Note the text of the *Washington State Labor*

News' union label guide in January 1928: It (the guide) represented "a splendid array of firms and institutions friendly to organized labor," its author averred. "The purpose of this page is to promote friendlier feeling between members of organized labor and the business institutions of Seattle who have expressed their desire to deal fairly with organized labor."[61] On another occasion a filler item explained, "The Union Label is a bid for friendship. It carries no sting of malice. . . . No red fire or excitement marks its progress. . . ."[62] Such rhetoric not only assumed that good employers existed, but it also asked true unionists to shape their shopping habits to support them. Campaign material from a 1924 statewide label campaign asked unionists along these lines to "help create a larger market" for the pro-union employer. "Help Employer Who Employes Union Labor," a half-page advertisement in the *Labor News* summarized.[63]

Such "help" could be of concrete economic value to the "good" employer. Ernest Spedden, who surveyed label promotion nationwide in 1910, observed that through label promotion unions absorbed their employers' advertising costs. The label endorsement could often be so lucrative as to allow a manufacturer to forgo advertising altogether, as the free publicity more than compensated for higher production costs.[64] An agent for the Tobacco Workers' International Union at the turn of the century discovered "a great lack of enterprise on the part of union label tobacco firms. . . . [T]hey seem to do no advertising at all."[65] Seattle employers, too, could reap economic advantages from the label. An organizer for Typographers' #202 reported in May 1923, "It is conservative to estimate that the use of the [printers'] label meant $5,000 to the shops holding it last fall."[66] After the formerly "unfair" Olympic Theatre settled with Seattle's amusement trades in 1923, the unions put on a "labor week" to restore the theater's patronage and paid for 50 percent of the advertising expenses. Like the standardized wages and respite from inter-firm competition the teamsters and building trades unions offered their employers, the union label came as part of a package of solid economic benefits to the employer who bought it.[67]

Label promotion was only the tactical vanguard of a broad citywide thrust in the Seattle AFL movement after 1922 toward cooperation with employers. As cross-class cooperation emerged at the level of the locals, the Central Labor Council's leadership actively reinforced those emerging politics citywide. John Jepson of the teamsters, when he was reelected to the council's presidency by a big majority in 1925, "praised the harmony that marked the council's activities and the spirit of cooperation existing between labor and employers."[68] The term "cooperation" took on new meaning. By mid-decade it meant not the Cooperative Commonwealth but cooperation between labor and capital, in implicit contrast to the non-cooperative approaches of 1917–20. Such was the message of the editors of the state federation's *Yearbook* for 1926, who devoted the publication's first page to profusely thanking its advertisers and then concluded, "[C]ooperation is a great vehicle for advancement."[69] By 1929 the leadership's commitment to friendly relations with the city's employers had climaxed in efforts to sweep any possible suggestion of opposing interests under the rhetorical rug. In an article entitled "Employee Loyalty," for example, Gertrude Ledwich, wife of Central Labor Council reading clerk Leo Ledwich, told the story of a worker who didn't want to join a union because to do so would be disloyal to her employer. Ledwich affirmed, "[O]ur first duty is to ourselves." Workers had the right to organize, she asserted. "And must our employer suffer?" she asked. "No, a thousand times no!"[70]

Seattle leaders' emphasis on cooperation with employers paralleled a national thrust within the AFL leadership in this period. At the 1923 AFL convention in Portland, Oregon, the Executive Council introduced a resolution entitled "Industry's Manifest Duty" that called for "cooperation and collaboration" between the "functional elements" of industry – organized labor and employers – to manage society and obviate state interference.[71] In 1925 the Executive Council again advocated union–management cooperation. In doing so, historian Louis Lorwin argued, the federation assumed that "industrial relations were shifting from a basis of conflict to one of continuous co-operation." Lorwin identified within the AFL in the mid-twenties a shift away from reliance on strikes. "In recent years [the AFL] has stressed converting employers to unionism by promising business gain from co-operative relations with unions."[72] The newly institutionalized structures of labor–management cooperation forged by local-market craft unions throughout the country in the mid-1920s underlay this ideological shift.

Seattle AFL leaders' arguments for cross-class cooperation stemmed in part from pro-employer machinations hatched years before by union conservatives in response to the radicalism of the immediate postwar years. William Short, president of the state federation, began meeting secretly with representatives of employers' associations as early as 1919, when he conferred, for example, with lumber baron Mark Reed to discuss how best to nurture a "community of interest" between labor and business, in opposition to the radical elements then dominating labor.[73] By 1922 Short openly advocated, as in a letter to the *Seattle Post-Intelligencer*, that "the best thing that could happen to Seattle would be the elimination of the open-shop war and the industrial strife between employers and workers, and the substitution of joint cooperation for their mutual goods and for the good of the whole community."[74] He commenced a regular round of speeches before the Rotary and Kiwanis Clubs, Chamber of Commerce, contractors' association, and other employer organizations, singing the praises of harmony and promising labor's docility. He served on boosterist bodies such as the Seattle Civic Federation, on which he collaborated on reform of the city charter alongside Frank Waterhouse (of the Bon Marche and Associated Industries) and Roy Kinnear (an industrialist who in 1919 and 1920 had two spies reporting daily to him about the labor movement).[75] Short's allies in the Seattle AFL concurred in his sentiments. C. O. "Dad" Young, AFL organizer for the region, in 1925 praised "an attitude of cooperation" abroad in labor circles.[76] After a speech by Young in 1923, Charles Doyle, business agent of the Central Labor Council, similarly affirmed, "The [central labor] council could rest assured he would do everything in his power to promote harmony." ("If there were not harmony," he growled, he would "place responsibility where it belonged.")[77]

By the late twenties the Seattle AFL movement had entered into an amicable relationship with local capital that would have been unthinkable in 1919–20. In 1919 the least suggestion of participation in any project with which the Chamber of Commerce was in any way connected had sparked denunciations. In 1927 Short, Harry Ault, Charles Doyle, and David Levine (then Central Labor Council president) served on a Chamber of Commerce committee alongside Waterhouse, Frank McDermott (of the Bon Marche's formerly boycotted McDermott Building), and the presidents of major business organizations.[78] Dave Beck swam happily in this sea. "Beck's forums are the American Legion, the Elks, the chambers of commerce, the Rotary clubs, and the realty," a journalist noted.[79] Individual union locals came to participate in these exchanges as well. The white musicians' union, for example, joined the Chamber of Commerce in 1928. In return, and much to the pleasure of Local #76's leadership, the Chamber entertained the entire Seattle Symphony Orchestra at luncheon.[80]

The city's employers and financial interests, not surprisingly, greeted organized labor's new attitude with delight. This was precisely the outcome they had sought in 1919 when they began strategizing against the unions. They had hoped to split off the business–unionist conservatives from the radicals, and then to encourage the one while obliterating the other. By late 1920 the open shop drive and postwar repression had accomplished much of the second goal. Thereafter the Associated Industries evidently lost steam, as less antagonistic attitudes prevailed in management circles. In July 1921 its newsletter, the *Square Deal*, ceased publication. By that point the association's greatest concern was not organized labor's alleged evils but the deepening depression. In August it moved to new, cheaper offices. By the winter of 1921–22 the Associated Industries "went off the industrial field," in the words of contemporary observer Earl Shimmons.[81] Robert Dunn concluded aptly in a 1927 national study of the open shop drive, "The employers were certainly more openly and generally militant in 1920–21 than they are to-day. A stronger labor movement forced them at that time to show their teeth."[82]

Seattle employers' appreciation of the AFL's new posture was open. "CONGRATULATIONS! TO ORGANIZED LABOR" twenty Seattle firms exulted in a full-page advertisement in the 1926 *Labor News*, "[t]here were no strikes in 1925." The public, they affirmed, was now confident, and all sides had benefited.[83] H. V. Bogert, secretary of the Associated General Contractors, in a 1928 interview attributed "stabilized conditions for both employer and employe . . . to the honesty and fairness of the labor leaders now in authority."[84] Summarizing the Central Labor Council in a 1927 article, president David Levine noted approvingly, "The prestige of the council amongst the citizens of Seattle is now the highest ever enjoyed."[85] "There is no labor problem in Seattle; labor and capital go hand in hand," a Chamber of Commerce representative exulted after a 1927 speech in Seattle by AFL president William Green. From the audience, part labor, part business, "no word of disapproval" arose.[86]

Hugh Grant Adam, an Australian trade unionist who visited Seattle as part of a tour of the U.S. labor movement in 1927, had only "harsh" words on what he saw throughout the Northwest: "[T]rade unionists crawl to the employers and, in return, are allowed a little place in public life. They get a seat on the Chamber of Commerce, and that gives them the right to attend midday luncheons and make speeches."[87] On the leadership's language of cooperation between labor and capital, he observed:

> The only sort of co-operation I found was the sort of co-operation that was established between the Tiger and the Young Lady from Riga when they returned from that famous ride. You will remember that the Young Lady from Riga was inside the Tiger.[88]

One final tactic employed by the AFL in the mid- and late twenties synthesized this blend of cross-class cooperation, label promotion, and local-market unionism. Beginning in 1925 the Central Labor Council, Washington State Federation of Labor, the *Union Record*, and several locals began to join in annual "Northwest Products Exhibitions" and other joint employer–labor fairs promoting local products. "Spend Northwest Dollars for Northwest Products," the labor press now regularly exhorted.[89] These campaigns cast label advocacy not just as promotion of union-made products but that of local products, too, especially those made in Seattle. The "workers' money power" of 1919 became "Northwest Dollars" to be spent on behalf of local, albeit unionized, firms. The AFL leadership presented these campaigns in part as an aid to the selection of union-made goods. Because all Seattle cigarmakers were unionized, for example, any cigar produced in Seattle could be guaranteed to be "fair". More often, though, the unions promoted local products in order to expand employment for their members and to deliver on their promise to help unionized employers reach local-market consumers. Seattle's District Council of Carpenters demanded that Rhodes department store buy fixtures for its new store not from a Portland, Oregon, firm, as planned, but from local manufacturers. Seattle's metal trades unions as well as the label trades engaged in these campaigns. The boilermakers, for example, protested when the city awarded the contract for a new seventeen-mile pipeline to a firm from California. The Metal Trades Council in 1926 "went on record favoring the construction of Seattle's eighty new street cars in Seattle, by Seattle people."[90] While local-products campaigns could, as in these cases, be cast in a somewhat oppositional mode, in general, and in the hands of the new leadership, they embedded the labor movement once again in cooperative activities with the city's employers. The model inherent in such campaigns was one of local prosperity, in which the local economic pie would expand to the benefit of both labor and capital, which would work together for ever-enhanced mutual benefit. Local-products campaigns suggested that a city or regional identity transcend that of class. They allied Seattle workers with their employers against the unorganized and even organized mass of workers outside the city, whose interests, now, opposed those of Seattle's workers. Local-products campaigns, in sum, followed logically from label unionism in the local-market sector of the economy. They contrasted almost diametrically with the wartime strategies of mass-market industrial unions in the metal trades, in which success depended structurally upon solidarity with other workers nationwide and even internationally. Out of the structural imperatives of each approach emerged concomitant philosophies about the relationship between labor and capital and about the place of organized labor in the community and its future.[91]

The Seattle AFL's new relationship to the Bon Marche symbolized nicely its new posture, and that of the employers. After the Central Labor Council lifted its boycott in 1922, the local AFL and the Bon Marche moved swiftly to reconciliation. By June the unions had replaced the 1920 "Bible in Window Condemning Bon Marche" with an immense cake constructed by the bakers' union in anticipation of its annual ball. Advertising dollars flowed once again from the Bon Marche to the labor press. At mid-decade the Bon Marche appeared on the list of "friends of organized labor" who had assisted in the publication of a special Labor Day issue of the *Labor News*. When the musicians asked the store to stop hiring scab musicians to play at functions of its company union, the store's management complied.[92]

In 1929 the Bon Marche erected itself yet another, still more lavish establishment downtown at 4th and Pine, in which it resides today. Union labor raised its walls, installed its locally union-made fixtures, cut its customers' locks, and served its meals (though it did not sell the goods). Store officials pledged that "whenever possible" they would give preference to local manufacturers in selecting goods.[93] When the store opened, the *Labor News* greeted it with a page-one article accompanying a cover photo captioned "Beautiful New Home of Bon Marche."[94] The store reciprocated with a series of three-column advertisements culminating in a huge headline (complete with a sketch of noble white male workers standing proudly before the glistening new store) that summed up far more than its author intended: "The New Bon Marche. A Monument to Seattle LABOR."[95] The edifice that had once so fully symbolized the class enemy, in other words, now symbolized the labor movement itself.

Conclusion

The "real trades unionism" that retail clerk Louis Nash had heralded turned out to be shaped, above all, by the logic of business unionism in the local-market sector. Where a mulitiplicity of small firms competed ruthlessly with one another, as in construction, local transportation, and food service, the closed shop could bring a measure of stability to employer and union alike. Standardized wages and, in the case of the teamsters, prices as well meant to employers a respite from cutthroat competition; to the unions, a shelter from employers' efforts to cut costs by slashing wages. Much of the local-market sector was also characterized by small firm size and low barriers to entry. In retail meat sales, barbering, restaurants, and building contracting, this meant a fluidity between employer and employee, as wage earners imagined themselves becoming employers one day. At the same time, they worked alongside employers who shared many of the same concerns over hours of work or sanitary conditions. That same context also meant that striking could be ineffectual, because the owner could cover operations himself or herself. All these factors offered powerful incentives to labor–management cooperation and label unionism. Promotion of the union label institutionalized the new harmony, as it offered a way to politicize consumption to the benefit of employer and union alike.[96]

At the same time, alternative voices that might have suggested other paths to working-class advancement had been silenced. That silence was crucial to the nature of the Seattle labor movement in the second half of the decade. Now, unionists imagined the purpose of politicized consumption in sharply narrowed terms. Unions in transportation, construction, skilled service work, and printing used the union label and their collective power to achieve union recognition and a measure of economic security for their members. But they only rarely looked beyond that. The future they envisioned was one more or less like the present. They had made their peace with capitalism. Far in the distant past (or deep in the plots of communist subversives) lay the vision of ever-advancing powers and dreams of the "workers' state."

9

Label unionism

THE LEADERS OF SEATTLE'S AFL envisioned their movement as a finely tuned machine that would deliver working-class shoppers to the city's unionized employers: On command, the dollars of rank-and-file union members and their families would flow into the cash registers of sanctified employers. Label unionism thus embodied more than just a relationship between union and employers; it structured new relationships between leadership and the rank and file. The leaders faced two contradictory tasks: persuading individual workers to buy labeled goods, and ensuring those same workers' docile acquiescence to their command.

There was the catch. Like the women who failed to respond to the Bon Marche boycott in 1920, rank-and-file workers and their families in the second half of the decade were not so easily handed over to the chosen pro-union employer or to their union officials. Identifying and explaining their response highlights the state of the Seattle AFL movement by the end of the decade. The movement had traveled a long distance from the cooperatives of 1919 and the Bon Marche boycott of 1920, and much of the explanation for the rank and file's lack of enthusiasm for the label lies in that transformation. Yet many of the reasons for the label's limited appeal had been just as entrenched in 1919 as in 1929. Race and gender exclusion constrained the movement's ability to politicize consumption at both moments. Efforts had been made to transcend those limits after the war, but by the decade's end any gains had largely been erased. Solidarity disintegrated further as craft unionism reigned triumphant. Label unionism brought more limitations to the movement as part of a broad process of professionalization that made the rank and file almost superfluous. Practically their only function was to pay their dues, observe union regulations, and spend their dollars as directed. Seattle's workers figured this out, and stayed home.

Buying union?

The Seattle AFL leadership's efforts to organize the shopping habits of union families began as part of a national-level AFL label campaign in

1925. The AFL's Union Label Trades Department sponsored a seven-month-long campaign that year which produced impressive-sounding numbers: Unions in 30 states held 591 meetings that an estimated 479,000 workers attended. In Seattle, local officials from the label trades began meeting weekly in early 1925 as a "House and Shop Card Council" within the Central Labor Council. At midyear, representatives from the most heavily label-dependent locals proposed the formation of a new citywide body, the Trade Union Promotional League. They got the idea from E. J. Helck, a tobacco-company agent who traveled across the country in 1925 promoting such leagues, aided by missives from the Union Label Trades Department. Seattle locals outside the label trades, though, lacked enthusiasm for the league idea and contributed only marginal funding for it. Undaunted, the label trades, whose delegates numerically controlled the Central Labor Council by this point, responded by voting in a mandatory per capita tax on all locals belonging to the council. That act institutionalized the power of the label-using trades to control the resources of the citywide movement. Not only in the leadership's theories, but in practice, "trade union promotion" became "label and shop card promotion." Moreover, a mere two years after the fight with Gompers the Seattle Central Labor Council's program was now identical to that of the national-level AFL.[1]

The Seattle Trade Union Promotional League's goal was to marshal the dollars of union members on behalf of the AFL. "The Trade Union Promotional League . . . presumes to influence the workers to support their friends," one member put it.[2] Throughout the second half of the decade the Trade Union Promotional League sponsored rallies, dances, speeches, and label promotions in the labor press. It placed a monthly "Label Guide" in the Seattle-based *Washington State Labor News* listing all unionized goods and services in the city, ran annual exhibits at the state fair in Puyallup, and stocked a permanent union label display at the Labor Temple. Organizers placed special hopes on community meetings in Seattle's white working-class neighborhoods in 1925 and 1926. These meetings presented the usual suspects of the mid-1920s local AFL leadership. At an October 1925 meeting, for example, speakers included officers of the laundry and dye wagon drivers, bakers, and butchers (the ubiquitous Joe Hoffman) and national organizer Hugh J. Glover of the United Hatters' Union. League members distributed pledge forms on which the signer promised to "do all that is possible to advance the use of the union label."[3] These events all combined general speeches on the virtues of the labor movement with specific exhortations to observe the label and card.[4]

The Trade Union Promotional League (TUPL) also expanded the movement's use of the mass media. As in 1919, the unions turned to film, this time in coordination with national-level AFL efforts. In 1925 the league sponsored a screening of "His Brother's Keeper," a pro-label film produced by the International Typographical Union. The next year it screened the five-reel AFL-produced film "Labor's Reward." As did AFL unions in Chicago and Los Angeles, the league experimented with pro-labor shows on local radio. A weekly TUPL program initiated in 1927 interspersed music ("Harp, vocal, and whistling numbers") with short hortatory speeches on behalf of organized labor and its products. By 1928 the TUPL had expanded its radio programs to three fifteen-minute slots a week.[5]

As with the Bon Marche boycott, it is difficult to assess the response of rank-and-file workers to these constant exhortations to shop union. But a range of evidence indicates the general pattern of responses. To begin with, label and shop-card promotion could not have been completely ineffective in persuading rank-and-file workers and their families to shop union or it would have died out as a tactic. More substantively, numerous examples of employers' efforts to counterfeit union labels indicate some level of demand for labeled products. In 1919 Seattle union members caught both non-union candy makers and tailors falsifying union labels, which could be authorized only by the unions. Two years later, members of Musicians' Local #76, playing at a unionized dance, discovered that a handbill for the event carried a falsified label from the Allied Printing Trades Council.[6] Sometimes these "fake" labels were actually the insignia of employers' associations. In 1925 Charles Ferries of the butchers charged that non-union meat markets were "deluding" housewives by pointing to the Master Butchers' Association card in their stores and insisting, "See, here's our union card."[7] All these instances suggest that some employers did believe that carrying the label or shop card would help their sales.[8]

Throughout the decade individual locals reported to the Central Labor Council that consumer pressure from unionists had aided their causes. In August 1921, for example, the garment workers "thank[ed] members of organized labor for their assistance," concluding that "the demand for the label has made it possible to sign up the Western Dry Goods Co."[9] In May 1925 they interpreted brisk sales as "an indication that there has been considerable demand for the label."[10] The streetcar men and butchers repeatedly thanked organized labor for their help in demanding the button and shop card.[11]

But just as often locals complained of the inadequate support other unionists had lent their cause. The same garment local wrote accusingly in a 1923 letter to all Seattle locals that despite the "commendable spirit" of their employers, "the complaint is registered by these employers that unionists, instead of encouraging [high wage] policies by loyally demanding union label products, are spending their money . . . for the purchase of inferior goods made under non-union or sweat-shop conditions."[12] The laundry workers similarly charged that they were "[f]inding it difficult to hold wage scale on account of lack of patronage of union laundries by unionists."[13] Observers agreed that the problem was not confined to any particular trade. "One of the greatest problems that the trade union movement has to meet is the indifference of members of the movement to demanding the union label, the union card," granted TUPL organizer Robert Harlin at the onset of the 1925 campaign.[14] The Women's Card and Label League agreed: "[T]he local movement is extremely lax in the matter of demanding the label."[15]

Label promoters who sought to quantify label observance found the same indifference. "We have watched several scab [meat] markets and found that union men patronize them," one label activist told the boilermakers' union in 1919.[16] *Musicland*, the newsletter of Musicians' Local #76, reported five years later the boast of a non-union meat seller that 75 percent of his trade came from trade unionists.[17] A 1925 survey of Seattle retailers "did not find them averse to carrying union made goods, but . . . some of the merchants did point out that there was an apparent laxity on the part of the members of organized labor in calling for these goods," reported the TUPL's Robert Harlin.[18] Perhaps most revealing was the story Harlin recounted a year later of a representative of the United Hatters' international union, who had spoken to the Seattle meeting of a local whose international "spends thousands of dollars in advertising its union label." While waiting in the anteroom to be called into the meeting for his speech, the visitor checked twenty to thirty hats hanging there. None carried the label. Harlin refused to reveal the name of the organization because "the same experience could have been had with any of them."[19]

The minutes of Musicians' Local #76 offer a rare glimpse into individual workers' decisions to ignore the label. The local regularly charged its members with violation of union precepts in spending their money. In June 1921 it called up member A. P. Adams on the charge of patronizing an "unfair" streetcar. Adams admitted his guilt. "On question if he had a good reason for his action he stated that he wanted to get to the University and he did not intend to wait until a union machine came along as a matter of fact he was tired and got into a machine to rest up, he did not look to see if it was union or non union," the minutes recount. Adams expressed no regrets. "He was not going to ask the Master Driver which was a union machine and that was the way he felt about it." Charged with the same offense, another member "stated he was in a hurry and could not wait for a union machine. He was asked if he had done this before and stated yes right along."[20]

Many Seattle merchants asserted that they spurned labeled goods because working people did not buy them. When *Union Record* representatives called on Ernst Hardware in 1922, "calling attention to the big union trade they have," Ernst responded, "We should worry about your paper, which we don't like, your people come in here and spend their money

anyhow."[21] In 1928 new cut-rate barber shops boasted that they did not
need to recognize the barbers' union because they already enjoyed union
patronage.[22] The *Washington State Labor News* admitted the breadth of
the problem: "A complaint often made to the representatives of labor unions
by union manufacturers and merchants is that it means but little to their
business to recognize and deal with unions."[23] "The only demand for union-
made goods is before they are placed in stock by the merchants," summed
up John Hayes, president of the AFL's union label department.[24]

Initially organizers of the 1924–25 pro-label campaign claimed a heightened observance of the label and card as a result of their efforts. One
investigation showed "a marked increase in demands for the label ... by
the retail stores."[25] The 1926 state federation yearbook noted that the
TUPL had produced "great progress," with "a much greater demand for
the label being reported by many retail stores."[26] But label promoters' reports
swiftly receded thereafter into pre- and early-TUPL observations of the
sorry state of union shopping. The TUPL's label guide in June 1928 lamented the "apathetic condition" of label observance.[27] An article the next
year referred to "the indifference of many workers" toward the label.[28]

Seattle workers' sluggish interest in buying union reflected national patterns in the 1920s. Albert Helbing, who studied the AFL's Union Label
Trades Department in 1931, found that after rosy reports of growing
demand for the label in the period 1909–12, by the 1920s the department's secretary-treasurer "reported the usual yearly complaint that most
union men were not spending their money on union label products." In
1923 the secretary entitled his report "The Apathy of Union Members."[29]
Louis Lorwin found label observance impossible to quantify but noted that
even manufacturers who were eligible to print the union label on their
products often failed to do so.[30]

The housewife must be sold on unionism

Many factors explain why organized workers and their families did not
"look for the union label." One set lay in the nature of union-labeled
goods and services themselves. First, shoppers did not buy union label
garments "because such inferior products can at times, possibly be purchased for a few cents less," the Central Labor Council acknowledged in
a 1923 letter to its constituent locals.[31] A *Union Record* reporter agreed:
"It is hard to convince a worker to pay a little more money for goods in
a union store, when he can buy them cheaper in the non-union stores."[32]
By the end of the decade label promoters began openly to acknowledge
higher prices as a problem, in order to argue that price shouldn't be one's
only consideration. We all know the phrase "penny wise, pound foolish,"
Gertrude Ledwich reminded her readers in a 1928 article in the *Labor
News*.[33]

Not all goods and services a worker might want to purchase came with a union label or card attached. The availability of a particular labeled commodity depended upon the strength and strategies of the labor movement in that given industry. Union label cars, for example, did not exist in the 1920s because the auto industry was not organized at the time. Even if union-made goods of a particular sort did exist, the loyal shopper might have to restrict sharply his or her selection to ensure a label. The General Manufacturing Company of Seattle pointed out to prospective buyers that its phonograph was the only one in the whole United States to carry a union label.[34] Its union-labeled phonograph, however, might not have been the equivalent in quality of a "scab" phonograph. Contemporary observers noted that labeled goods or services could be of inferior quality. Combined with price, inferior quality helps explain why frequency of purchase was one of the key variables in the willingness (or not) of workers to buy a union-labeled product. When it came to big-ticket, infrequent purchases such as stoves, workers were least likely to respect the label, because the stakes were higher.[35]

The distribution of union-made goods narrowed their availability further. "Storekeepers do not make any efforts to push such articles and often they are not available even if the customer insists," Louis Lorwin found in a national study.[36] The president of the Union Label Trades Department conceded in 1919: "[I]t is not an exaggeration to say that there are very few localities in the jurisdiction of the American Federation of Labor where it is possible for a man to successfully conduct a business of any character if he handles nothing but goods bearing the union label."[37] New developments in marketing practices in the 1920s further restricted the availability of labeled goods. Chain stores claimed an increasing share of dry goods and food dollars and proved unwilling to carry union-made goods. Despite the entreaties of the bakers' international the Atlantic and Pacific (A & P) chain, for example, refused to carry union-made bread.[38]

These restrictions on availability meant that even individual workers who wanted to look for the union label had to do some hard looking. They had to spend more time and use more car fare or gas to go on longer trips to find union-made shoes or suspenders or scissors that might not even exist. Providers displaying the union shop card, including the barbers, butchers, and retail clerks, observed earlier closing hours than did non-union shops. Label promoters granted that accessibility played a significant role in luring workers from the fold of pro-union spending. Unionists might "carelessly" enter scab theaters "located in parts of the city that make them easily accessible," acknowledged the *Labor News*.[39] Label promoters displayed little patience, however, with unionists' pleas that labeled goods and services took more than a little work to track down. Such efforts, the promoters maintained, were part and parcel of a loyal unionist's responsibility. "The only way to get a union label is to hunt for that union label like you would hunt for a job," dismissed John J. Manning of the AFL.[40]

Powerful allures were simultaneously at work to attract union members and their families to non-union goods and services. By the 1920s corporate-level marketers mustered new, glittering tactics to sell their products. The Bon Marche serves as a good example. Such "palaces of consumption" offered a richly varied array of goods and services in a setting designed to suggest glamour, self-fulfillment, and the illusion of ascendance of the class ladder.[41] A very few of those goods and services could be purchased with union label affixed. But at no point did the union shop card grace the store's fancy window displays. Working-class shoppers flocked to the Bon Marche nonetheless. Union leaders conceded in 1920 that they couldn't stop women from shopping at Seattle's department stores – they could hope only to divert them from one to another.[42] Chain stores, department stores, and products with national markets all poured vast sums of money into slick mass-market advertising campaigns in the 1920s. The Bon Marche's full-page advertising displays in the *Union Record* offer only one small example. While the effect of such advertising remains under sharp debate among historians and sociologists, Seattle workers surely felt the pull of the promises mass-market advertising held before them of sexy womanhood, tough manhood, and individualized self-fulfillment. Next to these glamours, union-labeled overalls and the only union-made phonograph in the country might seem puny and drab indeed. The saturation campaign through which the AFL leadership sought to imbue organized workers with loyalty to the union label could mount only weak competition to the highly capitalized advertising campaigns of corporate producers and distributors such as the A & P, Bon Marche, or RCA Victor. The AFL's insistence on selection of local products in the late 1920s would only have limited still further its ability to compete with national-market advertising.[43]

When label promoters in Seattle complained that "unionists" failed to ask for the union label, they usually referred to both union members and the women of their families. Numerous complaints and national surveys, though, charged that the worst culprits were women. "It would be difficult to name a single article ordinarily purchased by women in which there is a strong demand for label goods," Ernest Spedden found in his 1910 national survey.[44] There were women's commodities, and men's commodities, and when women purchased the object or service the label had little effect. The broommakers had difficulty pushing their label because brooms sold to women, for example. The boot and shoe workers found that the men bought labeled shoes, but women didn't. Similarly, the garment workers' label sold well nationally on men's clothing, but not on women's. In retail meat sales, men might buy meat in a union shop, but women were far more difficult to convince. These gender dynamics mattered especially because women did more shopping than did men. Observers usually estimated women's share of their family's shopping at 80 to 90 percent.[45] While men proved also reluctant to shop union, in dollar totals women's still greater reluctance mattered four times as much.[46]

This situation produced discussions that replicated those conducted during the Bon Marche boycott. Label promoters explicitly talked about women's importance as shoppers. "The American housewife is the purchasing agent of the home. It is her privilege and duty to spend the wages earned by her husband in the fields of union endeavor, and to withhold her patronage from unfriendly institutions," the Trade Union Promotional League observed.[47] Male leaders once again acknowledged the task of reaching women. The typographers, for example, wrote the Central Labor Council in 1923 to request that "union men educate their wives to ask for [the] union label."[48] *Musicland* chimed in: "Persistent consistency will win. 80 percent of the shopping is being done by women. Talk it over with the wife."[49]

But women were no more easily convinced of the desirability of pro-union shopping in 1927 than they had been in 1920, perhaps even less. For every paean to woman's shopping bag there was an admission of the impossibility of influencing her choice of what to put in it. "Even good union men find it hard to get their wives interested in asking for union made goods," a man wrote to Ruth Ridgeway's column in 1920.[50] The Central Labor Council agreed in 1928, reporting with a slight hint of despair: "It is up to each member to *try* and educate his own immediate family upon the value of patronizing the shop card and label."[51] Women throughout the country agreed with their Seattle sisters. "The women are notoriously hard to win over to the cause," one scholar concluded.[52] The strength of women's resistance can be measured in the confession by *Musicland*'s editor, in a 1923 editorial entitled "Where Does Your Wife Spend Your Money, Mr. Union Man?" that it had taken him eleven years to convince his wife of the validity of union shopping.[53] If this were the case with the wife of a staunch devotee of the label at the leadership level, we can imagine the recalcitrance of the wife of an average rank-and-file member.

Union label shopping, like boycott observance, made women's work harder. All those extra trips to the store, queries of the clerk as to the status of the establishment, objects turned upside down and inside out in search of the usually absent label – women performed most of those tasks. The AFL's John Manning preached to union workers that they should "hunt for that union label like you would hunt for a job," but to hunt for that label was precisely women's job. Women's assigned task was spending their family's money. They weighed many factors other than just union label status in deciding which goods and services to purchase.

As in their encounter with cooperatives and boycotts, chief among women's concerns was price. Ernest Spedden drew out this point in explaining the difficulty of selling union-made stoves nationwide: "[B]esides calling for a considerable outlay of money," stoves were "generally bought by women who, no doubt, are controlled more by the price than any other consideration."[54] The more expensive union-made stove dropped by the wayside. Seattle labor promoter Gertrude Ledwich complained in 1928, "Wives are not interested in the wage-earners' problems, being blind to all but the size of the paycheck."[55] Housewives, indeed, inhabited what has been called "the other side of the paycheck," where they were responsible for translating wages into goods and services.[56] The union label, shop card, and button were everywhere, potentially, in their daily tasks of managing that arena of family consumption. At the same time, at a practical level unionized goods and services were nowhere – hard to find, more expensive, ugly, and unfashionable. For a Seattle working-class housewife to have placed unionized shopping at the top of her concerns would have taken a supreme level of identification with and commitment to the AFL movement that in the majority of cases did not exist.

Evidence indicates that wives did not look for the union label in large part because they remained alienated from their men's union activities. In 1928 the Central Labor Council's label committee concluded its report with the story of a union man who "up to the present . . . had not patronized the label, as his wife did all the shopping and his belonging to a union had always been a bone of contention in the family." The committee then recounted how the man had finally won his wife over by making her calculate, with pencil in hand, the exact financial benefits that accrued to his family from his union membership. Similar stories appeared elsewhere in label promotion materials and can be summarized as "tips on how to win your wife over" stories. They indicate that union men exercised by no means complete control over their wives, who often held independent opinions. Note, for example, the alternately pleading and commanding tone the editor of *Musicland* recommended to his union brothers: "Don't say you can't. They're human and they're reasonable. . . . Make them see it – show 'em."[57] His choice of words suggests that "showing them" could be quite a task. William Bailey, secretary of the Promotional League, implicitly acknowledged in 1926 the effect feminism might have had on working-class women's compliance with their husbands' demands:

> Union men must be alive to the changing conditions and exigencies of the times, the woman, he helped more than any other group to throw off the shackles that bound her for centuries must be enlisted with him, economically and politically, for since she will no longer be denied, she must be abided and counselled with.[58]

In other words, before she would "buy union" a woman had to "buy" trade unionism, and usually she did not.

Many, perhaps even most, male union members were themselves alienated from the trade-union movement by the mid-1920s. The open shop defeats, collapse of cooperation, and labor capitalist scandals had all damaged individual men's faith in the movement and the efficacy of sacrifice on its behalf. Even in 1919, moreover, men's commitment to shopping union had been limited. Activists in the label trades recounted that year many stories of union men who ignored the label: hundreds who ate at "scab" restaurants in 1919, dozens who bought meat from non-union butcher shops, or the many who purchased milk from cheaper, non-cooperatively owned dairies. The defeats and disillusionments of 1920–24 would have cut deeply into an already shallow level of commitment to unionized shopping.

Two individual stories indicate that alienation from the AFL movement might have prompted leadership-level activists to spurn the union label as well. In June 1923 Charles Doyle, business agent of the Central Labor Council, registered a complaint against Sophie Pugsley, the council's former organizer for women, whose funding had been cut off in 1921 in part because of her affiliation with the left. Pugsley had hired non-union labor to build a new house, Doyle charged. In corroborating this story delegates from the carpenters added that "she had refused to even allow a union contractor to bid on [the job]."[59] It seems plausible that Pugsley was not enamored of the conservative building trades unions, which had brought about her dismissal, and chose not to respect their card. Two years later council president David Levine, of the jewelers' union, accused the barbers' local of buying a signet ring for its retiring secretary at a jewelry store that lacked his union's shop card. The retiring recipient was none other than Phil Pearl, the Socialist barber who had just been driven out of the AFL by the same David Levine, who had once been his closest political associate. "The union jewelry shops were hardly of the class that would warrant the consideration of his organization when making such an important purchase," the barbers' delegate retorted.[60] No equivalent stories of rank-and-file alienation are available. We can imagine, though, innumerable similar stances based on feelings of distrust, anger, or frustration at experiences with organized labor.

The Women's Card and Label League had long been assigned the task of persuading wives to shop union. But by mid-decade its composition and role in the movement had changed dramatically from the expansive, independent, often feminist organization of 1919–20. In 1921 that earlier incarnation had still been very much alive, as the league's most enthusiastic campaign in late spring illustrates. Through it, the members of the Card and Label League sought to create a literal women's space within the trade-union movement, exactly as the cooperative women had constructed their own independent space. When the *Union Record* bought its new building overlooking Elliot Bay and the Olympic Mountains and began renting the extra space to individual locals, "The possibilities of the top floor . . . captured the imagination of the women of the labor movement who have dreamed of a social headquarters," the paper reported.[61] League members here echoed exactly cooperators' concern with homelike qualities. "The wall around the edge is waist high, making it safe even for the children, and we dream of window boxes here filled with flowers and trailing vines that in time will cover the walls and become a riot of color when they bloom." They felt the room "would make a fine, 'homey' living room with a fireplace on one side," windows with a view, "and last but not least a kitchenette" so the women could prepare refreshments for meetings and parties.[62] The members of the Card and Label League, in sum, wanted a room with a view; they envisioned a labor movement with lovely flowers, pleasant for parties, safe for children. That vision also involved concerns with their own labors: The kitchenette would make food preparation for movement functions easier; the waist-high wall meant children couldn't fall into the bay, and women could therefore let them run about unattended; and the space would be one "where the women of organized labor may come for an hour of rest during their shopping tour down town."[63] This time, they reversed the usual gender roles in the movement and asked men to "help your own cause" by helping the women find a place to rest their tired feet.[64]

That campaign turned out to be the independent Card and Label League's swan song, however. By the end of 1921 it had begun to sharply limit its activities. In the fall and during the following winter league members concentrated almost all their energies on support work for the long, disastrous western Washington coal miners' strike and on soliciting donations of shoes, clothes, and food and distributing them to the miners and their families. When the label league emerged from the depression in 1922 and 1923 it became what the men had long sought. Two activities occupied its time, promotion of the label and shop card and the provision of social affairs for the movement, especially parties for the leadership. The league rarely engaged in support work for wage-earning women; its membership narrowed to the wives of male unionists only; and only occasionally did it take a stand on political issues, and those solely in support of campaigns officially sanctioned by the state federation of labor. Mark Litchman, the Communist lawyer, reported that his wife, Sophie, was attempting to bore from within the Card and Label League "but intends shortly to quit for the reason that it is merely a social organization for the Ladies of the labor movement to get together and gossip."[65]

This new league defined its role above all in terms of service to the men's trade unions. "WHAT CAN WE DO FOR YOU?" appeared as its new slogan in 1923.[66] "Most organizations are organized to get better working conditions and higher wages for their members," Gertrude Millson, an active member, noted in 1925; "not so with the league. Our sole aim is to bring about better conditions for all and our individual members have no way of profiting from their membership in the league."[67] Mary Friermood, corresponding secretary, felt the need to insist similarly: "[O]ur members have no way of profiting directly from their membership."[68] Such conscious self-effacement to their men's concerns stood in stark contrast to the women's rest rooms envisioned in 1921, in which women asked men to recognize their own tired feet.[69]

A number of factors converged to produce this new, far more subservient Card and Label League. The league's leadership changed almost completely between 1920 and 1922. It had always drawn most of its constituency from the wives of the AFL movement's leadership. As the movement overall shifted, so too did the league. Before the depression it was composed of women affiliated with the cooperative movement or married to socialist or other radical men, such as Lola Lunn (married to Carl Lunn, the cooperative leader), or Mary Nauman (married to Ben Nauman, a member of Boilermakers' Local #104 and Ault's ally in the swamplands scam). The new league's leaders, by contrast, were the wives of staunch conservatives, such as Gertrude Millson (wife of the cooks' officer Fred Millson) and Maud Doyle (married to Central Labor Council business agent Charles Doyle). A few women such as Minnie Ault, Kate McMahon, and Hattie Titus spanned both periods. But they seem to have shifted rightward along with the league. At the same time, the general narrowing of the Seattle AFL movement's vision and loss of organizational zeal after 1921 must have contributed to the league's constriction of scope.[70]

One final factor must also have contributed to the league's transformation. By late 1925, male trade union leaders had themselves taken over the league's original and core purpose of label and shop-card promotion. The Trade Union Promotional League, its forerunner the House and Shop Card Council, and the Central Labor Council's label committee all supplanted wives' work in promoting union-made products. As men carried label promotion to the center of the AFL movement's overall strategic agenda, they would have pushed non–wage-earning wives out of the independent turf on which they had long found a valued place in the movement. Women were now subordinated to men in precisely the one task they had called their own. The wives were caught in a bind. They had embraced precisely the subservient service role men had prescribed for them, but even there they had become superfluous.

The women did not, apparently, protest this usurpation. By the time of the TUPL's formation in 1925 these wives had defined their own role so completely in term of service that to object would have been inconceivable. "Cooperation is the watchword of the League," they assured in the fall of 1925, this time meaning cooperation between women and men.[71] League members may also have shared their husbands' belief that professionalization was in the best interests of the movement. More practically, the label league's numbers were so reduced by 1925 that they were in no position to offer to shoulder the burden of label promotion themselves.

A 1925 incident illustrates the league women's situation. In March, the *Labor News* reported, the league planned a big dance for the AFL movement and spent a great deal of money on providing music and entertainment. But only a handful attended. "This has a discouraging effect on the membership of the league and makes them feel that their time, energy and money is often wasted." The paper called on other women to attend the next week's league meeting to inject it with new "pep." "They are a real help to the movement and should be supported accordingly."[72] Who was helping whom here? The league had taken on the task of providing social events for the trade union movement, but others in that movement did not necessarily want to attend. The state of the movement was such that even entertainments did not draw out the members. The women were understandably discouraged.[73]

By mid-decade even the wives who sought to be active in the movement found themselves in a narrow space in which to maneuver. Having embraced the men's preferences for their activities, they were left with little room in which to assert their own point of view, or even to contribute in useful ways to the male-defined movement. Its earlier vision lost, its membership evaporating, in November 1929 the Women's Card and Label League disbanded.[74]

The other fellow's label

We can gain further insight into the indifference of Seattle rank-and-file workers, female and male alike, to the union label by turning the question on its head and asking why they should have sought the label. The answer returns us to a central issue in the story of the Seattle AFL movement: solidarity. Solidarity depended upon an understanding of one's class position in collective terms, and a faith that union label observance would serve those collective interests. The many Seattle working people who, even on occasion, spent by union precepts acted upon such a faith. They were deciding that it was worth their time, effort, and money to invest in the collective advancement to which union label observance might contribute. Such commitments could override the counterincentives stacked against label shopping.[75]

In the mid- and late-1920s Seattle AFL, solidarity was not entirely dead. The leaders of many locals watched out for one another's interests somewhat and from time to time engaged in acts of intertrade solidarity. In June 1928, for example, the musician's union refused to supply a dance promoter with union musicians if his advertisements did not carry the typographers' union label.[76] The printers, musicians, carpenters, streetcar employees, waitresses, and many other locals declared fines on members found purchasing non-union products or services produced by trades other than their own. Organized workers also sought tools carrying the union label. Carpenters, for example, insisted on union-made saws, barbers on union-made barber chairs, butchers on union-label aprons.[77] Solidarity could also be structurally embedded in a given trade's use of the label. The cooks could not place the shop card in a restaurant if the waitresses and waiters at the establishment were not also recognized. The shop card enforced a degree of solidarity between the skilled, male cooks and the less skilled female waitresses, to the waitresses' benefit. In other trades, though, male workers proved quick to reject the possibilities for solidarity structured into label promotion. The retail clerks, for example, refused to encourage shoppers to purchase union-label goods.[78]

But more often the institutionalized fragmentation inherent in craft unionism ate away at label solidarity. Since 1905 the Industrial Workers of the World (IWW) had called for a "universal label," one single label common to all unions that would do away with craft distinctions. AFL affiliates at the local and regional levels carried similar proposals for a universal AFL label to the federation's annual convention repeatedly during the first three decades of the century. But efforts to institute the universal label always foundered on the sacred principle of trade autonomy on which the AFL had been built. The internationals' officers were not interested in working for another union's label, only for their own. The AFL's Label Trades Department ran into the same problem: While the internationals were all for general, nationwide promotion of the union label in principle, when it came time to coughing up dues to the Label Trades Department they often defaulted. They preferred to spend the money promoting the labels or cards of their individual trades.[79]

Seattle's AFL unions in the postdepression 1920s replicated that fragmentation locally. The movement contracted in smaller and smaller circles, as individual trades increasingly turned to their own concerns. Not only did the ascendance of label promotion split off the metal trades and dock workers from the rest of the movement, but increasingly label promotion itself was fragmented by trade. Label promoters began to complain that none of the city's individual trades cared much about the labels of any trades other than their own. Each trade just wanted to make sure that those other unionists observed their own label. As a 1924 poem in the *Labor News* needled:

> Each member of a Union thinks
> His Label is o.k.
> They agitate for it and sound
> Its praises night and day.
> The other fellow's Label, though,
> Too often they forget,

But makes an awful howl
When theirs is overlooked, you bet.[80]

Visiting the locals for the Trade Union Promotional League in 1928, secretary William Bailey entitled his pro-label speeches "The Other Fellow's Problem."[81]

Discussions of the "problem" indicate that unionists' failure to observe other trades' labels only made visible a larger problem of lack of solidarity. In her column Gertrude Ledwich in 1928 pleaded with union members and their wives to help out not just their own unions but others' as well.[82] Such forced pleas for solidarity had been rare in 1919. Contrast, for example, these small, scaled-down calls for solidarity with the great debates on the meaning of solidarity on the eve of the general strike. But solidarity had not entirely evaporated by the late 1920s. Rather, the minutes of the locals indicate that it ran in a very narrow circle, as specific locals traded solidarity in a self-consciously self-interested manner. H. G. Adam, the Australian trade unionist who visited in 1927, found this to be true throughout the country. He was startled by the U.S. labor movement's lack of solidarity.

> Unionism in America is not a political creed or a social movement; it is the grouping of workers in different trades to obtain practical advantages for their own trade; but no group is anxious that its advantages should be extended to the other.[83]

Smack in the middle of the tension between solidarity and label promotion lay the craft unions' eternal problem of jurisdiction. Seattle's industrial-unionist *Forge* wisecracked about this in 1919: "When a worker who is striking because of a jurisdictional dispute reaches into the pocket of a coat that bears no union label and pulls out three different kinds of union cards, none of them printed on union made paper, that proves he is a good union man, doesn't it?"[84] The problem was that individual unions wanted to be able to name a firm "fair" without waiting for other workers at the same firm, represented by other unions, to achieve recognition. It was the same tension that had sapped the Bon Marche boycott.[85] Matters got stickier when more than one union claimed jurisdiction over a given establishment or group of workers. In many cases Seattle locals declared "unfair" the products or services of unionized firms that in fact carried the union label or card, but of an international other than their own. In 1929, for example, Seattle's electrical engineers and stationary engineers got into a jurisdictional dispute over which union could claim the workers at the heating plants of a group of theaters. At the same time, Musicians' Local #76 had declared the theaters fair to their own local. The white musicians convinced the Central Labor Council to order the dissenting engineers to stop distributing leaflets declaring the theaters "unfair." Locals could also fling "unfair" charges in the course of disputes within the same international.

When the International Longshoremen's Association revoked the charter of Local #38–12 after its unsanctioned 1921 strike and chartered a new local, #38–16, in its place, Local #38–12 asked the Seattle Central Labor Council to put #38–16 on the "unfair" list. Other jurisdictional fights dragged the label into national-level rivalries between competing internationals. In one such fray Seattle's William Short warned pro-union shoppers in 1926 not to be deceived by the Amalgamated Clothing Workers' label. It was not, he asserted, a union label. The highest level of such rivalry was that between the AFL and the IWW. Both refused to recognize each others' labels. In Seattle, where AFL–IWW tensions ran especially high, representatives of each camp picketed restaurants bearing the other's card throughout the 1920s. All these activities created a confusing and often contradictory map of unionized goods and services that must have been nearly impossible to decode for even the most loyal AFL member, who had to keep track of no less than fifty-seven different cards and labels. To the average union member this swirl of messages would have sent a powerful message as well: Solidarity is not universal, let alone forever.[86]

The teamsters had their own solution to the problem of jurisdiction and solidarity. They simply took over other locals, obviating the need to work in cooperation with them. Carl Westine, their historian, characterized Seattle's teamsters as an example of "predatory unionism."[87] After consolidating their control over local transportation, the teamsters moved in on nontransportation workers in the industries for which they drove trucks. Chief among these was the laundry industry. By the end of the decade the "Beck gang" had taken over the Mutual Laundry and used it to control the 1,400-member laundry workers' union and thus the entire laundry trade. In the same years the teamsters moved in on inside workers in the city's dairies. When it came to the bakery salesmen, the teamsters had a tougher job. Unlike the laundry or dairy workers, the bakery workers were skilled white men with a long-established, powerful international to back them up. It took a jurisdictional fracas lasting nearly the entire decade, and rulings all the way up to the AFL Executive Board, for the Seattle teamsters to finally achieve their claim to the bakery salesmen. In each of these cases, the Seattle teamsters' behavior presaged their international's organizing style in the decades to follow, as they built from a base of transportation workers into a vast network of dues-paying inside workers, most prominently in canneries, for the interests of whom the international cared little. Such institutionalized co-subservience was anything but solidarity.[88]

White solidarity?

Craft unionism was not the only culprit. Racism continued to slice off African-, Japanese-, and Chinese-American workers from the conceived "solidarity" on which label promotion necessarily rested. Yet it is too easy simply to say racial distinctions undermined union label promotion, for within the white sector of the working class racial exclusion simultaneously strengthened solidarity as well.

In 1921–22 white barbers, butchers, and shoe repairers had chosen to adapt to the growth of the Japanese-American service sector by recognizing Japanese-American unions. Seattle's culinary locals, though, chose the opposite path. Their response was to work harder at exclusion, and it was they who most vigorously carried racial politics into the center of label promotion in the Seattle AFL. Seattle's restaurant workers had built their unions since the turn of the century by actively excluding workers of Asian descent. In 1915 the Hotel and Restaurant Employees and Bartenders International Union officially banned all "Orientals" from membership. During the 1920s Alice Lord of the Seattle waitresses continued to agitate actively within the international on behalf of racial exclusion, protesting, for example, the proposed admission of Asian-American workers who were U.S. citizens. Lobbying the Washington state legislature as well, she condemned "Japanese business aggression in the past 15 years"[89] and proclaimed that "the American workmen could not compete with the Jap and maintain American standards."[90]

The Japanese-American presence in the Seattle restaurant industry grew in the war and postwar years. Restaurants owned by Japanese-Americans, serving either western-style or Japanese food, numbered seventy-three in 1920. White restaurant owners also proved eager to hire Japanese- and Chinese-American workers. From their point of view Asian-American workers were cheaper, more amenable to command, and more willing than whites to work longer hours with fewer holidays. They were easier to obtain and less likely to quit. This was in part because workers of Asian descent lacked the collective power that white workers had in their unions. Those same white exclusionary unions made it hard for Japanese-American workers to find other jobs, which then forced them to accept undesirable terms of employment.[91]

Seattle's Japanese-American restaurant laborers were well aware of racial disparities in the terms of their employment. Fifty years later Chuichi Sunohara remembered that Japanese-American workers had received only half or two-thirds the wages of whites performing the same job. Whites worked only eight hours; Japanese-Americans worked ten or eleven.[92] "We had no holidays all year long," recalled Kyutaro Fukui. "Meanwhile the white employees seemed to have one day off a week."[93] Tohachi Suzuki did not have a single day off from his dishwashing job for seven years and worked from five in the morning until nine at night.[94] Japanese-American restaurant workers had to put up with racial epithets as well. Although they were without union protection, Japanese-American workers nonetheless engaged in informal collective actions against their employers. In 1928 Suzuki and fifteen Japanese-Americans who worked at the Libby Cafe got fed up with their low salaries, and when one day the manager called them "Goddam Japs," Suzuki's brother walked out in protest. Because the brother was hard to replace, the manager relented, promising not to use the term "Japs" in the future and agreeing to raise the salaries of all the Japanese-American workers.[95]

Rather than embrace these restaurant workers as union members, the white culinary unions instead employed boycotts and the union shop card to force them out of their jobs. In 1919, for example, the waiters pronounced two delicatessans unfair "because of Jap cooks."[96] They regularly used the Central Labor Council's "unfair" list to force employers to fire Asian-American workers and then hire whites in their places. The culinary unions put Joe Dizard's Card Room and Joe Wood's Lunch Counter onto the list in 1926 after the union's officers had "tried time after time to induce the proprietors to place white help in the kitchen, without avail."[97] For white restaurant workers, then, the purpose of the union shop card was largely to keep out Asian-Americans.[98]

On the question of African-American restaurant employees the culinary unions presented a less united front. At a national level, the hotel and restaurant employees' international left racial policy up to its locals, who were free to exclude, include, or sponsor separate locals of African-American workers. The responses of Seattle's three locals can be attributed in part to their divergent positions in the industry. The waitresses continued to exclude African-American members. Waitress employment boomed during the 1920s, at the same time as employers increasingly replaced African-American women with whites in an effort to please white customers. As a result, the waitresses should have been able to enforce exclusion without great effort or sacrifice. The waiters, by contrast, were more stable in the 1920s in total numbers. They lost ground to waitresses, as hotel employment, the traditional turf of male waiters, gave way to new mass cafeterias and restaurants that preferred to hire women. We can speculate that the less powerful waiters' union lacked the strength actively to exclude from the industry African-American waiters, who counted one in five Seattle waiters in 1920. White cooks, by contrast, boasted a strong union of skilled workers that faced competition from non-union African-American cooks. In 1924 white cooks initiated the formation of an all–African-American cooks' local that sent delegates to the Central Labor Council but then evidently disappeared, leaving no information as to its composition or position in the movement. However much their approaches diverged, the culinary unions never used the union shop card or boycott to force out African-Americans. They may not have felt threatened by African-American restaurant workers, whose numbers were not on the increase, and who were not accompanied by a growing sector of African-American–owned restaurants, as were Japanese-Americans.[99]

For the culinary workers, then, the union shop was a white shop, more specifically a white, anti-Asian shop. The front of their international's magazine summed up the meaning of its union button tidily: "Skilled, Well-paid Bartenders and Culinary Workers Wear Them. Chinks, Japs and Incompetent Labor Don't."[100] Not only was "union" thus actively equated with "white," but the converse as well: "Nonwhite" functioned as an easily accessible code for "non-union." A Japanese-American–owned restaurant was by definition a "scab" restaurant.

Many of Seattle's exclusionary craft unions similarly used race to identify non-union goods and services. A 1920 advertisement in the *Union Record* that listed "SCAB BREAD," for example, named four white-owned non-union firms by their individual names, plus "All Jap Groceries" as scab.[101] "All white laundries now fair," Dave Beck reported in 1926.[102] These campaigns asked rank-and-file union members to identify with a specific form of white racial consciousness and then carry it with them every time they spent a dollar. "There are a number of good, fair eating places in this vicinity, displaying the union card and button, employing Americans; bear this in mind when looking for a place to eat," cautioned Pauline Newman of the culinary crafts' joint board in 1925, reporting on two Seattle cafes that employed Asian-American kitchen workers.[103] In 1923 the musicians printed a list of sixteen "unfair" restaurants for the use of "unionists, their friends and all others who believe in the principles of organized labor and the American standard of living."[104] Both their "American standard of living" and Newman's "Americans" served as an easily understood code for "white," in contradistinction to "low Asiatic living standards." The use of the shop card, label, and boycott to exclude Asian-Americans, in sum, infused class identity with white racial identity. Seattle's white workers employed anti-Asian consumer campaigns precisely to reinforce "class" solidarity within their subsector of the working class. As David Roediger has argued, racism served as "a pole around which white workers' consciousness takes shape."[105]

The full effect of these campaigns on the consciousness and shopping choices of rank-and-file workers remains unclear. Race-based label campaigns may have helped solidify white working-class solidarity. Many AFL locals embedded racial consciousness in their structures of intertrade solidarity. Note, for example, the musicians' willingness to ask members of their own union to help the white culinary workers fight Asian-American advancement. Carpenters' Local #131 likewise placed its internal disciplinary machine at the service of the restaurant unions: "Upon investigation report untrue that carpenters on Busy Bee [job] patronized Jap Cafe, however, would like to have names of any carpenters patronizing unfair places," it reported in July 1929.[106] Throughout the decade the Central Labor Council allowed exclusionary unions to employ its collective "unfair" list in their efforts to force out workers of Japanese and Chinese descent, thus placing the legitimacy and power of the citywide AFL boycott and label promotion machinery at the service of racial exclusion. And the Card and Label League shared in this racial program. Jean Stovel, speaking on behalf of the label league to the Commonwealth Club in 1921, recounted proudly the origins of the union label: "[I]n 1874 in San Francisco several cigar manufacturers tried to import coolie labor, and it was agreed by the workers that boxes must be labeled white to indicate that white hands had made the cigars."[107] Racially identified consumer organizing was both a goal of intertrade solidarity (i.e., forcing out Asian-Americans) and a source of it (unions bonded as workers commonly oppressed by Asian-Americans).[108]

Some workers may not have "bought white," however. Members of the white butchers', barbers', and shoe repairers' locals, all of whose cards hung in shops with both white and Asian-American workers, may have felt uneasy about observing a label, card, or boycott the purpose of which was to exclude Asian-Americans. It seems safe to assume that Japanese-American members of those unions never sought the label except deliberately to avoid it. And white industrial-unionist radicals, whether of early 1920s' leadership stratum or of the rank and file, may have been overtly critical of the exclusionary practices of the culinary workers and other unions and even deliberately patronized firms owned by Japanese-Americans because they rejected racist campaigns as much as they rejected conservative business unionism.

The musicians offer another, different story of the ongoing tensions between solidarity, exclusion, and consumer organizing. African-American musicians were the only group of African-American workers in Seattle in a position to force recognition by a white union. Their situation in many ways paralleled the negotiations between Japanese-American and white unions in the skilled service trades. By World War I African-Americans had established an increasing presence in the provision of popular music in Seattle. The American Federation of Musicians' policy was to recommend separate locals for African-Americans, while allowing for individual African-Americans to join white locals. In 1917 Seattle's white local, #76, had one African-American member, Powell Barnett. Other African-American musicians refused to join, charging that it would be impossible for them to receive a fair shake in the white local. Their numbers were simply too small – fifty or sixty, compared with several hundred white members. In 1921 they chose instead to form their own new separate local, #458.[109] The status of African-American women in Local #458 remains unclear. All officers in the decade were male, though one of five African-American signatories to a key negotiating letter in 1924 was a married woman.[110]

The two separate, racially segregated locals immediately began a tense, conflictual relationship that would persist through the remainder of the decade. Most of Seattle's African-American musicians worked part-time and moved in and out of the trade. Employers would hire them only if they were cheaper than whites or if they acceded to inferior working conditions. Yet African-American musicians, like Japanese-American dishwashers, wanted the same union protection and powers vis-à-vis employers that white union musicians could get. Union recognition would also mean access to the union shop card, and therefore the jobs on which only union members could work. At the same time African-American musicians, we can surmise, did not easily identify with the white AFL movement that had spurned them and other African-American workers for decades.[111]

Their experience after unionization would only have reinforced such suspicions. White musicians wanted African-American musicians organized so that they could not underbid whites. As a result, they initially were all for solidarity with the new local, #458, and even sponsored its formation. Soon, though, the relationship degenerated. After an early round of mutual thank-yous for help in enforcing union standards, each union began to charge the other with betrayal. In May 1921, members of #458 accused white union musicians of "underhanded behavior" in securing engagements over African-Americans. In 1923 white workers successfully forced African-American union members out of their jobs at Gatt's, because, they charged, members of #458 were working below the white union's official scale. In 1925 members of #76 again accused African-American union musicians of taking their places at the Lodge Cafe after trouble broke out with management. White musicians charged that members of #458 worked seven days a week, played alongside non-union musicians, and accepted wages below scale.[112]

In 1924 these tensions erupted in a particularly fierce fight. The white musicians' idea of a solution was to increase their power over the African-American local. Local #458 rarely met, they concluded; its officers were engaged in a fratricidal internal fight, and its members were largely un-informed as to the white unions' work rules, regulations, and wage stand-ards. The whites first persuaded their international to revoke #458's charter. Then, when the international restored the charter as Local #493, the white local got an explicit statement granting #76 supervisory powers over the officers and members of the African-American local. Through the rest of the decade officers of the white local dragged African-American union musicians and their officers before them and put them on disciplinary trial for an array of transgressions. But the situation changed little. Because the white union was not interested in fighting for the rights of #493's members, only in using it to ensure the closed shop, African-American union musicians understandably continued to violate #76's rules. White workers thus de-fined "trade unionism" in their own interest, then yelped when African-American workers defined it in theirs.[113]

The musicians' situation underscores how rocky was any middle ground between inclusion and exclusion. Because the whites were unwilling to grant complete equality and fight for the equal rights of African-American musicians to union protection, a single harmonious interracial union was impossible. The creation of a separate local did not resolve the question in part because it remained unequal, like unions of Japanese-Americans in Seattle's service sector. Sterling Spero and Abram Harris, in their classic study of African-American workers and the labor movement, argued that segregated, subordinate locals "vitiate solidarity." Such locals, they argued, made it difficult to persuade African-American workers of the intentions of white unions.[114]

The white musicians' treatment of Local #458 tainted the label still further. When they sought to revoke #458's charter in 1924, the white musicians asked the Central Labor Council to put employers onto the council's "unfair" list simply because they had hired members of the African-American local. In so doing #76 arrogated to itself the right to determine which shop was a union shop.[115] Again, the union card was a white card, if white unionists so chose. And again, jursidictional fratricide undermined the solidarity on which union shopping depended.[116]

The experience of Filipino immigrants illustrates how very unresolved were questions of exclusion and solidarity in the mid- and late 1920s. By 1924 federal law had cut off Chinese, Japanese, and most European immigration to the United States. In response employers, seeking to replace their ebbing supply of cheap labor, encouraged the immigration of single male workers from the Philippines. By the end of the decade the Filipino immigrant population of Seattle had grown to 1,614, from 458 in 1920. Most worked in canneries or domestic service or migrated to agricultural jobs in the hinterland.[117]

For a brief moment Seattle's AFL unions greeted Filipino-American workers with open arms. In 1925 officials of the Central Labor Council met with a group of Filipino-American cannery workers in the Labor Temple, pledged their whole-hearted support, and published in the *Labor News* stories celebrating a new coastwide organizing drive among Filipino-American cannery workers. Three years later, though, the white leadership completely reversed its stance and threw itself into a vicious local, state, and national campaign against Filipino immigration. "Stop Filipino Horde," screamed one headline in the *Labor News*. Filipinos were an "economic menace," their standard of living threatened "American standards," and they could not be assimilated, AFL unionists charged. The unionists also claimed that Filipino-Americans carried meningitis and were an imminent threat to the public health.[118]

Because of their "morals," moreover, Filipino-American men constituted a "social menace" in the unionists' eyes. Filipino-American men were trapped by this charge. Because the United States barred Filipinas from immigrating, miscegenation laws barred Filipinos from relationships with white women, and homosexuality was condemned, much sexual activity by Filipino immigrant men was by definition illegal and "immoral." AFL activists used this atmosphere to cast Filipino exclusion in the guise of protection of white women. C. O. "Dad" Young, Northwest organizer for the AFL, in a speech at the 1928 state federation of labor convention claimed that his investigation of Filipino-Americans in Yakima, Washington, had unearthed "a moral condition so revolting among the Filipinos that the presence of women delegates prevented his giving the details to the convention." Seattle unionists melded such inflammatory hints with charges that Filipino immigrant men were taking jobs away from white women. In 1929, the Central Labor Council sensationalized the YWCA's replacement of white female elevator operators with Filipino-American men and tried to force the men's removal.[119]

A new tone of general anti-Asian hostility crept into the late 1920s AFL movement. The *Labor News* condemned a Longview, Washington, firm for employing Japanese-American workers, carried approving stories on the anti-Filipino campaign, and implicitly endorsed a federal bill banning "Oriental" labor from ships. The Central Labor Council gladly welcomed representatives of the bookbinders' and cigarmakers' international as they passed through town on anti-Asian lecture circuits. Overall, the story of race relations in the 1920s AFL movement underscores that forward motion on the race question was by no means assured. The unions continued to vacillate between solidarity, negotiation, and exclusion. Usually exclusion won out, in part because it contained an added benefit: Racial solidarity could prompt white workers to "look for the union label" precisely because it was the product of "white hands."[120]

Taking in members by card

A final set of reasons why rank-and-file workers did not shop union lay in the nature of label unionism itself. Dependence upon label promotion set up internal dynamics between leadership and rank and file that vitiated solidarity as surely as did racial exclusion.

After the depression a new wave of professionalization swept the Seattle AFL movement. Paid staff members came to dominate, indulging, in the process, in blatant self-glorification. From 1926 onward the *Washington State Labor News* ran regular articles praising the excellent work done by business agent Tom, local secretary Dick, or organizer Harry. The epitome of this was the cover of the Central Labor Council's special Labor Day edition in 1926. Framing a sketch of "Labor" personified pushing a globe toward "Progress" were glossy photographs of council officers David Levine, John Jepson, Charles Doyle, and J. J. Murray.[121] The predepression movement had certainly had its leaders, but they had never been celebrated self-consciously as such. James Duncan, for example, had been deeply loved and respected, just as Harry Ault had enjoyed tremendous trust and respect before his fall. But neither had been singled out for beatification. Dave Beck, by contrast, exemplified the new leaders of the mid- and late twenties. He believed that union leaders should be professionals, not elected but appointed "by individuals (such as himself) that had the capacity for determining good leadership," as Donald Garnel puts it. "Elections were, therefore, just so much window dressing." Beck believed that "the workers knew what was best for themselves (and that a competent union leader could sense this without having to ask the membership), but they did not know how best to go about achieving their goals."[122] In her memoir of a visit to Seattle, Rose Pesotta, an organizer for the International Ladies' Garment Workers' Union, captured the style of these professionals and their attitude toward the rank and file:

> Union officers, quartered in the Labor Temple, were largely of the type portrayed in the capitalist press – chair-warmers and cigar-smokers. I learned that rank-and-file members were not encouraged to hang around the union offices.[123]

As part of this process the Trade Union Promotional League professionalized cross-trade union label work. The city's business agents, local secretaries, and presidents originally formed the league. A paid male executive secretary performed most of its work. The shift from volunteer to paid labor was thus a gendered one. And the movement's professionalization must have contributed another factor to the Card and Label League's demise. In the late twenties, as the TUPL's activities waned, a new, even more elite professional body, the Board of Business Agents, took responsibility for label promotion. It met in secret weekly sessions to discuss the fight against unfair firms, label campaigns, and the general welfare of the labor movement. Rank-and-file members were not welcome.[124]

The nature of the union label was integral to this process of professionalization. The label focused a given union's attention on convincing an employer to recognize the union, and then, in turn, sign up his or her employees into it. The butchers serve as a good example. Consumers pressured shop owners, who in turn capitulated to the union official; but the rank-and-file butcher worker had little to do with the transaction. Business agent Joe Hoffman, describing his weekly activities to the Central Labor Council, would report that he "put several cards in and took others out."[125] Shop-card promotion thus directed the butchers away from a member-defined, member-run local. It contributed to the union's professionalization and bureaucratization. "A corps of careerists" managed the nation's strongest butchers' locals in the 1920s, David Brody found; he singled out Seattle's Hoffman as a prime example.[126] Officials from Seattle's white male barbers' union similarly described their activities in terms of shop-card placement; speaking of the union's activities in relation to the employers' status, not that of the employees. When the employer agreed to recognize the union's card, and its conditions, then the workers were in the union. The cooks explicitly acknowledged this process: "Taking in members by card," they reported.[127]

This approach meant that it was management, not union organizers, who induced individual workers to join a given union. Stuart Kaufman argues that for the tobacco workers' international, label dependence "meant that the Union sold a firm on the benefits of using the label and the workers joined the Union more or less with the understanding that this was what the employer expected them to do."[128] This same dynamic was evident when Musicians' Local #76 placed member Irene Parker on trial for playing below the union scale at the Class A Theatre: She "denied knowing what [the union] scale was," admitted to performing non-union work in the suburbs, and said she had "only joined at the solicitation of the manager to keep his house in good repute with Organized Labor."[129] Culinary unions found that "picketing could be successful even if the potential union members working inside were indifferent or hostile to unionism," Dorothy Cobble argues.[130] Label unionism, in sum, could produce locals in which rank-and-file workers never even met their union officials or were suspicious of them if they had. It undermined the union's rank-and-file base while simultaneously strengthening the position of its staff in relation to management.[131]

Only nominally responsible to their locals' rank and file, officials in label unions were free to cut deals with management at the expense of their members. The boot and shoe workers' international union awarded union labels in this period to firms that did not even pay the union scale.[132] William Z. Foster charged in his 1927 book *Misleaders of Labor* that in return for the label, "[T]he bosses permit the union leaders to maintain a semblance of organization through a compulsory check-off, with the understanding that there will be no 'unreasonable' demands from the workers."[133] Indeed, without a tightly organized rank and file committed to union militance the locals were in no position to make any such "unreasonable" demands.

Gender dynamics further intensified the hierarchy embedded in this internal structure. In many cases, the leaders were male, the rank-and-file members female. Recall the retail clerks' attitude toward the 1920 Bon Marche boycott. The union's male leaders supported it precisely because they were frustrated with trying to convince female department-store clerks to join their union. They hoped to use the boycott to force management to compel women clerks to join. Irene Parker, the errant musician, belonged to a local all of whose officials were male. Nationally, unions heavily dependent on label promotion were often those in which male leaders represented an overwhelmingly female rank and file, such as the Boot and Shoe Workers, Tobacco Workers, and United Garment Workers.[134]

The garment workers' union went so far as to issue its label to plants in which only highly skilled male workers were organized, but female operatives were not. In Seattle, the largest such case was that of the laundry workers. White male teamster leaders held tight control over the overwhelmingly female laundry workers' union. In the mid-1920s the city's laundries had a labor turnover rate of 357 percent – meaning that in order to retain a labor force of 1,272 workers in 1924, the employers had to hire 3,559 people. The laundries with the worst working conditions replaced their entire work force five times during a single year. With a revolving door that turned so swiftly, and a leadership that didn't really want to talk to rank-and-file members, the contact between an individual laundry worker and her union officials must have been minimal, and in the vast majority of cases nonexistent.[135]

The top-down nature of label unionism sheds light on the AFL movement's race dynamics as well. When the white butchers, barbers, and shoe repairers proved willing to "sign up" and "put the card in" Japanese-American shops in 1921 and 1922, their officials were merely negotiating with a new set of employers; they were not necessarily embracing Japanese-American fellow workers. White unionists could look the other way in placing the shop card in firms owned by Japanese-Americans in part because they were not looking at rank-and-file workers at all. Similar dynamics may explain the presence in the laundry workers' local of African-American workers, who counted 1 percent of the total membership (or about a dozen workers) at the decade's end. Dave Beck may have been so distant from his own membership that he didn't even care.[136]

Understanding the internal dynamics of label unionism helps explain the place of wage-earning women in the AFL movement by the end of the decade. Female trade unionists were almost all entrapped within the narrow logic of label unionism. The laundry workers' local counted the single largest body of women, but they were in thrall to the teamsters. The garment workers elected female leaders, but in their case label unionism meant subservience to paternalistic male employers. The waitresses, by contrast, retained a great deal of independence and gained advantages from the cooks' dependence on a shared shop card. Yet their success was built upon white solidarity and racial exclusion institutionalized through that same shop card. The lady barbers' union had once been independent, but by the decade's end it had been absorbed into a male-dominated local that subordinated their concerns as women workers. Nor did Japanese-American women barbers find sympathy among their male peers. Women in two other mixed-gender locals, the cooks' and the typographers', fared no better, possessing little power or presence in the officialdom. While a male delegate from the cooks reported in 1919 that its women members were "a lively bunch" that participated in the local's meetings "like regular fellows," the women had no such "regular fellow" status overall in the local.[137] A lone woman who ran for vice president in 1921 lost. At mid-decade female cooks were joining with wives of male cooks to organize social events.[138] The tailors' union appears to have been the only mixed-gender local in which women held leadership positions. It revived some-what after the depression and in 1923 sent a woman delegate to the Central Labor Council. In 1925, while its officers and trustees were all male, its executive board was half male, half female.[139]

The case of the white musicians' union demonstrates, though, that women union members could still kick up a storm in the late 1920s' AFL move-ment. Local #76 counted 700 male members in 1920, 125 female. While figures for the gender breakdown for the rest of the decade are not available, women retained a strong numerical presence in the local and worked in a variety of jobs in the trade. Nineteen-twenty-seven members included Edna Ward, organist at the Queen Anne Theatre; Cecile Baron, piano instructor; and "Alberta Bailey and her Girls Orchestra." Up to that point, though, no women served as officers of the local or as members of its key govern-ing committee.[140]

Rank-and-file women's attitudes toward the local appear to have been ambivalent. They evidently did not attend the local's meetings in the pre-war or early war years. In response, president W. E. Murray proposed in September 1918 that the local "encourage the lady members to attend the next General meeting and that each member should make himself a com-mittee of one to try and get them up."[141] When women did show up in January 1919, a Mrs. Glidden protested that the local was giving prefer-ence to new members transferring from other locals outside Seattle, over "members who had brought conditions up to where they are," and she announced that "some of the women members [are] considering quitting" the local. The local had evidently been dispatching newly arriving male workers rather than longstanding female members.[142] Her protest suggests that white women musicians, like African-American musicians, vacillated between fighting for equality within the union and staying away in frus-tration at the discriminatory treatment they experienced within it.

In late 1926, 1927, and 1928 the women in #76 finally staged a little revolution. "A crowd of them big enough to make any man think twice" showed up at the November 1926 monthly meeting.[143] By the late spring of 1927 women outnumbered men at some local meetings and had begun to participate in general debates.[144] Then, in November 1927, they an-nounced the formation of a new Women's Club of musicians. It counted fifty-three charter members and stated its purpose as both social and "the progress of the lady musicians."[145]

The first thing the Women's Club did was to replicate exactly the co-operatives' women's clubs and the Card and Label League. It organized its own place within the union, once again, literally – setting up club rooms. Historians have noted that male unionists tended to call union meetings in male-defined cultural spaces such as saloons, making it difficult for women members to participate.[146] The Musicians' Hall was clearly such a place. Male members smoked, put their feet up on the tables, and gambled all night in the hall.[147] "It is only when luncheon is served that the feminine members of the association dare to enter the sacred portals," observed an anonymous contributor to *Musicland*.[148] In January and February 1928, the Women's Club claimed for itself two "delightfully cheery and comfortable" rooms in the hall. Redecorating came first. "The walls are done in a flowered pattern, the furniture is wicker and upholstered, and the curtains are the homelike, ruffled kind."[149] Again, they created within the musician's union a "homelike" space in which they sewed, played cards, put on showers and skits, and swapped recipes.[150] Angella Santucci "prepared Italian spaghetti and demonstrated to the girls just how it should be eaten."[151] Men were not admitted.[152]

The Women's Club also supported women's efforts to achieve equality as working musicians. Members reported on the progress of an all-female symphony orchestra, for example, and celebrated a woman's performance as director of a fifteen-piece orchestra.[153] Most actively, though, the women agitated for a powerful place in their own union. One of the first things they did at their meetings was to study parliamentary law so that they could play the complex parliamentary game male leaders used to manipulate local meetings. Their most spectacular feat was to elect Ida Dillon to the local's supreme five-member Executive Board in November 1928. She received the highest number of votes of any candidate and was reelected in 1929.[154]

The male members of Local #76 sat up and took notice of all this. "The stronger sex . . . better turn out or they are liable to have a lady president next time," warned member Charlie Morris after observing the female majority at the May 1927 meeting.[155] A story in the December 5 *Musicland* (possibly written by Dillon) suggested that "if you have aspirations political or otherwise, you'd better take the girls into consideration because they are going to be right there to let you know what they want."[156] Male members appear to have reacted with either uncomfortable jokes or statements of warm support, sometimes tinged with condescension or gender-based stereotypes. A two-page spread in the Christmas 1927 newsletter, in which male unionists took out little advertisements greeting the new Women's Club, offers a glimpse into men's reactions, though men truly hostile to the women's activities apparently refrained from placing ads. "To the ladies; God Bless them," contributed Jack Wolenschlager, trumpet player. Ed McKenzie, "Pianist at the Orpheum," seconded, "More Power to You, Girls." "I wish you success, Girls. I may be old but I have young ideas," contributed another. O. R. McLain, though, could not resist cracking: "I'm for the Women And with the Women (When I get the chance)."[157]

"Greetings to the Women's Club. I'm for the ladies, but don't let my wife know it," supplied Frank Myers, drummer.[158] Myers' remarks suggest possible tensions over the question of married men's fraternization with female union members. In March 1929 – well over a year after its founding – the Women's Club invited wives to visit its meetings. "The Women's Club extends you a cordial invitation to take lunch and play bridge or five hundred with them at any of their meetings. . . . Come and get acquainted."[159] The female musicians may have extended the invitation to defuse possible tensions, or simply out of a sincere desire to connect socially with the wives of their co-workers. *Musicland* reported that several wives did attend a March meeting. "However," it went on, "the husbands need not worry, as the members of the club have sworn to 'tell the wives nothing.' "[160] We can only wonder what it was that the female musicians were not going to reveal, and whether their possession of such information gave them bargaining power within the local. It is also worth noting that while half the Women's Club members were married, no mention was made in the newsletter of their husbands.[161]

The story of the women musicians shows feminism to be alive, even in this case advancing in the late 1920s AFL movement. Like women participants in the cooperatives and the citywide movement earlier in the decade, the women musicians envisioned a "homelike" movement that shaded over from wage earners' concerns to those of workers in the home. They wanted to both be conductors and learn how to cook spaghetti. As long as the men smoked, gambled, and put their feet up on the tables of the movement, they wanted their own rooms with tidy ruffled curtains. And like African-American musicians, they learned that if they organized separately, they could increase their bargaining power in relation to white male musicians. Sometimes, they could win.[162]

A contagion of indifference

The leadership's top-down, professionalized approach pushed the rank and file a little too far away, even from the leadership's point of view. A "contagion of indifference . . . seems to have gripped the whole labor movement," a representative of the cooks' union lamented on Labor Day, 1927.[163] Mass apathy plagued the postdepression movement at all levels. The Card and Label League evaporated. Individual union locals reported only a handful in attendance at meetings unless a major agreement was up for ratification. Of 600 members of Musicians' Local #76 only 22 attended the local's July 1923 monthly meeting; of those, half were members of the Board of Directors. The Trade Union Promotional League acknowledged in 1926 that the "vast majority of . . . members rarely attend union meetings." It estimated that only 5 to 25 percent of members attended meetings. The Central Labor Council, home to the most active, suffered a similar affliction. Subcommittees delayed meeting because they couldn't come up with enough delegates. By 1926 the problem had become so pronounced that the *Labor News* was reduced to pitiable editorials pleading with delegates to attend council meetings. Members stayed away from meetings at all levels in part because they were afraid that if they did show up, they would then be nominated for subcommittees and still more meetings. Such apathy was not unique to Seattle. "The appalling indifference of the workers themselves is a difficulty that seems unsurmountable," concluded AFL President William Green in 1929 of the movement nationwide.[164]

The unions did attempt to liven up their meetings. Social events for the committed increasingly supplanted political or economic action as labor organizations' main activity. The typographers in 1923 set aside for the first time an hour every three meetings for an "educational feature," excluding "partisan, political, or religious subjects."[165] The bakers organized increasingly elaborate balls at which the pièce de résistance was an immense decorated cake.[166] The Central Labor Council in 1922 voted to devote a half hour each month to entertainment; the next year it appointed a new "social committee.[167] The TUPL itself became almost purely a social provider for the movement. Its activities became social events only, with obligatory label speech appended. By the late 1920s label promoters were merely talking to one another to the extent that the TUPL began to spend its money organizing social occasions for Central Labor Council delegates.[168] Reinaugurating a dance series in June 1928, the league described the dances as "a start in an attempt to coordinate the social activities of the labor movement, under its own control and for the purpose of its own determining."[169] This was all a long way from the "workers' own" institutions of 1919.

Wives' activism followed the same path. In the late twenties Seattle's trade union wives reinvigorated a form of activism dating from the late nineteenth century, the ladies' auxiliary. Here was a final stage in the retreat of women's activism from the independently political to the subservient. Regular reports in Seattle's labor press show both a wave of newly founded auxiliaries in the mid- and late twenties and an expansion of the membership of extant auxiliaries.[170] Even more than the Card and Label League in its post-1922 incarnation, the ladies' auxiliary's basic function was to serve. In practice that meant organizing social functions at the level of the local. Typically, auxiliary members convened during their husbands' local meeting, and then, when the men were done, provided refreshments and entertainment, usually a card party or skits. Some auxiliary members engaged in label promotion work in their husbands' trades; others, whose husbands worked for the government, joined lobbying efforts. Still other auxiliary members announced quite firmly that their organizations' purpose was social and social only.[171] The auxiliaries, then, marked a final narrowing of women's activism: The wives now defined what they as women shared by their husbands' occupations and organized their activities to entertain only their husbands (and themselves). They neither defined their own interests beyond those of their husbands' trades nor extended their concerns to those of other women, wage-earning or not.[172]

Confronted with an apathetic rank and file but needing to enlist their dollars as union shoppers, the leadership came to speak of label observance and, increasingly, trade unionism itself, as an obligation. "Get in the harness," the Promotional League enticed in 1925.[173] It promised to give recalcitrant members "insight into what is really required of us as trade unionists."[174] Wives were included in this happy arrangement. It was their "duty" to spend according to union precepts and bear their "share of the burden of organized labor."[175] The demanding tone of these calls could spill over into the frustrated suggestion that it was unionists, not employers, who, in their failure to buy union, caused labor's problems. A box in the TUPL's monthly label guide argued along these lines that anti-union employers "stay scab employers only because union men buy their goods without demanding the label."[176] Demands that the rank and file "do their duty," however, cast the labor movement in a negative light. Union membership was now a restriction of members' and members' families' activities and choices, rather than a celebration, a liberation, or an expansion of working-class power or political potential. Trade unionism and label promotion both had become rather distasteful, undesirable "burdens."[177]

The leadership's task was then to coerce the reluctant rank and file into shouldering label observance. On the carrot side, the leadership attempted to lure rank and filers back into the fold with an array of alluring prizes. Locals awarded prizes for regular attendance, for label observance, for aid in label promotional campaigns, or just for showing up at union events at all. The printers, for example, in their 1924–25 label campaign awarded cash prizes to the members who turned in the greatest number of articles lacking the label.[178] In another TUPL drive that year the loyalist who displayed three labels on his or her clothing won a chance on a $35 suit of clothes (union labeled, of course).[179] Prizes were sometimes cash, sometimes articles donated by sympathetic merchants, but most often the ubiquitous samples of union-label clothing donated by sympathetic garment manufacturers, or else union label cigars liberally distributed by their makers.[180]

As for sticks, the leaders began with shame. Ernest Spedden argued in 1910 that much of the demand for the label depended on peer pressure from fellow unionists. He noted that the brewery workers' and cigarmakers' success in promoting their labels stemmed in part from the public nature of beer and cigar consumption. Working people bought union goods only in the presence of other unionists, because no one wanted to admit they didn't shop union. "It is a matter of frequent complaint among the Cigar makers that although unionists when in groups almost always buy union-made cigars, they are not so careful when they are alone and in places where the character of their purchases is not likely to be noted."[181] Evidence from Seattle corroborates this. A letter to the *Union Record* in 1919 observed that while "no real union man will patronize a scab house [establishment] . . . others claiming to be union would rather not be caught patronizing them. . . ."[182] The visual coding of postwar Seattle reinforced this pattern. Union buttons were common enough that two symbolic systems operated, one to identify union goods and services, the other to identify union persons. This made possible the surveys that counted, for example, one hundred men with union buttons buying scab milk. Label unions used this heightened visibility to promote their products by in effect de-privatizing shopping. The waitresses' union had thoroughly mastered this method, at one point even threatening to photograph union men caught patronizing an "unfair" restaurant.[183] In 1925 the musicians similarly menaced, "Keep away from Lonesome Club unless you want unfavorable publicity."[184]

Far more frequently, though, the leadership turned to the coercive mechanisms that had always been integral to craft unionism. Failing to convince members to shop union voluntarily, they declared fines on those who would not. Fines imposed on members found to be patronizing non-union firms ranged from $5 to $25. Violations could be quite specific. Electrical Workers' Local #944, for example, in 1924 declared a fine on any member caught buying the boycotted *Post-Intelligencer*. Or general: The milk wagon drivers' work rules included "Any member found guilty of purchasing unfair goods or patronizing unfair firms will be subject to a fine."[185] International unions also declared general fines. The hatters' international, for example, passed a resolution in 1900 forbidding the purchase of non-union cigars.[186] The regularity with which the unions declared such fines was matched, however, by the rarity with which they actually imposed them.[187] In the entire decade, Carpenters' #131, Typographers' #202, and Musicians' #76, three locals whose minutes are available, fined only two members, one of whom was Sophie Pugsley, the leftist backslider who built her house with non-union labor.[188] The infrequency of actual fining suggests not only the pervasiveness of violations but also the limited control the leadership had over its rank and file. After all, if the members wouldn't even attend meetings, imposing fines would only drive them further away. Some locals resolved that dilemma, however, by imposing fines for non-attendance at meetings.[189]

Ultimately, label observance was an ever-receding pot of gold that the leadership evidently believed was just within its reach. It was just effective enough to keep trying but never captured the enthusiasm of the rank and file or roused them to assiduously loyal shopping. Label unionism's basic problem was that in its internal structure it kept the rank and file at arm's length from direction of their movement but then needed all the loyalties and enthusiasm that a true mass movement would generate. Union shopping depended on class consciousness, but class consciousness was precisely what the business unionist leadership discouraged. Rather, they sold trade union consciousness – a much narrower, less conflictual, carefully regulated duty, augmented by white racial consciousness.[190]

Seattle's business unionist leadership in the end had no vision with which to ignite the rank and file. Irving Bernstein describes late-1920s AFL leaders nationwide as "bereft of ideas."[191] Note, for example, this speech by William Short to the Building Trades Council in 1923: "The progressive organization is the one that meets the immediate problems that face it from day to day and does not spend the major portion of its time in trying to solve problems that are impossible of solution in the near future."[192] A similar, but still more diminished version of this same "vision" graced the *Labor News* on Labor Day, 1929:

> We do not make war on society, we are not interested in changing governments. We occupy the lowest rung in the ediface [*sic*] of our civilization, but it is our paramount duty and purpose to improve the life and character of those who are occupying this fundamental position in this civilized structure.
>   Be proud and steadfast, dreams seldom come true but what men can vision can be accomplished, our influence for good is being recognized as time moves on, our economic philosophy, once scored by almost all employers is becoming accepted not alone by leading economists but by the employer himself. LET'S PRESS FORWARD.[193]

All too perfectly this vision matched Selig Perlman's description of the national AFL at decade's end: "a curious blending of 'defeatism' with complacency."[194]

Label unionism thus helped make the AFL a vacant shell. It helps explain the paradox of the Seattle labor movement in the late 1920s: high membership, but low militance. Formal membership in Seattle AFL locals grew every year after 1923, until by 1927 it had reached a total of 18,000, a pale figure beside the 60,000 to 65,000 of 1919, but 8,000 higher than in any year before 1917. Membership in American trade unions overall similarly exceeded prewar levels, growing from 2,582,600 in 1915 to 3,442,600 in 1929. But what those figures meant was entirely different in 1929 from in 1919. If in 1919 the whole of the Seattle labor movement had been far greater than the sum of its parts, in 1929 it was far less.[195]

Conclusion

In theory, the union label created a class-coded network that marked the entire city with its politics of production. Daily life became thick with opportunities for workers to extend their politics to every conceivable economic transaction. But in the context of the postdepression AFL movement, the label came to symbolize not working-class power but the benevolent issue of a friendly employer who acquiesced to Asian exclusion. One key to the difference lay in the relative importance of production- and consumption-based organizing by the mid-1920s. In 1919–20, politicized consumption had been in service to a broad vision of a workers' society tied to confrontational tactics at the point of production. But in the mid- and late 1920s business unionists severed consumer organizing from militance at the paid workplace. Instead, union label promotion was designed precisely to defuse such conflict. Seattle's new labor leadership employed the label not as a complement to the strike, boycott, and ballot box but as a replacement. The labor movement was reduced to union label promotion alone. Then, when rank-and-file workers and their families rejected union shopping, they rejected all that was left of the movement. As wives, especially, spurned the union label, the Seattle AFL more forcefully than ever confronted the Achilles' heel of its consumer organizing campaigns, the contradiction between its request that women "look for the label" and its disregard for the speedup of housewives' labor that such a search entailed.

Why did the leadership stick by the label if it was so apparently unsuccessful? The resolution to that apparent contradiction lies in our definition of success. Given the goals of the leaders who promoted the label, it was successful. Some Seattle unionists did spend by union precepts, helping the city's unionized garment firms stay in business, encouraging meat-shop owners to acquiesce to the butchers' unions, keeping some contracts inside the city, and helping maintain the typographers' position in job shops. The label also helped the leadership keep rank-and-file members in line, by enlisting the movement's remaining core of committed unionists as a police force exerting vigilance over the membership status of workers all over the city, such as the streetcar employees, retail clerks, musicians, and construction workers.

More important, though, the union label allowed the leadership to talk big about union loyalty without having to worry about a mass-based, rank-and-file movement that might get out of line or challenge its power. At the same time it defined a subservient place for women – whether as wives or as indentured union members – that, similarly, didn't challenge men's rights to govern. It solidified white supremacy in the name of solidarity. Best of all, label unionism provided a structure and ideology through which the leaders could befriend local capital and establish themselves as important men in the city, ostensibly as power brokers yet also as preachers of harmony and friendship. All the while they could appear as the most virtuous unionists in the city, right down to their union-label handkerchiefs. The union label, in other words, was eminently successful from the leadership's point of view. It had two faces: one a smile to the employers, the other a scowl to the rank and file. As long as the local-market industries that their locals represented prospered economically, the city's employers could smile back. They, too, remembered the unruly rank and file of 1919 and knew a good deal when it was offered to them. Similarly, the rank and file ignored the scowl, paid their dues money, and took their paychecks home. They didn't, though, spend them on union-labeled hats.

Conclusion

In RETROSPECT it is all too easy to see the unhappy ending as inevitable. A host of powerful forces conspired to bring down the early-1919 Seattle AFL movement: the open shop drive, state repression, the nationwide depression of 1921, and perhaps most important, the closing of the shipyards and resultant restructuring of the Seattle economy, returning it to the prewar world of services, distribution of natural resources, and small-scale production for a local market.

To include only these factors, though, is to suggest a version of history in which economic forces roll forward free of human restraints, in which state power is absolute, and in which employers get everything they want. It is to obscure the complex dynamics of labor and capital in the 1919–29 period. The employers, after all, constructed their own institutions of solidarity and mounted their counterattack in response to the gains won by trade unions during the war years. The government repressed the Wobblies, the Socialist Party, and the *Union Record* because they were becoming so popular and so threatening. Even Seattle's postwar depression was engineered, in part, by policymakers in Washington who defunded wartime shipbuilding and produced the postwar deflation through manipulation of the money supply.

Just as important, factors internal to the labor movement shaped organized labor's ability to respond to external assaults. The shift in the AFL movement from radical industrial unionists in the mass-production sector to conservative craft unionists in the local-market sector serves as just one example. Ostensibly a product of economic restructuring and state repression, that transition was also machinated by AFL conservatives who, as they rose to power within the city's AFL movement, cut the industrial unionists off from the resources of solidarity they needed to survive.

Each moment at which the AFL movement redefined solidarity to include fewer and fewer members of the working class, it vitiated the movement's ability to counter employers' assaults. The purges of "dual card" Wobbly sympathizers in late 1919, of Communists in 1925, and the gradual marginalization of socialists meant not only that the local movement would fail to transcend the jurisdictional barriers inherent in the AFL but also that the movement lost its ability to imagine a fundamentally different social and economic order. The rejection of married women workers in 1919 and the withdrawal of funds for a female organizer in 1922 helped push wage-earning women out of the movement or into a subordinate position within it, further weakening the movement as a whole. And the silencing of industrial-unionist voices meant the loss of explicit critiques of racial exclusion within the AFL, though Asian- and African-American workers would continue to contest exclusionary practices.

Finally, the leadership's continual failure to grasp the concerns of the wives of male union members meant that every time the movement adopted a consumer tactic, it stood on shaky ground. This was vitally important because the AFL movement continually turned to consumption to advance or defend its perceived interests. In many cases organized consumption nonetheless brought strength, if limited, to the AFL. When the Retail Grocers' Association cut off credit during the general strike, the cooperatives provided vital aid. Producer cooperatives and labor capitalist firms such as the Mutual Laundry harbored blacklisted activists throughout 1919 and provided an organized wedge with which unionists in a few cases could break employers' united front. The independent institutions of 1919–21 helped sustain rank-and-file dreams of a very different, worker-run society that might address the workplace concerns of women and men. And the *Union Record*, to quote the millmen's union again, was "a flaming sword in [the] battle for the legitimate rights and ideals of Labor." The 1920 boycotts, similarly, helped pressure employers to move from the open shop drive to more conciliatory approaches.

The pitfalls of consumer organizing were legion, however. Cooperatives and labor capitalist enterprises were organized on the premise of beating capitalism at its own game. One problem was that if labor started winning that game, it produced profits, which could spiral the working class right back into capitalism. More often labor lost, because the odds of the game were stacked both by noncooperative firms' superior business acumen and access to capital and by the cycles of boom and bust in which any business operated and to which small firms were especially vulnerable.

Boycotts highlighted jurisdictional tensions always lurking beneath the AFL's surface. In a movement in which male and female members occupied unequal positions of power, men resolved jurisdictional disputes over a given boycott's benefits to the detriment of women. Skilled workers sacrificed the unskilled. The limited visibility of shopping, moreover, meant that the success of a boycott was always hard to prove and observance hard to police. In a movement premised on whiteness and racial exclusion, boycotts infested class identities with racism and extended racial exclusion and identities from the waged workplace into a racial politics of shopping.

Label unionism was equally treacherous. In contrast to the boycott, whose stance was oppositional, the label enlisted trade unionists' shopping habits on behalf of "friendly" firms, potentially reinforcing identification of the labor movement's interests with those of employers. It could undermine rank-and-file involvement in an organization by focusing union activities on negotiations between employers and union officials. Such a top-down style was historically correlated with male leaders' aggrandizement of power over a female membership. Finally, union label promotion could slide over into campaigns identifying products based on the city, region, or nation in which they were produced, rather than on the common interests of working people across geographical lines.

The lesson, though, is not to eschew consumer tactics. Working people's purchasing power is real, and institution building an essential part of any movement for fundamental social change. I hope this study will contribute not to the avoidance of consumer tactics but to their more shrewd and effective application.

I also hope it will contribute to the ongoing efforts to redefine labor history. Once we begin the process of incorporating gender, race, and consumption into the history of working-class organizations, it seems difficult to imagine a story without them. The story of 1919–29 Seattle without the gender politics of cooperatives, without the racial politics of boycotts, and without the class politics of the union label would be a diminished, inaccurate one. A story discussing white male workers alone cannot hold, any more than one sector of the working class, which chose to speak in the name of the whole, could hold against the united powers of organized capital.

Integrating race and gender into the "main" story of labor history does not "splinter" class analysis. The skilled white male workers who constructed the movement and claimed to speak for the whole working class did that. They put the barriers up. They blackballed African-American potential members. They, along with white women, boycotted restaurants that hired Asian-American kitchen workers. They banned married women from serving as organizers and then fired the unmarried organizer. When we integrate gender and race we can see the ways in which the white and the male portions of the working class undermined their own cause. We can see the labors of the female half of the working class as they were shaped by the sexual division of labor in the labor force and the home alike, and the ways in which the male half benefited – or did not – from that division of labor. Finally, and most important, we can imagine "class" in a manner that includes all working people and all the work they perform and imagine a working-class social movement built by and addressing the interests of the entire working class.

Integrating this story into our larger, national-level understandings of the labor movement of the 1920s is not just a matter of assessing the degree to which Seattle is or is not "representative." Some dynamics I have identified were indeed specific to Seattle, most important the strong IWW influence on the AFL, the weak manufacturing base after the war, and the tripartite dynamics of race. Each of these characteristics, though, was shared by other cities in the period, though not all in a single location.[1] A different approach to the "uniqueness" question is to identify ways in which national-level developments affected Seattle's story at the time. To name just one example, federal edicts for postwar reconstruction, including the Macy Award granting only meager raises to shipyard workers after the war, impinged on any apparent local autonomy of Seattle's employers. Similarly, Seattle's Red scare was engineered from above – in Washington, D.C., as well as in Olympia. In the same period that Seattle's Associated Industries borrowed their "American Plan" campaign whole cloth from employers' associations in Toledo and elsewhere, officials of the AFL internationals constrained Seattle locals at every turn. And on a much broader scale, race relations deep in the fabric and institutions of American society set the stage for racial negotiations in Seattle.

Those national-level forces can be understood only if we also grasp the ways in which Seattle forces in turn shaped them. The Seattle general strike serves as a good example. It was reported in the daily press nationwide and further popularized by ex-Mayor Ole Hanson, who quit his office to hit the national lecture circuit fanning the post-strike flames.[2] Frightened elites, imagining a Bolshevik Revolution on American soil, then turned to the Red scare and open shop drive, of which Seattle, in turn, proved a victim. To give another, very different case, AFL activists on the Pacific coast, concerned about competition from Asian immigrant workers in their region, made Asian exclusion part of national AFL policy.[3]

The Seattle AFL's usage of consumer tactics also had national impact. Unionists from Seattle traveled to national conventions of cooperative activists in Springfield, Illinois, in 1919 and again in Cincinnati in 1920, at which they extolled the virtues of their expanding cooperative networks to delegates who then dispersed to communities throughout the nation.[4] Thousands of the *Union Record*'s 120,000 subscribers resided outside Seattle and learned in its pages of all the consumer campaigns I have described here. The dynamics of this story, in sum, are not only those between labor and capital, men and women, whites and those they identified as racially different, leaders and rank and file, but also between local and national forces.

This story of Seattle in the 1920s illuminates, lastly, our understanding of the "big picture" of labor history in the decades that followed. Labor historians often conceptualize the rise and institutionalization of the CIO as the center of their twentieth-century narrative. All roads lead to, or descend from, the CIO in 1936–37. The 1920s, from this perspective, become a blank space to skip over while waiting for the industrial unionists of the WWI era to turn into CIO organizers. An alternative view is to see the AFL as the norm, the CIO as the deviation from it. The picture I have drawn of the local-level AFL in the second half of the 1920s underscores AFL leaders' entrenched stakes by the early thirties. AFL business unionists were threatened by the challenge of the CIO in part because they had ensconced themselves in a comfortable rapprochement with local capital and had a lot to lose. Yet as the CIO grew in the late thirties and forties, the AFL did not decline. Instead, it boomed, doubling its membership between 1937 and 1943, in many ways because of the CIO.[5] In a complex dynamic similar to Seattle's in the period I have examined, the threat to employers posed by the CIO's more militant industrial-union model for trade unionism created the collaborationist space in which the AFL thrived. Pressed by the federal endorsement of workers' right to form unions of their own choosing, employers chose to make deals with the AFL rather than face the far more demanding and potentially disruptive CIO, much as Seattle employers identified conservative AFL leaders and cultivated a relationship with them. AFL leaders were all too pleased to enter into that arrangement.[6]

By the late 1940s, moreover, the CIO came increasingly to look like its former rival. CIO leaders negotiated longer and longer contracts, distanced themselves from rank-and-file dissidents, and developed increasingly amicable relationships with corporate management in a manner replicating that of Seattle's AFL in the late 1920s. To paraphrase Steve Fraser, Seattle proved a dress rehearsal not for the New Deal but for the Treaty of Detroit – that is, the 1950 contract with General Motors in which the United Auto Workers traded away control over production in exchange for an expanding package of wages and benefits. By the time the AFL and CIO merged in 1955, the CIO was more like the AFL than vice versa. To use the Australian's metaphor again, the lady was inside the tiger.[7]

Today progressives are still inside, kicking to get out. Those of us who support a democratic, militant labor movement as a step on the road to economic democracy still face the AFL's legacy of conservative business unionism. Lee Iaccoca and Owen Bieber appear side by side looking like twins on the cover of the *New York Times Magazine*, symbolizing "the Auto Workers' New Partnership With Management," and the AFL-CIO promotes "Buy American" campaigns that reinforce anti-Asian sentiments while calling on politicized shopping in support of organized labor.[8] The big difference between the history I have recounted in this book and the challenges of the present, however, is that our own story is not over yet. Whether the ending is happy or unhappy is up to us.

Notes

Introduction

1. Selig Perlman, *A Theory of the Labor Movement* (New York: Macmillan, 1928), p. 232.
2. J.B.S. Hardman, *American Labor Dynamics in the Light of Post-War Developments* (New York: Harcourt, Brace & Co., 1928), p. 10.
3. A sampling of studies of periods of growth includes Leon Fink, *Workingman's Democracy: The Knights of Labor and American Politics* (Urbana: University of Illinois Press, 1983); Susan Levine, *Labor's True Woman: Carpet Weavers, Industrialization, and Labor Reform in the Gilded Age* (Philadelphia: Temple University Press, 1984); Richard Oestereicher, *Solidarity and Fragmentation: Working People and Class Consciousness in Detroit, 1875–1900* (Urbana: University of Illinois Press, 1986); Michael Kazin, *Barons of Labor: The San Francisco Building Trades and Union Power in the Progressive Era* (Urbana: University of Illinois Press, 1987); Bruce Nelson, *Workers on the Waterfront: Seamen, Longshoremen, and Unionism in the 1930s* (Urbana: University of Illinois Press, 1988); Ronald Schatz, *The Electrical Workers: A History of Labor at General Electric and Westinghouse, 1923–60* (Urbana: University of Illinois Press, 1983); and Gary Gerstle, *Working-class Americanism: The Politics of Labor in a Textile City, 1914–1960* (New York: Cambridge University Press, 1989).

    Studies of the post–World War II era have of necessity focused on the question of decline; for example, Kim Moody, *An Injury to All: The Decline of American Unionism* (London: Verso, 1988); Michael Goldfield, *The Decline of Organized Labor in the United States* (Chicago: University of Chicago Press, 1987); David Brody, "The Uses of Power I: Industrial Battleground" and "The Uses of Power II: Political Action," in David Brody, ed., *Workers in Industrial America: Essays on the Twentieth-Century Struggle* (New York: Oxford University Press, 1980), pp. 173–257. For an example of my generation's interest in defeat and decline, see Colin Davis, "Bitter Storm: The 1922 National Railroad Shopmen's Strike," Ph.D. Diss., State University of New York at Binghamton, 1989.
4. I have never been quite sure if that Golden Aftermath referred to the postwar strike wave, referred to the supposed prosperity of the 1920s, or was intended ironically, given labor's defeats in the decade. See Maurice F. Neufeld, Daniel J. Leab, and Dorothy Swanson, *Working Class History: A Representative Biblio-*

graphy (New York: Bowker, 1983), and Swanson's annual bibliographies in the journal *Labor History*. Analyses of the 1920s include Irving Bernstein, *The Lean Years: A History of the American Worker, 1920–1933* (Boston: Houghton Mifflin, 1960); David Montgomery, *The Fall of the House of Labor: The Workplace, the State, and American Labor Activism, 1865–1925* (Cambridge: Cambridge University Press, 1987); Philip Taft, *The A.F. of L. in the Time of Gompers* (New York: Harper & Bros., 1957); Frank Stricker, "Affluence for Whom? – Another Look at Prosperity and the Working Classes in the 1920s," *Labor History* Vol. 24, No. 1 (Winter 1983), pp. 5–33; David Brody, "The Rise and Decline of Welfare Capitalism," in Brody, ed., *Workers in Industrial America*, pp. 48–81; Alice Kessler-Harris, "Problems of Coalition-Building: Women and Trade Unions in the 1920s," in Ruth Milkman, ed., *Women, Work, and Protest: A Century of US Women's Labor History* (Boston: Routledge & Kegan Paul, 1985), pp. 120–38; Alice Kessler-Harris, *Out to Work: A History of Wage-Earning Women in the United States* (New York: Oxford University Press, 1982), Ch. 7; John Bodnar, "Immigration, Kinship, and the Rise of Working-Class Realism in Industrial America," *Journal of Social History* 14 (Fall 1980), pp. 45–65; Cecelia Bucki, "The Pursuit of Political Power: Class, Ethnicity and Municipal Politics in Interwar Bridgeport, 1915–1936," Ph.D. Diss., University of Pittsburgh, 1991; Susan Levine, "Workers' Wives: Gender, Class and Consumerism in the 1920s United States," *Gender and History* Vol. 3, No. 1 (Spring 1991), pp. 44–64; Robert H. Zieger, *The Republicans and Labor, 1919–1929* (Lexington: University Press of Kentucky, 1969); Lizabeth Cohen, *Making a New Deal: Industrial Workers in Chicago, 1919–1939* (Cambridge: Cambridge University Press, 1990); Steven Fraser, *Labor Will Rule: Sidney Hillman and the Rise of American Labor* (New York: Free Press, 1991); David Montgomery, "Thinking about American Workers in the 1920s," and responses by Charles S. Maier and Susan Porter Benson, in *International Labor and Working Class History* No. 32 (Fall 1987), pp. 4–38.

Studies written at the time include Hardman, *American Labor Dynamics*; Perlman, *Theory of the Labor Movement*; and William Z. Foster, *Misleaders of Labor* (New York: Trade Union Educational League, 1927).

5. Leo Troy, *Trade Union Membership, 1897–1962* (New York: National Bureau of Economic Research, 1965), p. 8; Taft, *The A.F. of L. in the Time of Gompers*; Philip Taft, *The A.F. of L. from the Death of Gompers to the Merger* (New York: Harper & Bros., 1959).

6. For the importance of unions in the local-market sector in the 1920s, see Bernstein, *The Lean Years*, pp. 86–87; C. L. Christenson, *Collective Bargaining in Chicago, 1929–1930* (Chicago: University of Chicago Press, 1933); Louis B. Perry and Richard S. Perry, *A History of the Los Angeles Labor Movement, 1911–1941* (Berkeley: University of California Press, 1963), pp. 193–225.

7. Stuart Ewen, *Captains of Consciousness: Advertising and the Social Roots of the Consumer Culture* (New York: McGraw-Hill, 1976); Robert S. and Helen Merrell Lynd, *Middletown: A Study in American Culture* (New York: Harcourt Brace Jovanovich, 1929).

8. Cohen, *Making a New Deal*; Ronald Edsforth, *Class Conflict and Cultural Consensus: The Making of a Mass Consumer Society in Flint, Michigan* (New Brunswick, N.J.: Rutgers University Press, 1987); Levine, *Labor's True Woman*.

William Leach argues that early-twentieth-century mass consumption could liberate working-class women; see William Leach, "Transformations in a Culture of Consumption: Women and Department Stores, 1890–1925," *Journal of American History* Vol. 71, No. 2 (September 1984), pp. 319–42. Many scholars have shown the ways in which working-class leisure has served as an arena of class struggle, including Roy Rosenzweig, *Eight Hours for What We Will: Workers and Leisure in an Industrializing City, 1870–1920* (New York: Cambridge University Press, 1983); Kathy Peiss, *Cheap Amusements: Working Women and Leisure in Turn-of-the-Century New York* (Philadelphia: Temple University Press, 1986); Francis G. Couvares, "The Triumph of Commerce: Class Culture and Mass Culture in Pittsburgh," in Michael Frisch and Daniel Walkowitz, eds., *Working-Class America: Essays on Labor, Community, and American Society* (Urbana: University of Illinois Press, 1983), pp. 123–52; David Brundage, "The Producing Classes and the Saloon: Denver in the 1880s," *Labor History* 26 (1985), pp. 25–52; Richard Butsch, "Introduction: Leisure and Hegemony in America," in Richard Butsch, ed., *For Fun and Profit: The Transformation of Leisure into Consumption* (Philadelphia: Temple University Press, 1990), pp. 3–27.

9. For the concept of the "politicization of consumption," see Kathleen Blee, "Family Patterns and the Politicization of Consumption," *Sociological Spectrum* 5 (1985), pp. 295–316.

10. *Consumers' Cooperative Societies in the United States in 1920*, U.S. Bureau of Labor Statistics Bulletin No. 313 (October 1922) (Washington: Bureau of Labor Statistics, 1922); *Co-operation*, throughout 1921–22; *Tampa Citizen*, 27 June 1919. I am grateful to Eric Arnesen for sharing this last citation with me. For the Trade Union Promotional Leagues, see Chapter 9.

11. Cooperatives: Sean Wilentz, *Chants Democratic: New York City and the Rise of the American Working Class, 1788–1850* (New York: Oxford University Press, 1984), pp. 366–73, 381, 384–85; John R. Commons, *History of Labor in the United States*, Vol. I (New York: Macmillan, 1918), pp. 564–74; Gerald Grob, *Workers and Utopia: A Study of Ideological Conflict in the American Labor Movement, 1865–1900* (Evanston, Ill.: Northwestern University Press, 1961), pp. 44–57; Claire Anna Dahlberg Horner, "Producers' Cooperatives in the United States, 1865–1890," Ph.D. Diss., University of Pittsburgh, 1978.

Boycotts: Leo Wolman, *The Boycott in American Trade Unions* (Baltimore: Johns Hopkins University Press, 1916); Harry Wellington Laidler, *Boycotts and the Labor Struggle* (New York: John Lane, 1914); Michael Gordon, "The Labor Boycott in New York City, 1880–1886," *Labor History* 16 (Spring 1975), pp. 184–229; David Scobey, "Boycotting the Politics Factory: Labor Radicalism and the New York City Mayoral Election of 1884," *Radical History Review* Nos. 28–30 (September 1984), pp. 280–325; Gregory R. Zieren, "The Labor Boycott and Class Consciousness in Toledo, Ohio," in Charles Stephenson and Robert Asher, eds., *Life and Labor: Dimensions of American Working-Class History* (Albany: State University of New York Press, 1986), pp. 131–46; Linda C. and Theo J. Majka, *Farm Workers, Agribusiness, and the State* (Philadelphia: Temple University Press, 1982).

The union label: Ernest Spedden, *The Trade Union Label* (Baltimore: Johns Hopkins University Press, 1910).

12. Mari Jo Buhle, "Gender and Labor History," in J. Carroll Moody and Alice Kessler-Harris, eds., *Perspectives on American Labor History: The Problems of Synthesis* (De Kalb: Northern Illinois University Press, 1990), pp. 55–79; Alice Kessler-Harris, "A New Agenda for American Labor History: A Gendered Analysis and the Question of Class," in Moody and Kessler-Harris, eds., *Perspectives on American Labor History*, pp. 217–34; Ava Baron, "Gender and Labor History: Learning from the Past, Looking to the Future," in Ava Baron, ed., *Work Engendered: Toward a New History of American Labor* (Ithaca, N.Y.: Cornell University Press, 1991), pp. 1–46; and essays in *Work Engendered*; Joan Wallach Scott, "On Language, Gender, and Working-Class History," in Joan Wallach Scott, ed., *Gender and the Politics of History* (New York: Columbia University Press, 1988), pp. 53–67.

13. The literature theorizing women's labors in consumption and in reproducing the labor force is far too large to summarize here, but examples include Lise Vogel, *Marxism and the Oppression of Women: Toward a Unitary Theory* (New Brunswick, N.J.: Rutgers University Press, 1983); Margaret Benston, "The Political Economy of Women's Liberation," *Monthly Review* 21 (1969), pp. 13–27; Batya Weinbaum and Amy Bridges, "The Other Side of the Paycheck: Monopoly Capital and the Structures of Consumption," *Monthly Review* Vol. 28, No. 3 (July–August 1976), pp. 88–103; Nona Y. Glazer, "Servants to Capital: Unpaid Domestic Labor and Paid Work," *Review of Radical Political Economics* Vol. 16, No. 1 (1984), pp. 61–87. On adding housework to labor history, see Buhle, "Gender and Labor History." The distinction between housework and waged work becomes more complex when we consider the history of domestic service; see, for example, David M. Katzman, *Seven Days a Week: Women and Domestic Service in Industrializing America* (New York: Oxford University Press, 1978); Phyllis M. Palmer, *Domesticity and Dirt: Housewives and Domestic Service in the United States, 1920–1945* (Philadelphia: Temple University Press, 1989); Tera W. Hunter, "Household Workers in the Making: Afro-American Women in Atlanta and the New South, 1861 to 1920," Ph.D. Diss., Yale University, 1990. For the history of housework, see Susan Strasser, *Never Done: A History of American Housework* (New York: Pantheon, 1982); Ruth Schwartz Cowan, *More Work for Mother: The Ironies of Household Technology from the Open Hearth to the Microwave* (New York: Basic Books, 1983); S. J. Kleinberg, *The Shadow of the Mills: Working-Class Families in Pittsburgh, 1870–1907* (Pittsburgh: University of Pittsburgh Press, 1989). One rare example integrating the history of housewives and housework into working-class history is Christine Stansell, *City of Women: Sex and Class in New York City, 1789–1860* (New York: Knopf, 1986). For an analysis integrating women's family labors into labor history in the 1930s, see Elizabeth Faue, *Community of Suffering and Struggle: Women, Men, and the Labor Movement in Minneapolis, 1915–1945* (Chapel Hill: University of North Carolina Press, 1991). For the argument that in a society which assigns consumption to women, consumption becomes a workplace issue for women, see Robert Shaffer, "Women and the Communist Party, USA, 1930–1940," *Socialist Review* No. 45 (May–June 1979), p. 100.

14. Buhle, "Gender and Labor History," p. 67.

15. Harold Benenson, "Victorian Sexual Ideology and Marx's Theory of the Working

Class," *International Labor and Working Class History* No. 25 (Spring 1984), pp. 1–23. On the historical origins of gender biases inherent in Marxist notions of class, see also Jeanne Boydston's superb analysis in her *Home and Work: Housework, Wages, and the Ideology of Labor in the Early Republic* (New York: Oxford University Press, 1990); Sally Alexander, *Eve and the New Jerusalem: Socialism and Feminism in the Nineteenth Century* (New York: Pantheon, 1983); and Scott, "On Language, Gender, and Working-Class History."

16. For the history of white working-class housewives and the labor movement, see Levine, *Labor's True Woman*; Levine, "Workers' Wives"; Kathryn J. Oberdeck, "'Not Pink Teas': The Seattle Working Class Women's Movement, 1905–1918," *Labor History* Vol. 32, No. 2 (Spring 1991), pp. 193–230; Priscilla Long, "The Women of the Colorado Fuel and Iron Strike, 1911–1914," in Milkman, ed., *Women, Work, and Protest*, pp. 62–85; Marjorie Penn Lasky, "'Where I Was a Person': The Ladies' Auxiliaries in the 1934 Minneapolis Teamsters' Strikes," in Milkman, ed., *Women, Work, and Protest*, pp. 181–205; Elizabeth Jameson, "Imperfect Unions: Class and Gender in Cripple Creek, 1894–1904," in Milton Cantor and Bruce Laurie, eds., *Class, Sex, and the Woman Worker* (Westport, Conn.: Greenwood Press, 1977), pp. 166–202; Dana Frank, "Housewives, Socialists, and the Politics of Food: The 1917 New York Cost-of-Living Protests," *Feminist Studies* Vol. 11, No. 2 (Summer 1985), pp. 255–85.

17. Mary Blewett, in *Men, Women, and Work: Class, Gender, and Protest in the New England Shoe Industry, 1780–1910* (Urbana: University of Illinois Press, 1988), has illuminated important distinctions and divisions between different groups of female trade unionists, who could enter the labor movement from quite different structural positions in the family economy and waged-labor force. For the dynamics between wives and female trade unionists, see Maurine Wiener Greenwald, "Working-Class Feminism and the Family Wage Ideal: The Seattle Debate on Married Women's Right to Work, 1914–1920," *Journal of American History* Vol. 76, No. 1 (June 1989), pp. 118–49. On the relationship between the sexual division of labor in the family and the sexual division of labor in the trade-union movement, see Lasky, "'Where I Was a Person'"; Faue, *Community of Suffering and Struggle*; and the essays in Milkman, ed., *Women, Work, and Protest*. On wage-earning wives and the labor movement, see Carole Turbin, "Beyond Conventional Wisdom: Women's Wage Work, Household Economic Contribution, and Labor Activism in a Mid-Nineteenth-Century Working-Class Community," in Carol Groneman and Mary Beth Norton, eds., *"To Toil the Livelong Day": America's Women at Work, 1780–1980* (Ithaca, N.Y.: Cornell University Press, 1987), pp. 47–83.

18. For other efforts to integrate men's and women's labor history into a single account, see Blewett, *Men, Women, and Work*; Patricia A. Cooper, *Once a Cigar Maker: Men, Women, and Work Culture in American Cigar Factories* (Urbana: University of Illinois Press, 1987); and Ileen A. DeVault, *Sons and Daughters of Labor: Class and Clerical Work in Turn-of-the-Century Pittsburgh* (Ithaca, N.Y.: Cornell University Press, 1990). For a gendered rethinking of the ways in which the 1920s are conceptualized, see Susan Porter Benson, response to Montgomery in *International Labor and Working Class History*; on the barriers to wage-earning women's participation in the labor movement in the

1920s, see Kessler-Harris, "Problems of Coalition-Building," in Milkman, *Women, Work, and Protest*. For an analysis of the gender dynamics of business unionism in the 1930s, see Faue, *Community of Suffering and Struggle*.

19. David R. Roediger, "'Labor in White Skin': Race and Working-class History," in Mike Davis and Michael Sprinker, eds., *Reshaping the U.S. Left: Popular Struggles in the 1980s* (London: Verso, 1988), pp. 288–89.

20. On white racial identities and the U.S. labor movement, see Alexander Saxton, *The Indispensable Enemy: Labor and the Anti-Chinese Movement in California* (Berkeley: University of California Press, 1971); David Roediger, *The Wages of Whiteness: Race and the Making of the American Working Class* (London: Verso, 1991); and Gwendolyn Mink, *Old Labor and New Immigrants in American Political Development: Union, Party, and State, 1875–1920* (Ithaca, N.Y.: Cornell University Press, 1986). Yuji Ichioka has also underscored that "the working class of America was by definition the *white* working class"; see Ichioka, *The Issei: The World of the First Generation Japanese Immigrants, 1885–1924* (New York: Free Press, 1988), p. 107.

21. Tomás Almaguer, "Racial Domination and Class Conflict in Capitalist Agriculture: The Oxnard Sugar Beet Workers' Strike of 1903," *Labor History* Vol. 25, No. 3 (Summer 1984), pp. 325–50. Eric Arnesen and Yuji Ichioka, as well as earlier scholars, have pointed out white workers' pragmatic concerns in admitting workers of color. See Eric Arnesen, "Testing the Limits: Black Workers and Biracial Unions in the Age of Segregation," paper delivered at the American Historical Association Annual Convention, New York, 1990, p. 3; Eric Arnesen, *Waterfront Workers of New Orleans: Race, Class, and Politics, 1863–1923* (New York: Oxford University Press, 1991); Yuji Ichioka, "Asian Immigrant Coal Miners and the United Mine Workers of America: Race and Class at Rock Springs, Wyoming, 1907," *Amerasia Journal* Vol. 6, No. 2 (1979), pp. 16–17; William H. Harris, *The Harder We Run: Black Workers Since the Civil War* (New York: Oxford University Press, 1982), p. 53; and Herman D. Bloch, "Craft Unions and the Negro in Historical Perspective," *Journal of Negro History* 43 (1958), p. 11.

22. On Pacific coast patterns in labor history, see Michael Kazin, "The Great Exception Revisited: Organized Labor and Politics in San Francisco and Los Angeles, 1870–1940," *Pacific Historical Review* Vol. LV, No. 3 (August 1986), pp. 371–402.

1. Solidarity

1. C. H. Hanford, *Seattle and Environs, 1852–1924* (Chicago and Seattle: Pioneer Historical Publishing Co., 1924), pp. 238–40, 322, 441–46; Roger Sale, *Seattle Past to Present* (Seattle: University of Washington Press, 1976), pp. 61, 78, 104–05; Dorothy O. Johansen and Charles M. Gates, *Empire of the Columbia: A History of the Pacific Northwest* (New York: Harper & Bros., 1957), pp. 520, 526–27; Clare Tripp, *Monograph, Frye & Company* (Seattle: Washington Industries Education Bureau, 1927); Tripp, *Monograph, Fisher Flour Mills Co.* (Seattle: Washington Industries Education Bureau, 1927); Washington State Bureau of Statistics and Factory Inspection, *Tenth Biennial Report of the Bureau of Labor Statistics and Factory Inspection, 1915–16* (Olympia: State of

Washington, 1916), p. 142; United States Department of Commerce, Bureau of the Census, *Fourteenth Census of the United States* (1920) (Washington: Government Printing Office, 1920), Vol. IX, p. 1570; John Charles Miller, "A Statistical History of Manufacturing in the State of Washington to 1923," M.B.A. Thesis, University of Washington; Richard C. Berner, *Seattle 1900–1920: From Boomtown, Urban Turbulence to Restoration* (Seattle: Charles Press, 1991).

2. *Fourteenth Census*, Vol. III, pp. 1093, 1055; Vol. IX, pp. 222–38, 863, 1232–35, 1562, 1570, 1578–79; James Green, *The World of the Worker: Labor in Twentieth-Century America* (New York: Hill and Wang, 1980), pp. 6, 84.

3. Washington Bureau of Labor, *Ninth Biennial Report of the Bureau of Labor Statistics and Factory Inspection, 1913–14* (Olympia: State of Washington, 1914), pp. 13–17; Melvin G. DeShazo, "Radical Tendencies in the Seattle Labor Movement as Reflected in the Proceedings of Its Central Body," M.A. Thesis, University of Washington, 1925, p. ii.

4. United States Department of Commerce, Bureau of the Census, *Thirteenth Census of the United States* (1910) (Washington: Government Printing Office, 1910), Vol. III, p. 1004; *Fourteenth Census*, Vol. II, pp. 47, 58, 754, 947; Vol. III, p. 1093.

5. Jorgen Dahlie, *A Social History of Scandinavian Immigration: Washington State, 1895–1910* (New York: Arno Press, 1980), pp. 39, 42, 150–51, 171–72; Janice L. Reiff, "Urbanization and the Social Structure: Seattle, Washington, 1852–1910," Ph.D. Diss., University of Washington, 1981, pp. 213–15, 227, 230–31, 241, 245–47; Berner, *Seattle 1900–1920*, pp. 62–63; *Thirteenth Census*, Vol. III, p. 1004; *Fourteenth Census*, Vol. II, pp. 47, 58, 754, 947, 1093.

6. *Thirteenth Census*, Vol. III, p. 1004; *Fourteenth Census*, Vol. II, pp. 47, 58, 754, 947; David L. Nicandri, *Italians in Washington State: Emigration 1853–1924* (Tacoma: Washington State American Revolution Commission, 1978), pp. 47, 55, 59; Nellie Virginia Roe, "The Italian Immigrant in Seattle," M.A. Thesis, University of Washington, 1915, pp. 34–44; Lori Etta Cohn, "Residential Patterns of the Jewish Community of the Seattle Area, 1910–1980," M.A. Thesis, University of Washington, 1982, p. 32; Reiff, "Urbanization and the Social Structure," p. 210; Berner, pp. 69–72; Karyl Winn, "The Seattle Jewish Community," *Pacific Northwest Quarterly* Vol. 70, No. 2 (April 1979), p. 74.

7. *Fourteenth Census*, Vol. III, pp. 445, 691; Vol. II, p. 58; Reiff, "Urbanization and the Social Structure"; Berner, *Seattle 1900–1920*, pp. 61–64; Calvin F. Schmid, *Social Trends in Seattle* (Seattle: University of Washington Press, 1944).

8. Kazuo Ito, *Issei: A History of Japanese Immigration in North America* (Seattle: Japanese Community Service, 1973), p. 841. *Thirteenth Census*, Vol. III, p. 1004; *Fourteenth Census*, Vol. II, pp. 47, 58, 754, 947; Yuzo Murayama, "The Economic History of Japanese Immigration to the Pacific Northwest," Ph.D. Diss., University of Washington, 1982, pp. 141, 144, 255–56; Sylvia Junko Yanagisako, *Transforming the Past: Tradition and Kinship among Japanese Americans* (Stanford, Calif.: Stanford University Press, 1985), pp. 42–48; Evelyn Nakano Glenn, *Issei, Nisei, War Bride: Three Generations of Japanese American Women in Domestic Service* (Philadelphia: Temple University Press, 1986), pp. 68–79, 99–116; Katherine Dally Woolston, "Japanese Standards of Living

in Seattle," M.A. Thesis, University of Washington, 1927; Ito, *Issei*; Tokichi Tanaka, "The Japanese in Seattle," *The Coast* Vol. XII, No. 5 (November 1909), pp. 249–57; S. Frank Miyamoto, *Social Solidarity Among the Japanese in Seattle* (Seattle: University of Washington Press, 1981, reprint of 1931); S. Frank Miyamoto, "The Japanese Minority in the Pacific Northwest," *Pacific Northwest Quarterly* Vol. 54, No. 4 (October 1963). On residential segregation, see Woolston, "Japanese Standards of Living," p. 17; Murayama, "Economic History of Japanese Immigration," pp. 141, 144; Calvin F. Schmid, Charles E. Nobbe, and Arlene Mitchell, *Nonwhite Races, State of Washington* (Olympia: Washington State Planning and Community Affairs Agency, 1968), p. 62; Monica Sone, *Nisei Daughter* (Seattle: University of Washington Press, 1979), pp. 112–14; Ito, *Issei*, p. 96.

9. Robert E. Wynne, "Reaction to the Chinese in the Pacific Northwest and British Columbia: 1850 to 1910," Ph.D. Diss., University of Washington, 1964; *Thirteenth Census*, Vol. III, p. 1004; *Fourteenth Census*, Vol. II, pp. 47, 58, 754, 947; Schmid et al., *Nonwhite Races*, p. 69; Schmid, *Social Trends in Seattle*, p. 147; Art Chin, *Golden Tassels: A History of the Chinese in Washington: 1857–1977* (Seattle: Art Chin, 1977), pp. 98–100; John Herbert Geoghegan, "The Migratory Worker in Seattle: A Study in Social Disorganization and Exploitation," M.A. Thesis, University of Washington, 1923, pp. 58–59.

10. Horace Cayton, *Long Old Road* (New York: Trident Press, 1965), p. 129.

11. Quote: Esther Mumford, *Seattle's Black Victorians, 1852–1901* (Seattle: Ananse Press, 1971), p. 39, quoted in Quintard Taylor, "Black Urban Development – Another View: Seattle's Central District, 1910–1940," *Pacific Historical Review* Vol. LVIII, No. 4 (November 1989), p. 432; Quintard Taylor, "A History of Blacks in the Pacific Northwest, 1788–1970," Ph.D. Diss., University of Minnesota, 1977, pp. 430–35; *Fourteenth Census*, Vol. II, pp. 47, 58; Vol. IV, pp. 1132–35; Mumford, *Seattle's Black Victorians*; Robert Bedford Pitts, "Organized Labor and the Negro in Seattle," M.A. Thesis, University of Washington, 1941, pp. 2–4.

12. For background on the Seattle labor movement before the war, see Washington Bureau of Labor, *Ninth Biennial Report*, pp. 127–28; Washington State Bureau of Labor Statistics and Factory Inspection, *Tenth Biennial Report*, pp. 232–35; Washington State Federation of Labor, *Proceedings of the Twelfth Annual Convention* (Olympia: Washington State Federation of Labor, 1913), p. 79; *Proceedings of the Thirteenth Annual Convention* (1914), p. 110; *Proceedings of the Fourteenth Annual Convention* (1915), p. 77; Jonathan Dembo, "A History of the Washington State Labor Movement, 1885–1935," Ph.D. Diss., University of Washington, 1979; Carlos A. Schwantes, *Radical Heritage: Labor, Socialism and Reform in Washington and British Columbia, 1885–1917* (Seattle: University of Washington Press, 1979); Carlos A. Schwantes, "Leftward Tilt on the Pacific Slope: Indigenous Unionism and the Struggle Against AFL Hegemony in the State of Washington," *Pacific Northwest Quarterly* 70 (January 1979), pp. 24–34; Roll Books, Central Labor Council of Seattle and Vicinity, in Records of the King County Central Labor Council, University of Washington Manuscripts Collection.

13. Washington State Federation of Labor, *Yearbook*, 1927 (Seattle: Washington State Federation of Labor, 1927); *Washington State Labor News* (hereafter

WSLN) 20 February, 22 May 1925, 11 February 1927; Seattle *Union Record*, daily edition (hereafter SUR), 1 March 1919; Harry W. Call, *History of the Washington State Federation of Labor* (Seattle: Washington State Federation of Labor, 1954) p. 45; Robert L. Friedheim and Robin Friedheim, "The Seattle Labor Movement, 1919–1920," *Pacific Northwest Quarterly* Vol. 55, No. 4 (October 1964), p. 155; Seattle *Municipal News*, 15 February 1919; Solon DeLeon, ed., *The American Labor Who's Who* (New York: Hanford Press, 1925), pp. 8, 74, 103, 123, 183, 192, 212.

14. Melvyn Dubofsky, *We Shall Be All: A History of the IWW, Industrial Workers of the World* (New York: Quadrangle, 1969); Joyce L. Kornbluh, *Rebel Voices: An I.W.W. Anthology* (Ann Arbor: University of Michigan Press, 1964).

15. As Carlos Schwantes has shown, AFL domination was always weak in the pre–World War I Pacific Northwest. Seattle's organized workers, moreover, identified more with regional affiliations such as the Central Labor Council, the local Building Trades and Metal Trades Councils, and regional federations of their trades such as the Pacific Northwest Painters' Council, than they did with Gompers's AFL or their trade internationals. See Schwantes, *Radical Heritage*; Schwantes, "Leftward Tilt on the Pacific Slope"; Robert L. Friedheim, *The Seattle General Strike* (Seattle: University of Washington Press, 1964), pp. 23–54.

16. Margaret Jane Thompson, "Development and Comparison of Industrial Relationships in Seattle," M.B.A. Thesis, University of Washington, 1929), pp. 29–39; Barbara Winslow, "The Decline of Socialism in Washington, 1910–1925," M.A. Thesis, University of Washington, 1969, pp. 30–48; Harvey O'Connor, *The Revolution in Seattle* (New York: Monthly Review Press, 1964), pp. 85, 238–44; Schwantes, *Radical Heritage*, p. 209; Paul S. Parker to Harvey O'Connor, 21 June 1917, in Part II, Box 2, Harvey O'Connor Papers, Archives of Labor and Urban Affairs, Walter Reuther Library, Wayne State University.

17. Mary Joan O'Connell, "The Seattle Union Record: A Pioneer Labor Daily," M.A. Thesis, University of Washington, 1964, pp. 4, 6; DeShazo, "Radical Tendencies in the Seattle Labor Movement," pp. 24–25; Dembo, "History of the Washington State Labor Movement," Ch. 3; Winslow, "Decline of Socialism"; Schwantes, "Leftward Tilt on the Pacific Slope"; Schwantes, *Radical Heritage*; Paul B. Bushue, "Dr. Herman F. Titus and Socialism in Washington State, 1900–1909," M.A. Thesis, University of Washington, 1967.

18. Wynne, "Reaction to the Chinese"; Winslow, "Decline of Socialism," pp. 35–36; Carlos Schwantes, "Unemployment, Disinheritance, and the Origins of Labor Militancy in the Pacific Northwest, 1885–86," in G. Thomas Edwards and Carlos Schwantes, eds., *Experiences in a Promised Land: Essays on Pacific Northwest History* (Seattle: University of Washington Press, 1986); Washington State Federation of Labor, *Proceedings of the 8th Annual Convention* (1909), pp. 46–47, 53; *9th Annual Convention* (1910), p. 104; *10th Annual Convention* (1911), p. 78; *13th Annual Convention* (1914), pp. 38, 89–90; *15th Annual Convention* (1916), pp. 23–26, 58, 160; *17th Annual Convention* (1918), pp. 134–35; *18th Annual Convention* (1919), p. 13; DeShazo, "Radical Tendencies in the Seattle Labor Movement"; Pitts, "Organized Labor and the Negro"; Joseph Sylvester Jackson, "The Colored Marine Employees Benevolent Association of the Pacific, 1921–1934," M.A. Thesis, University of Washington, 1939; SUR, 10 April 1900; *Who's Who in Religious, Fraternal, Social,*

Civic and Commercial Life on the Pacific Coast (Seattle: Searchlight Publishing Co., 1926–27), p. 124.

19. Washington Bureau of Labor, *Ninth Biennial Report*, pp. 103–04; Roll Books, Seattle Central Labor Council.
20. SUR, 26 August 1919, 24 January 1921; Karl G. Yoneda, "Outline, 100 Years of Japanese Labor in U.S.A.," in Karl G. Yoneda Papers, University of Washington Manuscripts Collection; Berner, *Seattle 1900–1920*, p. 215; Tanaka, "Japanese in Seattle," p. 256; Yuji Ichioka, *The Issei: The World of the First Generation Japanese Immigrants, 1885–1924* (New York: Free Press, 1988), pp. 94–95, 140; Ito, *Issei*, pp. 144–46, 150, 153, 313, 315, 548, 860, 910, 916, 918; J. Watanabe to North American Japanese Association, 15 June 1920, in Records of Japanese Association of North America, Box 1, Folder 31.
21. Ito, *Issei*, p. 138. Karl Yoneda, *Ganbatte: Sixty-year Struggle of a Kibei Worker* (Los Angeles: UCLA Resource Development and Publications, Asian American Studies Center, 1983), p. xiv; Yoneda, "Outline"; Hyman Kublin, *Asian Revolutionary: The Life of Sen Katayama* (Princeton, N.J.: Princeton University Press, 1964); Sone, *Nisei Daughter*, p. 43; By-Laws, Japanese Shoemakers Association, n.d., in Records of the Japanese Association of North America, University of Washington Manuscripts Collection, Box 8, Folder 36; Katsutoshi Kurokawa, "The Seattle General Strike and Japanese Americans," Parts I–III, *Okayama Economic Review* Vol. 21, No. 4 (February 1990), pp. 31–50; Vol. 22, No. 1 (May 1990), pp. 73–89; Vol. 22, No. 2 (September 1990), pp. 149–66. My thanks to Yuji Ichioka for sharing these articles with me, and to Curtis Eberhard for translations.
22. Friedheim, *Seattle General Strike*, pp. 55–56.
23. Hanford, *Seattle and Environs*, pp. 356, 359; A. L. Kempster and successors (D. C. Barnes, W. H. McGrath, etc.), weekly reports to Stone and Webster Company (hereafter SW), in Box 122, Records of the Puget Sound Traction, Light and Power Company, University of Washington Manuscripts Collection, 13 August 1918; O'Connor, *Revolution in Seattle*, p. 108; Washington Bureau of Labor, *Eleventh Biennial Report* (1918), pp. 13–22; Friedheim, *Seattle General Strike*, pp. 56–58; Berner, *Seattle 1900–1920*, p. 273.
24. Hanford, *Seattle and Environs*, p. 356; O'Connor, *Revolution in Seattle*, p. 108; SW, 12 October 1918; 20 July 1918; Washington Bureau of Labor, *Twelfth Biennial Report*, pp. 17–18.
25. *Fourteenth Census*, Vol. IV, pp. 222–38, 1232–35; Vol. IX, pp. 1562, 1570, 1578.
26. Seattle Chamber of Commerce, "Seattle's Labor Shortage," pamphlet in Seattle Public Library, pp. 4–5; Friedheim, *Seattle General Strike*, p. 58. For a different perspective on the availability of jobs, see *Journeyman Barber* Vol. XIV, No. 3 (April 1918), p. 122.
27. Friedheim, *Seattle General Strike*, pp. 58–59; O'Connor, *Revolution in Seattle*, p. 90; Seattle Chamber of Commerce, "Seattle's Labor Shortage," p. 6 (quote), pp. 5–9; *Fourteenth Census*, Vol. II, p. 58.
28. Seattle Chamber of Commerce, "Seattle's Labor Shortage," pp. 8, 12.
29. "Seattle's Labor Shortage," quote, p. 6, pp. 9–11; Washington Bureau of Labor, *Eleventh Biennial Report*, pp. 155–56; Maurine Weiner Greenwald, "Working-Class Feminism and the Family Wage Ideal: The Seattle Debate on Married

Women's Right to Work, 1914–1920," *Journal of American History* Vol. 76, No. 1 (June 1989), p. 125.

30. Sone, *Nisei Daughter*, pp. 8–9; Yanagisako, *Transforming the Past*, p. 46; Schmid, *Nonwhite Races*, p. 62; Ito, *Issei*, pp. 153, 519–20, 548; *Cayton's Weekly* 28 February 1920; *Forge* 1 May 1919; SUR, 11, 30 April, 1 May, 25 August 1919, 30 April 1921; "Population," table compiled by Japanese Association of North America, Seattle Branch, 1 March 1922, Records of the Japanese Association of North America, Collection #1235–3, Box 5, Folder 21; *Reports of the Immigration Commission, Immigrants in Industries*, Part 25: Japanese and Other Immigrant Races in the Pacific Coast and Rocky Mountain States, Vol. I (U.S. Senate, 61st Congress, Second Session, Document No. 633) (Washington: Government Printing Office, 1911), pp. 100–43, 271–301.

31. Ito, *Issei*, pp. 188, 195–96, 200, and passim; Yanagisako, *Transforming the Past*, pp. 27–62; Glenn, *Issei, Nisei, War Bride*, pp. 42–50, 94–116; Sone, *Nisei Daughter*, pp. 5–7, 13; Ichioka, *The Issei*, pp. 5, 164–69; Yuji Ichioka, "*Amerika Nadeshiko*: Japanese Immigrant Women in the United States, 1900–1924," *Pacific Historical Review* 48 (1980), pp. 192–225.

32. Taylor, "History of Blacks in the Pacific Northwest," p. 436; Jackson, "Colored Marine Employees," pp. 13–17; Pitts, "Organized Labor and the Negro," pp. 4–5; Berner, *Seattle 1900–1920*, p. 251; *Cayton's Weekly*, 22, 29 December 1917; Horace R. Cayton, *Long Old Road: An Autobiography* (Seattle: University of Washington Press, 1963), p. 99.

33. Cayton, *Long Old Road*, pp. 36–37, 22–23.

34. Washington Bureau of Labor, *Twelfth Biennial Report*, pp. 17–18; *Seattle Times* 24, 27 January 1919; Thompson, "Industrial Relationships in Seattle," pp. 108–9; O'Connor, *Revolution in Seattle*, p. 109; Friedheim, *Seattle General Strike*, p. 59.

35. Louis Lorwin, *The American Federation of Labor: Policies and Prospects* (Washington: Brookings Institution, 1933), pp. 187–88; David Montgomery, *Workers' Control in America: Studies in the History of Work, Technology, and Labor Struggles* (Cambridge: Cambridge University Press, 1979), pp. 91–122.

36. Joe Pass to Harvey O'Connor, 14 January 1963, Harvey O'Connor Papers, Part II, Box 3, Folder "Joe Pass."

37. Friedheim, *Seattle General Strike*, 58–59; O'Connor, *Revolution in Seattle*, pp. 90, 108; Thompson, "Industrial Relationships in Seattle," p. 37; History Committee of the Seattle General Strike, *The Seattle General Strike* (Seattle: Seattle Union Record Publishing Co., [1919]), p. 8. See also SW, 12 October 1918.

38. Paraphrasing Plunkitt in William L. Riordan, *Plunkitt of Tammany Hall* (New York: Dutton, 1963), p. 3: "I seen my opportunities and I took 'em."

39. Thompson, "Industrial Relationships in Seattle," pp. 106, 112, 140; *Seattle Times* 30 January 1919; James Duncan to Robert Bridges, 12 April 1919, in Records of the Seattle Port Commission, Box 4, Folder 26, University of Washington Manuscripts Collection; SW, 30 August, 7 September 1918; Washington Bureau of Labor, *Eleventh Biennial Report*, pp. 64–70; Friedheim and Friedheim, "Seattle Labor Movement," pp. 146–56; Roll Books, Seattle Central Labor Council; Berner, *Seattle 1900–1920*, pp. 233–45; William Short, *A History of Activities of Seattle Labor Movement and Conspiracy of Employers to Destroy It and Attempted Suppression of Labor's Daily Newspaper* (Seattle: Seattle Union

Record Publishing Co., 1919), pp. 1–2, in William Short Papers, University of Washington Manuscripts Collection.

40. For characterization of the different locals, see Minutes, Central Labor Council of Seattle and Vicinity (hereafter CLC), in King County Central Labor Council Records; SUR, throughout 1917–19; and Thompson, "Industrial Relationships in Seattle." William Short, president of the Washington State Federation of Labor, wrote that many of the "ablest leaders of labor were absorbed into the employment service and other war emergency services. In addition to the inroads made on the experienced leadership . . . the old organization lost many of its most experienced members and leaders through the operation of the selective service act, due to the fact that they were engaged in what was [sic] regarded as non-essential industries, while the new membership was absorbed into what were denominated as 'war industries.'" Short, *History of Activities*, pp. 1–2. For internal dynamics of the locals, see also Reports of Agents #17 and #106, Broussais C. Beck Papers, University of Washington Manuscripts Collection.

41. David Montgomery, *The Fall of the House of Labor: The Workplace, the State, and American Labor Activism, 1865–1925* (Cambridge: Cambridge University Press, 1987), p. 332.

42. Ibid.

43. Washington Bureau of Labor, *Eleventh Biennial Report*, pp. 85–87; SUR, 8 December 1917, 29 April 1919; Washington State Federation of Labor, *Proceedings of the Eighteenth Annual Convention*, pp. 21–22; Greenwald, "Working-Class Feminism," p. 126. See Chapter 7 for a discussion of the lady barbers. On the hotel maids, a new all-female local formed in this period, see Ida L. Levi, "Hotel Maids Seek Protection in Organization," *Life and Labor* Vol. VII, No. 4 (April 1918), pp. 74–76.

44. *Cayton's Weekly*, 14 April 1919, 5 May 1920; *Forge*, 14 Oct. 1919; Cayton, *Long Old Road*, p. 118; Pitts, "Organized Labor and the Negro," pp. 39–42, 51.

45. SUR, 6 August 1919, 24 January 1921; Yoneda, "Outline, 100 Years of Japanese Labor in U.S.A."; Berner, *Seattle 1900–1920*, p. 215; Tanaka, "The Japanese in Seattle," p. 256; Ichioka, *The Issei*, pp. 94–95, 140; Ito, *Issei*, pp. 144–46, 150, 153, 313, 315, 548, 860, 910, 916, 918; J. Watanabe to North American Japanese Association, 15 June 1920, in Records of Japanese Association of North America, Box 1, Folder 31.

46. John Williamson, *Dangerous Scot: The Life and Work of an American "Undesirable"* (New York: International Publishers, 1969), p. 31; *Monthly Labor Review* Vol. XII, No. 2 (February 1921), p. 57.

47. Joe Pass, notes to Harvey O'Connor, 26 June 1962, O'Connor Papers, Part II, Box 3.

48. O'Connor, *Revolution in Seattle*, pp. 102, 109; Friedheim, *Seattle General Strike*, pp. 26–50; Winslow, "Decline of Socialism," pp. 40, 70; Roll Books, Seattle Central Labor Council; Thompson, "Industrial Relationships in Seattle"; Anna Louise Strong, *I Change Worlds: The Remaking of an American* (New York: Holt, 1935), pp. 64–65; Robert L. Tyler, *Rebels of the Woods: The I.W.W. in the Pacific Northwest* (Eugene: University of Oregon Press, 1967), pp. 77–78; Berner, *Seattle 1900–1920*, p. 248.

49. Williamson, *Dangerous Scot*, p. 34.

50. O'Connell, "Seattle Union Record"; Carlos A. Schwantes, "Washington State's

Pioneer Labor-Reform Press: A Bibliographical Essay and Annotated Check-list," *Pacific Northwest Quarterly* Vol. 71, No. 3 (July 1980), pp. 112–26; see SUR for visiting speakers; Strong, *I Change Worlds*, pp. 68–69. On the radical community, see also Sarah E. Sharbach, "A Woman Acting Alone: Louise Olivereau and the First World War," *Pacific Northwest Quarterly* Vol. 78, Nos. 1–2 (January–April 1987), pp. 32–40.

51. SW, 7 September 1918.
52. *Seattle Times*, 30 January 1919; Thompson, "Industrial Relationships in Seattle," p. 102; Short, *History of Activities*, p. 1.
53. Montgomery, *Fall of the House of Labor*, p. 332.
54. See SUR and CLC throughout 1918–19.
55. O'Connor, *Revolution in Seattle*, pp. 105–6.
56. Cayton, *Long Old Road*, p. 116.
57. SUR, 29 April 1919; see Chapter 7.
58. *Cayton's Weekly*, 16 March 1918.
59. *Cayton's Weekly*, 28 September 1918.
60. Seattle Chamber of Commerce, "Seattle's Labor Shortage," p. 14.
61. Lorwin, *American Federation of Labor*, p. 501; *Cayton's Weekly*, 22 December 1917, 26 October 1918; Sterling Spero and Abram Harris, *The Black Worker: The Negro and the Labor Movement* (New York: Columbia University Press, 1931; reprint New York: Atheneum, 1969); Herbert R. Northrup, *Organized Labor and the Negro* (New York: Harper & Bros., 1944); Herman D. Bloch, "Craft Unions and the Negro in Historical Perspective," *Journal of Negro History* 43 (1958), pp. 10–33; Herman D. Bloch, "Labor and the Negro, 1866–1910," *Journal of Negro History* 50 (1965), pp. 163–84; Herbert Hill, "Racial Practices of Organized Labor," *New Politics* IV (1965), pp. 26–46; Phillip Foner, *Organized Labor and the Black Worker, 1619–1974* (New York: Praeger, 1974); John R. Commons et al., *History of Labour in the United States*, Vol. II (New York: Macmillan, 1918), pp. 252–66; Gwendolyn Mink, *Old Labor and New Immigrants in American Political Development: Union, Party, and State, 1875–1920* (Ithaca, N.Y.: Cornell University Press, 1986), esp. Ch. 3.
62. *Fourteenth Census*, Vol. IV, pp. 228–38.
63. For IWW imagery, see Kornbluh, *Rebel Voices*; for images of women, see Ann Schofield, "Rebel Girls and Union Maids: The Woman Question in the Journals of the AFL and IWW, 1905–1920," *Feminist Studies* Vol. 9, No. 2 (Summer 1983), pp. 335–58; for AFL imagery, see Elizabeth Faue, *Community of Suffering and Struggle: Women, Men, and the Labor Movement in Minneapolis, 1915–1945* (Chapel Hill: University of North Carolina Press, 1991), pp. 69–99; and the journals published by the different internationals.
64. On the factors limiting white women's presence in the AFL in this period, see Alice Kessler-Harris, *Out to Work: A History of Wage-Earning Women in the United States* (New York: Oxford University Press, 1982), pp. 155–60; Alice Kessler-Harris, *A Woman's Wage: Historical Meanings and Social Consequences* (Lexington: University Press of Kentucky, 1990), pp. 6–32; Martha May, "Bread Before Roses: American Workingmen, Labor Unions, and the Family Wage," in Ruth Milkman, ed., *Women, Work, and Protest: A Century of US Women's Labor History* (Boston: Routledge & Kegan Paul, 1985), pp. 1–21; Patricia A. Cooper, *Once a Cigar Maker: Men, Women, and Work Culture in American*

Cigar Factories, 1900–1919 (Urbana: University of Illinois Press, 1987), pp. 219–21; Carole Turbin, "Beyond Conventional Wisdom: Women's Wage Work and Household Economic Contribution, and Labor Activism in a Mid-Nineteenth Century Working-Class Community," in Carol Groneman and Mary Beth Norton, eds., *"To Toil the Livelong Day": America's Women at Work, 1780–1980* (Ithaca, N.Y.: Cornell University Press, 1987), pp. 47–67; Susan Porter Benson, *Counter Cultures: Saleswomen, Managers and Customers in American Department Stores, 1890–1940* (Urbana: University of Illinois Press, 1986); Susan Levine, *Labor's True Woman: Carpet Weavers, Industrialization, and Labor Reform in the Gilded Age* (Philadelphia: Temple University Press, 1984); Mary Blewett, *Men, Women, and Work: Class, Gender, and Protest in the New England Shoe Industry, 1780–1910* (Urbana: University of Illinois Press, 1988); Ava Baron, "An 'Other' Side of Gender Antagonism at Work: Men, Boys, and the Remasculinization of Printers' Work, 1830–1920," in Ava Baron, ed., *Work Engendered: Toward a New Labor History* (Ithaca, N.Y.: Cornell University Press, 1991); Leslie Woodcock Tentler, *Wage-Earning Women: Industrial Work and Family Life in the United States, 1900–1930* (New York: Oxford University Press, 1979). For a superb analysis of structural discrimination against women in the CIO, see Sharon Hartman Strom, "Challenging 'Woman's Place': Feminism, the Left, and Industrial Unionism in the 1930s," *Feminist Studies* Vol. 9, No. 2 (Summer 1983), pp. 359–86.

65. *Fourteenth Census*, Vol. IV, p. 22; on domestics, see Donna L. Van Raaphorst, *Union Maids Not Wanted: Organizing Domestic Workers, 1870–1940* (New York: Praeger, 1988) and David M. Katzman, *Seven Days a Week: Women and Domestic Service in Industrializing America* (New York: Oxford University Press, 1978). On organizing housewives, see also Dana Frank, "Housewives, Socialists, and the Politics of Food: The 1917 New York Cost-of-Living Protests," *Feminist Studies* Vol. 11, No. 2 (Summer 1985), pp. 355–85.

66. Levine, *Labor's True Woman*, pp. 129–53.

67. For U.S. working-class opposition to World War I, see Phillip S. Foner, *History of the Labor Movement of the United States, Vol. 7: Labor and World War I, 1914–1918* (New York: International Publishers, 1987); Montgomery, *Fall of the House of Labor*, pp. 371–72; and Frank L. Grubbs, *Struggle for Labor Loyalty: Gompers, the A.F. of L., and the Pacifists, 1917–1920* (Durham, N.C.: Duke University Press, 1968). For opposition in Seattle, see Strong, *I Change Worlds*, pp. 55–60; Winslow, "Decline of Socialism," pp. 49–68, 70; Dembo, "History of the Washington State Labor Movement," pp. 140, 142–49, 188, 191; Berner, *Seattle 1900–1920*, pp. 229–32, 237.

68. William Preston Jr., *Aliens and Dissenters: Federal Suppression of Radicals, 1903–1933* (Cambridge, Mass.: Harvard University Press, 1963), pp. 153, 155–56, 160–62, 172; Sarah Sharbach, "Louise Olivereau and the Seattle Radical Community, 1917–1923," M.A. Thesis, University of Washington, 1986, pp. 80–82; Seattle Police Bulletin, 28 March, 4 October 1918, clippings in Michael T. Powers Papers, University of Washington Manuscripts Collection, Box 1, Folder 13; Berner, *Seattle 1900–1920*, pp. 255–59; Albert F. Gunns, "Civil Liberties and Crisis: The Status of Civil Liberties in the Pacific Northwest, 1917–1942," Ph.D. Diss., University of Washington, 1971, pp. 11, 18, 40 and Chapters I–II; SW, 18 January 1919; Lee Forrest Pendergrass, "Urban Reform and Voluntary Association: A Case Study of the Seattle Municipal League,"

Ph.D. Diss., University of Washington, 1972, pp. 82–83; O'Connor, *Revolution in Seattle*, pp. 11, 114, 151, 153, 206; Winslow, "Decline of Socialism," pp. 53, 59, 161–67; Strong, *I Change Worlds*, pp. 59–63; Friedheim, *Seattle General Strike*, pp. 11–12.

69. *Seattle Star*, 30 January 1919.
70. Friedheim, *Seattle General Strike*, pp. 64–67; History Committee of the Seattle General Strike, *The Seattle General Strike* (Seattle: Seattle Union Record Publishing Co., 1919), pp. 8–10; Alexander Bing, *Wartime Strikes and Their Adjustment* (New York: Dutton, 1921), p. 27; Wilfrid Harris Crook, *The General Strike: A Study of Labor's Tragic Weapon in Theory and Practice* (Chapel Hill: University of North Carolina Press, 1931), p. 541; *Monthly Labor Review* Vol. XII, No. 2 (February 1921), p. 57.
71. History Committee, *The Seattle General Strike*, pp. 8–12; Friedheim, pp. 64–69; Thompson, "Industrial Relationships in Seattle," pp. 44–47; Strong, *I Change Worlds*, p. 75; *Seattle Times*, 26, 27 January 1919.
72. Friedheim, *Seattle General Strike*, Chapters III–IV; O'Connor, *Revolution in Seattle*, Chapter VI; *Seattle Times*, 25–31 January 1919; History Committee, pp. 8–10.
73. *Seattle Times*, 30 January 1919.
74. Ibid.
75. *Seattle Star*, 23 January 1919.
76. *Mixer and Server* Vol. XXVIII, No. 4 (15 April 1919), p. 66.
77. *Journeyman Barber* Vol. XV, No. 6 (July 1919), p. 250. For the importance of solidarity to the strike, see also *Seattle Star*, 30 January 1919; History Committee, *The Seattle General Strike*, p. 18.
78. *Seattle Star*, 30 January 1919.
79. SW, 18 January 1919.
80. SW, 1 February 1919.
81. *Cayton's Weekly*, 8 February 1919. The *Star* similarly reported: "The entire United States is watching Seattle labor for the next move that is to determine the course of events during the transition period, according to at least half a dozen of the speakers" at a Central Labor Council meeting. *Seattle Star*, 23 January 1919.
82. *Seattle Times*, 26 January 1919.
83. *Seattle Star*, 23 January 1919.
84. *Seattle Times*, 30 January 1919.
85. CLC 29 January, 5 February 1919; *Seattle Star*, 1, 6 February 1919; Minutes, Local #76, American Federation of Musicians, 4 February 1919, in possession of Local #76, Seattle, Washington; Friedheim, *Seattle General Strike*, pp. 87–88.
86. History Committee, *The Seattle General Strike*, pp. 41–44; *Seattle Star*, 23, 27 January 1919.
87. SUR, 4 February 1919.
88. *Seattle Star*, 7 February 1919.
89. SW, 9 February 1919.
90. On the kitchens, see SUR, 4, 8, 11 February 1919; *Seattle Star*, 30 January, 3 February 1919; "Official Central Labor Council Strike Bulletin," 7 February 1919, pp. 1–2, in Seattle Public Library, Miscellaneous Labor Papers; *Seattle Times*, 5, 9 February 1919; History Committee, *The Seattle General Strike*,

pp. 41–45. The commissary system had additional problems. Because the city's public transportation systems had completely shut down, cooks and other volunteers had problems getting to and from their tasks. The cafeterias originally planned for each diner to bring his or her own utensils, but protests from diners forced them to purchase plates and cups. Some establishments withdrew their earlier offers of kitchens. Other "eating halls" failed to serve meals until late afternoon. Most serious, when the strike ended, the metal trades committee left with the bills absorbed a $6,000 to $7,000 loss. Bert Swain, secretary-treasurer of the Metal Trades Council, estimated that if the strike had lasted another four or five days the commissaries would have broken even on their investment in trucks and equipment; but they had sustained heavy losses in leftover bread and other incorrect estimates. The milk delivery system similarly sustained financial losses from over- and underestimates.

91. Taylor, "Black Urban Development," p. 437; *Seattle Star*, 3 February 1919; History Committee, *The Seattle General Strike*, p. 28; Ito, *Issei*, p. 152; Katherine Jane Lentz, "Japanese-American Relations in Seattle," M.A. Thesis, University of Washington, 1924, p. 82; *International Weekly*, 6 February 1919. For other accounts of the Seattle general strike, see Washington State Federation of Labor, *Proceedings of the Eighteenth Convention* (1919), pp. 19–21; for Seattle labor's official account, History Committee; for reminiscences, Strong, *I Change Worlds*, and O'Connor, *Revolution in Seattle*; for the most extended secondary account, Friedheim, *Seattle General Strike*; for employers' perspectives, SW, 25 January, 1, 10 February 1919; Ole Hanson, *Americanism versus Bolshevism* (Garden City, N.Y.: Doubleday, 1920).

92. Friedheim, *Seattle General Strike*, pp. 89, 105–06, 181; Kurokawa, "The Seattle General Strike."

93. See Crook, *The General Strike*, pp. 528–43, for another account of the end of the strike. Ed T. Levi of the cooks advised in the aftermath of the strike: "No general strike should be called until a date is set for its ending"; see *Mixer and Server* Vol. XXVII, No. 4 (15 April 1919), p. 66.

94. SUR, 4 February 1919; *Seattle Star*, 8 February 1919; O'Connor, *Revolution in Seattle*, p. 140; SW 17 February 1919; Friedheim, *Seattle General Strike*, pp. 123–45; Washington State Federation of Labor, *Proceedings of the Eighteenth Convention*, pp. 19–21. For an extended sociological analysis of the general strike and its after-effects on working-class consciousness, see also Rob Rosenthal, "After the Deluge: The Seattle General Strike of 1919 and its Aftermath," M.A. Thesis, University of California, Santa Barbara, 1980.

95. O'Connor, *Revolution in Seattle*, p. 132. On Strong, see her 1935 autobiography, *I Change Worlds*, and Tracy B. Strong and Helene Keyssar, *Right in Her Soul: The Life of Anna Louise Strong* (New York: Random House, 1983).

2. Cooperatives

1. Seattle *Union Record*, daily edition (hereafter SUR), 25 April 1919.
2. *Co-operation* V:1 (January 1919), p. 10.
3. Minutes, Central Labor Council of Seattle and Vicinity (hereafter CLC), 12 March 1919, in Records of the King County Central Labor Council, Box 8, University of Washington Manuscripts Collection.

4. John R. Commons et al., *History of Labour in the United States* (New York: Macmillan, 1918), Vol. I, pp. 564–74; Sean Wilentz, *Chants Democratic: New York City and the Rise of the American Working Class, 1788–1850* (New York: Oxford University Press, 1984), pp. 366–67, 373, 381, 384–85; Gerald Grob, *Workers and Utopia: A Study of Ideological Conflict in the American Labor Movement, 1865–1900* (Evanston, Ill.: Northwestern University Press, 1961), pp. 44–57; Claire Anna Dahlberg Horner, "Producers' Cooperatives in the United States, 1865–1890," Ph.D. Diss., University of Pittsburgh, 1978; Clifton K. Yearley, Jr., *Britons in American Labor* (Baltimore: Johns Hopkins University Press, 1957); Daniel J. Walkowitz, *Worker City, Company Town: Iron and Cotton-Worker Protest in Troy and Cohoes, New York, 1855–84* (Urbana: University of Illinois Press, 1978), pp. 92, 96–98, 184–85, 190.

5. Charles Pierce LeWarne, *Utopias on Puget Sound, 1885–1915* (Seattle: University of Washington Press, 1975); *John Swinton's Paper*, 13 June 1886 (for a Seattle cooperative in 1886); Doug Honig, *Experiments in Democracy: Cooperatives in the Seattle Area* (Seattle: Puget Consumers' Cooperative, 1981); *Pacific Grange News* January 1911; *Co-operator* (Burley, Wash.), January 1904; list of Washington State Cooperatives, 1904, clipping in possession of Doug Honig; photograph of Producers and Consumers Association, 1908, possession of Doug Honig; I am grateful to Doug Honig for sharing this material with me; Carl Lunn, "How We Cooperate Out West," *Life and Labor* Vol. X, No. 7 (September 1920), p. 205; *Northwestern Co-operative News* I:5 (1 September 1919); *Co-operative Consumer* IV:4 (April 1918), p. 6; *Proceedings of the First American Co-operative Convention*, Springfield, Ill., 25–27 September 1919 (Springfield: Co-operative Association of America, 1919), p. 109; Washington State Federation of Labor (hereafter WSFL), *Proceedings of the Sixteenth Convention* (Olympia, WSFL, 1917), p. 14.

On Swedish cooperatives: Peder Alex, "The Consumer Cooperative as Educator," paper delivered at the Conference on Consumers' Cooperation in the Western World, 1840–1950, Lawrence, Kansas, 7 April 1990; Gary DeLoss, "Making Change: Consumer Cooperatives in Sweden," in Ralph Nader Task Force on European Cooperatives, *Making Change? Learning from Europe's Consumer Cooperatives* (Washington: Center for the Study of Responsive Law, 1985), pp. 63–91.

6. SUR, 28 January, 3, 12 February, 7, 11, 12, 14, 20, 29 March, 2, 12, 23 April, 4, 7 June, 13, 14 November 1919; 7 January 1920; Seattle *Union Record*, weekly edition (hereafter SURW), 12 February, 1, 15 March 1919; Lunn, "How We Cooperate Out West," p. 205; *Co-operation* V:7 (July 1919), p. 108; V:9 (September 1919), pp. 135–36; *Co-operative Consumer* IV:1 (January 1918), p. 13; IV:4 (April 1918), p. 6; *Northwestern Co-operative News* I:5 (1 September 1919), p. 5; Earl Shimmons, "The Seattle Union Record," mss. in Harry Ault Papers, University of Washington Manuscripts Collection, Part I, Box 7, Folder 9, p. 31; *Forge*, 5 July 1919; First Co-operative Convention, p. 122.

7. Harry Ault to Roger Baldwin, 29 August 1922, Ault Papers, Box 4, Folder 17. On the CFPA see its monthly newsletter, *The Co-operator* (in Seattle Public Library); U. G. Moore, "The Rise and Fall of the Seattle Food Products Association," *Co-operation* IX:1 (January 1923), p. 9; *Co-operation* V:3 (March

1919), p. 48; First Cooperative Convention, pp. 109–23; and reports in Min-
utes of CLC and SUR throughout 1919–21, esp. SUR, 26 March, 7 June, 28
August, 23 October 1919; D. F. Stanley to SUR, 1 December 1919, in Ault
Papers, Part I, Box 3, Folder 63.

8. On the plumbers: History Committee, pp. 52–55; SUR, 1 April 1919; SURW,
   1, 8 March 1919; CLC, 12 March 1919; First Cooperative Convention, p. 114;
   Co-operation V:9 (September 1919), p. 136; V:10 (October 1919), p. 152.
   City employees: SUR, 20 March, 28 June, 3 July 1919. On Scandia Cooperative:
   SURW, 14 June 1919; SUR, 14 June 1919; Lunn, "How We Cooperate Out
   West," p. 205; First Cooperative Convention, pp. 113–114; *Co-operation* V:10
   (October 1919), p. 152. On Cooperative Cafe: *Forge*, 10 May, 5, 12 July
   1919, 21 February 1920; First Cooperative Convention, p. 113. On Equity
   Print Shop: *International Weekly*, 31 January 1919; *Forge*, 11 October 1919;
   Harvey O'Connor, *The Revolution in Seattle* (New York: Monthly Review
   Press, 1964), pp. 147, 238–39; Hays Jones to Harvey O'Connor, n.d. [1962],
   in Harvey O'Connor Papers, Part II, Archives of Labor and Urban Affairs,
   Walter Reuther Library, Wayne State University. On the cleaners and dyers:
   Report of Agent #106 (hereafter Agent #106) 17 October 1919, Broussais C.
   Beck Papers, Boxes 1–2, University of Washington Manuscripts Collection;
   SUR, 13 January, 30 October, 1 November 1919; SURW, 18 October 1919.
   On the barbers: SUR, 12, 17 February 1919; SURW, 20 February 1919; His-
   tory Committee, p. 52. On auto mechanics: SURW, 18 October 1919; CLC,
   10, 24 September 1919; *Forge*, 1 November 1919. On the longshoremen:
   Minutes, CLC, 28 January 1920; Agent #106 28, 30 January 1920, 26 February
   1920; Report of Agent #17 (hereafter Agent #17), 10 May 1920, Broussais
   C. Beck Papers, Boxes 1–2; Agent #17, 16 June 1920; SUR, 24 March, 28
   April 1919; Lunn, "How We Cooperate Out West," p. 207; *New Majority*
   [29?] May 1920, in Scrapbooks, Co-operative League of the United States,
   Boxes 25 and 26, Unprocessed collection, Archives of the State Historical
   Society of Wisconsin. On painters: SUR, 20 February 1919. On the carpenters:
   SUR, 17 May, 2, 10 September 1919. On the shoe repairers: Minutes, CLC,
   29 October 1919; First Cooperative Convention, p. 114. On fishermen: SUR,
   17 June 1919. On campers: SUR, 3 July 1919 (quote); 10 May 1919; Minutes,
   Local #202, International Typographers' Union (hereafter Minutes, Typo-
   graphers #202), in Records of Local #99, International Typographers' Union,
   Box 16, University of Washington Manuscripts Collection, 6 April 1919;
   flyers, Co-operative Campers, Pacific Northwest Collection, University of
   Washington Library. See also proposed or organized cooperatives in shipbuilding: *Co-operative Consumer* IV:4 (April 1918), p. 61; musicians: *Musicland*, 15 January, 1 March 1922 (in collection of Local #76, American
   Federation of Musicians, Seattle); coal mining: Minutes, CLC, 17 September
   1919; ferry service for farmers in Poulsbo: SUR, 4 April 1919.

9. Organization Committee Cooperative Food Products Association to the
   Members of Organized Labor, n.d. [1919], Box 2, Folder 19, Beck Papers;
   SUR, 15, 20 May, 26, 27, 30 June, 11, 15 July, 7 August 1919; SURW, 15,
   22 March, 26 April, 17 May 1919; Minutes, CLC, 9 April, 2 July, 6 August
   1919; Minutes, Typographers' #202, 4 May, 3 August 1919; *Co-operative
   Consumer* IV:4 (April 1918) p. 61.

10. SUR, 23 October 1919; Minutes, CLC, 18 February, 8, 22 September, 24 November 1920.

11. SUR, 11 July 1919; *Northwestern Co-operative News* I:5 (1 September 1919). On wholesale operations and statewide networks: SUR, 24 March, 7 April, 26 July, 2 August 1919; SURW, 13 September, 18 October 1919; Lunn, "How We Cooperate Out West," p. 206; *Co-operative Consumer* IV:1 (January 1918), p. 13; Minutes, CLC, 5 February 1919; *Co-operation* V:9 (September 1919), p. 134; VIII:4 (April 1922), pp. 68–69; Second Cooperative Convention, p. 57; Carl Lunn to Harry Ault, 7 May 1920, Ault Papers, Part I, Box 3, Folder 27; *Co-operator* I:12 (October 1920), p. 3.

12. Charles Neiderhauser and E. O. F. Ames should be included in this group; nationally, Albert Sonnichsen as well. *Northwestern Co-operative News* I:5 (1 September 1919), p. 1; SURW, 5 July 1919; SUR, 12 February, 11 April, 11 July 1919; 2 January 1920; First Cooperative Convention, pp. 109–23, 260; Second Cooperative Convention. For national theorists, see issues of *Co-operation* (formerly *Consumers' Co-operation*). On James Warbasse, see Kathleen G. Donohue, "'A Cheap Store is Not a Great Social Aim': Consumer Legitimacy in a Cooperative Society," paper delivered at the Conference on Consumer Cooperation in the Western World, 1840–1950, University of Kansas, Lawrence, 7 April 1990; James Peter Warbasse, *Cooperative Democracy Attained Through Voluntary Association of the People as Consumers*, 2d ed. (New York: Macmillan, 1927). On the national cooperative movement: Florence Parker, *The First 125 Years: A Study of Distributive and Service Cooperation in the United States, 1829–1954* (Chicago: Cooperative League of the U.S.A., 1956); Albert Sonnichsen, *Consumers' Cooperation* (New York: Macmillan, 1920); Russell Sage Foundation, *Consumers' Cooperation* (New York: Russell Sage Foundation, 1921); Ellis Cowling, *Cooperatives in America: Their Past, Present and Future* (New York: Coward-McCann, 1938).

13. SUR, 29 April 1919.

14. *Co-operator* I:14 (December 1920), p. 3.

15. Quote: *Co-operator* II:3 (March 1921), p. 4; see also p. 2; I:6 (June 1921), p. 4; First Cooperative Convention, p. 119; *Co-operation* V:8 (August 1919), p. 120; *Forge*, 5 July 1919.

16. SUR, 28 April 1919; WSFL, *Proceedings of the 17th Convention* (Olympia, WSFL: 1918) p. 153.

17. SUR, 26 June 1919; *Co-operation* V:9 (September 1919) p. 135. Almost every issue of the *Co-operator* ran an article on coops in Britain or Europe. See, e.g., I:13 (November 1920), p. 6. For evidence of rank-and-file awareness in Seattle of British coops, see, e.g., SUR, 30 April 1919. On British cooperatives, see G. D. H. Cole, *A Century of Co-operation* (Manchester: Co-operative Union, 1944); Stephen Yeo, ed., *New Views of Co-operation* (London, 1988: Routledge). For the World War I statistics, see Paddy Maguire, "Co-operation and Crisis: Government, Co-operation and Politics, 1917–22," in Yeo, *New Views of Co-operation*, p. 192.

18. SUR, 7 January 1919; *Co-operator* I:5 (May 1921), p. 2; I:6 (April 1920), p. 3.

19. Ellen Furlough, *Consumer Cooperation in France: The Politics of Consumption, 1834–1930* (Ithaca, N.Y.: Cornell University Press, 1991); Carl

Strikwerda, "Working Class Culture as a Battleground: The Political Economy of Consumer Cooperation in Belgium, 1880–1980," paper presented at the Conference on Consumers' Cooperation in the Western World. For Seattle cooperators' awareness of European cooperatives, see *Co-operation* VI:1 (January 1920), p. 12; SUR, 30 April 1919, 2 January 1920; *Co-operator*, all issues.

20. James Weinstein, *The Decline of Socialism in America, 1912–1925* (New York: Vintage, 1967); David A. Shannon, *The Socialist Party of America, A History* (New York: Macmillan, 1955); Julia Greene, "The Strike at the Ballot Box: Politics and Partisanship in the American Federation of Labor, 1881–1916," Ph.D. Diss., Yale University, 1990; Marc Karson, *American Labor Unions and Politics* (Carbondale: Southern Illinois University Press, 1958).

21. For a survey of consumers' cooperation nationwide, see *Consumers' Co-operative Societies in the United States in 1920*, U.S. Bureau of Labor Statistics Bulletin no. 313 (October 1922) (Washington: Bureau of Labor Statistics, 1922); *Co-operation* (formerly *Consumers' Co-operation*) carries reports from cooperatives; for other references to cooperatives, see *Northwestern Co-operative News* I:5 (1 September 1919), p. 5; Minutes, CLC, 22 December 1920; Agent #106, 7 March 1920; *Co-operation* V:10 (October 1919), pp. 152–53, for Washington State; *New Orleans Times-Picayune*, 24 February–23 April 1920; *Houston Labor Journal*, 4 October, 22 November 1919; *Savannah Morning News*, 10 May 1919, 1 May 1920; *Virginia Pilot and Norfolk Landmark*, 19, 21 October 1917; Augusta, Ga., *Labor Review*, 4 January 1919; *Boilermakers' and Iron Ship Builders' Journal* Vol. XXXI, No. 6 (May 1919), p. 469; *Brotherhood of Locomotive Firemen and Enginemens' Journal* Vol. 6, No. 9 (1 November 1922), p. 14, and the journal's "Consumers' Co-operation Department," many issues in this period. My thanks to Eric Arnesen for sharing this information.

22. See *Consumers' Co-operation.*

23. SUR, 10, 13 February, 25, 29 April, 1, 6 May, 31 October 1919; 24 May 1921; *Co-operation* V:9 (September 1919), p. 135; For citywide educational campaigns, see, e.g., Agent #106 6 May, 19 September 1919.

24. The proselytizers indeed complained that rank-and-file workers often failed to heed their advice; First Cooperative Convention, p. 122; SUR, 12, 14 February, 11 March 1919; *Co-operation* V:9 (September 1919) p. 135.

25. O'Connor, *The Revolution in Seattle*, p. 128; *Co-operation* V:3 (March 1919), p. 48.

26. Alanson Sessions to James Warbasse, 18 February 1919, Co-operative League of the U.S.A. Records, Box 1, New York Public Library Manuscripts Collection; A. L. Kempster, and successors, weekly reports to Stone and Webster Company (hereafter SW), Box 122, Records of the Puget Sound Traction, Light and Power Company, University of Washington Manuscripts Collection, 25 January 1919; *Co-operation* V:3 (March 1919), p. 28; SUR, 28 January 1919; O'Connor, *The Revolution in Seattle*, p. 128.

27. Agent #106, 4 November 1919; *Seattle Star*, 25, 27 January 1919; SUR, 5 February 1919. For this motivation behind cooperatives, see also SUR, 19 September 1919, 19 May 1921.

28. History Committee, p. 6.

29. Ibid., p. 52.
30. Sessions to Warbasse, 18 February 1919; History Committee, pp. 53, 58.
31. O'Connor, *The Revolution in Seattle*, p. 128; *Co-operation* V:3 (March 1919) p. 48.
32. History Committee, pp. 53–54. The *Record* reported, "The recent camouflaged 'booze raid' resulted in a landslide for the meat markets and grocery in the Co-op Market" (SUR, 12 February 1919). The Central Labor Council's History Committee similarly traced the cooperatives' "sudden growth not only to the strike, but to [the] raid" (pp. 53–54).
33. SUR, 28 January 1919.
34. History Committee, pp. 52–55; SUR, 4 February, 1 March, 1, 26 April 1919; SURW, 1, 8 March 1919; Minutes, CLC, 12 March 1919; First Cooperative Convention, p. 11.
35. National Industrial Conference Board, *The Cost of Living in the United States* (New York: National Industrial Conference Board, 1926), pp. 30, 174–75; Paul Douglas, *Real Wages in the United States, 1890–1926* (New York: Houghton Mifflin, 1930), pp. 389–400; Eugene Rotwein, "Post World War I Price Movement and Policy," *Journal of Political Economy* Vol. 53, No. 3 (September 1945), pp. 234–57.
36. SURW, 8 March 1919; SUR 4 February 1919; *Co-operator* I:6 (April 1920), p. 3. The Bureau of Labor Statistics' study found that the high cost of living was the impetus behind cooperatives across the country in 1919–20; *Consumers' Cooperative Societies*, p. 2. On inflation and Seattle cooperatives, see also Agent #17, 8 October 1919, Beck Papers, Box 1, Folder 30.
37. *Co-operator* II:6 (June 1921), p. 4. Another asserted, "It is useless for unionists to agitate for better wages if they do not see to it that they get really higher pay; for after all, a real improvement in wages means better purchasing power" (ibid. I:7 [May 1920]), p. 2; see also I:8 (June 1920), p. 2; II:6 (June 1921), p. 7.
38. Harry Ault to Roger Baldwin, 29 August 1922, Ault Papers, Part I, Box 4, Folder 17.
39. Quote: SUR, 2 February 1920 (in Wisconsin Scrapbooks); SURW, 26 April 1919; Lunn, "How We Cooperate Out West," p. 206; First Cooperative Convention, p. 122.
40. SUR, 10, 18, 20 October, 1 November 1919; SURW, 18 October 1919; Agent #106, 17 October 1919. For the same argument by the tailors, see SUR, 10 October 1919; Agent #106, 17 October 1919.
41. *Journeyman Barber* XV:5 (June 1919); SUR, 12, 17 February 1919; SURW, 20 February 1919; History Committee, p. 52. For a sociological analysis of the aftereffects of the general strike on working-class consciousness, see Rob Rosenthal, "After the Deluge: The Seattle General Strike of 1919 and its Aftermath," M.A. Thesis, University of California, Santa Barbara, 1980.
42. SUR, 2, 10 October 1919. For building trades cooperatives in Boston, see Mark Erlich, *With Our Hands: The Story of Carpenters in Massachusetts* (Philadelphia: Temple University Press, 1986), pp. 91–94.
43. Quote: Agent #106, 30 January 1920; Minutes, CLC, 12 March 1919, 28 January 1920; Lunn, "How We Cooperate Out West," p. 207; *New Majority* 29[?] May 1920 (in Wisconsin Scrapbooks); SUR, 24 March, 22, 28 April

1919; Agent #106, 16 June 1920; Agent #17, 10 May 1920; Agent #106, 28 January 1920; Robert Bridges to the Members of the Executive Committee of the Cooperative Longshoremen's Association, 15 June 1919, in Records of the Seattle Port Commission, Box 4, Folder 27, University of Washington Manuscripts Collection.

44. History Committee, pp. 53, 63; see also pp. 7–8.

45. SUR, 4 February 1919.

46. SUR, 20 May, 30 June 1919; SURW, 22 March 1919; *Co-operative Consumer* IV:4 (April 1918), p. 61.

47. Agent #106, 30 April 1920; Joe Pass to Harvey O'Connor, 14 January 1963, Part II, Box 3, O'Connor Papers.

48. "Semi-Annual Report, Boilermakers' Local #104, April 1919," in Beck Papers, Box 1; Lunn, "How We Cooperate Out West," p. 206; Interview with Reinhold Loewe by Doug Honig, April 1981, in possession of Doug Honig.

49. First Cooperative Convention, pp. 121–22.

50. SUR, late April–early May 1919.

51. *National Co-operative News*, 21 January 1920 (in Wisconsin Scrapbooks).

52. *Co-operation* V:8 (August 1919), p. 120.

53. One of their opponents charged in 1924, "The same group of 'reds' in control of the Central Labor Council got control of the Rochdale Co-operative stores." See Shimmons, "The Seattle Union Record," p. 29.

54. *Co-operation* V:9 (September 1919), p. 136. See also Minutes, CLC, 3 December 1919.

55. O'Connor, *The Revolution in Seattle*, pp. 11, 114, 151, 153, 163, 206; Anna Louise Strong, *I Change Worlds: The Remaking of an American* (New York: Henry Holt, 1935), pp. 60, 66; Barbara Winslow, "The Decline of Socialism in Washington, 1910–1925," M.A. Thesis, University of Washington, 1969.

56. SUR, 16 March, 17 June 1921 (Short); SURW, 6 July 1918 (Hoffman); CLC, 3 December 1919 (Pearl).

57. SURW, 6 July 1918; Minutes, Local #131, 13, 20 January, 13, 20 April, 7 October 1920; 15 February, 1 March, 21, 28 June, 15, 16 November 1921, Box 2, Records of Carpenters and Joiners Local #131, University of Washington Manuscripts Collection.

58. Minutes, Musicians' Local #76, 7 May 1918; Minutes, Typographers' #202, 4 May, 3 August 1919.

59. E.g., SUR, 23 April 1919.

60. SUR, 20 May, 30 June 1919; SURW, 22 March 1919; *Co-operative Consumer* IV:4 (April 1918), p. 61.

61. SURW, 6 July 1918; Lunn, "How We Cooperate Out West," pp. 207–8; WSFL, *Proceedings of the 16th Convention* (1917), p. 4; Moore, "Rise and Fall," p. 9; *Co-operative Consumer* IV:9 (September 1918), p. 143; *Co-operation* V:1 (January 1919), p. 10; V:4 (April 1919), p. 63; SUR, 5 February 1919; First Cooperative Convention, p. 120. On the western Washington Grange movement, see Harriet Crawford, *The Washington State Grange* (Portland, Oreg.: Binfords & Mort, 1940). On farmer–labor political campaigns in Seattle and Washington state in the early and mid-twenties, see Jonathan Dembo, "A History of the Washington State Labor Movement, 1885–1935," Ph.D. Diss., University of Washington, 1978, pp. 271–94; and Chapter 7. See also Carlos

Schwantes, "Farmer–Labor Insurgency in Washington State: William Bouck, the Grange, and the Western Progressive Farmers," *Pacific Northwest Quarterly* Vol. 76, No. 1 (January 1985), pp. 2–11.

On June 28, 1919, a *Union Record* editorial, calling the reader's attention to the "union milk from organized cows milked by union men" advertisements, observed that while this was ostensibly a new idea, "Alas, again we discover there is nothing new under the sun! For cows were organized some few thousand years ago, according to one E. Sop, a noted Greek Co-op, and he tells the story, whose effect the 'capitalistic press' has neutralized through the centuries by calling it a 'fable.' E. Sop says there were some cows feeding in a pasture in Greece. They had the habit of scabbing on each other by each one trying to get the juicy grasses, with no thought of the others. (It was open-shop conditions.) The result was that they were scattered and this in turn resulted in the wild beasts from the jungles attacking them separately, which resulted in the cow-casualty list mounting up. The idea got into the skull of one cow that solidarity would be fine. They organized and got together in their process of consumption. They elected a walking delegate to keep an eye on the jungle, so when the wild beasts attacked them, they 'bunched up' their horns and legs and the casualty list mounted up on the jungle side of the list.

"E. Sop relates that the members of this Ancient Order of United Cows adopted as their class motto: 'What great good there is in Cooperation!'

"Now the age of cooperation has come again among the cows. We take off our hats to the new combination of union men and union milk from Organized Cows!

"All manner of animals – even Elks, Eagles, Moose – believe in organization – except Donkeys."

62. SUR, 3 March, 24 July 1919.
63. Ibid., 22 February 1919.
64. *Seattle Star*, 6 February 1919. See letter to the editor from A. Bergh (of the typographers), SUR, 21 October 1919, for a similar argument about cooperatives as an alternative to radical measures.
65. Agent #106, 30 January 1920.
66. This estimate is based on the names of over 300 persons involved in Seattle's working-class cooperatives I accumulated.
67. SUR, 6, 30 June 1919.
68. Roll Books, CLC; WSFL, *Proceedings of the 19th Convention* (Olympia: WSFL 1920), pp. 33–34.
69. Leslie Tentler, *Wage-Earning Women: Industrial Work and Family Life in the United States, 1900–1930* (New York: Oxford University Press, 1979); Alice Kessler-Harris, *Out to Work: A History of Wage-Earning Women in the United States* (New York: Oxford University Press, 1982), p. 154.
70. SUR, 4 January 1919.
71. Joanne Meyerowitz, *Women Adrift: Independent Wage Earners in Chicago, 1880–1930* (Chicago: University of Chicago Press, 1988); Kathy Peiss, *Cheap Amusements: Working Women and Leisure in Turn-of-the-Century New York* (Philadelphia: Temple University Press, 1986), p. 68; Tentler, *Wage-Earning Women*, pp. 115–35; S. J. Kleinberg, *The Shadow of the Mills: Working-Class*

Families in Pittsburgh, 1870–1907 (Pittsburgh: University of Pittsburgh Press, 1989).

72. E.g., SUR, 23 June, 24 September 1919.

73. Martha May, "Bread Before Roses: American Workingmen, Labor Unions and the Family Wage," in Ruth Milkman, ed., *Women, Work and Protest: A Century of US Women's Labor History* (Boston: Routledge & Kegan Paul, 1985), pp. 1–21; Tentler, *Wage-Earning Women*, pp. 85–114.

74. Lunn, "How We Cooperate Out West," pp. 209–10; First Cooperative Convention, pp. 256–60; SUR, 9 March, 24 April, 7 June, 28, 29 August, 3 October, 4 November 1919; SURW, 6 July 1918, 12 April 1919; *National Cooperative News*, 21 January 1920 (in Wisconsin Scrapbooks); *Co-operator* I:7 (May 1920) p. 8; I:10 (August 1920), pp. 1–2; I:11 (September 1920), p. 7; I:13 (November 1920), pp. 2–3; II:5 (May 1921), p. 3.

75. SUR, 28 August, 24 September 1919.

76. Ibid., 9 August 1919.

77. Ibid., 12 March 1919.

78. University district: Ibid., 11 March 1919; Duwamish: Ibid., 8 April 1919. See also ibid., 12 February, 27 May, 28 June, 22 September, 1 October, 7 November 1919; SURW, 26 April 1919; *Co-operator* I:7 (May 1920), p. 7; I:11 (September 1920), p. 2; II:2 (February 1921), p. 2; Organization Committee, CFPA, to the Members of Organized Labor.

79. *Co-operator* I:4 (December 1920), p. 5; I:10 (August 1920), p. 2; I:12 (October 1920), p. 7; I:13 (November 1920), pp. 2–3.

80. Ibid., I:14 (December 1920), p. 5.

81. SUR, 11 July 1919; see also 25 September 1919.

82. Ibid., 2 May 1919.

83. *Co-operation* VI:1 (January 1920), p. 12.

84. *Co-operator* I:14 (December 1920), p. 5; II:1 (January 1921), p. 2.

85. SUR, 26 April 1921. For more on the importance of women's shopping, see ibid., 14 June 1919.

86. *Co-operator* I:8 (June 1920), p. 3; I:9 (July 1920), p. 3.

87. Ibid., I:10 (August 1920), p. 6.

88. *Co-operation* VI:2 (February 1921), p. 32.

89. *Co-operator* II:3 (March 1921), p. 3.

90. SUR, 14 June 1919.

91. Margaret Llewelyn Davies, *The Women's Co-operative Guild, 1883–1904* (Westmorland: Women's Co-operative Guild, 1904); Margaret Llewelyn Davies, ed., *Life as We Have Known It, by Co-operative Women* (London: Virago, 1977 repr. of 1931); Gill Scott, " 'Working Out Their Own Salvation': Women's Autonomy and Divorce Law Reform in the Co-operative Movement, 1910–1920," in Stephen Yeo, ed., *New View of Co-operation* (London: Routledge, 1988), pp. 128–53. For statistics on members, see Yeo, introduction to Scott, "Working Out Their Own Salvation," p. 128; Jean Gaffin and David Thomas, *Caring & Sharing: The Centenary History of the Co-operative Women's Guild* (Manchester: Co-operative Union, 1983). On women and French cooperatives, see Furlough, *Consumer Cooperation in France*, pp. 199–224.

92. *Co-operator* I:6 (April 1920), p. 3; I:7 (May 1920), p. 6; I:14 (December 1920), p. 6; II:3 (March 1921), p. 3.

93. SUR, 22 April 1919.

94. SURW, 15 February 1919; SUR, 2 February 1920. On the SCCA's Women's Guild and citywide cooperative women's activities, see also SUR, 22 April, 23 June, 1, 8, 15 July, 9, 18 August, 6, 24 September 1919; 2 February 1920. A Washington State Women's Cooperative Guild was formed in January 1920, its "chief purpose" "to develop the educational and recreational phases of the Co-operative Movement." *Co-operation* VI:2 (February 1920), p. 28.

95. SUR, 7, 14, 19, 26, 28 January 1921; *Co-operator* throughout 1920–21, monthly reports of women's clubs, e.g., I:8 (June 1920), p. 5; I:11 (September 1920), pp. 6–7; II:5 (May 1921), p. 2.

96. *Co-operator* I:13 (October 1920), pp. 6–7; see also I:14 (December 1920), pp. 5–6.

97. *Co-operator* meeting reports; SUR, 11 June 1919, 5 May 1921; *Co-operation* V:9 (September 1919), p. 135.

98. SUR, 27 August 1919.

99. Ibid., 14 January 1921.

100. *Co-operator* I:6 (April 1920), p. 7; I:8 (June 1920), p. 7; I:9 (July 1920), p. 6; I:11 (September 1920), pp. 1, 6; I:13 (October 1920), p. 5; I:13 (November 1920), p. 5; I:14 (December 1920), p. 7; II:1 (January 1921), p. 4; II:2 (February 1921), p. 4; II:3 (March 1921), p. 5; II:6 (June 1921), p. 5; *Co-operation* VI:2 (February 1921), p. 32.

101. SUR, 26 January, 24 February, 19, 23 March, 6 April, 1, 9 June 1921.

102. SUR, 25 June 1921.

103. SUR, 11 April 1919.

104. *Union Labor Bulletin* (Little Rock, Ark.), 12 September 1919. My thanks to Eric Arnesen for this reference.

105. SUR, 27 August 1919.

106. *Co-operator* II:3 (March 1921), p. 7; II:4 (April 1921), p. 1.

107. SUR, 18 August 1919.

108. Ibid., 1 April 1921.

109. Ibid., 9 June 1921.

110. Joan M. Jensen, "Cloth, Butter and Boarders: Women's Household Production for Market," *Review of Radical Political Economics* Vol. 12, No. 2 (Summer 1980), pp. 14–24.

111. *Co-operator* I:6 (April 1920), p. 5; I:8 (June 1920), p. 3; I:11 (September 1920), p. 1; I:12 (October 1920), pp. 1, 7; II:5 (May 1921), p. 2.

112. SUR, 21 August 1920.

113. *Co-operator* I:14 (December 1920), p. 3.

114. SUR, 1 April 1919. Paul Johnson, in a study of saving and spending habits among the English working class in the early twentieth century, found that English workers used cooperatives as a form of enforced savings accounts, awaiting their dividends every six months. See *Saving and Spending: The Working-Class Economy in Britain, 1870–1939* (Oxford: Clarendon, 1985), p. 128. For the importance of dividends to women in English cooperatives, see Davies, *Women's Co-operative Guild*, p. 38.

115. Maurine Wiener Greenwald, "Working-Class Feminism and the Family Wage Ideal: The Seattle Debate on Married Women's Right to Work, 1914-1920," *Journal of American History* Vol. 76, No. 1 (June 1989), pp. 137–38.

116. *Co-operator* I:9 (July 1920), p. 5; II:2 (February 1921), p. 4; II:6 (June 1921), p. 1.

117. Organizational Committee CFPA to the Members of Organized Labor; *Co-operator* I:7 (May 1920), p. 7; II:3 (March 1921), p. 2; see letter to the editor from T.D.E., SUR, 30 April 1919. For SUR debates on profiteering, see, e.g., SUR, 18 March 1919, and SURW as late as 3 January 1920 reporting on the prosecution of "sugar profiteers" in Washington, D.C.

118. WSFL, *Proceedings of the 16th Convention* (1917), p. 14; *Co-operator* I:7 (May 1920), p. 7; SURW, 30 August 1919. For the concept of efficiency, see *Co-operator* I:14 (December 1920), p. 4; II:6 (June 1921), p. 5.

119. SUR, 9 June 1921; *Co-operator* II:3 (March 1921), p. 4; II:4 (April 1921), p. 1; SUR, 17 June 1919; SURW, 6 July 1918; History Committee, pp. 54–55.

120. *Co-operator* II:8 (June 1920), p. 2.

121. SUR, 26, 27 June 1919; for further debates, see also 26 June 1919.

122. Ibid., 26 March, 1 April 1919; *Co-operative Consumer* IV:4 (April 1918), p. 6.

123. SUR, 7 June 1919.

124. *Co-operation* V:9 (September 1919), p. 136; Lunn, "How We Cooperate Out West," p. 206; *Co-operator* I:7 (May 1920), p. 7.

125. *Co-operator* I:6 (April 1920), pp. 4–5.

126. Organization Committee CFPA to the Members of Organized Labor.

127. For more, see *Co-operator* II:4 (April 1921), p. 1; II:3 (March 1921), p. 4; I:13 (November 1920), p. 6.

128. Ibid. I:14 (December 1920), p. 3.

129. Ibid. II:2 (February 1921), p. 4; II:6 (June 1921), p. 1.

130. Strong, *I Change Worlds*, p. 70.

131. Agent #106, 30 January 1920.

132. SUR, 24 March 1919.

133. *Co-operator* I:8 (June 1920), p. 2; see also I:14 (December 1920) p. 4.

134. Ibid. I:6 (April 1920), p. 2.

135. Ibid. II:6 (June 1921), p. 5. On 7 March 1919 a *Union Record* article similarly argued that the purpose of a new SCCA branch was "not to antagonize those already in business."

136. Olive M. Johnson, *The Cooperative Movement: An Infantile Disorder and an Old-Age Disease* (New York: New York Labor News Company, 1924), pp. 33–34.

137. Emphasis added. Agent #106, 30 January 1920.

138. *Forge*, 5 July 1919, 21 February 1920; see also 12 July 1919; SUR, 3 June 1919.

139. *International Weekly*, 31 January 1919; *Forge*, 11 October 1919. On the Equity Print Shop, see O'Connor, *The Revolution in Seattle*, p. 247; Hays Jones to Harvey O'Connor, n.d. [1962], in O'Connor Papers, Part II.

140. SURW, 14 June 1919; SUR, 11 June 1919.

141. SURW, 8 March 1919; SUR, 14 March 1919; *Co-operation* V:9 (September 1919), p. 136. The cooperative tailors advertised suits "made for USE and NOT FOR PROFIT." *Forge*, 12 July 1919. They used the Rochdale plan for dividends on purchases. See also SUR, 3 June 1919.

142. SUR, 16 January 1920.

143. Ibid., 3 June 1919. A third correspondent, Wm. A. H. Kirkholz, added, "Even the present co-operative plan is class conscious, as its aim is not to lower costs as much as to make profit for its shareholders" (SUR, 19 June 1921).
144. Ibid., 11 June 1921.
145. A SUR article (7 June 1919), for example, referred to the CFPA as "financed by approximately 40,000 organized farmers and union men of the Northwest."
146. Agent #106, 7 March 1920.
147. Debs said in a famous speech: "But I am no labor leader. I don't want you to follow me, or anyone else. If you are looking for a Moses to lead you out of this capitalist wilderness, you will stay right where you are. I would not lead you into the promised land if I could, because if I could lead you in someone else could lead you out." Quote in Ray Ginger, *Eugene V. Debs: A Biography* (New York: Collier, 1962, repr. of 1949), p. 260.

3. Labor capitalism

1. Photograph, Deep Sea Salvage Company Float, 1920, in Pemco Webster & Stevens Collection, #83.10.8579.2, Museum of History and Industry, Seattle; Seattle *Union Record* daily edition (hereafter SUR), 18 June 1919.
2. SUR, 24 July 1919.
3. Ibid., 3, 18 April, 2, 7 May, 21 July, 4 September, 18 December 1919; 14 January, 10 February, 3, 18 March, 10 April, 26 May, 20 July, 5 August 1920; Harvey O'Connor, *The Revolution in Seattle* (New York: Monthly Review Press, 1964), p. 208.
4. Selig Perlman and Philip Taft, *History of Labor in the United States, 1896–1932,* Vol. IV (New York: Macmillan, 1935), p. 572.
5. "Carpenters' Home," *American Federationist* Vol. 35, No. 1 (November 1928), pp. 1334–39; Maxwell C. Raddock, *Portrait of an American Labor Leader: William L. Hutcheson* (New York: American Institute of Social Science, 1955), pp. 156, 416–24. Joel Seidman, *The Needle Trades* (New York: Farrar & Rinehart, 1942), pp. 294–99; Steven Fraser, *Labor Will Rule: Sidney Hillman and the Rise of American Labor* (New York: Free Press, 1991), pp. 219–20, 230, 238; Charles Elbert Zaretz, *The Amalgamated Clothing Workers of America: A Study in Progressive Trades-Unionism* (New York: Ancon, 1934), pp. 273–84; Princeton University Industrial Relations Section, *The Labor Banking Movement in the United States* (Princeton, N.J.: Princeton University Industrial Relations Section, 1929); Lewis Corey, "The New Capitalism," and E. W. Morehouse, "Labor Institutionalism: Banking" in J.B.S. Hardman, ed., *American Labor Dynamics in the Light of Postwar Developments* (New York: Harcourt, Brace, 1928), pp. 43–70 and 310–19, respectively; William English Walling, *American Labor, American Democracy* (New York: Harper & Brothers, 1926); Richard Boeckel, *Labor's Money* (New York: Harcourt, Brace, 1923); William Z. Foster, *Misleaders of Labor* (Chicago: Trade Union Educational League, 1927). For local-level labor-owned businesses in this period, shading over into cooperatives, see, e.g., Louis B. Perry and Richard S. Perry, *A History of the Los Angeles Labor Movement, 1911–1941* (Berkeley: University of California Press, 1963), p. 202; Savannah, Ga., *Morning News,* 13, 31 January 1921.

6. Report of Agent #106, 27 March 1920 (hereafter Agent #106), in Boxes 1–2, Broussais C. Beck Papers, University of Washington Manuscripts Collection.
7. Hulet Wells, "I Wanted to Work," p. 215, mss. in Hulet Wells Papers, Box 2, Folder 2–3, University of Washington Manuscripts Collection.
8. SUR, 19 February 1919; Lewis Lorwin, *The American Federation of Labor: Policies and Prospects* (Washington: Brookings Institution, 1933), pp. 188, 318; Princeton University Industrial Relations Section, *Labor Banking Movement*, pp. 4–5.
9. Washington State Federation of Labor (hereafter WSFL), *Proceedings of the 18th Convention* (Olympia: WSFL, 1919), pp. 146–47; SUR, 18, 22, 23, 26, 30 April, 1, 6, 7 May 1919; O'Connor, *The Revolution in Seattle*, p. 119.
10. Reinhold Loewe, interview by Doug Honig, April 1981, in possession of Doug Honig.
11. Agent #106, 26 February 1920.
12. Seattle *Union Record*, weekly edition (hereafter SURW), 18 January 1919.
13. SUR, 23 February 1919.
14. SUR, 8 October 1919; Co-operative League of America, *Proceedings of the First American Co-operative Convention*, Springfield, Ill., 25–27 September 1919 (Springfield: Co-operative Association of America, 1919), pp. 115–16; *Northwestern Co-operative News* Vol. I, No. 5 (1 September 1919), p. 1; see also Frank Stricker, "The Wages of Inflation: Workers' Earnings in the World War One Era," *Mid-America* 63 (1981), p. 95; David Montgomery, *The Fall of the House of Labor: The Workplace, the State, and American Labor Activism, 1865–1925* (Cambridge: Cambridge University Press, 1987), pp. 384–85. For the importance of liberty bonds in bankrolling labor capitalism and co-operatives in Seattle, see Report of Agent #17 (hereafter Agent #17), 21 February 1920, Broussais C. Beck Papers, Boxes 1–2; SUR, 4, 15, 19 April, 2, 3 May 1919; SURW, 7 July 1918, 8 March, 3 May 1919; *Co-operative Consumer* Vol. IV, No. 9 (September 1918), p. 144; *Northwest Co-operative News* Vol. I, No. 5 (1 September 1919), p. 1. The Trades Union Savings and Loan Association held $58,552.44 in "Liberty Bonds Investments" on June 30, 1919; SUR, 18 July 1919.
15. SUR, 7 August 1920.
16. See, e.g., Minutes, Board of Directors, Local #76, American Federation of Musicians, 20 January 1920, in possession of Local #76, Seattle, Wash., for the question arising of dealing with the local's money.
17. SUR, 23 January 1920.
18. *Co-operator* Vol. II, No. 2 (February 1921), p. 7.
19. SUR, 13 May 1920.
20. *Co-operator* Vol. II, No. 2 (February 1921), p. 7; SUR, 22 May 1920. See also SUR, 3, 14 June 1919; 8 July 1920; Carl Lunn, "How We Cooperate Out West," *Life and Labor* Vol. X, No. 7 (September 1920), p. 208.
21. Agent #106, 14 January 1920.
22. SUR, 26 March 1920.
23. Ibid., 26 November, 19, 20, 24, 29 December 1919; 1 January, 17 July 1920; 21 January 1921; Minutes, Central Labor Council of Seattle and Vicinity (hereafter CLC), 14 January, 18 February, 17, 24 March, 7, 27 April, 5, 12 May 1920; 27 April, 8 June 1921; in Records of the King County Central

Labor Council, Box 8, University of Washington Manuscripts Collection; Agent #17, 17, 27 January, 14, 26 February, 18, 25, 26 March, 8, 17 April, 2, 19 June 1920; Minutes, Musicians' #76 Board of Directors, 11, 22 June 1920; "Receipt, Federation Film Corporation," 29 January 1920, in Harry Ault Papers, Part II, Box 1, Folder 31, University of Washington Manuscripts Collection; William Short to Whom it May Concern, 2 May 1923, Records of the Washington State Federation of Labor (hereafter WSFL Records), Box 35, University of Washington Manuscripts Collection; Minutes, Local #131, United Brotherhood of Carpenters and Joiners, 27 January, 16 March, 27 April, 4 May, 1, 8, 15 June, 23 November 1920, 3 May 1921, in Records of Local #131, United Brotherhood of Carpenters and Joiners, University of Washington Manuscripts Collection; Minutes, Local #202, International Typographers' Union, 28 March, 28 November 1920, in Records of Local #99, International Typographers' Union, Box 16, University of Washington Manuscripts Collection; Agent #106, 21 November 1919, 24 March, 2 April 1920; Records of Agent #172, 2 April 1920, Box 1, Folder 6, Roy John Kinnear Papers, University of Washington Manuscripts Collection.

24. Minutes, CLC, 27 April 1921; Agent #17, 2 June 1920.
25. See the *Union Record* itself, and Mary Joan O'Connell, "The Seattle Union Record: A Pioneer Daily," M.A. Thesis, University of Washington, 1964. On the importance of the SUR for internal communication, Reinhold Loewe, an officer of Machinists Local #79, recalled, "Instead of getting out a notice and mailing it to all of our members of some special meeting coming up or whatever, we'd put in an ad on the front page of the *Union Record* . . . little box notice." It wasn't necessary to handwrite addresses on postcards, then, or mail them out. Loewe, interview with Honig.
26. "Come Across," leaflet, n.d. [1920–21], in Ault Papers, Part II, Box 1, Folder 53; O'Connell, "The Seattle Union Record"; Harry Ault to William F. Gibbons, 5 July 1923, Ault Papers, Part I, Box 4, Folder 20; Ault to Roger Baldwin, 29 August 1922, Ault Papers, Part I, Box 4, Folder 17; "To the Stockholders," 14 August 1924, Ault Papers, Part I, Box 4, Folder 22; SUR, 29 March, 29 November 1919; "Approximate Statement of Per Capita Investment in the Seattle Union Record by Local Union Organizations Investing $5.00 or Over Per Capita" and charts following for locals' investments, in Ault Papers, Part I, Box 6, Folder 7.
27. Records of Local #131, including financial records of the local and of the Washington Benevolent Association; SUR, 2 April 1919.
28. SUR, 2 April 1919.
29. Minutes, Carpenters #131, 3 August 1920; I.A. [?] Ogden to the Washington State Federation of Labor, 8 February 1922, WSFL Records, Box 8, Folder 20; SUR, 24 March, 5, 21 April, 20 May 1920; *Musicland*, 1 September 1921, 27 December 1926, in possession of Local #76, American Federation of Musicians, Seattle; Mabel Abbott, "The Waitresses of Seattle," *Life and Labor*, February 1914, pp. 48–49; Labor Temple Business Records, in WSFL Records.
30. *Co-operation* VI:1 (January 1919), p. 9; VI:9 (September 1920), p. 143; VII:2 (February 1921), p. 25. *Musicland*, 1 December 1924, 5 November 1926; *Cooperative Consumer* IV:4 (April 1918), p. 61; Minutes, Carpenters Local #131, 20 July, 17 August 1920; SUR, 5 May, 19 August 1919; Co-operative League

of America, *Proceedings of the First American Co-operative Convention*, Springfield, Ill., 25–27 September 1919 (Springfield: Co-operative League of America, 1919), p. 120; Harry Ault to Roger Baldwin, 29 August 1922, Ault Papers, Part I, Box 4, Folder 17; Financial Statement of the Mutual Laundry Company, year ending 31 December 1920, Ault Papers, Part I, Box 3, Folder 23; WSFL, *Proceedings of the 15th Convention*, p. 76; Doug Honig, "Experiments in Democracy," pamphlet in possession of the author, accompanying radio show on the history of cooperatives in Seattle, Station KUOW, Seattle, Wash., p. A–4.

31. SUR, 19 August 1919; *Co-operation* VII:2 (February 1921), p. 25.
32. Anna Louise Strong, *I Change Worlds: The Remaking of an American* (New York: Holt, 1935), p. 70; SUR, 28 February 1919; *Co-operator* II:3 (March 1921), p. 8; *Musicland*, 27 December 1926; Carl S. Evans to the Union Addressed, 9 October 1922, Records of Local #1289, United Brotherhood of Carpenters and Joiners, Box 3, Folder 3, University of Washington Manuscripts Collection; Minutes, Typographers Local #202, esp. 1923; *Machinists' Monthly Journal* 33 (August 1921), p. 633. My thanks to Cecelia Bucki for the last reference.
33. For amounts on deposit: *Forge*, 26 June 1920; Minutes, CLC, 11 November 1920; SUR, 2, 20 May, 2, 3, 23, 25, 27 June, 1, 11, 25 July, 1, 19 August 1919; 22 March, 3, 22 April, 1, 6, 13, 29 May, 1, 8 July, 4, 9 August, 9 September, 9 October, 12 November 1920; 11 January 1921; SURW, 8 March, 26 May, 5 July, 28 August, 4 October 1919; *Musicland*, 1 February 1924; WSFL, *Official Yearbook of Organized Labor* (Seattle: Washington State Labor News, 1927), p. 18; *Washington State Labor News* (hereafter WSLN), 6 January 1927; 5 October, 7 December 1928; 11 January, 28 June, 26 July 1929.

On the founding and policies of the savings and loan: SUR, 28, 31 March, 14, 18 April, 27 June 1919; *Musicland*, 20 January 1927; Minutes, CLC, 8 January 1919; Ault to Baldwin, 29 August 1922; Articles of Incorporation, Trades Union Savings and Loan Association, in Pacific Northwest Collection, University of Washington Library.

34. SUR, 28 February 1919.
35. Ibid.
36. Minutes, CLC, 12 March 1919.
37. SUR, 31 March 1919.
38. Ibid., 19 September 1919; see also 29 March 1919.
39. Ibid., 2 January 1920.
40. Agent #106, 9 December 1919.
41. For the officers and policies of the Trades Union Savings and Loan, see Articles of Incorporation, Trades Union Savings and Loan; Earl Shimmons, "The Seattle Union Record," mss. in Ault Papers, Part I, Box 7, Folder 9, p. 23; SUR, 28, 31 March, 14, 18 April, 27 June 1919; *Musicland*, 20 January 1927; Minutes, CLC, 8 January 1919; Ault to Baldwin, 29 August 1922.
42. Shimmons, "The Seattle Union Record," p. 39; SUR, 12, 15 May 1920, and May 1920 passim.
43. Shimmons, "The Seattle Union Record," pp. 39, 43; O'Connell, "The Seattle Union Record," p. 142; Saul Haas to Harry Ault, 26 May 1920, Ault Papers, Part I, Box 2, Folder 43; George Listman to Harry Ault, 7 June 1920, Ault

Papers, Part I, Box 3, Folder 11; William Short to Samuel Gompers, 19 April 1920, WSFL Records, Box 35; Washington State Federation of Labor Executive Council Minutes, 7 May 1920, WSFL Records, Box 60; WSFL, *Proceedings of the 19th Convention*, p. 74; "The Seattle Union Record – What It is ...," draft pamphlet, n.d. [1921–22], Ault Papers, Part II, Box 3, Folder 26; Minutes, Carpenters Local #131, 13, 27 July, 31 August 1920; Agent #17, 26 May 1920; Agent #106, 7 March 1920; Minutes, CLC, 19 May, 7, 14, 21 July, 4, 18 August 1920; SUR, 31 March, 2, 4 December 1919; 2 January, 23, 27, 28 April, 12, 13, 15, 19 May, 12 June, 8, 12, 16, 17, 19, 31 July, 19 August, 4, 6 December 1920; 7 January 1921; SUR, 6 December 1919.

44. On the distinction between cooperatives and labor banking, see David Saposs, "Labor Banks and Trade-Union Capitalism," *American Review* Vol. 1 (September–October 1923), pp. 534–36.

45. Agent #106, 14 January 1920.

46. SUR, 4 December 1919, 2 January 1920; SURW, 6 December 1919.

47. *Co-operator*, 1920–21.

48. SUR, 19 March 1919; Articles of Incorporation, Trades Union Savings and Loan Association; see also SUR, 28 February 1919; *Co-operation* V:4 (April 1919), p. 63.

49. SURW, 18 January 1919.

50. SUR, 12 March 1919; see also 14 June 1919.

51. Ibid., 7 June 1919.

52. Ibid.

53. Ibid., 14 June 1919; see also *Co-operator* II:5 (May 1921), p. 9; II:1 (January 1921), p. 8; SUR, 12 March 1919.

54. *Co-operator* II:1 (January 1921), p. 8; SUR, 1 May, 21 June (want ad) 1919; 23 January, 12 June 1920; SURW, 3 May 1919; Ault to Baldwin 29 August 1922; *Tacoma Labor Advocate*, clipping, n.d. [April 1921], in Ault Papers, Part II, Box 1, Folder 1; Ault to Arthur Nelson, 10 January 1922, Ault Papers, Part I, Box 4, Folder 16; "Statement of the Resources and Liabilities of the Listman Service Company, July 2nd 1921," in Ault Papers, Part I, Box 5, Folder 48; Minutes, Carpenters Local #131, 29 April 1919; George Listman to Harry Ault, 7 June 1920, Ault Papers, Part II, Box 3, Folder 11; A. W. Johnston to William Short, 21 September 1922; WSFL Records, Box 14, Folder 25. On the United Finance Company: SUR, 6, 12 March, 26, 30 May, 7 June, 3, 28 July, 29 November 1919; 23 January 1920; SURW, 5 January 1919.

55. Harry Ault to Arthur Nelson, 10 January 1922, Ault Papers, Part I, Box 1, Folder 16; Ault to Saul Haas, 20 November 1924, Ault Papers, Part I, Box 4, Folder 23; Ault to Haas, 2 February 1925, Ault Papers, Part I, Box 4, Folder 29; Ault to Collector, Internal Revenue, n.d. [1921], Ault Papers, Part I, Box 4, Folder 15; Haas to Harvey O'Connor, 24 September 1921, in Harry O'Connor Papers, Archives of Labor and Urban Affairs, Wayne State University, Detroit, Mich., Part II, Box 1, Folder "Haas, S."; Padilla Bay Development Association to Ault, 11 September 1922, Ault Papers, Part I, Box 3, Folder 23; Padilla Bay Development Association to Haas, 30 August 1920, Saul Haas Papers, Box 41, Folder 15, University of Washington Manuscripts Collection; *Tacoma Labor Advocate* clipping n.d. [April 1921], in Ault Papers, Part I, Box 1, Folder 1; SUR, 26, 27, 30 June 1920; O'Connor, *The Revolution in Seattle*, p. 208.

56. SUR, 22 August, 8 November 1919.

57. SUR, 2 October 1919; see also 22 August 1919.

58. Harry Ault to C. A. Mann, 5 January 1921, Ault Papers, Part I, Box 4, Folder 14.

59. "In the Matter of the Seattle Union Record," Ault Papers, Part I, Box 5, Folder 19; Phil Pearl and Frank Clifford to the Seattle Central Labor Council, 2 February 1921, King County Central Labor Council Records, Box 7; Ault to Baldwin 29 August 1922.

60. For investigating committees, see, e.g., SUR, 3 September 1919. Individual representatives called on the locals to plead their causes; see, e.g., Minutes, Musicians' Local #76, 23 April 1918.

61. Minutes, Musicians' Local #76, Typographers' Local #202. See Chapter 5 for a more extended discussion of women's power within the locals.

62. Abbott, "The Waitresses of Seattle," pp. 48–49; SUR, 21 April, 20 May 1919.

63. WSLN 3 September 1926; Lunn, "How We Cooperate Out West," p. 207; *Co-operation* VI:9 (September 1920), p. 143; financial statement, Mutual Laundry Company, year ending 31 December 1920, in Ault Papers, Part I, Box 3, Folder 23. See the latter for agitation by the local Women's Trade Union League, trying to bring women's wages up at the firm.

64. Leslie Woodcock Tentler, *Wage-Earning Women: Industrial Work and Family Life in the United States, 1900–1920* (New York: Oxford University Press, 1979), pp. 115–35; Joanne Meyerowitz, *Women Adrift: Independent Wage Earners in Chicago, 1880–1930* (Chicago, University of Chicago Press, 1988), pp. 33–41. For evidence that white women working as live-in domestics were able to save money, see Hasia Diner, *Erin's Daughters in America: Irish Immigrant Women in the Nineteenth Century* (Baltimore: Johns Hopkins University Press, 1983), pp. 71, 73.

65. See Tentler, *Wage-Earning Women*, pp. 177–78, for the argument that wives controlled financial decisions in working-class families.

66. See the *Record*'s women's pages throughout 1919; Maurine Wiener Greenwald, "Working-Class Feminism and the Family Wage Ideal: The Seattle Debate on Married Women's Right to Work, 1914–1920," *Journal of American History* Vol. 76, No. 1 (June 1989), pp. 118–49.

67. SUR, 2, 5, 6, 7 August 1920.

68. One piece of evidence suggests a possible exception. In June 1921, Dora Hayward reported to the CLC that "sleeping and dining car waiters and porters have offered their assistance in maintaining the Cooperative Food Products Association." These waiters and porters were probably all African-American, though it is possible they were white or of mixed race. SUR, 23 June 1921.

69. Yuji Ichioka, *The Issei: The World of First Generation Japanese Immigrants, 1885–1924* (New York: Free Press, 1988), p. 95; Forrest B. Washington, "Chicago Negroes Launch Cooperative Store," *Life and Labor* Vol. IX, No. 7 (July 1919), pp. 179, 184; James R. Barrett, *Work and Community in the Jungle: Chicago's Packinghouse Workers, 1894–1922* (Urbana: University of Illinois Press, 1987), p. 209; St. Louis *Argus*, 26 October, 26 December 1919; 26, 29 March 1920; *Crisis*, July 1919, p. 152, and editorial, November 1917, p. 9.

70. Horace R. Cayton, *Long Old Road: An Autobiography* (Seattle: University of Washington Press, 1963), pp. 35–36; *Forge*, 27 March 1920; Kazuo Ito, *Issei*

(Seattle: Japanese Community Service, 1973), pp. 97–98; *Crisis*, June 1913, p. 69.

71. Monica Sone, *Nisei Daughter* (Boston: Little, Brown, 1953), pp. 112–15; Ito, *Issei*, pp. 97–98. For segregation of African-Americans in hotel accommodations, see *Cayton's Weekly*, 16 December 1920.

72. Katherine Dally Woolston, "Japanese Standards of Living in Seattle," M.A. Thesis, University of Washington, 1927, pp. 24, 27–30; Ito, *Issei*, p. 96; Quintard Taylor, "Black Urban Development – Another View: Seattle's Central District, 1910–1940," *Pacific Historical Review* Vol. LVIII, No. 4 (November 1989), pp. 432–44; *Seattle Republican* Vol. XVI, No. 24 (12 November 1909), p. 1.

73. Ito, *Issei*, p. 708; SUR, 29 January 1921; H. A. Millis, *The Japanese Problem in the United States* (New York: Macmillan, 1915), pp. 56–78; See also Chapter 1.

74. Sylvia Junko Yanagisako, *Transforming the Past: Tradition and Kinship Among Japanese Americans* (Stanford, Calif.: Stanford University Press, 1985), pp. 45–46; Yuzo Murayama, "The Economic History of Japanese Immigration to the Pacific Northwest," Ph.D. Diss., University of Washington, 1982, pp. 141, 255–56; Ito, *Issei*, pp. 266–67, 863–64. For a comparative perspective on the Los Angeles Japanese-American community, see John Modell, *The Economics and Politics of Racial Accommodation: The Japanese of Los Angeles, 1900–1942* (Urbana: University of Illinois Press, 1977).

75. Taylor, "Black Urban Development;" Calvin F. Schmid, *Social Trends in Seattle* (Seattle: University of Washington Press, 1944), p. 140; *Cayton's Weekly*, throughout 1917–21, esp. 29 December 1917, 3 July 1920, 22 May 1920.

76. *Cayton's Weekly*, 26 October, 23 November 1918; 4 January 1919.

77. Tokichi Tanaka, "The Japanese in Seattle," *Coast* Vol. XIII, No. 5 (November 1909), p. 253; Yuzo Murayama, "The Economic History of Japanese Immigration," p. 256; H. A. Millis, "Some Economic Aspects of Japanese Immigration," *American Economic Review* Vol. 5, No. 4 (December 1915), p. 803; idem, *The Japanese Problem in the United States*, pp. 56–78. Quintard Taylor reaches many of the same conclusions in a recent, much more extensive comparative study of the Seattle African-American and Japanese-American communities. See his article, "Blacks and Asians in a White City: Japanese Americans and African Americans in Seattle, 1890–1940," *Western Historical Quarterly* Vol. XXII, No. 4 (November 1991), pp. 401–29, for an insightful analysis of the barriers facing both communities and their strategies for advancement. For comparative development of African-American business communities in the late nineteenth and early twentieth centuries, see Joe William Trotter, Jr., *Black Milwaukee: The Making of an Industrial Proletariat, 1915–1945* (Urbana: University of Illinois Press, 1985); Kenneth L. Kusmer, *A Ghetto Takes Shape: Black Cleveland, 1870–1930* (Urbana: University of Illinois Press, 1976); David M. Katzman, *Before the Ghetto: Black Detroit in the Nineteenth Century* (Urbana: University of Illinois Press, 1973).

4. Counterattack

1. Minutes, Central Labor Council of Seattle and Vicinity (hereafter CLC), in Records of the King County Central Labor Council, Box 8, University of Washington Manuscripts Collection, Seattle, 12 February 1919.

2. Washington State Federation of Labor (hereafter WSFL), *Proceedings of the 18th Convention* (Olympia: WSFL, 1919) p. 21.

3. Seattle *Union Record*, daily edition (hereafter SUR), 14, 18 April 1919; see also 12 March 1919; Minutes, CLC, 12, 26 February, 12 March 1919.

4. SUR, 11 June 1919.

5. Ibid., 25 April 1919.

6. *Co-operation* V:8 (August 1919), p. 120; SUR, 19, 29, 30 April, 2, 12, 27 May, 11, 18 June, 6 August 1919; Minutes, Local #76, American Federation of Musicians, July–August 1919, in possession of Local #76, Seattle.

7. SUR, 28 February, 13 May, 2, 12, 25, 30 June, 7 July, 15 September 1919; Report of Agent #106 (hereafter Agent #106), 20 May 1919, in Broussais C. Beck Papers, Boxes 1–2, University of Washington Manuscripts Collection; *Forge*, 15 July 1919; WSFL, *Proceedings of the 18th Convention* (1919), pp. 21–22; Minutes, CLC, 14 May 1919.

8. Dorothy Sue Cobble, "Sisters in the Craft: Waitresses and Their Unions in the Twentieth Century," Ph.D. Diss., Stanford University, 1986, pp. 29–30.

9. Harvey O'Connor, *The Revolution in Seattle* (New York: Monthly Review Press, 1964), p. 235. The waitresses were known to reciprocate the kindness of such efforts. One Seattle leftist recalled, "For a long time afterward left wing organizers got small checks in some of the expensive restaurants." Another remembered, "When four or five of us would drop in for a late evening bite, the biggest part of the check was on the boss." Joe Pass to Harvey O'Connor, 13 March 1963, Harvey O'Connor Papers, Part II, Box 3, Folder "Joe Pass," Archives of Labor and Urban Affairs, Walter Reuther Library, Wayne State University.

10. Agent #106, 4 June 1919; Minutes, CLC, 4 June 1919, 1 September 1920; SUR, 28 June, 7 July, 30 September 1919; 7 January 1920.

11. *Forge*, 10 May 1919.

12. Ibid.

13. SUR, 6 May 1919.

14. Ibid.

15. SUR, 5 June 1919.

16. Ibid., 3 July 1919.

17. Minutes, Board of Directors, Local #76, American Federation of Musicians, 1 July 1919, in possession of Local #76.

18. Minutes, CLC, 2 July 1919; SUR, 15, 24 May, 28 June, 1, 2, 3 July 1919; Margaret Jane Thompson, "Development and Comparison of Industrial Relationships in Seattle," M.B.A. Thesis, University of Washington, 1929, p. 60; A. L. Kempster and successors, weekly reports to Stone and Webster Company (hereafter SW), Box 122, Records of the Puget Sound Traction, Light and Power Company, University of Washington Manuscripts Collection, 9, 26 July 1919; *Forge*, 5 July 1919.

19. Minutes, CLC, 30 April, 17 September 1919; SUR, 28–30 April 1919 and passim March–August 1919; Mary Joan O'Connell, "The Seattle Union Record, 1918–1928: A Pioneer Labor Daily," M.A. Thesis, University of Washington, 1964, p. 98; SUR, 19 June 1919; John Williamson, *Dangerous Scot: The Life and Work of an American "Undesirable"* (New York: International Publishers, 1969), pp. 33–34.

20. SUR, 22 February, 5 March, 11 April, 2, 3 July 1919; Report of Agent #17

(hereafter Agent #17), 3 July, 23 September 1919, Broussais C. Beck Papers, Boxes 1–2; SW, 12 July 1919; Mark Litchman to Eugene Belmont, 13 October 1919, in Mark Litchman Papers, Part I, Box 1, Folder 26, University of Washington Manuscripts Collection; O'Connor, *The Revolution in Seattle*, pp. 122–24; David Montgomery, *The Fall of the House of Labor: The Workplace, the State, and American Labor Activism, 1865–1925* (Cambridge: Cambridge University Press, 1987), pp. 389–91; "List of Unions Which Have Voted for Mooney Strike" [June 1919], Harry Ault Papers, Part I, Box 4, Folder 10, University of Washington Manuscripts Collection.

21. SUR, 30 June 1919.

22. James Hinton, *The First Shop Stewards' Movement* (London: Allen & Unwin, 1973).

23. SUR, 8 April 1919.

24. *Forge*, 12 July 1919.

25. Those instituting the shop steward's movement were all among Seattle's radical-led locals. Thompson, "Industrial Relations in Seattle," p. 93; Agent #106, 19 September 1919; *Forge*, 4 October 1919; SUR, 22 August, 25 October 1919. On the shop steward movement in Seattle, see also James Robertson, "Labor Unionism, Based Upon the American Shop Steward System," n.p., n.d., copy in Department of Labor Library; my thanks to David Montomery for sharing this document with me.

26. SUR, 12 May 1919.

27. Ibid., 18 April, 1, 5, 8, 15, 22, 24, 29 May 1919; Agent #106, 18 April, 16 May 1919; Minutes, CLC, 21 May 1919.

28. Minutes, CLC, 5 March 1919; SUR, 22 February, 5, 19 March 1919; Copy of Duncan Plan in Ault Papers, Part I, Box 1, Folder 54 (Central Labor Council of Seattle and Vicinity to All Organizations Affiliated with the American Federation of Labor, 12 March 1919); also in O'Connor Papers, Box II, with letter attached.

29. David Jay Bercuson, "The One Big Union in Washington," *Pacific Northwest Quarterly* Vol. 69, No. 3 (July 1978), pp. 127–34; Montgomery, *Fall of the House of Labor*, pp. 427–30.

30. Montgomery, *Fall of the House of Labor*, p. 429.

31. Minutes, Local #131, United Brotherhood of Carpenters and Joiners, 20 May 1921, Records of Local #131, United Brotherhood of Carpenters and Joiners, University of Washington Manuscripts Collection; Minutes, CLC, 9, 16 April, 28 May 1919; Agent #17, 14, 21 August 1919; Agent #106, 14 August 1919; SUR, 25 March, 12 July, 9, 11 August 1919; Seattle *Union Record*, weekly edition (hereafter SURW), April 1919; *Forge*, 5 July 1919; Duncan plan.

32. "Bulletin," Clyde Van Hemert to Mark Allison Matthews, n.d. [c. 17 February 1919], Mark Allison Matthews Papers, Box 1, Folder 5, University of Washington Manuscripts Collection.

33. Minutes, CLC, 26 February 1919.

34. SW, 19 April 1919.

35. Bercuson, "One Big Union," pp. 132–34; *Seattle Star*, 6 March 1919; *Seattle Times*, 14 February 1919; Montgomery, *Fall of the House of Labor*, pp. 429–30; Agent #106, 4, 14, 20, 21 August 1919; Minutes, CLC, 5 March 1919.

36. SW, 9 April 1919.

37. Ibid., 12 May 1919; SUR, 18 March, 2 April 1919; SW, 10 March, 3 May 1919.
38. SW, 19 February 1919.
39. Ibid.
40. Ibid., 17 February 1919.
41. Agent #106, 30 April 1919. Agent #17, 21 January 1920; SUR, 10, 14 February 1919; SW, 12 February, 28 June 1919, 24 January 1920; Wilfred Harris Crook, *The General Strike* (Chapel Hill: University of North Carolina Press, 1931), pp. 532, 54; Albert F. Gunns, "Civil Liberties in Crisis: The Status of Civil Liberties in the Pacific Northwest, 1917–1942," Ph.D. Diss., University of Washington, 1971, p. 42; Robert L. Tyler, *Rebels of the Woods: The IWW in the Pacific Northwest* (Eugene: University of Oregon Press, 1967), p. 193; William Preston, Jr., *Aliens and Dissenters: Federal Suppression of Radicals, 1903–1933* (Cambridge, Mass.: Harvard University Press, 1963), pp. 198–99; O'Connor, *The Revolution in Seattle*, p. 200; Bulletin, Clyde Van Hemert to Mark Allison Matthews, n.d. [c. 17 February 1919], Matthews Papers, Box 1, Folder 5; History Committee, p. 57; Hays Jones mss., n.d. [c. 1962], O'Connor Papers, Part II, Box 3.
42. SW, 15 March 1919; see also 17 February, 11 March 1919.
43. Francis R. Singleton, "Seattle and the American Plan," reprint from *Business* n.d., n.p., in Ault Papers, Part I, Box 5, Folder 17; Thompson, "Industrial Relations in Seattle," pp. 16, 69–70; Warren Stanley Gramm, "Employers Association Development in Seattle and Vicinity," M.A. Thesis, University of Washington, 1948, pp. 5–6; "How Seattle Fights Unfair Labor Unions," *Iron Age* 106 (21 October 1920), pp. 1055–56; Savel Zimand, *The Open Shop Drive* (New York: Bureau of Industrial Research, 1921), p. 14; Associated Industries of Seattle, *The American Plan: Seattle's Answer to the Challenge of Bolshevism* (Seattle: Associated Industries of Seattle, 10 December 1919); O'Connell, "The Seattle Union Record," p. 137; SUR, 18 October 1918; SW, 6 December 1919.
44. Lee F. Pendergrass, "Urban Reform and Voluntary Association: A Case Study of the Seattle Municipal League, 1910–1929," Ph.D. Diss., University of Washington, 1972 (quote, pp. 92–93); Pendergrass, "The Formation of a Municipal Reform Movement: The Municipal League of Seattle," *Pacific Northwest Quarterly* Vol. 66, No. 1 (January 1975), pp. 13–25; Charles Byler, "Austin E. Griffiths: Seattle Progressive Reformer," *Pacific Northwest Quarterly* Vol. 76, No. 1 (January 1985), pp. 22–32; Minutes, 1919–21, Seattle Chamber of Commerce, (in Seattle Public Library); "Declaration of Industrial Situation by Seattle Chamber of Commerce and Commercial Club," 27 October 1919, in Austin Griffiths Papers, Box 9, Folder 8, University of Washington Manuscripts Collection; Thompson, "Industrial Relations in Seattle," p. 131; Anna Louise Strong, *I Change Worlds: The Remaking of an American* (New York: Henry Holt, 1935), pp. 49–50.
45. SUR, 24 April 1920.
46. O'Connell, "The Seattle Union Record," pp. 84, 201; Harry Ault to Roger Baldwin, 3 October 1922, Records of the American Fund for Public Service, Box 18, New York Public Library Manuscripts Collection; SUR, 18 February 1919, 24 April 1920; Earl W. Shimmons, "The Labor Dailies," *American*

Mercury 15 (September 1928), pp. 85–93; *Business Chronicle* 25 January 1919, in Harvey O'Connor's notes for *The Revolution in Seattle*, O'Connor Papers, Part II, Box 3; Ault to Baldwin, 10 March, 29 August 1922, in Ault Papers, Box 18; Earl W. Shimmons, "The Seattle Union Record," p. 19, manuscript in Ault Papers, Part I, Box 7, Folder 9. For a list of firms boycotting the *Record*, see SUR, 18 February 1919; for financial effect of the boycott, see Minutes of Joint Meeting of Union Record Employees and Board of Directors, 27 December [1921], Ault Papers, Part I, Box 6, Folder 53; Telegram, Seattle *Union Record* to *Labor Age*, 21 June 1922, Ault Papers, Part I, Box 4, Folder 17. For an extended discussion of the boycott and the *Record*'s response, see Dana Frank, "At the Point of Consumption: Seattle Labor and the Politics of Consumption, 1919–1927," Ph.D. Diss., Yale University, 1988, pp. 221–53.

47. O'Connell, "The Seattle Union Record," pp. 83–84, 132–33; SUR, 14, 15 February 1919; 24 April 1920; Minutes of Joint Meeting of Union Record Employees and Board of Directors; William Short, *History of Activities of Seattle Labor Movement and Conspiracy of Employers to Destroy It and Attempted Suppression of Labor's Daily Papers, the Seattle Union Record* (Seattle: Union Record Publishing, 1919), pp. 12, 23.

48. O'Connell, "Seattle Union Record," p. 131.

49. SUR, 22 August 1919.

50. Mark Litchman to Miss Baritz, 3 February 1920, Litchman Papers, Part I, Box 1, Folder 27; Thompson, "Industrial Relations in Seattle," pp. 65–68; O'Connell, "Seattle Union Record," p. 131; Washington State Bureau of Labor, *Twelfth Biennial Report*, 1920, pp. 18–20; *American Union*, 1 November 1919; *Forge*, 8 November 1919; Zimand, *Open Shop Drive*, p. 13; Singleton, "Seattle and the American Plan"; SUR, 2 September 1919; O'Connor, *The Revolution in Seattle*, p. 158; O'Connell, "Seattle Union Record," pp. 131–32; Short, *History of Activities*, pp. 9–10; Agent #17, 23 September, 1 November 1919; Agent #106, 29 August, 2, 4, 8, 13, 17, 20, 21, 23 September, 11, 17, 21, 23 October, 6, 19 November, 18 December 1919; 10, 15, 17 March, 5 April 1920; Agent #181, 10 March 1920, Roy John Kinnear Papers, Box 1, Folder 6, University of Washington Manuscripts Collection; SUR, 2, 15, 23 September, 17 October, 4 December 1919; 10 March 1920; Minutes, CLC, 24 September 1919; Mark Litchman to Percy Sparks, 19 September 1919, Litchman Papers, Part I, Box 1, Folder 8; WSFL, *Proceedings of the 19th Convention* (Olympia: WSFL, 1920), p. 9.

51. Zimand, *Open Shop Drive*, p. 14.

52. Ibid.; SW, 12 November 1919; Thompson, "Industrial Relations in Seattle," pp. 63, 69; Associated Industries of Seattle, *The American Plan*, p. 4; Singleton, "Seattle and the American Plan"; *Square Deal*; Christy Thomas, "Seattle's New Labor Policy," *Review of Reviews* Vol. 62 (November 1920), pp. 516–20; *Seattle Times, Seattle Post-Intelligencer, Seattle Star*, Fall 1919; O'Connell, "Seattle Union Record," p. 129; *Labor and Industrial Journal*, 3 April 1920; "How Seattle Fights Unfair Labor Unions," p. 1056.

53. Associated Industries of Seattle, *The American Plan*, pp. 21–22.

54. Singleton, "Seattle and the American Plan"; *Square Deal*; Zimand, *Open Shop Drive*, p. 14; SUR, 30 August, 8 October 1919.

55. Robert E. Ficken, *The Forested Land: A History of Lumbering in Western Washington* (Durham, N.C.: Forest History Society; Seattle: University of Washington Press, 1987), p. 154.

56. Ibid., pp. 154–56.

57. Mark Allison Matthews to George W. Baker, Jr., 8 October 1919, Mark Allison Matthews Papers, Box 1, Folder 6, University of Washington Manuscripts Collection.

58. Matthews to Baker, 5 November 1919, Matthews Papers, Box 1, Folder 6; Dale Soden, "Mark Allison Matthews: Seattle's Minister Rediscovered," *Pacific Northwest Quarterly* Vol. 76, No. 1 (January 1985), pp. 50–58.

59. Francis Russell, *A City in Terror: 1919, the Boston Police Strike* (New York: Viking, 1975); William Z. Foster, *The Great Steel Strike and Its Lessons* (New York: Huebsch, 1920); Interchurch World Movement of North America, *Report on the Steel Strike of 1919* (New York: Harcourt, Brace, 1920); David Brody, *Steelworkers in America: The Nonunion Era* (Cambridge, Mass.: Harvard University Press, 1960), pp. 231–62; Foster Rhea Dulles and Melvyn Dubofsky, *Labor in America: A History*, 4th ed. (Arlington Heights, Ill.: Harlan Davidson, 1984), pp. 223–29.

60. Alan M. Wakstein, "The Origins of the Open Shop Movement, 1919–1920," *Journal of American History* Vol. 51 (December 1964), pp. 460–75; Robert W. Dunn, *The Americanization of Labor: The Employers' Offensive Against the Trade Unions* (New York: International Publishers, 1927), pp. 17–80; Zimand, *Open Shop Drive*.

61. Mark Allison Matthews to Woodrow Wilson, 13 September 1919, Matthews Papers, Box 5, Folder 13; Associated Industries of Seattle, *The American Plan*, p. 21; Singleton, "Seattle and the American Plan," p. 4.

62. SW, 6 December 1919, 10 January 1920; Singleton, "Seattle and the American Plan"; Associated Industries of Seattle, *The American Plan*, p. 20.

63. Associated Industries of Seattle, *The American Plan*, p. 21; Singleton, "Seattle and the American Plan"; Thomas, "Seattle's New Labor Policy"; "How Seattle Fights Unfair Labor Unions."

64. SW, 4 October 1919.

65. Ibid.

66. Mark Allison Matthews to George W. Baker, Jr., 5 November 1919, Matthews Papers, Box 1, Folder 6.

67. SW, 3, 24 January 1920; see also 20 September, 4, 8, 11, 13, 15 October, 8 November, 10 December 1919.

68. SW, 10 September 1919.

69. "How Seattle Fights Unfair Labor Unions," p. 1056; Washington State Bureau of Labor, *Twelfth Biennial Report* (1920), pp. 18, 20; Thompson, "Industrial Relations in Seattle," p. 68; Singleton, "Seattle and the American Plan"; O'Connell, "Seattle Union Record," p. 131; Minutes, Seattle Chamber of Commerce, 19 October 1920; Mark Litchman to Miss Baritz, 3 February 1920, Litchman Papers, Part I, Box 1, Folder 27.

70. O'Connell, "Seattle Union Record," pp. 132–33.

71. SW, 1 November 1919.

72. Shimmons, "Seattle Union Record," p. 36.

73. SUR, September–October 1919.

74. Agent #106, 16 October 1919.
75. Ibid.
76. Ibid., 28 October 1919; see also 18, 25 October 1919; *American Union*, 8 November 1919.
77. *Forge*, 8 November 1919.
78. Agent #106, 17 October 1919.
79. Ibid., 26 October 1919; see also 8 November 1919.
80. Ibid., 28 October 1919.
81. Ibid., 16 October 1919.
82. SUR, 20, 27, 28 October 1919; Agent #17, 20, 30 March 1920; O'Connell, "Seattle Union Record," pp. 131–32; Minutes, Executive Board, CLC, 5 November 1919, in Box 15, Records of the King County Central Labor Council; *American Union*, 8 November 1919; Agent #181, 2 April 1920, Kinnear Papers, Box 1, Folder 6; Jonathan Dembo, "A History of the Washington State Labor Movement, 1885–1935," Ph.D. Diss., University of Washington, 1978, pp. 264–65; SUR, January, February 1920. Progressive Jimmy Duncan said of the Committee of Fifteen: "The trouble is that we can't agree and can't trust each other.... The fact is there should only be three good men on the committee, – A radical, a conservative, and a reactionary." Agent #106, 20 October 1919.
83. SUR, 29 August, 23 September, 9 October 1919; *Forge*, 11 October 1919; Agent #106, 17 September 1919.
84. *American Union*, 25 October 1919; SUR, 1 July 1919; Minutes, CLC, 22 October 1919; Maurine Weiner Greenwald, "Working-Class Feminism and the Family Wage Ideal: The Seattle Debate on Married Women's Right to Work, 1914–1920," *Journal of American History* Vol. 76, No. 1 (June 1989), pp. 118–49.
85. *American Union*, 25 October 1919; SUR, 10 June, 29 July, 23, 25, 30 October 1919; Greenwald, "Working-Class Feminism."
86. O'Connor, *The Revolution in Seattle*, pp. 170–97; Friedheim, *Seattle General Strike*, pp. 172–73; Robert L. Tyler, "Violence at Centralia, 1919," *Pacific Northwest Quarterly* Vol. 45 (October 1954), pp. 116–24.
87. SW, 15 November 1919.
88. William Short to Samuel Gompers, 5 November 1919, WSFL Records, Box 3; Gunns, "Civil Liberties in Crisis," pp. 42–43; *Seattle Times*, 10 December 1919; O'Connor, *The Revolution in Seattle*, pp. 170–97.
89. SUR, 24 April 1920; O'Connell, "Seattle Union Record," pp. 101–22. Eventually the cases against the *Record*'s managers were thrown out of court.
90. O'Connor, *The Revolution in Seattle*, pp. 200–1; O'Connell, "Seattle Union Record," pp. 114, 118–20, 134; *Seattle Times*, 7 April 1920; Shimmons, "The Labor Dailies," p. 91; Ault to Baldwin, 29 August 1922, American Fund for Public Service Records, Box 18.
91. Minutes, Monthly Meeting, Local #76, American Federation of Musicians, 14 November 1919, in possession of Local #76, Seattle.
92. Minutes, CLC, 19 November 1919.
93. Agent #106, 18 November 1919; *American Union*, 22 November 1919; see also 1 November, 25 December 1919.
94. Quoted in Jonathan Dembo, "A History of the Washington State Labor

Movement, 1885–1935," Ph.D. Diss., University of Washington, 1979, p. 216; see also *Seattle Times*, 14 February 1919.

95. SW, 9 July 1919.
96. Agent #106, 19 November 1919.
97. E.g., *American Union*, 8 November 1919.
98. Barbara Winslow, "The Decline of Socialism in Washington, 1910–1925," M.A. Thesis, University of Washington, 1969, p. 102.
99. Report of Agent #181, 2 April 1920, Roy John Kinnear Papers, Box 1, Folder 6.
100. *American Union*, 25 October 1919.
101. For the term "disruptionists," see, e.g., Minutes, CLC, 19 November 1919.
102. Agent #106, 14 January 1920.
103. *American Union*, 13 December 1919; Minutes, CLC and SUR, November–December 1919; Agent #106, 9 December 1919.

5. Boycotts

1. *Square Deal*, 14 August 1920.
2. Report of Agent #106, (hereafter Agent #106), 19 December 1919, Broussais C. Beck Papers, Boxes 1–2, University of Washington Manuscripts Collection.
3. Agent #106, 1 December 1919. See 9 February 1920 for the same argument by McPherson of the plasterers.
4. Agent #106, 15 December 1919. For a similar point of view expressed by Sam Arena of the shoemakers, see Agent #106, 18 December 1919. For the range of views, see Agent #106, 23 October 1919 and November–December 1919.
5. Seattle *Union Record*, daily edition (hereafter SUR), 8, 29 January 1920; Minutes, Central Labor Council of Seattle and Vicinity (hereafter CLC), in Records of the King County Central Labor Council, Box 8, University of Washington Manuscripts Collection, 28 January 1920; Agent #106, 7, 10, 15, 29 January 1920. For the same argument that workers should "strike on the job," see Agent #106, 1 December 1919.
6. SUR, 20 September 1920; Agent #106, 19 September 1920.
7. SUR, 18 November 1919.
8. Agent #106, 16 November 1919; see also SUR, 26 December 1919.
9. Agent #106, 29 November 1919.
10. On the boycott campaign, see also Minutes, CLC, 17, 19 December 1919; SUR, 17, 18, 19 November, 4, 16, 17, 19, 22 December 1919; Report of Agent #17 (hereafter Agent #17), 29 November, 18 December 1919, Broussais C. Beck Papers; Agent #106, 16, 17 November.
11. Margaret Jane Thompson, "Development and Comparison of Industrial Relationships in Seattle," M.B.A. Thesis, University of Washington, 1929, p. 36; Harvey O'Connor, *The Revolution in Seattle* (New York: Monthly Review Press, 1964), pp. 101–2; Tracy B. Strong and Helene Keyssar, *Right in Her Soul: The Life of Anna Louise Strong* (New York: Random House, 1984), pp. 65, 68–69; Jonathan Dembo, "A History of the Washington State Labor Movement, 1885–1935," Ph.D. Thesis, University of Washington, 1978, p. 145.
12. Mary Joan O'Connell, "The Seattle Union Record, 1918–1928: A Pioneer

Labor Daily," M.A. Thesis, University of Washington, 1964, p. 87; "Story of Union Record," p. 3 [1924–25] in Saul Haas Papers, Box 41, Folder 5, University of Washington Manuscripts Collection; A. L. Kempster and successors, weekly reports to Stone and Webster Company (hereafter SW), in Box 122, Records of the Puget Sound Traction, Light and Power Company, University of Washington Manuscripts Collection, 12 February, 8, 11 March 1919; SUR, 4, 12 February 1919.

13. O'Connell, "Seattle Union Record," p. 116; SUR, 18 June, 27 October, 4 November 1919; Agent #106, November, December 1919; Earl Shimmons, "The Seattle Union Record," manuscript in Harry Ault Papers, Part I, Box 7, Folder 9, University of Washington Manuscripts Collection, p. 32; William J. Dickson, "Labor in Municipal Politics: A Study of Labor's Political Policies and Activities in Seattle," M.A. Thesis, University of Washington, 1928, p. 53; Agent #17, 29 August 1919; William Short to Samuel Gompers, 5 November 1919, Records of the Washington State Federation of Labor (hereafter WSFL), Box 35, University of Washington Manuscripts Collection.

14. Agent #106, 20 February 1920. SUR, 30 August 1919; January–March 1920; Agent #106, 16 November 1919, January–March 1920; O'Connell, "The Seattle Union Record," pp. 116, 151–58; Dembo, "History of the Washington State Labor Movement," pp. 275–79; Mark Litchman to Miss Baritz, 3 February 1920, Mark Litchman Papers, Part I, Box 1, Folder 27, University of Washington Manuscripts Collection.

15. Agent #106, 21 January 1920.

16. Ibid., 12 January 1920. See also SUR, 30 August, 27 October 1919; William MacDonald, "Where Labor Points the Way," *Nation* Vol. 108 (5 April 1919), p. 500; Shimmons, "The Seattle Union Record," p. 34.

17. *Forge*, 6 March 1920; Agent #106, 9, 17 January 1920. Seattle's African-American business community, despite the labor movement's exclusionary record on race relations, evidently chose as well to support Duncan, who gained the endorsement of the weekly *Searchlight*. A "delegation of Japanese" visited the campaign office to deliver $125 for the campaign fund and "pledge their support", evidently having concluded that Duncan would be preferable to his probusiness opponent, Caldwell. Agent #106, 1 March 1920.

18. O'Connell, "The Seattle Union Record," pp. 156–58; Dembo, pp. 275–79.

19. Minutes, CLC, 3, 10 March 1920; Executive Board Minutes, CLC, 10 March 1920, in Records of the King County Central Labor Council.

20. SUR, 27 August 1919; 3, 9, 29 March 1920; Minutes, CLC, 13 August 1919. On the identification of the Bon Marche with the Associated Industries, see also Agent #17, 31 October 1919; SUR, 18 October 1919; Agent #106, 3 March 1920. On the decision to boycott the Bon Marche, see also Minutes, CLC, 28 January 1920; Executive Board Minutes, 2 February, 10, 15 March 1920; Thompson, "Development and Comparison," pp. 66–67; SUR, 29 January, 5 February 1920; Agent #106, 28 February, 3 March 1920; Agent #17, 6 February 1920.

21. Agent #106, 24 March 1920.

22. Ibid., 6 January, 3 March, 26 April 1920. In a speech at the CLC, Harry Ault argued similarly: "Bon March [*sic*] caters to the trade of the workers and the workers do trade there. The Bon is not like Frederick & Nelson's and

McDougall's but in spite of that the Bon Marche is the leading aggressor against the very people that patronize the store." Agent #106, 3 March 1920; see also 5 March 1920. Women activists in the Cooperative Food Products Association reported: "We are building up our dry-goods department and hope some day to occupy a larger building than the Bon Marche. They say we built the Bon. Why can we not build one for ourselves" (*Co-operator* II: 2 [February 1921]). A woman who wrote to Ruth Ridgeway in February, 1920, seeking Butterick patterns, said she had looked for them at the Bon but had been unable to find them there – which would further indicate that working-class people shopped at the store. SUR, 19 February 1920.

23. Leo Wolman, *The Boycott in American Trade Unions* (Baltimore: Johns Hopkins University Press, 1916), p. 22; Michael Gordon, "The Labor Boycott in New York City, 1880–1886," *Labor History* Vol. 16, No. 2 (Spring 1975), p. 184.

24. Wolman, *Boycott in American Trade Unions*, pp. 23–24; Norman J. Ware, *The Labor Movement in the United States, 1865–1895* (New York: D. Appleton, 1929), p. 334; Harry Wellington Laidler, *Boycotts and the Labor Movement* (New York: John Lane, 1914), p. 58; David Scobey, "Boycotting the Politics Factory: Labor Radicalism and the New York City Mayoral Election of 1884," *Radical History Review* 28–30 (September 1984), p. 298.

25. Agent #106, 23 April 1920.

26. Scobey, "Boycotting the Politics Factory," p. 298; Ware, *Labor Movement*, p. 334.

27. Agent #106, 21 April 1920.

28. See SUR, early 1920.

29. Ware, *Labor Movement*, p. 335. Gregory Zieren, in a study of Toledo, Ohio, in the late nineteenth century, argues that the boycott's usage provides "a gauge for workers' solidarity and class consciousness." See "The Labor Boycott and Class Consciousness in Toledo, Ohio," in Robert Asher and Charles Stephenson, eds., *Life and Labor: Dimensions of American Working-Class History* (Albany: State University of New York Press, 1986), pp. 131–49. James Cronin has shown consumer organizing to be crucial to European labor's solidarity and militance in the immediate post–World War I years. "Labor Insurgency and Class Formation: Comparative Perspectives on the Crisis of 1917–1920 in Europe," *Social Science History* Vol. 4, No. 1 (February 1980), pp. 125–52.

30. Agent #106, 13 April 1920.

31. Ibid., 20 March 1920; see also 12, 16, 19 March 1920; Report of Agent #317, 11 March 1920, Roy John Kinnear Papers, University of Washington Manuscripts Collection.

32. Minutes, CLC, 10, 31 March 1920; Executive Board Minutes, 10 March 1920; Agent #17, 18 March, 3 June 1920; Agent #106, 10 March, 11 April 1920 (leaflet attached to report); SUR, 29, 31 March, 15 April 1920; Minutes, Local #202, International Typographers' Union, 28 March, 25 April 1920, in Records of Local #99, International Typographers' Union, Box 16, University of Washington Manuscripts Collection.

33. SUR, 16 April 1920. SUR, 4 February, 12, 15, 19, 27, 31 March, 1, 2, 3 April, 18 May 1920.

34. Ibid., 26, 27 March, 12, 15 April, 7 May, 19 June, 27 July, 10 August 1920.
35. Ibid., 27 March 1920.
36. John Commons, *History of Labour in the United States*, Vol. I (New York: Macmillan, 1918), p. 130; Laidler, *Boycotts and the Labor Movement*; Wolman, *Boycott in American Trade Unions*.
37. Philip Taft, *The A.F. of L. in the Time of Gompers* (New York: Harper & Bros., 1957), pp. 266–71.
38. Laidler, *Boycotts and the Labor Movement*, pp. 112–15; Wolman, *Boycott in American Trade Unions*, p. 108; Minutes, CLC, 1919–22; correspondence files, WSFL Records.
39. Wolman, *Boycott in American Trade Unions*, p. 115; Michael Kazin, "The Great Exception Revisited: Organized Labor and Politics in San Francisco and Los Angeles, 1870–1940," *Pacific Historical Review* Vol. 55, No. 3 (August 1986), pp. 371–402; Julia Greene, "The Strike at the Ballot Box: Politics and Partisanship in the the American Federation of Labor, 1881–1916," Ph.D. Diss., Yale University, 1990, pp. 74–99; Lloyd Ulman, *The Rise of the National Trade Union* (Cambridge, Mass.: Harvard University Press, 1955), pp. 341–48.
40. Executive Board Minutes, 1919–20.
41. "Revised Central Labor Council Unfair List," Seattle, February 1923, in Records of Local #1289, United Brotherhood of Carpenters and Joiners, Box 12, Folder 14, University of Washington Manuscripts Collection.
42. Agent #106, 5 February 1920.
43. SUR, 28 July 1919.
44. Ibid., 8 May 1919; Agent #106, 7 May 1919.
45. SUR, 4 August 1919; see also Agent #106, 27 May 1919; SUR, 5 June 1919; Minutes, CLC, 4 March 1921.
46. Minutes, CLC, 7 May 1919.
47. SUR, 10 June 1920; see also Minutes, CLC, 4 June 1919, 2 June 1920; August 1920.
48. For fines routinely imposed by craft locals, see Minutes, Typographers #202, and Minutes, Local #76, American Federation of Musicians, in possession of Local #76, Seattle. Infractions included working alongside nonunion members, failure to attend meetings, working below scale, and other failures to observe the union's work rules. See also David Bensman, *The Practice of Solidarity: American Hat Finishers in the Nineteenth Century* (Urbana: University of Illinois Press, 1985), p. 83; Patricia Cooper, *Once a Cigar Maker: Men, Women, and Work Culture in American Cigar Factories, 1900–1919* (Urbana: University of Illinois Press, 1987), pp. 99, 108–110, for fines imposed by AFL affiliates at the local level.
49. SUR, 7 August 1920; *Musicland*, 4 April 1924; *Co-operator* I:10 (August 1920), p. 6.
50. Agent #17, 29 March 1920.
51. Ibid.
52. Agent #106, 12 March 1920.
53. SUR, 1 November 1919.
54. *Forge*, 14 October 1919.
55. SUR, 11 February 1921.
56. Ibid.

57. Ibid., 1 November 1919.
58. *Forge*, 14 October 1919.
59. SUR, 9 October 1919; see also SUR, 6 July 1921. For the origins of this point of view, see Susan Levine, *Labor's True Woman: Carpet Weavers, Industrialization, and Labor Reform in the Gilded Age* (Philadelphia: Temple University Press, 1984), pp. 151–53; and Mari Jo Buhle, *Women and American Socialism, 1870–1920* (Urbana: University of Illinois Press, 1981), p. 180.
60. For the concept of "emotional labor," see Arlie Russell Hochschild, *The Managed Heart: Commercialization of Human Feeling* (Berkeley: University of California Press, 1983).
61. *Journeyman Barber* Vol. XV, No. 11 (December 1918), p. 391.
62. Minutes, Musicians' #76 Board of Directors, 21 September 1920.
63. Minutes, #76 Board of Directors, 5 February 1929.
64. SUR, 9 October 1919.
65. *Forge*, 14 October 1919.
66. SUR, 25 October 1919.
67. Ibid., 10 June 1919.
68. For a challenging analysis of working-class wives' point of view on the English labor movement in the 1940s and 1950s, see Nicky Hart, "Gender and the Rise and Fall of Class Politics," *New Left Review*, No. 195 (May–June 1989), pp. 19–47.
69. Kathryn Oberdeck, "'Not Pink Teas': The Seattle Working Class Women's Movement, 1905–1918," *Labor History* Vol. 32, No. 2 (Spring 1991), pp. 193–230; Mary Friermood to Carpenters #1289, 29 March 1923, Box 3, Folder 4, Records of Carpenters #1289; SUR, 10 June 1919; Harry Call, *History of the Washington State Federation of Labor, 1902–1954* (Seattle: WSFL, 1954), p. 36; Ernest Radcliffe Spedden, *The Trade Union Label* (Baltimore: Johns Hopkins University Press, 1909), p. 66; Albert Helbing, *The Departments of the American Federation of Labor* (Baltimore: Johns Hopkins University Press, 1931), pp. 104–10; WSFL, *Proceedings of the 12th Convention* (Olympia: WSFL, 1913), p. 63; *Proceedings of the 14th Convention* (Olympia: WSFL, 1915), pp. 4, 109; WSFL, *Proceedings of the 16th Convention* (Olympia: WSFL, 1917), p. 53.
70. SUR, 10 June 1919. I am assuming that all the members were white, given the pattern of racial exclusion in the unions of which these women's husbands were members.
71. Ibid., 5 June 1919.
72. Ibid., 5 February 1919.
73. See also ibid., 28 February 1919.
74. Minutes, CLC; Roll Books, CLC, in Records of the King County Central Labor Council.
75. For a theoretical discussion of the question of housewives' acceptance of the sexual division of labor and the activism that may evolve from that, see Temma Kaplan, "Female Consciousness and Collective Action: The Case of Barcelona, 1910–1918," *Signs* Vol. 7 (Spring 1982), pp. 545–66. For an analysis of working-class family strategies of which women's labors were a part, see Jane Humphries, "Class Struggle and the Persistence of the Working-Class Family," *Cambridge Journal of Economics* Vol. 1, No. 3 (September 1977),

pp. 241–58; see also Ron Rothbart, "'Homes are What Any Strike Is About': Immigrant Labor and the Family Wage," *Journal of Social History* Vol. 23, No. 2 (Winter 1989), pp. 267–84.

76. Agent #17, 13, 22 May 1920; SUR, 20 May 1920; Minutes, CLC, 19 May 1920.

77. SUR, 21 April 1920.

78. Ibid., 5, 6, 7, 12 August 1920.

79. For the activities of the Card and Label League, see WSFL, *Proceedings of the 18th Convention* (1919), pp. 68, 109; Seattle *Union Record*, weekly edition (hereafter SURW), 8 March, 3 May 1919; SUR, 6 January, 15, 22 February, 17, 20, 31 March, 2, 14, 22 April, 7, 10, 16, 17, 19, 20, 23, 31 May, 5, 10, 16, 19, 24 June, 5, 9 July, 20 November, 3, 18 December 1919; 7, 29 January, 21 April, 2 June 1920; Minutes, CLC, 29 January, 12, 26 February, 19 March, 2, 23 April, 18 June, 19 November 1919; 28 January, 17, 24, 31 March, 7 April, 12 May, 2 June, 4 August 1920; 20 April, 18, 25 May, 22 June, 27 July, 17 August, 7, 14 September, 5, 12 October, 9, 23 November, 7 December 1921; Jonathan Dembo, "John Danz and the Seattle Amusement Trades Strike, 1921–35," *Pacific Northwest Quarterly* Vol. 71, No. 4 (October 1980), pp. 172–82.

80. WSFL, *Proceedings of the 18th Convention* (1919), p. 150; SUR, 10 January 1919, 7 January 1920; Minutes, CLC, 31 March, 7 April, 12 May 1920.

81. Minutes, CLC, 12, 19 November 1919; SUR, 24 June 1919; Oberdeck, " 'Not Pink Teas.' "

82. For the Women's Modern Study Club: SUR, 17 April, 31 July, 4 September 1919; 6 January, 20 April, 5, 9 May, 2 July 1921. For the Business Women's Civic Club: SUR, 19, 22, April, 17 May 1919. For the Women's Trade Union League: SUR, 13 May, 29 July, 5 August, 16 October 1919; 7, 12 January, 7 February, 9 March, 12 May, 18 June 1921; Seattle *Post-Intelligencer*, 15 July 1920. For the Workers', Soldiers' and Sailors' Council Women's Club: *Forge*, 4, 14 October 1919. For the Farmer–Labor Party Women's Club: SUR, 3, 18 March, 17 May 1921. For the Ladies' Auxiliaries: SUR, 21 March, 29 April, 16 August, 1 November 1919; see also Chapter 9.

83. *Co-operator* I:11 (September 1920), p. 7; I:10 (October 1920), p. 7; SURW, 1 March 1919.

84. For the mix of concerns within a given group, see, e.g., SUR, 6 May 1919.

85. The Seattle women's situation confirms Estelle Freedman's argument identifying the efficacy of separate organization by women in "Separatism as Strategy: Female Institution-Building and American Feminism, 1870–1920," *Feminist Studies* Vol. 5 (Fall 1979), pp. 512–29.

86. SUR, 24 June 1919.

87. See Chapter 4; see also SUR, 26 February 1919 for such tensions.

88. A third much smaller group of clerical workers included the postal clerks and railway clerks; the latter were not affiliated with the Central Labor Council. Washington State Bureau of Labor, *Twelfth Biennial Report of the Bureau of Labor Statistics and Factory Inspections, 1919–1920* (Olympia: Washington State Bureau of Labor, 1920), pp. 32–34.

89. Agent #106, 18 February 1920; Seattle *Times*, 21, 27 May, 6 October 1920; SUR, May 1920 in general; Seattle *Post-Intelligencer*, clipping, n.d. [1920], in

Seattle Public Library clipping file; SUR, April, May 1920; Minutes, CLC, 28 February, 17 March, 21 April, 5, 12, 26 May 1920; Alice Kessler-Harris, *Out to Work: A History of Wage-Earning Women in the United States* (New York: Oxford University Press, 1982), p. 204, and Ch. 7 in general. On the minimum wage in Washington State, see Joseph F. Tripp, "Toward an Efficient and Moral Society: Washington State Minimum-Wage Law, 1913–1925," *Pacific Northwest Quarterly* Vol. 67, No. 3 (July 1976), pp. 97–112; and Joseph F. Tripp, "Progressive Labor Laws in Washington State, 1900–1925," Ph.D. Diss., University of Washington, 1973.

90. Minutes, CLC; Roll Books, CLC.
91. For the percentage of each union that was male or female, see Washington State Bureau of Labor, *Twelfth Biennial Report*, pp. 32–34. Information as to the officers of the unions comes from CLC (CLC delegates and reporting officers from the locals); SUR (see, e.g., 24 April 1919 on the candy workers, 26 March 1921 for the failure of a woman to win the vice-presidency of the cook's union, although the union was 30 percent female); reports of Agents #106 and #17; Minutes of Typographers' Local #202, and Musicians' Local #76.
92. Theresa Schmid McMahon, notes to accompany "My Story," in Theresa Schmid McMahon Papers, Box I, University of Washington Archives.
93. SUR, 18 March 1921; see also 17 May 1921, and Chapter 2.
94. Ibid., 17 March 1919; ibid., 4 February, 1, 28 May 1919; 8 February 1921; Seattle *Star*, 31 January 1919.
95. SUR, 17 March 1919.
96. Seattle Typographical Union #202, Card, "Officials for 1920–21," in Records of Typographers' #99, Box 4; SUR, 29 May 1919. For similar dynamics within the cook's union, see SUR, 22 January 1921.
97. Minutes, CLC, 11 June 1919; Agent #106, 11 June 1919.
98. Agent #106, 10 February 1920.
99. Ibid., 19 March 1920.
100. Ibid., 9 March 1920; see also 19 April 1920.
101. Ibid., 21 April 1920. For debates over restricting the list, see also *Labor and Industrial Journal* Vol. II, No. 21 (25 September 1920), p. 7.
102. Report of Agent #181 (hereafter Agent #181), 10 March 1920, Roy John Kinnear Papers, Box 1, Folder 6, University of Washington Manuscripts Collection.
103. Agent #106, 10 March 1920.
104. Ibid., 10 March 1920; Agent #181, 10 March 1920.
105. Agent #106, 10 March 1920; Agent #181, 10 March 1920.
106. Executive Board Minutes, 3 March 1920.
107. Agent #106, 10 March 1920; Agent #181, 10 March 1920.
108. Washington State Bureau of Labor, *Twelfth Biennial Report*, pp. 32–34; SUR, 24 April 1919.
109. SUR, 1 April, 6, 17 March, 18 May, 5 June 1920.
110. Agent #106, 24 January 1920; War Camp Community Service, *Temporary Survey of the Conditions Surrounding the Employed Girl of Seattle*, February 1919 (Seattle: War Camp Community Service, 1919), in Seattle Public Library Pamphlet File.

111. Agent #106, 19 November 1919; Retail Clerks' Association Local 174 Resolution to Seattle Central Labor Council, 25 February 1919, in Harry Ault Papers, Part II, Box 3, Folder 48, University of Washington Manuscripts Collection.
112. Agent #106, 13 March 1920. Ibid., 6 June, 5, 8 November, 17 December 1919; 24 January 1920; SUR, 1 April 1920.
113. Agent #106, 4 June 1919.
114. Ibid., 5 November 1919.
115. Ibid., 6 March 1920.
116. Ibid., 21 April 1920.
117. Associated Industries of Seattle, *Revolution, Wholesale Strikes, Boycotts* (Seattle: Associated Industries of Seattle, 1920), p. 4.
118. The Associated Industries continued to claim the open shop in the building trades throughout the year. But the State Federation of Labor's annual report for 1920 reported to the contrary that "the Building Trades have succeeded, despite the assault made on them by the Associated Industries, in restoring almost completely a 100 percent organization in all of the trades involved." WSFL, *Proceedings of the 19th Convention* (Olympia: WSFL, 1920), p. 9. See also Agent #106, 9 February 1920.
119. Ware, *Labor Movement*, p. 334.
120. Minutes, Board of Directors, Musicians Local #76, 13 July 1920, in possession of Local #76, Seattle.
121. Minutes, CLC, March–May 1920; *Labor and Industrial Journal* Vol. II, No. 8 (26 June 1920), p. 14. See CLC for other internal disputes; see also Agent #106, 11 June 1919.
122. On the Von Herberg Theater boycott: Agent #17, 29 April 1920; SUR, 20, 28, 29 July, 13, 21 August, 11, 18 November 1920; Minutes, CLC, 4, 11, 18 August, 1, 8 September, 6, 13 October 1920; Minutes, Typographers' #202, 25 July 1920; Associated Industries of Seattle, *Revolution, Wholesale Strikes, Boycotts*, pp. 6–7.
123. Executive Board Minutes, 22 September 1920; Minutes, CLC, 17 November 1920; 12 January, 9 February, 4 May, 15, 22 June, 17, 24, 31 August, 21, 28 September, 26 October, 16, 23, 30 November 1921; 8 February, 8 March 1922; Minutes, Carpenters #131, 6 November 1920; 7, 14 June, 1 November 1921; SUR, 18, 20 November, 8 December 1920; 13 January 1921; *Square Deal*, 25 December 1920.
124. SUR, 1, 2, 17 April, 3, 18 May 1920; Agent #106, 19 April 1920. For evidence of self-conscious lies by *Record* writers, see Chapter 6.
125. Seattle *Times*, 14 April, 2 May 1920. The *Record* charged that the Associated Industries' department store members had pressured the *Times* and other dailies to take a strong anti-union stance or else they would withdraw their advertising dollars. SUR, 18 October 1919; O'Connell, "The Seattle Union Record," p. 133.

    The pro-employer Seattle *Times* never once mentioned the boycott, despite a usual tendency to respond to labor's initiatives with both alacrity and hostility. Instead, it ran prominent stories on the Bon Marche's thirtieth anniversary, on the grand opening of the McDermott building, and on the virtues of the Bon's employee representation plan. On April 14 it quoted the company union's new president exulting, "As a store family we are as happy and contented a bunch as can be found anywhere, and the reason for that happiness lies in the fact that we receive fair and generous treatment from those for whom we work." Seattle *Times*, 14 April, 2 May 1920.

126. Associated Industries of Seattle, *Revolution, Wholesale Strikes, Boycotts*, p. 4.

127. Associated Industries of Seattle, Bulletin No. 5, n.d. [1920], in Seattle Public Library.

128. "How Seattle Fights Unfair Labor Unions," p. 1056.

129. Associated Industries of Seattle, *Revolution, Wholesale Strikes, Boycotts*; see *Square Deal*, 11 September 1920 for the same three-stage analysis.

130. *Square Deal*, 14 August 1920. See also "Weekly Bulletin No. 1 – Associated Industries of Seattle," leaflet in WSFL Records, Box 6, Folder 37.

131. Associated Industries of Seattle, *Revolution, Wholesale Strikes, Boycotts*, pp. 9–10.

132. *Square Deal*, 14 August 1920.

133. Associated Industries of Seattle, *Revolution, Wholesale Strikes, Boycotts*, p. 10.

134. *Square Deal*, 21 August 1920.

135. Ibid., 14 August, 18 September, 9 October, 25 December 1920; 22 January 1922; Associated Industries of Seattle, *Revolution, Wholesale Strikes, Boycotts*, p. 11; *Labor and Industrial Journal* Vol. II, No. 6 (12 June 1920), p. 5; Associated Industries of Seattle, "Reference and Membership List of Associated Industries," n.d. [1920], in Seattle Public Library; SUR, 27 May, 2 July 1920.

136. Associated Industries of Seattle, *Revolution, Wholesale Strikes, Boycotts*, pp. 3–4.

137. Associated Industries of Seattle, "To Our Members," 21 July 1920, in Ault Papers, Part I, Box 2, Folder 4.

138. *Square Deal*, 9 October 1920.

139. Shimmons, "The Seattle Union Record," p. 57; Thompson, "Development and Comparison," p. 22; Warren Stanley Gramm, "Employer Association Development in Seattle and Vicinity," M.A. Thesis, University of Washington, 1948, p. 6; Bulletin, Associated Industries of Seattle, 23 August 1921, WSFL Records, Box 6, Folder 37; Committee on Labor Relations, Seattle Chamber of Commerce and Commercial Club, *Profitism, Slackism, and You* (Seattle: 15 October 1920); Minutes, Seattle Chamber of Commerce, 1919–1920 (in Seattle Public Library).

140. SUR, 14 December 1920; Savel Zimand, *The Open Shop Drive* (New York: Bureau of Industrial Research, 1921), p. 17.

141. Seattle Chamber of Commerce Minutes, 19 October 1920; SUR, 23 March 1920; O'Connell, "The Seattle Union Record," p. 143; Christy Thomas, "Seattle's New Labor Policy," *Review of Reviews* Vol. 62 (November 1920), pp. 518–20; Zimand, *The Open Shop Drive*, pp. 16–17; Seattle Chamber of Commerce and Commercial Club, *Profitism, Slackism, and You*.

142. *Seattle Times*, 14 April 1920; The Bon Marche Co-operative Association, History, Constitution and By-Laws, 1918, in Seattle Public Library pamphlet file; ZIZZ, "Published Monthly in the Interests of the Employees of the Standard Furniture Company, Seattle," various issues, 1910–1918, in Schoenfeld Family Papers, Box 1, Folder 10, University of Washington Manuscripts Collection.

143. SUR, 7 March, 6 May 1919.

144. Seattle *Times*, 11 April 1920; C. T. Conover to Ellery Sedgwick, 24 December 1920, in C. T. Conover Papers, Box 1, Folder 19, University of Washington Manuscripts Collection; Seattle Chamber of Commerce and Commercial Club, *Profitism, Slackism, and You*, p. 19; Francis R. Singleton, "Seattle and the American Plan," p. 4, reprint from *Business*, n.d., n.p., in Ault Papers, Part I, Box 5, Folder 17. See also *Forge*, 27 March 1920, for Waterhouse's imposition of profit sharing and a company union at the Vulcan Iron Works. Not all such efforts were successful; an attempt to introduce a company union at the tailors' shops failed. Thompson, "Development and Comparison," pp. 67, 94.

145. Lee Johnston to Austin E. Griffiths, 10 March 1919, in Austin E. Griffiths Papers, Box 9, Folder 16, University of Washington Manuscripts Collection; H. Alvin Moore to Austin E. Griffiths, 15 January 1920, in Griffiths Papers, Box 10, Folder 17; Lee Johnston to Griffiths, 10 March 1919, Griffiths Papers, Box 9, Folder 16; Seattle *Municipal News* Vol. VIII, No. 30 (July 1919), pp. 1–2; Vol. IX, No. 1 (3 January 1920), p. 1; David Brody, "The Rise and Decline of Welfare Capitalism," in David Brody, ed., *Workers in Industrial America: Essays on the Twentieth-Century Struggle* (New York: Oxford University Press, 1980), pp. 48–81; Sanford M. Jacoby, *Employing Bureaucracy: Managers, Unions, and the Transformation of Work in American Industry, 1900–1945* (New York: Columbia University Press, 1985), pp. 49, 52, 196–98.

146. Selig Perlman and Philip Taft, *History of Labor in the United States*, Vol. IV (New York: Macmillan, 1935), pp. 489–514; Irving Bernstein, *The Lean Years: A History of the American Worker, 1920–1933* (Boston: Houghton Mifflin, 1960), pp. 154–57; David Montgomery, *The Fall of the House of Labor: The Workplace, the State, and American Labor Activism, 1865–1925* (Cambridge: Cambridge University Press, 1987), pp. 394–410, 438–455; Eric Arnesen, *Waterfront Workers of New Orleans: Race, Class, and Politics, 1863–1923* (New York: Oxford University Press, 1991), pp. 228–52; Louis B. Perry and Richard S. Perry, *A History of the Los Angeles Labor Movement, 1911–1941* (Berkeley: University of California Press, 1963), pp. 193–211; Michael Kazin, *Barons of Labor: The San Francisco Building Trades and Union Power in the Progressive Era* (Urbana: University of Illinois Press, 1987), pp. 245–64; James R. Barrett, *Work and Community in the Jungle: Chicago's Packinghouse Workers, 1894–1922* (Urbana: University of Illinois Press, 1987), pp. 240–63.

6. Depression

1. A. L. Kempster and successors, weekly reports to Stone and Webster Company (hereafter SW), in Box 122, Records of the Puget Sound Traction, Light and Power Company, University of Washington Manuscripts Collection, 31 May 1919; 3 January, 11 June, 18 September 1920; 12 January 1921; Walter Woehlke, "Is the Seattle Spirit Dead?" *Sunset* Vol. 42, No. 4 (April 1919), pp. 13–16, 64; Robert L. Friedheim, *The Seattle General Strike* (Seattle: University of Washington Press, 1964), pp. 162–65.

2. SW, 11 June 1920.

3. Minutes, Central Labor Council of Seattle and Vicinity (hereafter CLC), 12 May 1920, in Records of the King County Central Labor Council, Box 8, University of Washington Manuscripts Collection; Seattle *Union Record* (hereafter SUR), 6 March 1919, 17 November 1920; Report of Agent #17 (hereafter Agent #17), 15 January, 20 April 1920, Broussais C. Beck Papers, Boxes 1–2, University of Washington Manuscripts Collection; Report of the Metal Trades Committees, Washington State Federation of Labor, 7 May 1920, Box 20, Records of the Washington State Federation of Labor (hereafter WSFL), University of Washington Manuscripts Collection.

4. SUR, 18 February, 1919; Minutes, CLC, 29 October 1919, 17 November 1920; Roll Books, CLC, Box 11, Records of the King County Central Labor Council.

5. Agent #17, 7 February, 20 March 1920; Report of Agent #106, (hereafter Agent #106), 22 March 1920, Broussais C. Beck Papers, Boxes 1–2; Margaret Jane Thompson, "Development and Comparison of Industrial Relations in Seattle," M.B.A. Thesis, University of Washington, 1929, p. 109.

6. Melvin G. DeShazo, "Radical Tendencies in the Seattle Labor Movement as Reflected in the Proceedings of its Central Body," M.A. Thesis, University of Washington, 1925, p. 63; Mary Joan O'Connell, "The Seattle Union Record, 1918–1928: A Pioneer Labor Daily," M.A. Thesis, University of Washington, 1964, p. 131; *Square Deal*, 22 April 1920; SUR, 5 June 1920; Report of Agent #172, 12 March 1920, Box 1, Folder 6, Roy John Kinnear Papers, University of Washington Manuscripts Collection; Minutes, Seattle Chamber of Commerce, 7 December 1920, in Seattle Public Library.

7. Mark Litchman to Emmanuel Slater, 21 December 1921, in Mark Litchman Papers, Part I, Box 1, Folder 32, University of Washington Manuscripts Collection.

8. W. Elliot Brownlee, *Dynamics of Ascent: A History of the American Economy*, 2d ed. (Chicago: Dorsey, 1988), p. 380; "Unemployment Survey – 1920–21," *American Labor Legislation Review* Vol. 11, No. 3 (September 1921), pp. 191–217; SUR, 1 February, 9, 25 May 1921; Chamber of Commerce Minutes, 7 December 1920; for the vicissitudes of the Seattle economy, see also SW, 1919–22. The 10 percent figure is very rough, based on a total of 153,876 wage earners in Seattle (1920 census) and an estimated 15,000 unemployed. United States Department of Commerce, Bureau of the Census, *Fourteenth Census of the United States*, Vol. IV (Washington: Government Printing Office, 1920), p. 222.

9. *Square Deal*, 25 December 1920.

10. Chamber of Commerce Minutes, 14 December 1920.

11. SW, 5 February, 24 September 1921.

12. SUR, 6 March 1920.

13. Ibid.

14. Ibid.

15. Ibid., 10 March 1920; WSFL, *Proceedings of the 19th Convention* (Olympia: WSFL, 1920), p. 9.

16. John Williamson, *Dangerous Scot: The Life and Work of an American "Undesirable"* (New York: International Publishers, 1969), pp. 28–29, 38; SW, 12 February 1920.

17. Minutes, CLC, 18 August 1921.

18. Agent #106, 24 December 1919.

19. Ibid., 9 April 1920.

20. SUR, 5, 6 March 1920. On the exodus and its potential virtues, see also Joseph Pass to Harvey O'Connor, 14 January 1963, in O'Connor Papers, Part II, Box 3; Agent #106, 15, 27, 30 March, 27 April 1920; William Short to Frank Morrison, 5 March 1920, WSFL Records, Box 35.

21. SUR, 22 February 1921.

22. Ibid., 1, 24 January, 23 March, 7 April, 7 July 1921. For workers' organized responses to unemployment in the 1930s, see Roy Rosenzweig, "Organizing the Unemployed: The Early Years of the Great Depression, 1929–1933," *Radical America* 10 (1976), pp. 37–62; David Montgomery and Ronald Schatz, "Facing Layoffs," in David Montgomery, *Workers' Control in America: Studies in the History of Work, Technology, and Labor Struggles* (Cambridge: Cambridge University Press, 1979), pp. 138–52.

23. SW, 12 February 1921.

24. Ibid., 6 December 1919, 10 January 1920; "Bulletin of the Associated Industries of Seattle," 15 September 1921, in Seattle Public Library; Associated Industries of Seattle, *The American Plan: Seattle's Answer to the Challenge of Bolshevism* (Seattle: Associated Industries of Seattle, 10 December 1919), p. 20.

25. SUR, 16 July 1921.

26. Ibid., 1, 5 February 1921.

27. Minutes, CLC, 17 August 1921; see Minutes, CLC, throughout 1921.

28. See also *Square Deal*, 1921; SUR, 21 April, 21 July 1921; Minutes, CLC, 2, 9 November 1921; WSFL, *Proceedings of the 20th Convention* (Olympia: WSFL, 1921), p. 11.

29. *Pacific Caterer* Vol. IV, No. 16 (November 1921), pp. 30–32; SW, 2, 15 October, 8, 19 November, 9 December 1921, 3 February 1922; WSFL, *Proceedings of the 21st Convention* (Olympia: WSFL, 1922), p. 14.

30. Roll Books, CLC; SUR, 21 April 1921. Some of these locals may have been absorbed into other, stronger locals. This list is based on those who disappeared from the roll books of the Central Labor Council. Some may also have withdrawn for other reasons. The total may have been augmented, on the other hand, by the disappearance of locals that were never affiliated in the first place.

31. SUR, 23 May 1919.

32. Ibid., 17 December 1919; see also 4 July 1919.

33. *Forge*, 8 November 1919.

34. On the minimum wage, see, e.g., *Seattle Times*, 29 April 1920; Chapter 5. On the wage–price question in 1919, see also SUR, 31 May, 27 June, 20 September 1919.

35. SUR, 15 January 1921.

36. Ibid., 11 April 1921.

37. See also ibid., 22 January 1921.

38. David Montgomery, *The Fall of the House of Labor: The Workplace, the State, and American Labor Activism, 1865–1925* (Cambridge: Cambridge University Press, 1987), pp. 241, 407–409, 452–53; Selig Perlman and Philip

Taft, *History of Labor in the United States, 1896–1932*, Vol. IV (New York: Macmillan, 1935), pp. 482–88; Foster Rhea Dulles and Melvyn Dubofsky, *Labor in America: A History*, 4th ed. (Arlington Heights, Ill.: Harlan Davidson, 1984), pp. 230–32; Colin Davis, "Bitter Storm: The 1921 National Railroad Shopmen's Strike," Ph.D. Diss., State University of New York at Binghamton, 1989.

39. Harry Ault to Roger Baldwin, 29 August 1922, Harry Ault Papers, Part I, Box 4, Folder 17, University of Washington Manuscripts Collection; Agent #106, 23 May 1919; U. G. Moore, "The Rise and Fall of the Seattle Food Products Association," *Co-operation* IX:1 (January 1923), pp. 9–10; *Co-operator* I:10 (August 1920), p. 2.

40. *Co-operator* II:3 (February 1921), p. 2.

41. Olive M. Johnson, *The Co-operative Movement: An Infantile Disorder and an Old-Age Disease* (New York: New York Labor News, 1924), p. 19.

42. Moore, "Rise and Fall," p. 9; Anna Louise Strong, *I Change Worlds: The Remaking of an American* (New York: Henry Holt, 1935), p. 84; *Co-operation* VI:1 (January 1920), p. 13.

43. Robert Jackall and Henry M. Levin, eds., *Worker Cooperatives in America* (Berkeley: University of California Press, 1984), p. 9.

44. *Co-operator* I:1 (May 1920), p. 6; I:10 (August 1920), p. 2; II:2 (February 1921), p. 7; II:5 (May 1921), p. 3.

45. *Monthly Labor Review* Vol. XIV, No. 2 (February 1922), p. 60; Brownlee, *Dynamics of Ascent*, p. 380.

46. *Co-operator* I:8 (June 1920), p. 8; Minutes, CLC, 8 June 1921; 25 February, 29 March 1922.

47. Minutes, CLC, 5 November 1921.

48. Seattle *Union Record*, weekly edition (hereafter SURW), 18 November 1919.

49. Carl Lunn, "How We Cooperate Out West," *Life and Labor* Vol. X, No. 7 (September 1920), p. 206.

50. *Co-operator* II:3 (February 1921), p. 4; emphases in original.

51. Ibid.

52. Ibid.; I:6 (April 1920), p. 2.

53. Lizabeth Cohen, *Making a New Deal: Industrial Workers in Chicago, 1919–1939* (New York: Cambridge University Press, 1990), p. 112.

54. SUR, 4 August 1919. For the attitudes of the national cooperative movement toward credit, see *Co-operative Consumer* IV:5 (May 1918), pp. 71–72; IV:6 (June 1918), pp. 194–95. For Seattle cooperatives and credit, see *Northwestern Co-operative News* I:5 (1 September 1919), p. 4; *Co-operator* I:12 (October 1920), p. 5. The balance sheets of the CFPA show entries under "Customer Charge Accounts" amounting to several thousand dollars; *Co-operator* I:7 (May 1920), pp. 4–5; I:10 (August 1920), pp. 4–5; II:2 (February 1921), p. 6; II:5 (May 1921), p. 5.

55. Minutes, CLC, 1921–22; see, e.g., 17 May 1922.

56. *Co-operator* I:8 (June 1920), p. 3.

57. Moore, "Rise and Fall," p. 11.

58. *Co-operator* I:10 (August 1920), p. 2; II:2 (February 1921), p. 2; II:6 (June 1921), p. 4; Minutes, CLC, 22 March 1922.

59. *Co-operator* II:2 (February 1921), p. 2.

60. Moore, "Rise and Fall," p. 11.
61. Ibid.; emphasis in original.
62. *Co-operator* I:10 (August 1920), p. 2; I:12 (October 1920), p. 7; II:4 (December 1920), p. 5. See also *Co-operator* I:11 (September 1920), p. 3, on reactions to internal criticism.
63. See also Moore, "Rise and Fall," p. 11; *Co-operator* I:8 (June 1920), p. 3.
64. In the 1930s, though, cooperatives were central to organizing by the unemployed in Seattle. See Arthur Hillman, *The Unemployed Citizens' League of Seattle* (Seattle: University of Washington Press, 1934); Clark Kerr, "Productive Enterprises of the Unemployed, 1931–1938," Ph.D. Diss., University of California, Berkeley, 1939, pp. 1188–1215.
65. Minutes, Local #131, United Brotherhood of Carpenters and Joiners, 1 March 1921, Records of Local #131, United Brotherhood of Carpenters and Joiners, University of Washington Manuscripts Collection; *Co-operator* II:3 (March 1921), pp. 1, 3; II:5 (May 1921), p. 2; SUR, 3, 4 February 1921; Minutes, CLC, 19 January 1921.
66. Moore, "Rise and Fall," pp. 9–10; *Co-operator* I:10 (August 1920), p. 2.
67. Co-operative League of America, *Proceedings of the Second National Co-operative Convention*, Cincinnati, Ohio, 1920 (Cincinnati: Co-operative Association of America, 1920), p. 41.
68. Moore, "Rise and Fall," p. 10; *Co-operation* VI:2 (February 1921), p. 32.
69. Ault to Lunn, 26 August 1920, Ault Papers, Part I, Box 3, Folder 27.
70. Ibid.
71. Lunn to Ault, 16 June 1920, Ault Papers, Part I, Box 3, Folder 27.
72. Lunn, "How We Cooperate," p. 209; Co-operative League of America, *Second Co-operative Convention*, p. 33; Agent #17, 17 June 1920; Minutes, CLC, 9 February, 30 March, 21, 28 July, 4 August 1920; SUR, 6 August 1920.
73. Co-operative League of America, *Second Co-operative Convention*, p. 41; see also pp. 32–34, 42; Minutes, CLC, 23 June, 27 October 1920.
74. Moore, "Rise and Fall," p. 10; Minutes, CLC, 25 May, 8, 15, 22, 29 June 1921; 29 March, 12, 19, 25 April 1922; *Co-operator* II:2 (February 1921), p. 2; II:3 (March 1921), p. 1; II:4 (April 1921), p. 1; II:5 (May 1921), p. 1; Associated Grange Warehouse Co. to Union Cooperators, 25 April 1922, in Records of Local #1289, United Brotherhood of Carpenters and Joiners, Box 3, Folder 1, University of Washington Manuscripts Collection; M.W.C., "The Grange Co-operative Wholesale at Seattle, Washington," *Co-operation* XII:9 (September 1926), pp. 162–64; Harriet Crawford, *The Washington State Grange, 1880–1924* (Portland: Binfords & Mort, 1940), pp. 221–22, 224, 298.
75. Ed. Coenen to William Short, 15 July 1921, WSFL Records, Box 10, Folder 25; "Asst. to President Short" to Ed. Coenen, 27 July 1927, WSFL Records; R.M.B. to C.W. Brassington, n.d., WSFL Records, Box 35; Minutes, CLC, 8 February 1922; Neil Roy Knight, "History of Banking in Washington," Ph.D. Diss., University of Washington, 1935, p. 379. See also CLC for examples of the financial straits in which the locals found themselves, e.g., the plumbers and plasterers, 1 December 1921.
76. Litchman to Albert Belmont, 4 June 1921, in Mark Litchman Papers, Part I, Box 1, Folder 32, University of Washington Manuscripts Collection.

77. SUR, 13 September 1920.
78. Ibid., 9 December 1920.
79. *Save the Record*, 21 May 1921.
80. Earl Shimmons, "The Seattle Union Record," p. 46, manuscript in Ault Papers, Part I, Box 7, Folder 9.
81. SUR, 13 July 1920; Agent #106, 10 September 1919.
82. Agent #106, 10 September 1919.
83. Ibid.; see also ibid., 20 August, 1, 10 September 1920; Minutes, CLC, 14 July, 13, 20, 27 August, 3, 10 September 1920.
84. *Forge*, 26 June 1919; see also 10 May, 6 September 1919.
85. Litchman to Emmanuel Slater, 18 March 1921, Litchman Papers, Part I, Box 1, Folder 31.
86. Ibid.; Litchman to Joseph Gilbert, 8 July 1921, Litchman Papers, Part I, Box 1, Folder 32; A. W. Swenson to Ault, 5 February 1921, Ault Papers, Part I, Box 3, Folder 62; Minutes, CLC, 14, 21 July, 1 September, 13 October, 24 November 1920; 26 January, 2 February 1921, for the early history of the investigating committee. See Minutes, CLC, March 1921, on the committee's report, and the report itself, "In the Matter of the Seattle Union Record," in Ault Papers, Part I, Box 5, Folder 19; Mark Litchman to Slater, Brewett & Belmont, 25 April 1921, Litchman Papers, Part I, Box 1, Folder 31; *Save the Record*, 21 April 1921; Washington State Federation of Labor Executive Council to Affiliated Unions, 29 April 1921, Ault Papers, Part I, Box 1, Folder 62.
87. "In the Matter of the Seattle Union Record"; *Save the Record*, 21 April, 21 May 1921; *Tacoma Labor Advocate*, clipping, n.d. [1921], in Ault Papers, Part I, Box 1, Folder 1.
88. *Save the Record*, 21 April, 21 May 1921; Phil Pearl and Frank Clifford to Seattle Central Labor Council, 2 February 1921, King County Central Labor Council Records, Box 7; Investigating Committee to Delegates, Seattle Central Labor Council, n.d. [1921], in Ault Papers, Part I, Box 1, Folder 54; "A Plain Reply," leaflet by Philip Pearl, William Kennedy, and Frank Clifford, n.d. [1921], in Ault Papers, Part I, Box 5, Folder 35; Litchman to Slater, 22–23 March 1921, Litchman Papers, Part I, Box 1, Folder 31.
89. "In the Matter of the Seattle Union Record"; Pearl and Clifford to CLC, 2 February 1921; "Save the Labor Movement," pamphlet by the Committee of One Hundred, n.d. [1921] in Ault Papers, Part I, Box 4, Folder 13; Ault to Baldwin, 29 August 1922.
90. *Save the Record*, 21 May 1921.
91. Ibid., 21 April 1921.
92. Ibid. See also "In the Matter of the Seattle Union Record"; Shimmons, "The Seattle Union Record," p. 40.
93. SUR, 9, 10, 13, 18, 19 November 1920; *Save the Record*, 21 May 1921; Litchman to Emmanuel Slater, 22–23 March 1921.
94. *Save the Record*, 21 May 1921; SUR, 21 May 1921; "In the Matter of the Seattle Union Record"; Executive Board, United Mine Workers' District #10 to the Seattle Central Labor Council, 6 April 1921, in Ault Papers, Part I, Box 3, Folder 67; Shimmons, "The Seattle Union Record," p. 46; "To the Officers and Members of Seattle Central Labor Council," signed by 47 delegates, 30

March 1921, in King County Central Labor Council Records, Box 7; *Save the Record,* 21 April 1921.

95. O'Connell, "The Seattle Union Record," pp. 182, 189; Litchman to Slater, 22–23 March 921; Litchman to Albert Brilliant, n.d. [April 1921], in Litchman Papers, Part I, Box 1, Folder 32; for a full list of the names of those support- ing the critics, see the signers of "To the Officers . . ." and CLC votes, March and April 1921 in Minutes, CLC; Shimmons, "The Seattle Union Record," pp. 28–29. On the Communists, see Litchman's letters and the file in the King County Central Labor Council Records on the purges of Communist delegates from the council in 1925. For a different interpretation of the critics and their motives, see Jonathan Dembo, "A History of the Washington State Labor Movement, 1885–1935," Ph.D. Diss., University of Washington, 1978, p. 297.

96. Agent #106, 29 November 1919; SUR, 7 January 1921; Minutes, CLC, 14 July 1920; "In the Matter of the Seattle Union Record."

97. Resolution from Millmen #338 to Central Labor Council and Union Record Board of Directors, 11 July 1921, Ault Papers, Part I, Box 2, Folder 18.

98. Minutes, CLC, 24 March 1921; "In the Matter of the Seattle Union Record."

99. "Polymorphous" [Hays Jones] to Harvey O'Connor, 7 January 1922, Harvey O'Connor Papers, Part II, Box 1, Archives of Labor and Urban Affairs, Wayne State University. "In the Matter of the Seattle Union Record"; Minutes, CLC, 24 March 1921; Harvey O'Connor, *The Revolution in Seattle* (New York: Monthly Review Press, 1964), p. 208; Litchman to Slater, 18 March 1921; W. P. Dyer to Ault, 24 March 1921, Ault Papers, Part I, Box 4, Folder 3; Dembo, "History of the Washington State Labor Movement," Ch. 7.

100. Litchman to Eugene Belmont, 27 May 1921, Litchman Papers, Part I, Box 1, Folder 31; Litchman to Albert Brilliant, n.d. [1921]; Strong, *I Change Worlds,* pp. 87–88; *Save the Record,* 21 May 1921; Telegram, Seattle *Union Record* to *Labor Age,* 21 June 1922, Ault Papers, Part I, Box 4, Folder 17.

101. Harry Ault to Officers and Delegates of the Central Labor Council, 30 March 1921, King County Central Labor Council Records, Box 7; "The Seattle Union Record – What It is – What It is Not," draft pamphlet, n.d. [1921], Ault Papers, Part II, Box 3, Folder 26; O'Connor, *Revolution in Seattle,* p. 208; Board of Directors Union Record to the Members, 19 December 1921, Ault Papers, Part I, Box 1, Folder 54; Ault to J. A. Kiderlen, 22 February 1922, Ault Papers, Part I, Box 4, Folder 16; Ault to Baldwin, 29 August 1922; F. A. Rust to Delegates and Officers of Central Labor Council of Seattle and Vicinity, 30 March 1921, King County Central Labor Council Records, Box 7, reprinted in Minutes, CLC, 30 March 1921.

102. Litchman to Belmont, 27 May 1921, Litchman Papers, Part I, Box 1, Folder 31; Litchman to Slater, 22–23 March 1921; Litchman to Slater, Browett and Belmont, 25 April 1921; O'Connor, *Revolution in Seattle,* p. 208; Shimmons, "The Seattle Union Record," pp. 49, 50; DeShazo, "Radical Tendencies," p. 89; *Save the Record,* 21 April 1921; Maud Weismantel to James L. Barrie, 30 March 1921, in Ault Papers, Part I, Box 3, Folder 38.

103. Litchman to Slater, 22–23 March, 25 June 1921; Litchman to Belmont, 27 May 1921; Minutes, CLC, 21 May, 12 October 1921, and April–May in general; *Tacoma Labor Advocate,* 21 October 1921.

104. DeShazo, "Radical Tendencies," p. 90.

105. *Tacoma Labor Advocate*, 21 October 1921; Litchman to Slater, 18 March 1921.

106. Minutes, CLC, 29 June 1921.

107. J. W. Von Carnop to W. P. Dyer, 14 July 1921, in Ault Papers, Part I, Box 2, Folder 55. For the locals and their responses, see Minutes, CLC, 16, 30 March, 6 April, 8, 15 May, 29 June, 13, 20 July, 19 October 1921; *Save the Record*, 21 April, 21 May 1921; United Association of Plumbers and Steamfitters Local #473 to Hans Evers, 31 August 1921, Ault Papers, Part I, Box 3, Folder 41; Resolution from Millmen Local #338 (United Brotherhood of Carpenters and Joiners) to Central Labor Council and Union Record Board of Directors, 11 July 1921, in Ault Papers, Part I, Box 2, Folder 18; United Mine Workers District #10 to Seattle Central Labor Council, 6 April 1921, in Ault Papers, Part I, Box 3, Folder 67; "To the Officers & Members of the Typographical Union #202," n.d. [1921], in Ault Papers, Part I, Box 6, Folder 6; Minutes, Local #202, International Typographers' Union, 27 March, 24 April 1921, in Records of Local #99, International Typographers' Union, Box 16, University of Washington Manuscripts Collection; telegram, Bruce Rodgers to J. T. Sullivan, 5 June 1921, in Ault Papers, Part I, Box 3, Folder 49.

108. Walter Price to Harry Ault, 21 February 1928, in Ault Papers, Part II, Box 3, Folder 47.

109. Shimmons, "The Seattle Union Record," p. 56.

110. William Benson to Harry Ault, 19 June 1922, in Ault Papers, Part I, Box 2, Folder 18.

111. A. W. Blumenroth to Ault, 6 October 1922, 19 March 192[?], Ault Papers, Part I, Box 2, Folder 7; Ault to Blumenroth, 21 March 1923, Ault Papers, Part I, Box 4, Folder 19.

112. Laundry Workers International Union Local #24 to Harry Ault, 2 May 1922, Ault Papers, Part I, Box 3.

113. S. J. Stamp to Ault, 14 June 1921, Ault Papers, Part I, Box 3, Folder 49. See also Minutes, CLC, 8, 29 June, 13, 20 July, 19 October, 30 November 1921; Shimmons, "The Seattle Union Record," p. 59; Minutes, Carpenters' #131, 12 April 1921; Litchman to Slater, 25 June, 21 December 1921.

114. O'Connor, *Revolution in Seattle*, p. 212.

115. Ault to Blumenroth, 17 October 1922; William Z. Foster, *Misleaders of Labor* (New York: Trade Union Educational League, 1927), pp. 86–87; Ault to M. C. Barry, 6 May 1922, Ault Papers, Part I, Box 4, Folder 17; *Vanguard*, April–May 1931; *Washington State Labor News*, 9 October 1925, 3 September 1926, 4 November 1927, 27 January 1928; Doug Honig, *Experiments in Democracy: Cooperatives in the Seattle Area* (Seattle: Puget Consumers' Cooperative, 1981); Memorandum of Agreement, Trades Union Savings and Loan Association, n.d. [1922], Ault Papers, Part I, Box 6, Folder 39; Washington State Department of Taxation and Examination, Division of Banking to the Officers and Directors of the Trades Union Savings and Loan Association, 21 June 1921, Ault Papers, Part I, Box 3, Folder 76; Ault to William F. Gibbons, 5 July 1923, Ault Papers, Part I, Box 4, Folder 20; Minutes, CLC, 19 July, 20 September, 10 October 1922, 15 April 1925; Litchman to Slater, 21 December 1921; Litchman to Adele Bennett, 7 March 1924, Litchman Papers, Part I, Box 1, Folder 35; William Short to J. D. Minaglia, 22 September 1923,

WSFL Records, Box 36; M. W. Sills to Typographers #202, 24 February 1923, Records of Typographers #99; Minutes, Typographers #202, 27 May 1923.

116. Shimmons, "The Seattle Union Record," p. 75.

117. Litchman to Slater, 26 December 1921, Litchman Papers, Part I, Box 1, Folder 34; punctuation as in original.

118. DeShazo, "Radical Tendencies," p. 64.

119. Shimmons, "The Seattle Union Record," p. 56.

120. Ibid., p. 217. See also Litchman to Brilliant, n.d. [1921], Litchman Papers, Part I, Box 1, Folder 32.

121. Strong, *I Change Worlds*, p. 87.

122. Minutes, CLC, 8 August, 14, 21, 28 September, 5, 19 October, 2, 16 November, 28 December 1921; 8 November 1922; Roll Books, CLC. Total membership of unions affiliated with the Central Labor Council declined from 65,000 in 1919 to 25,707 in 1920 to 11,948 in 1921. Thompson, "Development and Comparison," p. 102.

123. Minutes, CLC, 27–28 April, 10 May, 16 September, 25 October, 16 November 1921; 25 January, 1 February 1922; Litchman to Slater, 21 December 1921; SUR, 10 May, 16, 18, 23 June 1921; Minutes, Local #76, American Federation of Musicians, 8 April 1921, in possession of Local #76, Seattle.

124. Shimmons, "The Seattle Union Record," p. 57; Thompson, p. 74; Minutes, CLC, 1921–22.

125. J.B.S. Hardman, *American Labor Dynamics in the Light of Post-War Developments* (New York: Harcourt, Brace, 1928), p. 10. David Montgomery, writing on the United Mine Workers in this period, observes similarly: "The steam of working-class hopes and daring had gone out of its engines" (Montgomery, *The Fall of the House of Labor*, p. 409).

7. Accommodations

1. "Statement of the Seattle Central Labor Council Relative to its Controversy with the Executive Council of the American Federation of Labor," n.d. [June 1923], in Harvey O'Connor Papers, Part II, Archives of Labor and Urban Affairs, Walter Reuther Library, Wayne State University; Jonathan Dembo, "A History of the Washington State Labor Movement, 1885–1935," Ph.D. Diss., University of Washington, 1978, pp. 370–78; Harvey O'Connor, *The Revolution in Seattle* (New York: Monthly Review Press, 1964), pp. 213–14; Hamilton Cravens, "A History of the Washington Farmer–Labor Party, 1918–1924," M.A. Thesis, University of Washington, 1962, p. 194.

2. Seattle *Union Record*, daily edition (hereafter SUR), 11 June 1921.

3. Washington State *Labor News* (hereafter WSLN), 3 September 1926; see also SUR, 12 January 1921; WSLN, 31 August 1928.

4. George Michael Jones, "Longshore Unionism on Puget Sound: A Seattle–Tacoma Comparison," M.A. Thesis, University of Washington, 1957, pp. 61–63; Melvin G. DeShazo, "Radical Tendencies in the Seattle Labor Movement as Reflected in the Proceedings of its Central Body," M.A. Thesis, University of Washington, 1925, p. 68; Washington Bureau of Labor and Industry (hereafter WBLS), *Tenth Biennial Report* (Olympia: Bureau of Labor and Industry, 1916), pp. 209–23; A. L. Kempster and successors, weekly reports

to Stone and Webster Company (hereafter SW), in Box 122, Records of the Puget Sound Traction, Light and Power Company, University of Washington Manuscripts Collection, 12, 19, 26 April, 10 May, 30 August, 10 September 1919; SUR, 8, 14, 17, 18, 19 April, 16 May, 5, 25, 30 June 1919; Charles P. Larrowe, *Shape-up and Hiring Hall: A Comparison of Hiring Methods and Labor Relations on the New York and Seattle Waterfronts* (Berkeley: University of California Press, 1955), pp. 89–90; Margaret Jane Thompson, "Development and Comparison of Industrial Relations in Seattle," M.B.A. Thesis, University of Washington, 1929, p. 64.

5. M. E. Wright to T. V. O'Connor, 14 January 1920, Records of the Washington State Federation of Labor (hereafter WSFL), Box 3, Folder 12, University of Washington Manuscripts Collection; Jones, "Longshore Unionism," pp. 63–68; Report of Agent #106 (hereafter Agent #106), 29 October 1919, 27 January 1920.

6. SW, 8, 15 May, 11 June, 3 July 1920; Jones, "Longshore Unionism," pp. 64–67; President, #38–12 ILA to T. V. O'Connor and Executive Council International Longshoremen's Association, 2 July 1920, WSFL Records, Box 15, Folder 63; Associated Industries Bulletin No. 2 [1920]; No. 4 [1920] in Seattle Public Library; Mary Joan O'Connell, "The Seattle Union Record, 1918–1928: A Pioneer Labor Daily," M.A. Thesis, University of Washington, 1964, p. 140; SUR, 6 May 1920; "How Seattle Fights Unfair Labor Unions," *Iron Age* Vol. 106 (October 1920), p. 1056; *Square Deal*, 23 October 1920; Report of Agent #17 (hereafter Agent #17), 7 May 1920, Broussais C. Beck Papers, Boxes 1–2, University of Washington Manuscripts Collection; Agent #106, 8, 9 April 1920, Broussais C. Beck Papers, Boxes 1–2.

7. Quoted in Thompson, "Development and Comparison," p. 155.

8. Jones, "Longshore Unionism," pp. 67–68.

9. Thompson, "Development and Comparison," pp. 151–68; *Seattle Times*, 2 July 1926, 13 May 1927; Jones, pp. 69–70; Larrowe, pp. 91–93; "Stabilizing Longshore Work," *Monthly Labor Review* Vol. XV, No. 6 (December 1922), p. 40; "Decasualizing the Beach in Seattle," *Survey*, Vol. 49 (15 October 1922), pp. 96–97; Francis P. Foisie, *Decasualizing Longshore Labor and the Seattle Experience* (Seattle: Seattle Waterfront Employers Union, 1934), pp. 70–72. For ILA activism after the imposition of the Foisie Plan, see Larrowe, "Shape-up and Hiring Hall," p. 94; Jones, "Longshore Unionism," pp. 72–73; WSLN, 10 April 1925, 18 March 1927; Minutes, Central Labor Council of Seattle and Vicinity (hereafter CLC), 17 May, 26 July, 6 September, 22 November 1922; 23 July 1924; 8 April 1925, Records of the King County Central Labor Council, Box 8, University of Washington Manuscripts Collection. For conditions, see Thompson, "Development and Comparison," pp. 157, 167; SW, 5 January 1924; Jones, "Longshore Unionism," pp. 72–74; Minutes, CLC, 24 January 1922; Larrowe, *Shape-up and Hiring Hall*, p. 94; William Short to Joseph Sheedy, 30 July 1924, WSFL Records, Box 36, Folder 17.

10. Horace R. Cayton, *Long Old Road: An Autobiography* (Seattle: University of Washington Press, 1963), p. 118.

11. Cayton, *Long Old Road*, pp. 110–18; Robert Bedford Pitts, "Organized Labor and the Negro in Seattle," M.A. Thesis, University of Washington, 1941, p. 42; *Forge*, 14 Oct. 1919; *Cayton's Weekly*, 19 April 1919, 15 May 1920.

12. Pitts, "Organized Labor and the Negro," pp. 46–51, 102.

13. Roll Books, CLC, Records of the King County Central Labor Council; Thompson, "Development and Comparison," p. 108; O'Connor, *Revolution in Seattle*, p. 109; Robert Friedheim, *The Seattle General Strike* (Seattle: University of Washington Press, 1964), p. 59; *Cayton's Weekly*, 19 April 1919; WBLS, *Twelfth Biennial Report*, pp. 17–18. For the fate of Seattle's seamen's unions in the West Coast maritime strike of 1921, see Giles T. Brown, "The West Coast Phase of the Maritime Strike of 1921," *Pacific Historical Review* Vol. 19 (November 1950), pp. 385–86, 392–95; SW, 7, 10 May, 9, 25 June 1921; Minutes, CLC, 8, 15 June, 7 July 1921; SUR, 5, 25 May, 23 June, 14 July 1921; Bruce Nelson, *Workers on the Waterfront: Seamen, Longshoremen and Unionism in the 1930s* (Urbana: University of Illinois Press, 1988), p. 56.

14. By mid-decade, 85 percent of building trades work in the city was under the closed shop, and carpenters' wages were up to 1919 levels by 1923. WSFL, *Proceedings of the 19th Convention* (Seattle: WSFL, 1920), p. 9; *Associated Industries Bulletin*, 11 October 1922; Thompson, "Development and Comparison," p. 141; William Short to A. S. Goss, 5 April 1926, Box 37, Folder 5, WSFL Records; Minutes, CLC, throughout the decade, esp. March 1922, April 1923; WSFL, *Proceedings of the 23rd Convention* (Olympia: WSFL, 1924), p. 11. The total value of building permits issued in the first six months of 1924 was up 74 percent from the preceding period in 1923; see WSLN, 13 June 1924. By 1926, permit levels were between two and three times 1920 levels. WSLN, 2 September 1927. On the carpenters: Minutes, CLC, 4 April 1923; 16 January, 2 April 1924; 18 February, 6 May 1925; WSLN, 13 June 1924; 24 April, 4 September 1925. On plumbers: William Short to D. Campbell, 26 November 1924, Box 26, Folder 27, WSFL Records. On painters: WSFL, *Official Yearbook of Organized Labor, State of Washington* (Seattle: WSFL, 1925); WSLN, 13, 27 February 1925; Minutes, CLC, 2, 25 April 1923; 12 March, 27 August 1924; 18 February 1925. On plasterers: WSFL, *Yearbook*, 1925, p. 31; WSLN, 1 May, 4 September 1925; 3 September 1926. On building laborers: WSLN, 4 September 1925, 3 September 1926; Minutes, CLC, 28 September 1921. On electricians: WSLN, 4 September 1925, 4 September 1926; Minutes, CLC, 25 December 1922, 2 January 1924. On millmen: WSLN, 3 September 1926; Minutes, CLC, 21 March, 25 April 1923. On pile drivers: WSLN, 4 September 1925. For seasonal unemployment, see, e.g., WSLN, 13 February 1925; Minutes, CLC, 21 January 1925.

On the typographers: Minutes, Local #202, International Typographers' Union, in Records of Local #99, International Typographers' Union, Box 16, University of Washington Manuscripts Collection. On the musicians: *Musicland* and Minutes, Local #76, American Federation of Musicians, and Minutes, Board of Directors, Local #76, in possession of Local #76, Seattle. On the teamsters: Carl Gustaf Westine, "The Seattle Teamsters," M.A. Thesis, University of Washington, 1937, pp. 24, 28, 55; WSLN, 13 June 1924; 23 January, 27 March, 1, 15 May, 14 August, 4 September 1925; 3 September 1926; 2 September 1927; Minutes, CLC, 21 January 1925; Thompson, "Development and Comparison," p. 112. For general statistics and reports of AFL locals in the decade, see Minutes and Roll Books, CLC, Records of the

King County Central Labor Council; Thompson, "Development and Comparison," esp. pp. 113–15.

15. Minutes, CLC; see Chapter 4.

16. For the longshoremen's politics: *Forge*, 5 July 1919; SW, 12 April 1919; Jones, "Longshore Unionism," p. 63; Agent #17, 28 August 1919; Thompson, "Development and Comparison," p. 79.

17. Paul Mohr, for example, hailed from the bakers; Phil Pearl from the barbers; the painters and millmen sent Communist delegates to the Central Labor Council.

18. Short to R. Lee Guard, 29 July 1919, WSFL Records, Box 35.

19. Agent #106, 26 November 1919; see also Report of Agent #172, 12 March 1920, Roy Kinnear Papers, Box 1, Folder 6, University of Washington Manuscripts Collection; Thompson, "Development and Comparison," pp. 48, 66, and Minutes, CLC, voting patterns for officers.

20. SUR, 20 May 1919.

21. Ibid., 4, 7 July 1919.

22. Agent #106, 2 July 1919.

23. Ibid., 20 June 1919. In general, see Minutes, CLC, for delegates' voting patterns over the course of the decade, and SUR, Thursday reports of CLC meetings.

24. O'Connor, *Revolution in Seattle*, p. 207. Melvin DeShazo, in a 1920s thesis on the Central Labor Council, noted the radicals' loss of power and similarly attributed it to the depression. See "Radical Tendencies in the Seattle Labor Movement as Reflected in the Proceedings of Its Central Body," M.A. Thesis, University of Washington, 1925.

25. Agent #106, 24 April 1920.

26. See also DeShazo, "Radical Tendencies," p. 62; O'Connor, *Revolution in Seattle*, pp. 129–30; O'Connell, "The Seattle Union Record," p. 89.

27. Michael Kazin points out the centrality of local-market industries to pre–World War I California and in general to the region west of the Rockies, and the resultant vulnerability of employers to strikes and boycotts. See "The Great Exception Revisited: Organized Labor and Politics in San Francisco and Los Angeles, 1870–1940," *Pacific Historical Review* Vol. LV, No. 3 (August 1986), p. 374.

28. Report of Agent #181, 2 April 1920, Kinnear Papers, Box 1, Folder 6.

29. Minutes, CLC, 30 June, 7, 14, 21 July 1920.

30. Irving Bernstein, *The Lean Years: A History of the American Worker, 1920–1933* (Boston: Houghton Mifflin, 1960), pp. 86–87.

31. C. L. Christenson, *Collective Bargaining in Chicago, 1929–30* (Chicago: University of Chicago Press, 1933).

32. Michael Kazin, *Barons of Labor: The San Francisco Building Trades and Union Power in the Progressive Era* (Urbana: University of Illinois Press, 1987), p. 273.

33. Louis B. Perry and Richard S. Perry, *A History of the Los Angeles Labor Movement, 1911–1941* (Berkeley: University of California Press, 1963), pp. 193–225.

34. SUR, 11 April 1919; 7 January 1920; 26 February, 9 March 1921; 22 August 1922; Katherine Jane Lentz, "Japanese-American Relations in Seattle," M.A. Thesis, University of Washington, 1924, p. 90; Kazuo Ito, *Issei: A History of*

Japanese Immigration in North America (Seattle: Japanese Community Service, 1973), pp. 124–25, 148, 155, 158, 245–25; Yuzo Murayama, "The Economic History of Japanese Immigration to the Pacific Northwest," Ph.D. Diss., University of Washington, 1982, pp. 291–92; Interview with Shigeru Osawa, by Richard Berner and Sally Kazama, May 1968, in University of Washington Manuscripts Collection.

35. Ito, *Issei*, p. 148.
36. Ibid., pp. 147–48.
37. Ibid., p. 148. Murayama, "Economic History," pp. 291–92; Ito, *Issei*, pp. 147–48, 150, 158; Yuji Ichioka, *The Issei: The World of First Generation Japanese Immigrants, 1884–1925* (New York: Free Press, 1988), p. 2.
38. Lentz, "Japanese-American Relations in Seattle," p. 90.
39. SUR, 26 January 1921.
40. Minutes, CLC, 26 May 1920.
41. *Musicland*, 1 September 1923.
42. Minutes, Executive Board, CLC, 22 January 1919, in Records of the King County Central Labor Council. For anti-Japanese sentiments, see also Agent #106, 14 April 1920; Minutes, CLC, 7, 14 April 1920.
43. Minutes, CLC, 5 December 1923.
44. SUR, 11 April 1919.
45. Ibid., 30 July 1919.
46. Ibid., 18 February 1919; see also 7 July, 26 August 1919.
47. Ibid., 22 January 1921.
48. Ibid., 25 February 1921.
49. Ibid., 29 January 1921.
50. Japanese Labor Association to Harry Ault, 30 July 1921, Harry Ault Papers, Part I, Box 2, Folder 61, University of Washington Manuscripts Collection.
51. Harry Ault to the Secretary, Japanese Hotel Keepers' Association, 23 May 1922, Ault Papers, Part I, Box 4, Folder 17. On the relationship between the Japanese-American community and the *Record*, see also Katsutoshi Kurokawa, "The Seattle General Strike and Japanese Americans," Parts I–III, *Okayama Economic Review* Vol. 21, No. 4 (February 1990), pp. 31–50; Vol. 22, No. 1 (May 1990), pp. 73–89; Vol. 22, No. 2 (September 1990), pp. 149–66.
52. On Ault, see Friedheim, *Seattle General Strike*, p. 52; Charles Pierce LeWarne, *Utopias on Puget Sound, 1885–1915* (Seattle: University of Washington Press, 1975), pp. 88–89.
53. *Industrial Worker*, 11 October 1919.
54. *Forge*, 1 May 1919.
55. SUR, 11 August 1919.
56. Quoted in Lentz, "Japanese-American Relations in Seattle," p. 75. For advocates of the admission of Japanese, see also Agent #106, 2 April 1920.
57. SUR, 14 February 1919.
58. Lentz, "Japanese-American Relations in Seattle," pp. 73–74.
59. Minutes, CLC, 12 September 1923, 26 May 1926; see also 5 September 1923.
60. Ito, *Issei*, pp. 98, 525, 868; S. Frank Miyamoto, *Social Solidarity Among the Japanese in Seattle* (Seattle: University of Washington Press, 1984), esp. p. 19; Sylvia Junko Yanagisako, *Transforming the Past: Tradition and Kinship Among Japanese Americans* (Stanford: Stanford University Press, 1985), pp. 41–46 and

passim; William S. Hall, *The Journeyman Barbers' International Union of America* (Baltimore: Johns Hopkins University Press, 1936), p. 10; Quintard Taylor, "Blacks and Asians in a White City: Japanese Americans and African Americans in Seattle, 1890–1940," *Western Historical Quarterly* Vol. XXII, No. 4 (November 1991), p. 412, and in general; Japanese Association of North America to Phillip Tindall, 22 July 1920, in Records of the Japanese Association of North America, Box 5, Folder 20, University of Washington Manuscripts Collection; *Polk's Seattle City Directory*, 1920–1929 (Seattle: R. L. Polk, 1920–29). For a comparative analysis with Japanese business growth in Los Angeles, see John Modell, *The Economics and Politics of Racial Accommodation: The Japanese of Los Angeles, 1900–1942* (Urbana: University of Illinois Press, 1977).

61. Minutes, CLC, 26 January 1921.
62. Ibid., 22 March 1922.
63. Ito, *Issei*, p. 152.
64. Ibid.
65. Ibid., pp. 152, 910; see also Tokichi Tanaka, "The Japanese in Seattle," *Coast* Vol. XII, No. 5 (November 1909), p. 256; Ito, *Issei*, p. 98.
66. Minutes, CLC, 18 June 1919.
67. SUR, 26 May 1921; Minutes, CLC, 26 January 1921, 4 March, 1 April 1925.
68. WSLN, 30 January 1925; SUR, 26 January 1920, 24 January 1921, 26 January 1925.
69. SUR, 24 January 1921; Lentz, "Japanese-American Relations in Seattle," pp. 73–74; Minutes, CLC, 5 September 1923; *Seattle Star*, 2 February 1919.
70. SUR, 25 April 1919.
71. Ibid., 27 January 1921.
72. Minutes, CLC, 22 March 1922; Lentz, "Japanese-American Relations in Seattle," pp. 8–10; see also Minutes, CLC, 1 May 1919, 26 January 1921; Ichioka, *Issei*, p. 94; "Japanese Shoemakers Association Rules" [1921], in Japanese Association of North America (hereafter JANA) Records, Box 8, Folder 36, translated for the author by Reiko Terai.
73. Minutes, CLC, 17 January 1923.
74. Agent #106, 24 February 1920.
75. SUR, 1 April 1921.
76. Quote: SUR, 5 May 1921. Minutes, CLC, 1 April 1920; 4 April, 4 May 1921; 22 March 1922; SUR, 30 April 1921; WSLN, 24 April 1925; Lentz, "Japanese-American Relations in Seattle," pp. 8–10; Joseph Hoffman to JANA, 15 April 1921, JANA Records, Box 1, Folder 2; Secretary, JANA to J. S. Hoffman, 25 April 1921, JANA Records, Box 2, Folder 2; Joseph Hoffman to G. S. Horiuchi, 26 April 1921, JANA Records, Box 1, Folder 2. On the admission of Chinese: SUR, 14 July 1921; Minutes, CLC, 13 July 1921; see also SUR, 12 January 1925 for the white butchers and Japanese-owned fish markets.
77. Roll Books, CLC, 1919–1929, in Records of King County Central Labor Council.
78. Herman D. Bloch, "Craft Unions and the Negro in Historical Perspective," argues that "partial" entry was more effective than "full restriction," since it allowed greater control by the unions over African-American workers. See *Journal of Negro History* Vol. 43 (1958), p. 11.

79. "Statement of the Seattle Central Labor Council . . ."
80. Minutes, CLC, 27–28 April, 10 May, 16 September, 25 October, 16 November 1921; 25 January, 1 February 1922; Mark Litchman to Emmanuel Slater, 21 December 1921, Mark Litchman Papers, Part I, Box 1, University of Washington Manuscripts Collection; SUR, 10 May, 16, 18, 23 June 1921; Minutes, Musicians #76, 8 April 1921; Roll Books, CLC.
81. Roll Books, CLC; WSFL, *Proceedings of the 19th Convention* (1920), pp. 33–34.
82. SUR, 29 April, 25 July 1919; Blanche Johnson, "What Organization Means to the Woman Barber," *Life and Labor* Vol. VIII, No. 2 (February 1919), pp. 27–28.
83. Johnson, "What Organization Means," p. 28.
84. John Herbert Geoghegan, "The Migratory Worker in Seattle: A Study in Social Disorganization and Exploitation," M.A. Thesis, University of Washington, 1923, p. 39.
85. Johnson, "What Organization Means," p. 27.
86. SUR, 29 April 1919. For insinuations about the morals of the lady barbers, and their defense, see SUR, 22, 23 June 1921; Minutes, CLC, 22 June 1921.
87. Minutes, CLC, 20 April, 18 May 1921; SUR, 19 May 1921.
88. SUR, 29 April 1919; United States Department of Commerce, Bureau of the Census, *Fourteenth Census of the United States*, Vol. IV (Washington: Government Printing Office, 1920), p. 1235.
89. No evidence indicates beauticians or hairdressers serving women customers were admitted to the lady barbers' union. All discussion of the lady barbers' work, including those regarding sexual "temptations" or harassment, spoke of male customers only. In 1927, though, Seattle's joint male–female local of white barbers launched an organizing drive among white female employees of "beauty shops." See WSLN, 11 February, 1, 29 April, 6 May 1927.
90. Bureau of the Census, *Fourteenth Census*, Vol. IV, p. 1235.
91. Ito, *Issei*, p. 866.
92. Bureau of the Census, *Fourteenth Census*, Vol. IV, pp. 1234–35; Ito, *Issei*, pp. 98, 152; Tanaka, "The Japanese in Seattle," p. 256; SUR, 26 January 1925; WSLN, 30 January 1925.
93. Ito, *Issei*, p. 866.
94. SUR, 10 April 1900; Bureau of the Census, *Fourteenth Census*, Vol. IV, pp. 1234–35; *Cayton's Weekly*, 29 December 1917; 20 May, 27 November, 18 December 1920; "Lincoln Industrial Fair Association Edition," n.d. [1920s], refers to ten African-American–owned barber shops employing twenty-five barbers; in Fred Woodson Papers, University of Washington Manuscripts Collection, no box or folder number. Lacunae in the situation still remain: whether Japanese-American barbers refused to serve African-American customers; whether African-American barbers cut white men's hair, and if yes, whether they constituted a threat to white barbers as a result. For additional evidence, see Quintard Taylor, "Blacks and Asians in a White City," *Western Historical Quarterly* Vol. XXII, No. 4 (November 1991), p. 412.
95. SUR, 29 April 1919.
96. For a cryptic comparative reference, see *Journeyman Barber* XIX:10 (November 1923), p. 403.

97. On pre-1923 efforts to gain admission of the lady barbers: "Statement of the Seattle Central Labor Council ..."; *Journeyman Barber* XIV (1918), debates all year; Vol. XV, No. 5 (June 1919), p. 186; XV:6 (July 1919), p. 249; Vol. XVII, No. 8 (September 1921), p. 333; Minutes, CLC, 13, 20 August, 26 November 1919, 21 January, 4 February 1920; SUR, 21 August 1920; *American Union*, 29 November 1919; Johnson, "What Organization Means," p. 28. On the 1923 fight: "Statement of the Seattle Central Labor Council ..."; Minutes, CLC, 23 May, 13, 27 June, 1, 8 August 1923; *Journeyman Barber* Vol. XIX, No. 10 (November 1923), p. 402; O'Connor, *Revolution in Seattle*, pp. 213–14; *Musicland*, 15 August 1923; Minutes, Musicians #76 Board of Directors, 14 August 1923; Seattle Central Labor Council to All Local Unions of Seattle and Vicinity, 1 August 1923, in Records of Local #1289, United Brotherhood of Carpenters and Joiners, Box 2, Folder 18, University of Washington Manuscripts Collection.
98. Emphases added. Quote: WSLN, 3 September 1926. Minutes, CLC, 21 May, 6, 13, 30 August, 10, 24 September, 15, 26 October, 26 November 1924; 14 January, 18 February 1925; WSLN, 26 September 1924; 16 January, 20 February 1925, 30 July, 3 September 1926; 14 January, 11 February, 1, 29 April, 6 May 1927.
99. On the lady barbers, see also Minutes, CLC, 16 May 1919; 7, 14 January, 4 February, 5 May, 29 September 1920; 18 May, 17 August 1921, 28 March, 18 April, 16 May 1923; SUR, 18 February, 20 March, 29 April, 18, 25, 26 June, 1 July, 10 October 1919; 19 May 1921; *Forge*, 11 October 1919.
100. "Statement of the Seattle Central Labor Council. ..."
101. Hamilton Cravens, "A History of the Washington Farmer–Labor Party," M.A. Thesis, University of Washington, 1962, pp. 114–15.
102. Cravens, "Washington Farmer–Labor Party," pp. 82–138; O'Connor, *Revolution in Seattle*, p. 206; SUR, 5 July 1919; Dembo, "History of the Washington State Labor Movement," pp. 271–94; Mark Litchman to Joseph Gilbert, 21 September 1920, Litchman Papers, Part I, Box 1, Folder 29; Litchman to Emmanuel Slater, 2 October 1920, Part I, Box 1, Folder 30.
103. Barbara Winslow, "The Decline of Socialism in Washington, 1910–1925," M.A. Thesis, University of Washington, 1969, p. 116; Dembo, "History of the Washington State Labor Movement," pp. 379–408; Cravens, "Washington Farmer–Labor Party," pp. 141–42, 144, 153–54, 159, 163–64, 185, 203; Minutes, CLC, 27 April, 25 May 1921, 17 May 1922; WSLN, 30 July, 6 August 1926; Ault to Baldwin, 29 August 1922, Box 18, Records of the American Fund for Public Service, New York Public Library Manuscripts Collection; James Duncan, "To All Labor Organizations ...," 23 May 1923, Records of Carpenters #1289, Box 2, Folder 22; John C. Kennedy, "The Outlook for a Labor Party," reprinted from *The American Labor Monthly*, in Harvey O'Connor Papers, Part II, Box 4; John C. Kennedy, *Winning Washington for the Producers* (Farmer-Labor Party of Washington, Seattle, n.d.), in O'Connor Papers, Part II, Box 4; Carlos Schwantes, "Farmer–Labor Insurgency in Washington State: William Bouck, the Grange, and the Western Progressive Farmers," *Pacific Northwest Quarterly* Vol. 26, No. 1 (January 1985), pp. 2–11.

104. David Montgomery, *The Fall of the House of Labor: The Workplace, the State, and American Labor Activism, 1865–1925* (Cambridge: Cambridge University Press, 1987), pp. 434–35.

105. Weinstein, *Decline of Socialism*, pp. 272–323; Montgomery, *Fall of the House of Labor*, pp. 406–07, 434–37; Cravens, "Washington Farmer–Labor Party," pp. 199–200, 212; Minutes, CLC, 15 February 1922.

106. Cravens, "Washington Farmer–Labor Party," pp. 157–86; Dembo, "History of the Washington State Labor Movement," pp. 379–408.

107. Cravens, "Washington Farmer–Labor Party," p. 142.

108. Ibid., p. 162. On the power shift and the Farmer-Labor Party, see also Dembo, "History of the Washington State Labor Movement," pp. vi–vii.

109. William J. Dickson, "Labor in Municipal Politics: A Study of Labor's Political Policies and Activities in Seattle," M.A. Thesis, University of Washington, 1928, pp. 37–38.

110. "Statement of the Seattle Central Labor Council. . . ."

111. Ault to Baldwin, 29 August 1922, Ault Papers, Part I, Box 4, Folder 17.

112. O'Connell, "The Seattle Union Record," pp. 196, 213–18; James Duncan to Roger Baldwin, 23 September 1922, Records of the American Fund for Public Service, Box 18, New York Public Library Manuscripts Collection. For post-labor-capitalism defections, see Chapter 6. On the SUR and Farmer–Labor Party, see also Cravens, p. 132; Ault to Baldwin, 29 August 1922, Box 18, Records of the American Fund for Public Service.

113. O'Connell, "The Seattle Union Record," p. 210.

114. Ibid., pp. 203–4, 210–38; Roger Baldwin to Harry Ault, 7 March 1925, Ault Papers, Part I, Box 2, Folder 2.

115. O'Connell, "The Seattle Union Record," p. 245.

116. "Statement of the Seattle Central Labor Council. . . ."

117. Ibid.

118. Minutes, CLC, 1 August 1923 (quote); Cravens, "Washington Farmer–Labor Party," p. 196; SW, 30 March 1925.

119. Mark Litchman to Emmanuel Slater, 11 May 1922, Litchman Papers, Part I, Box 1, Folder 23; Litchman to Frank H. Hall, 19 March 1920, Folder 27; Litchman to Slater, 2 November 1920, Folder 30; Litchman to Slater, n.d. [late October–early November 1920], Folder 30; Litchman to Slater, 21 January 1921, Folder 30; Litchman to Slater, 3 March 1922, Folder 33; Litchman to Slater, 11 May 1922, Folder 23; Litchman to Slater, 25 May 1922, Folder 23; Litchman to Slater, 26 December 1922, Folder 34; Litchman to Slater, 20 February 1923, Folder 34; O'Connor, *Revolution in Seattle*, p. 206; WSLN, 30 January, 13 February 1925; SUR, 27 April 1922; David M. Schneider, *The Workers' (Communist) Party and American Trade Unions* (Baltimore: Johns Hopkins University Press, 1928), pp. 14, 18; Kennedy, "The Outlook for a Labor Party," p. 1; Jonathan D. Bloom, "Brookwood Labor College and the Progressive Labor Network of the Interwar United States, 1921–1937," Ph.D. Diss., New York University, 1992, pp. 232–33. On the demise of the Socialist Party, see Winslow, "Decline of Socialism," pp. 95, 112, 117; Litchman to Eugene Belmont, 2 September 1920, Part I, Box 1, Folder 29; Cravens, "Washington Farmer–Labor Party," p. 201.

120. WSLN, 27 March 1925; Minutes, CLC, 24 February, 18, 25 March 1925. For events leadings to the purge, see Minutes, CLC, 28 January, 4, 11 February

1925; WSLN, 30 January, 6, 13, 20, 27 February 1925. For the vote itself, see "Result of Vote to Adopt Committee's Report on Unseating of Communists as Delegates to the Central Labor Council," in Box 6, Folder "Communist Trials and Data, 1925," in Records of the King County Central Labor Council; O'Connor, *Revolution in Seattle*, p. 216; Minutes, CLC, 25 March 1925, and all meetings February–March 1925. On the purges, see also Seattle Building Trades Council to the Seattle Central Labor Council, 3 February 1925, Box 6, Records of the King County County Central Labor Council; *Daily Worker*, 7, 14 February 1925. For transcripts of the purge trials, see Box 6, Folder "Communist Trials and Data, 1925," Records of the King County Central Labor Council. For delegates' reelection and return despite their purges, see Minutes, CLC, 25 February, 8, 15 April 1925; WSLN, 17 April, 15 May, 10 July 1925; 19 August 1927; Resolution, Painters' Local #300 to Seattle Central Labor Council, 16 January 1929, Box 6, King County Central Labor Council Records; C. W. Doyle to Frank Morrison, 23 January 1926, Box 6, King County Central Labor Council Records.

121. E.g., WSLN, 27 May 1927; 29 March, 5, 19, 26 April, 20 September 1929.

122. Karl G. Yoneda, "Outline, 100 Years of Japanese Labor in U.S.A.," speech of 24 April 1969, pp. 10, 16, in Yoneda Papers, University of Washington Manuscripts Collection; U.S. Congress, House of Representatives, 71st Congress, 2d session, *Investigation of Communist Propaganda*, Pt. 5, Vol. 1 (Washington: Government Printing Office, 1930), pp. 1–105, esp. pp. 104–105.

123. "Result of Vote to Adopt Committee's Report on Unseating of Communists as Delegates to the Central Labor Council"; for Pearl's attitude toward the Communist Party, see *Daily Worker*, 14 February 1925; SUR, 5 February 1925.

124. WSLN, 20 March, 2 October 1925; *Journeyman Barber* XXI:8 (September 1928), p. 356; XVIII:5 (June 1922), p. 203; *Seattle Times*, 14 July 1925; William Short to Rae Last, 28 July 1925, Washington State Federation of Labor Records, Box 36, Folder 42; Short to James C. Shanessy, 1 October 1925, WSFL Records, Box 36, Folder 46; Shanessy to Short, 21 November 1925, WSFL Records, Box 1, Folder 6; WSFL, *Proceedings of the 24th Convention* (Olympia: WSFL, 1925), pp. 44–45, 48–49. William Short had plotted this "housecleaning" operation since before the general strike. In a November 1918 letter to Samuel Gompers, he anticipated the entire postwar transformation of the Seattle AFL: "There is danger ahead and when the crash comes, there will be some scalps lifted, but it won't be the ones [the radicals] have in mind. We will have to clean out a few Judases, but it can't be done until after the crash." Short foresaw his own future in the movement: "I will be at the helm yet when the sea calms, but some of my former friends won't be on board." Short, of course, was the first to push them overboard. See William Short to Samuel Gompers, 29 November 1918, Washington State Federation of Labor Records, Box 41.

125. Anna Louise Strong, *I Change Worlds: The Remaking of an American* (New York: Henry Holt, 1935), pp. 84–86.

126. Walter J. Henry to Harry Ault, 1 March 1928, Ault Papers, Part II, Box 3, Folder 38; see also Agent #106, 21 March and 24 April 1920 for exodus of activists, and letters to O'Connor from Hays Jones in O'Connor Papers.

127. SW, 6 June 1919; Wilfred Harris Crook, *The General Strike* (Chapel Hill: University of North Carolina Press, 1931), pp. 540–41.
128. Minutes, CLC, September–October 1923; "Statement of the Seattle Central Labor Council . . ."; Dembo, "History of the Washington State Labor Movement," pp. 374–76.

8. Harmony

1. *Newsboys' American*, 15 October 1919 (in Seattle Public Library).
2. On the definition and origin of business unionism, see Philip Taft, "On the Origins of Business Unionism," *Industrial and Labor Relations Review* Vol. 17, No. 1 (October 1963), pp. 20–38.
3. Alexander Saxton, *The Indispensable Enemy: Labor and the Anti-Chinese Movement in California* (Berkeley: University of California Press, 1971), pp. 215–18; John R. Commons et al., *History of Labour in the United States*, Vol. II (New York: Macmillan, 1918), pp. 266–67; Ernest R. Spedden, *The Trade Union Label* (Baltimore: Johns Hopkins University Press, 1910); Patricia A. Cooper, *Once a Cigar Maker: Men, Women, and Work Culture in American Cigar Factories, 1900–1919* (Urbana: University of Illinois Press, 1987), pp. 104–07, 137–39; David Bensman, *The Practice of Solidarity: American Hat Finishers in the Nineteenth Century* (Urbana: University of Illinois Press, 1985), pp. 57, 152–65, 185–90, 199–201; Stuart B. Kaufman, *Challenge and Change: The History of the Tobacco Workers International Union* (Urbana: University of Illinois Press, 1986), pp. 11–23, 26–35, 61; Stuart B. Kaufman, *A Vision of Unity: The History of the Bakery and Confectionery Workers International Union* (Urbana: University of Illinois Press, 1987), pp. 49–50, 52, 55, and illustrations throughout; Sally F. Zerker, *The Rise and Fall of the Toronto Typographical Union, 1832–1972: A Case Study of Foreign Domination* (Toronto: University of Toronto Press, 1982), pp. 112, 116, 133–34, 137, 139–42, 154–56, 198–99, 242; George Barnett, *The Printers* (Cambridge, Mass.: American Economic Association, 1909), pp. 273–78; Albert Helbing, *The Departments of the American Federation of Labor* (Baltimore: Johns Hopkins University Press, 1931), pp. 104–11; Louis Lorwin, *The American Federation of Labor: History, Policies, Prospects* (New York: Brookings Institution, 1933), pp. 368–69; Mary H. Blewett, *Men, Women, and Work: Class, Gender and Protest in the New England Shoe Industry, 1780–1910* (Urbana: University of Illinois Press, 1988), pp. 290–92, 299–301.
4. For prewar promotion of the union label and shop card, see Minutes, Central Labor Council of Seattle and Vicinity (hereafter CLC), Records of the King County Central Labor Council, University of Washington Manuscripts Collection; Seattle *Union Record*, weekly edition (hereafter SURW); Seattle *Union Record*, daily edition (hereafter SUR); Washington State Federation of Labor (hereafter WSFL), *Proceedings of the Annual Convention* (Seattle: WSFL, 1907–16); Kathryn J. Oberdeck, " 'Not Pink Teas': The Seattle Working-class Women's Movement, 1905–1918," *Labor History* 32:2 (Spring 1991), pp. 193–230.
5. SUR, 10 June 1919.

6. *Musicland*, 26 June 1925, and passim, in possession of Local #76, American Federation of Musicians, Seattle. For the musicians and building trades both, a union members' card could serve the same function as his or her button. The Building Trades Council abolished the union button in October 1923. See Minutes, Seattle Building Trades Council, 5 October 1923, in Records of Local #1289, United Brotherhood of Carpenters and Joiners, Box 1, Folder 2, University of Washington Manuscripts Collection; for previous use of the button, see Minutes, Seattle Building Trades Council, 9 March 1923, Box 1, Folder 2. At some point before the 1950s, the council reinstated quarterly buttons; 1953 and 1963 quarterly buttons, Seattle Building Trades Council, in possession of the author.

7. CLC, 17 January 1919; 26 May, 3 November 1920; 26 January, 23 February, 16 March, 14 December 1921; 1, 18 January 1922; 29 August, 7 November 1923; 6 February, 14 May, 20 August 1924; 21 January, 11, 18 February, 1, 29 April 1925; Minutes, Local #202, International Typographers' Union, 27 March 1921, in Records of Local #99, International Typographers' Union, Box 16, University of Washington Manuscripts Collection; Margaret Jane Thompson, "Development and Comparison of Industrial Relationships in Seattle," M.B.A. Thesis, University of Washington, 1929, pp. 85, 112; WSFL, *Official Yearbook of Organized Labor, State of Washington* (Seattle: Washington State Labor News, 1925), p. 31; WSFL, *Proceedings of the 23rd Convention* (1924), p. 11; *Washington State Labor News* (hereafter WSLN), 20 February, 20 March, 10 April 1925; SUR, 15 April 1925; Denzel C. Cline, "The Street Car Men of Seattle," M.A. Thesis, University of Washington, 1926.

8. Emphasis added. Report of Agent #106 (hereafter Agent #106), 20 February 1920, Broussais C. Beck Papers, Boxes 1–2, University of Washington Manuscripts Collection. On another occasion Hoffman similarly argued: "The Butchers as well as other business establishments where labor expects to organize depend entirely on the public and public alone can make union houses out of all business establishment" (*sic*). Agent #106, 3 July 1919.

9. Seattle's butchers' local (#81) and assistants' (#186) merged in 1923; I refer to both here as the butchers. David Brody, *The Butcher Workmen: A Study of Unionization* (Cambridge, Mass.: Harvard University Press, 1964), pp. 18–19, 107, 114; Minutes, CLC, 30 April, 4 June, 19 November, 22 December 1919; 16 March, 18 May 1921; 17 May, 4 October 1922; 17 January, 7 November 1923; 6 February, 19, 24 March 1924, 7, 28 January 1925; SUR, 25 April 1919; WSLN, 20 November 1925, 7 May, 23 July, 3 September 1926; Meat Cutters Local #81 to Organized Labor, 16 February 1924, in Records of Carpenters Local #1289, Box 3, Folder 3; Agent #106, 21 July 1919, 24 February 1920.

10. Brody, *The Butcher Workmen*, pp. 116–17.

11. Ibid., pp. 18–19. WSFL, *Proceedings of the 27th Convention* (Olympia: WSFL, 1928), p. 70; WSLN, 4 September 1925; 20 July 1928; Minutes, CLC, 15 March 1922; 8 October 1924; Brody, *The Butcher Workmen*, pp. 11, 112–13, 116–17.

12. WSLN, 3 September 1926; Blanche Johnson, "What Organization Means to the Woman Barber," *Life and Labor* Vol. VIII, No. 2 (February 1919), p. 28; *Musicland*, 25 July 1928; Minutes, CLC, 22 December 1920; 5 October 1921;

19 September, 17 October 1923; W. Scott Hall, *The Journeymen Barbers' International Union of America* (Baltimore: Johns Hopkins University Press, 1936), pp. 9–11, 115–18. On the barbers' strength in the middle and late 1920s, see Minutes, CLC, 4 January, 13 September 1922; 21 February, 27 June 1923; 26 March, 14, 21 May, 10 September 1924; 7, 28 January, 8 April 1925; WSLN, 19 March 1926; WSFL, *Yearbook*, 1925, p. 31.

13. WSLN, 19 August 1927.

14. Ibid., 3 September 1926 (quote); see also 15 May, 10 July, 16 October, 20 November 1925; 22 January, 5 February, 1 June, 2 July, 3 September 1926; 17 June, 1 August, 4 November 1927; Minutes, CLC, 6 October 1920; 5 October 1921; 18, 25 April, 16 May, 6 June, 18 July 1923; 18 June 1924; SUR, 20 February 1919; Minutes, Typographers Local #202, 26 June 1926; H. J. Conway to A. Alford, 10 November 1922, Records of Carpenters #1289, Box 3, Folder 4. The clerks also cooperated with employers on early closing campaigns; WSLN, 27 March, 3 April 1925; Minutes, Seattle Building Trades Council, 16 May 1924, Records of Carpenters #1289, Box 1, Folder 4; Frank Kannair to "Dear Sir" (Carpenters #131), 15 May 1924, in Records of Local #131, United Brotherhood of Carpenters and Joiners, Box 1, University of Washington Manuscripts Collection.

15. Dorothy Sue Cobble, "Sisters in the Craft: Waitresses and Their Unions in the Twentieth Century," Ph.D. Diss., Stanford University, 1986, p. 205. For the culinary unions' dependence on the shop card: Minutes, CLC, 1 December 1920; 2 November 1921; 22 March, 21 August, 15 November 1922; 28 November 1923; 5 March, 15 October 1924; WSLN, 14 March 1926; Robert Hesketh to William Short, 18 October 1924, WSFL Records, Box 21, Folder 50, University of Washington Manuscripts Collection; Matthew Josephson, *Union House, Union Bar: The History of the Hotel & Restaurant Employees and Bartenders' International Union, AFL-CIO* (New York: Random House, 1956); SUR, 17 February 1919; Robert Hesketh to Harry Ault, n.d., Harry Ault Papers, Part I, Box 2, Folder 46, University of Washington Manuscripts Collection.

16. Cobble, "Sisters in the Craft," p. 137.

17. Ibid., pp. 137, 341–42.

18. Ibid., p. 342.

19. Ibid.

20. WSLN, 2 February 1926.

21. Ibid., 15, 22 May, 4 September 1925; 21 May, 3 September 1926; 31 August 1928; *Pacific Caterer* VIII:4 (April 1925), p. 34. On the culinary workers, see also WSLN, 15 May 1925; WSFL, *Yearbook*, 1925, pp. 25, 31; Mabel Abbott, "The Waitresses of Seattle," *Life and Labor* Vol. 10 (February 1914), pp. 48–49; Minutes, CLC, 12, 19 October, 2 November, 21 December 1921; 18 April 1923; 18 June 1924; 27 May 1925; C. M. Baker to R. M. McCullough, 13 May 1929, Box 4, Typographers' #99 Records; SUR, 25 May 1926.

22. Unions using the Allied Printing Trades label included the bookbinders (until their demise), typographers, pressmen and assistants, web pressmen, stereotypers and electrotypers, lithographers, mailers, and photo engravers.

23. WSLN, 31 July 1925, 2 September 1927, 30 March 1928; Barnett, *The Printers*, pp. 273–78; Zerker, *Toronto Typographical Union*, pp. 133–34, 137–40, 154–56; Roll Books, CLC, Records of the King County Central Labor Council;

Minutes, Typographers' #202, 28 July 1925; Seattle Typographical Union #202, *Seventy-Fifth Anniversary Album,* in Records of Typographers Local #99, Box 27.

24. Minutes, Typographers' #202, 29 April 1923.

25. Ibid., 31 August 1924 (quote); Zerker, *Toronto Typographical Union,* Ch. 9; Minutes, Typographers #202, 4, 25 May 1921, 2 February 1922, 30 December 1923 and throughout the decade; Minutes, CLC, 20 July 1921, 13 February 1924.

26. Minutes, Typographers #202, 25 October 1925; see also 30 August 1925.

27. WSLN, 2 September 1927; "Report of Organizer," 27 May 1923, in "Minutes January–June 1923," Box 16, Records of Typographers #99; Minutes, CLC, 9, 15 August 1922; 14 January, 17 September 1924; for background on the ITU and the label, see Spedden, p. 20; Barnett, *The Printers,* pp. 273–78.

28. Minutes, CLC, 12 May 1919, 21 December 1921, 15 August 1923; Cooper, *Once a Cigar Maker,* pp. 111–14; Kaufman, *Challenge and Change,* Ch. 2, esp. p. 19; WSFL, *Proceedings of the 27th Convention* (Olympia: WSFL, 1928), p. 16; Minutes, Typographers #202, 2 March 1919; 29 June 1924; 26 April 1925; 30 January, 27 February 1927; Minutes, CLC, 22 March, 1 November 1922; 15 August 1923; 4 June 1924; 15 April 1925; WSLN, 24 April, 8 May, 1 August, 18 September, 24 November 1925; 3 September 1926; 8 April 1927; Cigar Makers International Union Local #188 to Carpenters Local #1289, 5 February 1924, Records of #1289, Box 3, Folder 1; SUR, 10 July 1927; Minutes, Seattle Building Trades Council, 13 June 1924, in Records of Carpenters #1289, Box 1, Folder 4.

29. WSLN, 11 January 1927.

30. Ibid., 2 September 1927.

31. Ibid., 16 January, 6 March, 18 September 1925; 23 July, 10 September, 17 December 1926; 4 February, 25 March 1927; 6 March, 12 October 1928; 25 January 1929; Minutes, CLC, 4 June 1919; 18 February, 2 November 1920; 1 February 1922; 10, 31 October 1923; 14 January, 6 May 1925; SUR, 6 May 1919; Roll Books, CLC; Black Manufacturing Company to William Short, 14 April 1927, WSFL Records, Box 7, Folder 72; Harold C. Runions to Harry Call, 16 August 1927, WSFL Records, Box 22, Folder 52; WSFL, *Yearbook,* 1927, p. 33; Minutes, Typographers #202, 31 March 1929; for promotion of garment labels issued by internationals with no members in Seattle, see, e.g., Union Label Collar Co. to "Dear Sir," 18 and 23 May 1927, WSFL Records, Box 23, Folder 68.

32. A. L. Kempster and successors, weekly reports to Stone and Webster Company (hereafter SW), in Box 122, Records of the Puget Sound Traction, Light and Power Company, University of Washington Manuscripts Collection, 4 May 1922; 7 April, 17 November 1923; see SW throughout the period for construction industry growth statistics; *Seattle Times,* 13 March 1924, 2 April 1928; Thompson, pp. 102, 141; WSLN, 2 September 1927. On the building trades in general, see *Associated Industries Bulletin,* 11 October 1922; William Short to A. S. Goss, 5 April 1926, WSFL Records, Box 37, Folder 5; Minutes, CLC, throughout the decade; WSFL, *Proceedings of the 23rd Convention* (Olympia: WSFL, 1924), p. 11; on building permits, see also WSLN, 13 June 1924.

33. WSLN, 18 July 1924.

34. *Seattle Times*, 2 May 1926. SW, 24 May 1926; SUR, 8 January, 7 May 1925; WSLN, 18 July 1924; *Seattle Times*, 13 March 1924.

35. *Seattle Times*, 12, 13 May, 18 June 1927; 1, 2 April, 9, 12 May, 2 June 1928; SW, 18 April, 9, 17 May, 16 June 1927; 14 May, 14 June, 16 July 1928; WSLN, 13 May 1927, 18 May 1928.

36. Thompson, "Development and Comparison," pp. 106, 140.

37. Ibid., pp. 142–50; Kim Moody, *An Injury to All: The Decline of American Unionism* (London: Verso, 1988), pp. 62–64; Toni Gilpin, "Left By Themselves: A History of the United Farm Equipment and Metal Workers Union, 1938–1955," Ph.D. Diss., Yale University, 1992, pp. 279–80; Judith Stepan-Norris and Maurice Zeitlin, "'Red' Unions and 'Bourgeois' Contracts," *American Journal of Sociology* Vol. 96 (March 1991), pp. 1151–1200; "The Treaty of Detroit," *Fortune*, July 1950, p. 54.

38. Minutes, CLC, 12 May 1920; 5 April, 17 May, 7 June, 27 December 1922; 18 July, 17 October 1923; WSLN, 6 November 1925; 23 April, 18 June 1926; Minutes, Seattle Building Trades Council, 20 April, 3 August 1923, in Records of Carpenters #1289, Box 1, Folder 2; Minutes, Seattle Building Trades Council, 27 April 1928, in Records of Local #131, Box 1; Minutes, Carpenters #131, 10 June 1919, 30 August 1921; Minutes, District Council of Carpenters, 11 May, 28 July 1922, in Records of Local #1289, Box 1, Folder 9; John T. Cosgrove to All Local Unions and District Councils, 6 March 1923, in Records of #1289, Box 2, Folder 13; John T. Cosgrove to Severt Johnson, 12 May 1926, Records of #131, Box 1; District Council of Carpenters to J. Blake, 11 January 1928, Records of #131, Box 1.

39. Carl Gustaf Westine, "The Seattle Teamsters," M.A. Thesis, University of Washington, 1937, pp. 24, 26, 28, 55; WSLN, 13 June, 13 August, 19 December 1924; 23 January, 27 March, 1, 15, 29 May, 10 July, 14 August, 4 September 1925; 9 July, 13 August, 3, 9 September 1926; 25 February, 11 March, 2 September 1927; 30 August 1929; Minutes, CLC, 21 January 1921; Thompson, "Development and Comparison," p. 112.

40. WSLN, 24 April, 7 August 1925; 30 July, 1 October 1926; 27 May 1927; Westine, "The Seattle Teamsters," p. 20; John D. McCallum, *Dave Beck* (Mercer Island, Wash.: Writing Works, 1978); Richard L. Neuberger, "Labor's Overlords," *American Magazine* 125 (March 1938), p. 168; International Brotherhood of Teamsters, Chauffers, Stablemen and Helpers of America, *Proceedings of the 11th Convention*, Seattle, Wash., September 14–19, 1925, pp. 12–13; *Proceedings of the 12th Convention*, Cincinnati, Ohio, September 3–13, 1930, p. 40; *Seattle Times*, 13 July 1925; Murray Morgan, *Skid Road: An Informal Portrait of Seattle* (New York: Ballantine, rev. ed., 1971), p. 259.

41. Neuberger, "Labor's Overlords," p. 167.

42. Ibid.

43. Ibid.

44. Ibid.

45. Ibid., p. 167. WSLN, 13 August 1926; Neuberger, "Labor's Overlords," p. 17; Donald Garnel, *The Rise of Teamster Power in the West* (Berkeley: University of California Press, 1972), pp. 38, 53, 65–70 and Ch. 3 in general; Westine, "The Seattle Teamsters," p. 20; Harvey O'Connor, *The Revolution in Seattle* (New York: Monthly Review Press, 1964), pp. 216–17.

46. Neuberger, "Labor's Overlords," p. 167.
47. Ibid., p. 166; WSLN, 15 May 1925, 9 July 1926, 1 April 1927; Westine, "The Seattle Teamsters," pp. 12, 15; Dale Soden, "Mark Allison Matthews: Seattle's Minister Rediscovered," *Pacific Northwest Quarterly* 74:2 (April 1983), p. 58; Calvin F. Schmid, *Social Trends in Seattle* (Seattle: University of Washington Press, 1944), pp. 267–69; William J. Dickson, "Labor in Municipal Politics: A Study of Labor's Political Policies and Activities in Seattle," M.A. Thesis, University of Washington, 1928, pp. 130–31.
48. Neuberger, "Labor's Overlords," p. 167.
49. Ibid., p. 17. Westine, "The Seattle Teamsters," pp. 12, 14–15.
50. Westine, "The Seattle Teamsters," pp. 13–14.
51. Ibid., p. 8. For evidence of physical persuasion, see also WSLN, 12 July, 2 August 1929.
52. WSLN, 13 June 1924; 15 May, 4 September 1925; 3 September 1926; 21 June, 17 July 1929; Garnel, *Rise of Teamster Power*, pp. 52–53; Westine, "The Seattle Teamsters," pp. 1, 12, 13–14, 56, 77–78.
53. Westine, "The Seattle Teamsters," pp. 7–8.
54. WSFL, *Proceedings of the 26th Convention* (Olympia: WSFL, 1927), p. 17.
55. WSFL, *Proceedings of the 27th Convention* (1928), p. 16; Minutes, Typographers #202, 21 July 1921; WSFL, *Proceedings of the 20th Convention* (Olympia: WSFL, 1921), p. 65; WSFL, *Proceedings of the 23rd Convention* (1924), p. 16; WSLN, 4 July, 1 August, 19 September 1924, and esp. June–July 1924; Harry Ault to Joseph Schlossberg, 27 July 1929, Ault Papers, Part I, Box 4, Folder 28; Harry Call to A. W. Johnston, 22 April 1927, WSFL Records, Box 37, Folder 36; SUR, 17 June 1921.
56. *Musicland*, 1 June 1922.
57. WSLN, 13 November 1925.
58. WSLN, 1 August 1924.
59. Lorwin, *American Federation of Labor*, p. 240; Irving Bernstein, *The Lean Years: A History of the American Worker, 1920–1933* (Boston: Houghton Mifflin, 1960), p. 90; Rose Pesotta, *Bread upon the Waters* (New York: Dodd & Mead, 1944), p. 148; SW, 14 February 1929; WSLN, 4 September 1925.
60. *Journeyman Barber* XV:11 (December 1918), p. 393.
61. WSLN, 27 January 1928.
62. Ibid., 1 November 1925.
63. WSLN, 9 September 1924; see also 13 June, 12 September 1924.
64. Spedden, *Trade Union Label*, pp. 68, 76.
65. Quoted in Kaufman, *Challenge and Change*, p. 15.
66. Report of Organizer, 27 May 1923, in Records of Typographers #99, Folder "Minutes, January–June 1923," Box 16.
67. The theater then declared that the unions' aid was not enough and spurned the locals, who then called a boycott. See Theatrical Federation of Seattle to Fellow Unionists, n.d. [February 1923], in Records of Carpenters #1289, Box 3, Folder 5. For employers and union assistance, see also *Musicland*, 5 May 1927.
68. Thompson, "Development and Comparison," p. 84.
69. WSFL, *Yearbook*, 1926, p. 1.
70. WSLN, 22 February 1929; 4 September 1925; *Musicland*, 10 August 1928; Minutes, CLC, 27 July 1927.

71. American Federation of Labor, *Report of Proceedings of the Forty-Third Annual Convention*, Portland, Oreg., October 1–12, 1923 (Washington: Law Reporter Printing, 1923), pp. 31–34.
72. Lorwin, *American Federation of Labor*, pp. 240–41, 352.
73. Joseph F. Tripp, "Progressive Labor Laws in Washington State, 1900–1925," Ph.D. Diss., University of Washington, 1973, p. 144.
74. Short to Carlton Fitchett, 30 June 1922, WSFL Records, Box 35.
75. W. J. Hindley to Short, 26 March, 27 April 1923, WSFL Records, Box 33, Folder 26; E. F. L. Sturdee to Short, 17 January, 2 February 1923, WSFL Records, Box 16, Folder 4; N. B. Coffman to David Whitcomb, 25 March 1924, WSFL Records, Box 10, Folder 14; Seattle Civic Federation to Short, several letters, 1926, in WSFL Records, Box 21, Folder 57. Tripp, "Progressive Labor Laws," p. 232, observes, "Short's principal activity in 1924 was 'Explaining in every city of the state the true affinity of interests between the business elements and the unionists.'" Hugh Grant Adam, an Australian trade unionist who visited Seattle as part of a national tour in 1927, reported of a conversation with Short: "[H]e preached at me in platitudes about fostering the spirit of co-operation between employer and employee. I failed to get him to come down from oratory to particulars." See *An Australian Looks at America* (London: Allen & Unwin, 1928), p. 5.
76. WSFL, *Yearbook*, 1925, p. 11.
77. Minutes, CLC, 24 December 1923; see also WSLN, 3 September 1926.
78. Agent #106, 30 July 1919; "Executive Committee" list, Seattle Chamber of Commerce, January 1927, in WSFL Records, Box 10, Folder 14; Minutes, Seattle Building Trades Council, 21 December 1928, in Records of Carpenters #131, Box 3, Folder "Seattle Building Trades Council."
79. Neuberger, "Labor's Overlords," p. 17.
80. *Musicland*, 10 August, 10 October 1928. On cooperation with the Chamber of Commerce, see also Harry Ault, "Autobiographical Statement," 18 July 1935, in Ault Papers, Part I, Box 6, Folder 62. A Labor Day article in 1928 by the President of the Seattle Chamber of Commerce was entitled "Labor Benefits From Work of Seattle Chamber of Commerce," WSLN, 31 August 1928. In 1926 a long article entitled "Manufacturers' Association Performs a Useful Function," appeared in WSLN, 3 September 1926.
81. Earl Shimmons, "The Seattle Union Record," ms. in Ault Papers, Part I, Box 7, Folder 9, p. 57.
82. Robert W. Dunn, *The Americanization of Labor: The Employers' Offensive Against the Trade Unions* (New York: International Publishers, 1927), p. 35. Warren Stanley Gramm, "Employer Association Development in Seattle and Vicinity," M.A. Thesis, University of Washington, 1948, p. 6; Thompson "Development and Comparison," p. 75; *Bulletin*, Associated Industries of Seattle, 23 August 1921, in WSFL Records, Box 6, Folder 37.
83. WSLN, 22 January 1926.
84. Thompson, "Development and Comparison," p. 148.
85. WSLN, 2 September 1927.
86. Thompson, "Development and Comparison," p. 85.
87. Adam, *An Australian Looks at America*, p. 8.
88. Ibid., p. 49.

89. WSLN, 27 January 1928; see also 16 September 1927.

90. Ibid., 9 April 1926; see also Minutes, CLC, 21 February 1923.

91. Carpenters District Council to Rhodes Department Store, 1 December 1926, Records of Carpenters #131, Box 1, Folder "1924–27"; Minutes, CLC, 19 July 1922, 3 June 1925; Minutes, Typographers #202, 28 June 1925; Pieter Prins to William Short, 22 May 1924, WSFL Records, Box 32, Folder 19; *Seattle Spirit* (organ of the Chamber of Commerce), throughout the 1920s; E. H. Hatch to Harry Ault, 23 August 1927, Ault Papers, Part I, Box 3, Folder 43; Ault to Hatch, 23 September 1927, Ault Papers, Part I, Box 3, Folder 43; WSLN, 25 July 1924; 31 July 1925; 25 February, 25 March, 1 July, 16 September 1927; 12 October 1928; Minutes, CLC, 3 September 1924; Minutes, Seattle Building Trades Council, 25 January 1924, in Records of Carpenters #1289; WSFL, *Proceedings of the 21st Convention* (Olympia: WSFL, 1922), p. 78; *Proceedings of the 26th Convention* (1927), p. 82; Minutes, Typographers #202, 27 October 1929.

92. Minutes, CLC, 14 June, 20 September 1922, 18 March 1925; WSLN, 4 September 1925; *Musicland*, 15 October 1922.

93. WSLN, 15 March, 22, 29 November 1929.

94. Ibid., 2 August 1929; see also 8 February 1929.

95. Ibid., 9 August 1929. See also Earle M. Casey to William Short, n.d., WSFL Records, Box 7, Folder 73.

96. Michael Kazin, in *Barons of Labor: The San Francicso Building Trades and Union Power in the Progressive Era* (Urbana: University of Illinois Press, 1987), p. 19, points out that in the local-market sector, firms lacked the leverage of national-market firms.

9. Label unionism

1. Lewis Lorwin, *The American Federation of Labor: Policies and Prospects* (Washington: Brookings Institution, 1933), p. 243; Albert Helbing, *The Departments of the American Federation of Labor* (Baltimore: Johns Hopkins University Press, 1931), p. 110; Report of the Executive Council, Washington State Federation of Labor (hereafter WSFL), to the 25th Convention, WSFL Records, Box 60, University of Washington Manuscripts Collection; Minutes, Central Labor Council of Seattle and Vicinity (hereafter CLC), 15, 22, 29 April, 13, 27 May, 3 June 1925, Records of the King County Central Labor Council, Box 8, University of Washington Manuscripts Collection; *Washington State Labor News* (hereafter WSLN), 27 March, 17 April, 1, 8, 15 May, 12, 19 June, 3 July, 25, 28 August, 13 November 1925; 23 April, 28 May, 3 September 1926; 27 February 1927; Seattle *Union Record*, daily edition (hereafter SUR), 27 May 1926; Short to William Bailey, 26 February 1926, WSFL Records, Box 37, Folder 2; Minutes, Local #202, International Typographers' Union, 28 June, 26 July, 27 September 1925, 30 May 1926, in Records of Local #99, International Typographers' Union, Box 16, University of Washington Manuscripts Collection; *Musicland*, 21 October 1925, in possession of Local #76, American Federation of Musicians, Seattle, Wash. For the AFL and label promotion, see Minutes, CLC, 23 April, 23, 30 July, 12 November 1924; 18 February 1925; 26 May 1926; WSLN, 13 June, 14 August, 3, 10 October

1924; 30 January, 14 August 1925; 1 January, 28 May 1926; 27 May 1927; 29 June 1928; Minutes, Typographers #202, 25 February, 29 April 1923; 29 January 1928; John J. Manning, "To Organized Labor," November 1924, in Records of Local #1289, United Brotherhood of Carpenters and Joiners, Box 3, Folder 5, University of Washington Manuscripts Collection; Frank Morrison to William Short, 18 May 1926, WSFL Records, Box 4, Folder 8; Short to Martin Graff, 19 October 1925, WSFL Records, Box 36, Folder 47; Short to Ethel A. Liggett, 11 February 1924, WSFL Records, Box 36, Folder 9; "Resolution," 26 September 1926, Washington State Association of the National Association of Letter Carriers, WSFL Records, Box 15, Folder 47.

2. WSLN, 24 February 1928.

3. Ibid., 30 October 1925.

4. For more information on the TUPL, see Report of Executive Council of WSFL to the 25th Convention (Seattle: WSFL, 1926), WSFL Records, Box 60; WSLN, 1, 8, 22, 29 May, 26 June, 3, 24 July, 14, 21 August, 4, 25 September, 9, 23, 30 October, 6 November 1925; 1, 29 January, 19 February, 5 March, 30 April, 7, 14, 21, 28 May, 11 June, 2 July, 3, 17 September, 1, 29 October, 26 November, 10, 17, 31 December 1926; 14 January, 4 February, 22 April, 6 May, 17 June, 5 August, 4 November 1927; 27 January, 24 February, 30 March 1928; 9 August, 13, 27 September 1929. Minutes, Typographers #202, 26 July 1925, 27 March 1927; Washington State Federation of Labor, *Official Yearbook of Organized Labor, State of Washington* (Seattle: Washington State Labor News, 1927), p. 31.

5. WSLN, 6 November 1925; 30 September, 28 October, 4 November 1927; 27 July, 10, 24 August, 7 December 1928; Report of WSFL Executive Council to 25th Convention; Helbing, *Departments*, p. 110; Minutes, Seattle Building Trades Council, 8 December 1922, in Records of Carpenters #1289, Box 1, Folder 1; Steven J. Ross, "Struggles for the Screen: Workers, Radicals, and the Political Uses of Silent Film," *American Historical Review* Vol. 96, No. 2 (April 1991), p. 353; Lizabeth Cohen, *Making a New Deal: Industrial Workers in Chicago, 1919–1939* (Cambridge: Cambridge University Press, 1990), pp. 136–42; Louis B. Perry and Richard S. Perry, *A History of the Los Angeles Labor Movement, 1911–1941* (Berkeley: University of California Press, 1963), pp. 276–78.

6. Minutes, Musicians #76 Board of Directors, 25 January 1921.

7. SUR, 8 January 1925.

8. For other fake labels, see SUR, 11 June, 22 October 1919; Minutes, CLC, 7 November 1928.

9. Minutes, CLC, 31 August 1921.

10. Ibid., 6 May 1925.

11. See ibid. throughout the 1920s, especially 1923–24; SUR, 28 April, 28 July 1919, 6 July 1921.

12. Central Labor Council of Seattle and Vicinity to All Local Unions of Seattle and Vicinity, 8 February 1923, Records of Carpenters #1289, Box 2, Folder 18.

13. Minutes, CLC, 7 September 1921.

14. WSLN, 26 June 1925.

15. WSLN, 11 September 1925. See also SUR, 4 November, 4 December 1920;

WSLN, 3 September 1926; Report of Agent #106 (hereafter Agent #106), 13 April 1920, Boxes 1–2, Broussais C. Beck Papers, University of Washington Manuscripts Collection.

16. Agent #106, 16 May 1919.
17. *Musicland*, 1 March 1924.
18. WSLN, 16 October 1925.
19. Ibid., 3 September 1926. See also *Musicland*, 1 September 1923, 10 December 1928; SUR, 19 June 1919; *American Union*, 18 November 1919; WSLN, 20 November 1925, 5 February 1926; Minutes, CLC, 10 October 1923, 14 May, 11 June, 13 August 1924; Agent #106, 12 May, 13 December 1919.
20. Minutes, Monthly Meeting, Local #76, American Federation of Musicians, 10 June 1921 (both quotes), in possession of Local #76, Seattle. For other violators see Minutes, #76 Board of Directors, 2 December 1919. At the February 13, 1920, monthly meeting it came out that "the whole meeting was in ignorance as to where union made goods could be purchased."
21. Union Record Purchasing Service to John J. Hessler, 25 May 1922, in Records of Carpenters #1289, Box 2, Folder 31.
22. *Musicland*, 25 July 1928.
23. WSLN, 13 June 1924.
24. *Journeyman Barber* XVII: 7 (August 1921), p. 283.
25. WSLN, 8 August 1924.
26. WSFL, *Yearbook*, 1926, p. 27. See also WSLN, 12 March 1926. In June 1926, J. J. Graff of Clown Cigarettes claimed that local sales were the highest ever: "Mr. Graff states that he has found much to refute the often-repeated claim that union men will not purchase union-made goods." See WSLN, 11 June 1926. Note, however, the "often-repeated claim."
27. WSLN, 29 June 1928.
28. WSLN, 4 October 1926.
29. Helbing, *Departments*, p. 108; see also p. 110.
30. Lorwin, *American Federation of Labor*, p. 372. We can find evidence also in the dejected tone of a letter from John J. Manning, secretary of the the AFL's Label Trades Department, to AFL unions throughout the country in 1924: "Those who become discouraged and dejected or listless and shiftless, will never become successful.... No one was ever defeated who did not admit defeat and give up trying to make good." See John J. Manning to Organized Labor, November 1924, in Records of Carpenters #1289, Box 3, Folder 5.
31. Central Labor Council of Seattle and Vicinity to All Local Unions of Seattle and Vicinity, 8 February 1923, in Records of Carpenters #1289, Box 2, Folder 18. Union members bought non-union goods "just to save a few pennies," the *Labor News* objected five years later. See WSLN, 30 November 1928.
32. Agent #106, 17 November 1919.
33. WSLN, 5 May 1928. See also Lorwin, *American Federation of Labor*, p. 373; William Z. Foster, *Misleaders of Labor* (New York: Trade Union Educational League, 1927), p. 219; WSLN, 14 September, 5 October 1928; 29 March 1929. For the opposite view, see Ernest Spedden, *The Trade Union Label* (Baltimore: Johns Hopkins University Press, 1910), p. 75.
34. General Manufacturing Co., Inc., to Japanese Association of North America,

10 October 1920, Records of the Japanese Association of North America, Box 1, Folder 5, University of Washington Manuscripts Collection. The Yours Truly Biscuit Company boasted in 1919 that it was the only cracker manufacturer in the Northwest employing union labor. *Northwest Co-operative News* Vol. I, No. 5 (September 1919), p. 7.

35. Lorwin, *American Federation of Labor*, p. 373.
36. Ibid.
37. *Journeyman Barber* XV:7 (August 1919), p. 302.
38. Stuart B. Kaufman, *A Vision of Unity: The History of the Bakery and Confectionery Workers International Union* (Urbana: University of Illinois Press, 1987), p. 90; Lorwin, *American Federation of Labor*, p. 373; Cohen, *Making a New Deal*, pp. 106–20.
39. WSLN, 8 January 1926.
40. *Journeyman Barber* XV:11 (December 1918), p. 392.
41. The phrase "palaces of consumption" is Susan Porter Benson's, in *Counter Cultures: Saleswomen, Managers, and Customers in American Department Stores, 1890–1940* (Urbana: University of Illinois Press, 1986), pp. 81, 82; on the allure of department stores, see Benson, *Counter Cultures*; William R. Leach, "Transformations in a Culture of Consumption: Women and Department Stores, 1890–1925," *Journal of American History* Vol. 71, No. 2 (September 1984), pp. 319–42.
42. Report of Agent #17, 29 March 1920, Boxes 1–2, Broussais C. Beck Papers, University of Washington Manuscripts Collection.
43. Stuart Ewen, *Captains of Consciousness: Advertising and the Social Roots of the Consumer Culture* (New York: McGraw-Hill, 1976); Stuart Ewen and Elizabeth Ewen, *Channels of Desire: Mass Images and the Shaping of American Consciousness* (New York: McGraw-Hill, 1982); Roland Marchand, *Advertising the American Dream: Making Way for Modernity, 1920–1940* (Berkeley: University of California Press, 1985); Susan Strasser, *Satisfaction Guaranteed: The Making of the American Mass Market* (New York: Pantheon, 1989). Michael Schudson disputes the effects of advertising in *Advertising, the Uneasy Persuasion: Its Dubious Impact on American Society* (New York: Basic, 1984).
44. Spedden, *Trade Union Label*, p. 72.
45. WSLN, 30 October 1929; *Musicland*, 4 April 1924.
46. Spedden, *Trade Union Label*, p. 72.
47. WSLN, 25 January 1925.
48. Minutes, CLC, 10 October 1923; see also 31 January 1922.
49. *Musicland*, 4 April 1924.
50. SUR, 20 November 1920.
51. Emphasis added. WSLN, 12 October 1928.
52. Spedden, *Trade Union Label*, p. 373.
53. *Musicland*, 1 August 1923.
54. Spedden, *Trade Union Label*, p. 75.
55. WSLN, 7 December 1928.
56. Batya Weinbaum and Amy Bridges, "The Other Side of the Paycheck: Monopoly Capital and the Structure of Consumption," *Monthly Review* Vol. 28, No. 3 (July–August 1976), pp. 88–103.

57. *Musicland*, 1 August 1923.

58. WSLN, 3 September 1926; see also 7 December 1928, 8 March 1929.

59. Minutes, CLC, 6 June 1923.

60. WSLN, 23 October 1925.

61. SUR, 16 April 1921. Women wanted "a place where the young people could feel at home," "where the ever-present hunger for beauty might . . . be satisfied." Ibid.

62. Ibid.

63. Ibid., 18 June 1921.

64. Ibid.; see also 21 April 1921.

65. Mark Litchman to Albert Brilliant, n.d. [April 1921], in Mark Litchman Papers, Part I, Box 1, Folder 32, University of Washington Manuscripts Collection. For support for the miners' strike, see Minutes, CLC, Fall 1921, Winter 1922. For the transformation of the league, see Minutes, CLC, 4, 25 January, 8, 15 February, 8 March, 5, 26 April, 3 May, 7, 14 June, 18 October, 22, 29 November 1922; 10 January, 2, 28 February, 7, 14 March, 4, 11 April, 2, 16 May, 6, 13, 20 June, 1, 19 August, 3, 10 October, 5, 12, 19 December 1923; 9, 16 January, 27 February, 9, 16, 23, 30 April, 7, 21 May, 2, 24 September, 15, 31 October, 5, 26 November, 3, 10 December 1924; 7, 14 January, 4, 18 February, 4 March, 8, 22, 29 April, 27 May 1925; and Minutes, CLC, through the rest of the decade; WSLN, 6 March, 3, 10, 24 April, 19 June, 7, 28 August, 23 October, 4, 11, 25 December 1925; 8, 29 January, 5, 26 February, 5 March, 21 May, 18, 25 June, 23 July, 27 August, 17, 24 September, 26 November, 10 December 1926; 7 January, 18 February, 4 March, 22 April, 27 May, 10 June, 29 July, 30 September, 2 December 1927; 6, 27 January, 2, 9, 30 March, 6 April, 4 May, 1, 8, 15, 22 June, 30 November 1928; 18 January, 15 March, 28 June 1929; Minutes, Local #131, United Brotherhood of Carpenters and Joiners, 3 April, 19 June, 10 September 1923; 29 January 1924, Records of Local #131, United Brotherhood of Carpenters and Joiners, University of Washington Manuscripts Collection; Minutes, Typographers #202, 28 May 1922, 27 January 1924, 29 November 1925, 28 November 1926; Minutes, Seattle Building Trades Council, 8 August 1923, in Records of Carpenters #1289, Box 1, Folder 1; *Musicland*, 15 May 1923, 1, 15 March 1924, 24 December 1927; Gertrude Millson to Harry Call, 12 June 1927, WSFL Records, Box 4, Folder 2; Union Record Purchasing Service to "Dear Folks," 28 March 1923, Box 2, Folder 31, Carpenters #1289 Records; Mary Friermood to #1289, 29 March 1923, #1289 Records, Box 3, Folder 4.

66. Minutes, CLC, 18 April 1923; WSLN, 2 September 1923.

67. WSLN, 18 September 1925.

68. Mary Friermood to Carpenters #1289, 29 March 1923, Records of Carpenters #1289, Box 3, Folder 4.

69. In 1927 league members introduced a new feature at their meetings; each member recounted an instance of what she had done since the last meeting to help unions in Seattle. See WSLN, 8 July 1927; see also WSLN 6 November 1925, 28 December 1928.

70. Roll Books, CLC, 1920–22, in Records of the King County Central Labor Council, University of Washington Manuscripts Collection; Seattle *Union Record*, weekly edition (hereafter SURW), 5 November 1919; SUR, 19 June,

2, 7 July 1919; *Musicland*, 15 May 1923; WSLN, 20 June, 26 September, 5 December 1924; 9 January, 20 March, 18 September, 6 November 1925; 7 May, 8 October 1926; 9 December 1927; 11 January, 2, 23 March, 13 April, 31 August 1928; "Result of Vote to Adopt Committee's Report on Unseating of Communists as Delegates to the Central Labor Council, Box 6, King County Central Labor Council Records.

71. WSLN, 9 October 1925; see also 18 September 1925.

72. WSLN, 27 March 1925.

73. The phrase "bread and roses, too" comes from the Wobblies' 1912 Lawrence, Mass., textile strike; Joyce L. Kornbluh, *Rebel Voices; An I.W.W. Anthology* (Ann Arbor: University of Michigan Press, 1968, 1972), pp. 164, 196.

74. Minutes, CLC, 13 November 1929. For another incident reflecting tensions over the league's role and responsibilities, see WSLN, 25 September 1925.

75. Norman J. Ware argued further that "present-day distribution of commodities requires a wider and deeper solidarity to boycott successfully." See *The Labor Movement in the United States, 1865–1895* (New York: D. Appleton, 1929), p. 337. For evidence of workers' willingness to pay more for (IWW) union-made printing at the Equity Print Shop, see Hays Jones to Harvey O'Connor, 24 June 1919, Harvey O'Connor Papers, Part II, Box 1, Archives of Labor and Urban Affairs, Walter Reuther Library, Wayne State University.

76. Minutes, Musicians #76 Board of Directors, 12 June 1928.

77. Minutes, CLC, 4 May 1927; WSLN, 7 January 1927; *Journeyman Barber* Vol. XIV, No. 2 (March 1918), p. 59; David Montgomery, *The Fall of the House of Labor: The Workplace, the State, and American Labor Activism, 1865–1925* (Cambridge: Cambridge University Press, 1987), pp. 201, 275–76.

78. Agent #106, 25 June 1919.

79. Lorwin, *American Federation of Labor*, pp. 371, 373–74; Spedden, *Trade Union Label*, pp. 30–31; Forge, 5 July 1919; WSFL, *Proceedings of the 21st Convention* (Olympia: WSFL, 1922), pp. 55, 81; Minutes, CLC, 31 May 1922.

80. WSLN, 14 November 1924.

81. Ibid., 20 April 1928; see also 3 September 1926.

82. Ibid., 1 June 1928.

83. Hugh Grant Adam, *An Australian Looks at America* (London: Allen & Unwin, 1928), p. 10.

84. *Forge*, 10 May 1919.

85. At the 1927 AFL convention, a proposed resolution failed to pass that would have required that the union label could be issued to a firm only if it were fair to all the crafts involved. See Lorwin, *American Federation of Labor*, p. 374.

86. Ibid., p. 373; WSLN, 12 March, 23 July 1926; SUR, 1 July 1920; Minutes, CLC, 5 January 1921; Minutes, Musicians #76 Board of Directors, 9 May, 11 June 1929; Minutes, monthly meeting, 3 July 1929; AFL vs. IWW in Seattle: SUR, 1 June 1921; John S. Gambs, The Decline of the I.W.W. (New York: Columbia University Press, 1932), pp. 72–73; #76 Board of Directors, 9 August, 30 September 1923; A. E. Schwarz to Carpenters #1289, 18 September 1924.

87. Carl Gustaf Westine, "The Seattle Teamsters," M.A. Thesis, University of Washington, 1937, pp. 7–8.

88. *Vanguard*, June, July, August 1931 ("Beck Gang" quote); Westine, "The

Seattle Teamsters," pp. 3–4, 7–8, 55–56; Kaufman, *A Vision of Unity*, p. 96; Lorwin, *American Federation of Labor*, p. 525; Minutes, CLC, 1, 22 June 1927; WSLN, 15, 22 May 1925; 6 May, 3, 10, 24 June, 22 July, 16 December 1927; 21 December 1928. See also Rose Pesotta, *Bread upon the Waters* (New York: Dodd, Mead, 1944), pp. 149–50.

89. SUR, 8 February 1921.

90. Ibid.; WSLN, 25 January 1929; Dorothy Sue Cobble, "Sisters in the Craft: Waitresses and Their Unions in the Twentieth Century," Ph.D. Diss., Stanford University, 1986, pp. 58–59, 157–58. For waiters, see Minutes, CLC, 4 June 1919.

91. N.a. [Japanese Association of North America?] to Phillip Tindall, 22 July 1920, in Records of the Japanese Association of North America, Box 5, Folder 20. Kazuo Ito, *Issei* (Seattle: Japanese Community Service, 1973), pp. 541, 543–45, 549–50, 801; *Pacific Caterer* Vol. IV, No. 1 (1 December 1920), p. 14; Tokichi Tanaka, "The Japanese in Seattle," *Coast* Vol. XII, No. 5 (November 1909), pp. 249–51.

92. Ito, *Issei*, pp. 548–49.

93. Ibid., pp. 543–44.

94. Ibid., pp. 541–42.

95. Ibid., p. 126; see also p. 847.

96. SUR, 5 June 1919.

97. WSLN, 10 September 1926.

98. See also Minutes, CLC, 29 January, 4 June 1919; WSLN, 19 June, 3 July 1925, 1 October 1926, 15 February 1929; SUR, 18 June 1925; Interview with Shigeru Osawa by Richard Berner and Sally Kazama, May 1968, in University of Washington Manuscripts Collection; Ito, *Issei*, p. 95. For similar activities in San Francisco, see Michael Kazin, *Barons of Labor: The San Francisco Building Trades and Union Power in the Progressive Era* (Urbana: University of Illinois Press, 1987), p. 165.

99. Cobble, "Sisters in the Craft," pp. 12, 31, 36, 48–49, 156, 159–60; Minutes, CLC, 1, 15 October 1924; WSLN, 2 September 1927; *Pacific Caterer*, 1 April 1921; *Mixer and Server* Vol. XXVIII, No. 9 (September 1919), pp. 116, 119; United States Department of Commerce, Bureau of the Census, *Fourteenth Census of the United States*, Vol. IV (Washington: Government Printing Office, 1920), pp. 1233–35; *Fifteenth Census*, Vol. V, pp. 1709–11. On African-American workers and culinary unions nationally, see National Urban League, Department of Research and Investigation (Ira De. A. Reid, Director), *Negro Membership in American Labor Unions* (New York: Alexander Press, 1930), pp. 90–91.

100. Cobble, "Sisters in the Craft," p. 158.

101. SUR, 12 June 1920.

102. WSLN, 8 June 1928; see also Minutes, CLC, 15 September 1920, 20 April 1927; WSLN, 14 August 1925, 18 June 1926.

103. SUR, 18 June 1925.

104. *Musicland*, 15 November 1923.

105. David Roediger, "'Labor in White Skin': Race and Working-Class History," in Mike Davis and Michael Sprinker, eds., *Reshaping the U.S. Left: Popular Struggles in the 1980s* (London: Verso, 1988), pp. 288–89. For evidence that anti-Asian activities contributed to white working-class consciousness in the

1880s, see Carlos Schwantes, "Unemployment, Disinheritance, and the Origin of Labor Militancy in the Pacific Northwest, 1885–1886," in G. Thomas Edwards and Carlos Schwantes, eds., *Experiences in a Promised Land: Essays in Pacific Northwest History* (Seattle: University of Washington Press, 1986), pp. 179–94.

106. Minutes, CLC, 24 July 1929.

107. SUR, 18 January 1921.

108. See also Minutes, Typographers #202, 27 May 1928. Harry Laidler found that the most successful labor boycotts of the 1880s were those directed against Chinese workers. Harry Wellington Laidler, *Boycotts and the Labor Struggle* (New York: John Lane Company, 1914), p. 78.

109. Robert Bedford Pitts, "Organized Labor and the Negro in Seattle," M.A. Thesis, University of Washington, 1941, pp. 66–69; Musicians #76 Minutes, Board of Directors, 9, 20 August, 23 December 1918; 7 January 1919; Clark Halker, "A History of Local 208 and the Struggle for Racial Equality in the American Federation of Musicians," *Black Music Research Journal* Vol. 8 (Fall 1988), p. 209; National Urban League, *Negro Membership*, pp. 93–94.

110. Minutes, #76 Board of Directors, 26 February 1924.

111. Pitts, "Organized Labor and the Negro," pp. 66–69.

112. Minutes, Musicians #76 monthly meeting, 8 February, 11 April 1924; Board of Directors, 15, 29 June, 7 December 1920; 1 March, 5 April, 3 May, 29 November 1921; 27 December 1923; 15 January, 5, 12, 19, 26 February, 11, 19 March, 15 April 1924; Minutes, CLC, 26 March 1924. On Local #76 in this period, see also Jonathan Dembo, "John Danz and the Seattle Amusement Trades Strike, 1921–1935," *Pacific Northwest Quarterly* Vol. 71, No. 4 (October 1980), pp. 172–82.

113. Pitts, "Organized Labor and the Negro," pp. 66–67; #76 monthly meeting, 10 October 1924, 9 January 1925, 7 October 1926, 3 July 1929. Board of Directors: 11, 20, 27 May, 7 October, 9, 23 December 1924; 5 May, 15, 21, 31 July, 11, 26 August, 1, 29 September, 9, 13 October, 15, 24 November, 29 December 1925; 10 August, 2 November 1926; 17 January, 15 February, 5, 27 March, 15 May, 26 June 1928; 21 May, 4, 25 June, 2 July 1929; WSLN, 13 May 1927; Minutes, CLC, 4 May 1927.

114. Sterling D. Spero and Abram Harris, *The Black Worker: The Negro and the Labor Movement* (New York: Atheneum, 1931, repr. 1971), p. 75; Pitts, "Organized Labor and the Negro," pp. 69–70.

115. Minutes, Executive Board, CLC, 12 March 1924, Records of the King County Central Labor Council, University of Washington Manuscripts Collection.

116. For #76 and Asians, see Minutes, Board of Directors, 11 June 1918, 17 June 1919; monthly meeting, 19 November 1918, 8 August 1919; *Musicland*, 15 October 1921.

117. Calvin F. Schmid, *Social Trends in Seattle* (Seattle: University of Washington Press, 1944), p. 149; Pitts, "Organized Labor and the Negro," p. 83.

118. WSLN, 24 April, 1 May 1925, 29 March 1929; Minutes, CLC, 1, 30 January, 6 February, 13 March, 8 September 1929.

119. *Seattle Times*, 29 March 1929; WSLN, 8 June, 13 July 1928, 7 June 1929. See also *Seattle Times*, 4 July 1929; WSLN, 29 June 1928, 4, 11, 25 January, 1, 8 February, 5 April, 15 May, 30 August 1929.

120. WSLN, 25 July 1924, 15 October 1926, 4 March, 29 April 1927, 18 May 1928.

121. WSLN, 3 September 1926.

122. Donald Garnel, *The Rise of Teamster Power in the West* (Berkeley: University of California Press, 1972), p. 74. On Beck, see Richard L. Neuberger, "Labor's Overlords," *American Magazine* 125 (March 1938), p. 169; WSLN, 3 September 1926.

123. Pesotta, *Bread upon the Waters*, p. 149.

124. W. Guerin to William Short, 10 June 1925, WSFL Records, Box 4, Folder 14; WSLN, 4 May, 27 April 1928.

125. Minutes, CLC, 17 May 1922. See also Agent #106, 24 February 1920.

126. David Brody, *The Butcher Workmen: A Study of Unionization* (Cambridge, Mass.: Harvard University Press, 1964), pp. 108–109.

127. Minutes, CLC, 14 January 1925 (cooks); WSLN, 3 September 1926; Minutes, CLC, 22 December 1920, 19 September, 17 October 1923; William S. Hall, *The Journeyman Barbers' International Union of America* (Baltimore: Johns Hopkins University Press, 1936), pp. 115–18.

128. Stuart B. Kaufman, *Challenge and Change: The History of the Tobacco Workers International Union* (Urbana: University of Illinois Press, 1986), p. 13.

129. Minutes, Musicians #76 monthly meeting, 14 May 1918.

130. Cobble, "Sisters in the Craft," p. 205.

131. Phillip Foner points out that in the early twentieth century, the AFL national office spent more money promoting the union label than on organizing the unorganized. See *History of the Labor Movement in the United States, Volume III: The Policies and Practices of the American Federation of Labor, 1900–1909* (New York: International Publishers, 1964), p. 177.

132. Montgomery, *Fall of the House of Labor*, p. 278.

133. Foster, *Misleaders of Labor*, p. 51.

134. Montgomery, *Fall of the House of Labor*, p. 278.

135. Andrew William Lind, *A Study of Mobility of Population in Seattle* (Seattle: University of Washington Press, 1925), p. 49. As many as half of the laundry workers' unpaid officers were female, though. SUR, 25 July 1919, 23 July 1921. For the gender dynamics of label unionism, see Mary H. Blewett, *Men, Women, and Work: Class, Gender, and Protest in the New England Shoe Industry, 1780–1910* (Urbana: University of Illinois Press, 1988), pp. 267–317.

136. National Urban League, *Negro Membership*, p. 98. For the Seattle teamsters' union and African-Americans, see Pitts, "Organized Labor and the Negro," p. 95; for African-American teamsters, see *Cayton's Weekly*, 29 December 1917, 22 May 1920.

137. SUR, 11 April 1919.

138. WSLN, 23 January 1925; SUR, 19, 29 March 1921.

139. WSLN, 7 August 1925, 3 September 1926; Minutes, CLC, 10 January, 6, 10 June, 7 August 1923; *Polk's City Directory, Seattle, 1929* (Seattle: R. L. Polk & Co., 1929). For women in the typographers' union, see Minutes, Local #202.

140. The one exception was Hattie Titus, who had been married to pre–World

War I socialist agitator Herman Titus. The local's oldest member, Hattie Titus served as one of Local #76's delegates to the Central Labor Council in the middle and late 1920s. But her power extended no further, and she was excluded from the informal power structure of the local. See Minutes, #76 monthly meeting, 14 November 1919, 9 November 1923; Board of Directors, 9 December 1921; *Musicland*, 27 December 1926, 24 December 1927, special Christmas issue 1928 n.d., 25 December 1929.

141. Minutes, #76 Board of Directors, 13 September 1918.
142. Minutes, #76 monthly meeting, 9 January 1919.
143. *Musicland*, 20 November 1926.
144. Ibid., 3 June 1927.
145. Ibid., 20 November 1927. WSLN, 6 April 1928.
146. Alice Kessler-Harris, *Out to Work: A History of Wage-Earning Women in the United States* (New York: Oxford University Press, 1982), p. 158.
147. Throughout the decade the officers of #76 tried to curtail these activities; see Minutes, Board of Directors and monthly meetings.
148. *Musicland*, 20 January 1928.
149. Ibid., 25 February 1928; see also 25 April 1928 for use of "homelike."
150. Ibid., 25 April 1928.
151. Ibid., 25 February 1928.
152. Ibid., 20 January 1928; 5 February 1928.
153. Ibid., 10 May 1928.
154. Ibid., 25 February, 10 March, 25 September, 10 December and Christmas issue, n.d., 1928, 25 December 1929; Minutes, #76 monthly meeting, 7 November 1928. At the decade's end, the Women's Club counted a hundred members and was going strong; see *Musicland*, 25 December 1929.
155. *Musicland*, 20 May 1927.
156. Ibid., 5 December 1927.
157. Ibid., 24 December 1927.
158. Ibid.
159. Ibid., 25 March 1929.
160. Ibid.
161. Ibid., 25 November 1928.
162. For more on the gender dynamics in #76, see the regular jokes about hen-pecked husbands or out-of-control wives in *Musicland*, e.g., 5 December 1927, 10 September 1928.
163. WSLN, 2 September 1927.
164. Green quoted in Irving Bernstein, *The Lean Years: A History of the American Worker, 1920–1933* (Boston: Houghton Mifflin, 1960), p. 143. Rose Pesotta observed of the Seattle AFL: "At meetings of locals the officers would take up routine matters – reading of the local's minutes, CLC minutes, the local's correspondence, then adjournment. Dull proceedings, no new faces." See Pesotta, *Bread upon the Waters*, p. 149. On attendance issues, see WSLN, 17 April 1925; 2 April, 18 June, 3 September 1926; 23 November 1928; Minutes, CLC, 10 January 1923, 16 January 1924, 24 January 1925; *Musicland*, 1 July 1923; Minutes, Carpenters #131, 21 June 1921; Report of Executive Council to the Washington State Federation of Labor Convention, 1927, WSFL Records, Box 60; John J. Hessler to All Affiliated Locals, District

Council of Carpenters, 1 June 1922, in Records of Carpenters #1289, Box 2, Folder 11.

165. Minutes, Typographers #202, 30 December 1923, Box 16, Records of Typographers #99; Minutes, Carpenters #131, Records of Carpenters #131, Box 2.

166. Minutes, CLC, 14 June 1922.

167. Ibid., 31 January, 27 November 1922; 7 February, 24 October 1923; WSLN, 20 September 1929.

168. WSLN, 12 February, 10 December 1926; 25 February, 25 March 1927; 10 February 1928; 2 August 1929.

169. Ibid., 10 February 1928.

170. Of a total of fifteen active auxiliaries in 1928, four had been founded in 1903–05 (three of those railroad workers), two in 1915–17 (both postal workers); one each in 1921, 1922, and 1923 (streetcar employees, machinists, and firefighters); four in 1924–25 (building trades and cooks) and one in 1928 (milk wagon drivers).

171. On the ladies' auxiliaries in general: WSLN, 23 March, 13, 20, 27 April, 4, 11, 18, 25 May, 18, 29 June, 31 August 1928, 1, 8 February 1929. On individual auxiliaries: *IBEW #46:* WSLN, 9 March, 6 April, 1 June, 31 August 1928; *Cooks #33:* Ibid., 21, 28 November 1924, 2 January, 24 April, 29 May, 7, 14 August, 11 September, 13 November, 4 December 1925; 16 April, 19 November 1926; 11 March 1927; 9, 23 March 1928. *Carpenters #131:* Ibid., 13 May 1927, 16 March, 11 May, 10, 31 August 1928; Minutes, CLC, 10 May 1922; Minutes, Seattle Building Trades Council, 9 November 1924, Records of Carpenters #131, Box 3; Susan A. Bartlett to District Council of Carpenters, 6 December 1927, Records of Carpenters #131, Box 1. *Railroad Brotherhoods:* WSLN, 16 March, 22 June, 20 July, 3 August 1928. *Postal Workers:* WSLN, 16 March, 20 April, 31 August, 14 September 1928; SUR, 23 May 1919. *Streetcar Employees:* WSLN, 19 December 1924, 24 April 1925, 9 July, 17 December 1926, 16 March, 6, 27 April, 11 May, 15 June, 31 August 1928; Minutes, CLC, 27–28 April, 4 May, 7, 28 September 1921; 25 January, 22 March 1922; 21 March, 4 April 1923, 22 April 1925; Roll Books, CLC; Isabell Simenson to William Short, 29 October 1921, Box 22, Folder 52, WSFL Records. *Boilermakers #104:* SUR, 15 May, 27 June, 16 August 1919, 11 September 1920; SURW, 6 July 1918, 21 May 1919. *Machinists #79:* SUR, 21 March 1919; WSLN, 14 August 1925; 14 May 1926; 6 April, 11 May, 31 August 1928; 22 February 1929. For national IAM auxiliaries in this period, see "Program of Year's Work" – Grace Klueg, Chair, IAM Ladies' Auxiliary Educational Committee, n.d. [1927], and pamphlets, in Records of American Fund for Public Service, Box 14, New York Public Library Manuscripts Collection. *Plumbers and Steamfitters:* WSLN, 1 August 1924, 6 March, 3 April, 4 September 1925; 23 April, 30 July, 24 September, 26 October 1926; 4 February, 4 March, 29 April, 23 September 1927; 6, 7 January, 11 May, 22 June, 31 August 1928. *Milk Wagon Drivers:* WSLN, 31 August, 14 September 1928. *Firefighters:* WSLN, 16 March, 31 August 1928. *Bricklayers:* WSLN, 3 August 1928. *Typographers #202:* Minutes, CLC, 7 December 1921; WSLN, 21 May 1926, 2, 16 March, 20 April, 31 August 1928; Minutes, Typographers #202, 2 March 1919; 27 June 1920; 30 January, 29 May, 26 June, 25 September, 27 November 1921,

26 March, 30 April, 27 May, 24 September, 29 October 1922; 29 April, 30 September 1923; 27 January 1924; 25 January, 26 April 1925; 31 January, 26 April, 31 October 1926; 30 January, 27 February, 27 March, 18 December 1927; 29 April 1928; 28 April, 26 May, 27 October 1929; Typographers #202, "Summary of Minutes – Seattle Typographical Union #202," Box 27, Folder "75th Anniversary," Records of Typographers #99.

172. On the auxiliaries, see also Minutes, Typographers #202, 28 May 1922; WSLN, 21 November 1924, 8 March 1929; Minutes, Musicians #76, 21 November 1928.

173. WSLN, 22 May 1925.

174. Ibid., 29 May 1925. See also "Label a Very Potent Factor," in WSFL, *Yearbook*, 1927, p. 35.

175. WSLN, 9 November 1928, 25 January 1929.

176. Ibid., 30 November 1928.

177. Ibid., 2 November 1928.

178. Minutes, Typographers #202, 28 September 1924, Box 16, Records of Typographers #99.

179. WSLN, 7 September 1928.

180. See also WSLN, 10 April 1925, 27 January 1928.

181. Spedden, *Trade Union Label*, p. 73.

182. SUR, 28 November 1919.

183. Minutes, CLC, 7 May, 4 June 1919; SUR, 5 June 1919.

184. Minutes, CLC, 21 January 1925. On visibility, see also, e.g., Minutes, CLC, 1 November 1922, 21 October 1923, 16 April 1924, 25 March 1925. In a more defensive vein, the butchers' union in a 1924 letter to all locals both acknowledged the extent to which union people did not buy union and pleaded that those who did not at least not advertise it publicly: "If you will so far forget your union obligations as to trade at a scab market, please remove your union buttons and uniforms, so you will not be so noticeable as to make even the scab clerks blush with shame." See Meat Cutters #81 to All Organized Labor, 16 February 1924, reprinted in *Musicland*, 1 March 1924. For visibility, see also Osawa interview; *Pacific Caterer* Vol. IV, No. 16 (November 1921), p. 32; SUR, 28 April 1919; Agent #106, 14 August 1919; WSLN, 24 April 1925.

185. Minutes, CLC, 18 June 1924; Westine, "The Seattle Teamsters," pp. 5–6; WSLN, 16 April 1926; Minutes, CLC, 9 November 1921; 25 January, 22 November 1922; 12 September 1923; 27 February, 24 March, 16 April, 11, 18 June, 2 July, 8 October 1924; 18 February 1925; and throughout the period; *Musicland*, 15 July 1924, 25 December 1928; Patricia A. Cooper, *Once a Cigar Maker: Men, Women and Work Culture in American Cigar Factories, 1900–1919* (Urbana: University of Illinois Press, 1987), p. 115.

186. Spedden, *Trade Union Label*, p. 69.

187. As Spedden put it, "That they cannot very well be enforced does not prevent their enactment"; p. 69.

188. Minutes, CLC, 1 November 1922; *Musicland*, 1, 10 July, 14 August 1923. Pugsley did not pay the fine and was suspended from the union.

189. WSLN, 16 April 1926. For other fines see Minutes, Musicians #76, monthly meeting, 8 July 1921, Board of Directors, 14 October 1924. Locals also

imposed fines on members of families caught patronizing unfair firms; e.g., Minutes, Typographers #202, 25 July 1920. In general, fines were not a new phenomenon; locals imposed them for violation of a variety of union rules such as working hours. Many of the "mass" labor events of 1918–19 were possible because members faced fines if they did not attend. Painters #300, for example, placed a fine on any member who did not attend a meeting to vote on the Mooney strike. SUR, 24 September 1919. Musicians #76, Longshoremen #38–12, and Typographers #202 all fined members who did not attend Labor Day parades. *Forge*, 4 October 1919; Minutes, Typographers #202, 4 August 1918; Minutes, Musicians #76, 27 August 1918.

190. On the concept of trade union consciousness, defined differently, see V. I. Lenin, *What Is To Be Done? Burning Questions of Our Movement* (New York: International Publishers, 1969).

191. Bernstein, *The Lean Years*, p. 90.

192. Minutes, Seattle Building Trades Council, 8 June 1923, in Records of Carpenters #1289, Box 1, Folder 2; see also WSLN, 13 June 1924 (article by Sam Frazier on Carpenters' Union); James A. Taylor to All Affiliated Organizations, 10 December 1929, WSFL Records, Box 38, Folder 2; WSLN, 2 September 1927.

193. WSLN, 30 August 1929.

194. Selig Perlman, *A Theory of the Labor Movement* (New York: Macmillan, 1928), p. 232; see also Bernstein, *The Lean Years*, p. 84.

195. Margaret Jane Thompson, "Development and Comparison of Industrial Relationships in Seattle," M.B.A. Thesis, University of Washington, 1929, p. 100; Washington Bureau of Labor and Industry, *Twelfth Biennial Report*, 1919–1920, pp. 32–34; Leo Troy, *Trade Union Membership, 1897–1962* (New York: National Bureau of Economic Research, 1965), p. 1. These figures include Canadian members of U.S. internationals. David Montgomery, discussing the postdepression AFL, observes, "A membership matching that of 1913 might still have been there; the combativeness, diversity, and optimism were not." See Montgomery, "Thinking about American Workers in the 1920s," *International Labor and Working-Class History*, No. 32 (Fall 1987), pp. 4–24.

Conclusion

1. Cities with a strong IWW presence included Spokane, Wash.; Fresno, Calif.; Paterson, N.J.; and Lawrence, Mass. See Melvyn Dubofsky, *We Shall Be All: A History of the IWW: The Industrial Workers of the World* (New York: Quadrangle, 1969); Joyce L. Kornbluh, *Rebel Voices: An I.W.W. Anthology* (Ann Arbor: University of Michigan Press, 1972). Cities with a weak manufacturing base included Denver and New Orleans; see David Brundage, *The Making of Western Labor Radicalism: Denver's Organized Workers, 1878–1905* (Urbana: University of Illinois Press, in press); Eric Arnesen, *Waterfront Workers of New Orleans: Race, Class, and Politics, 1863–1923* (New York: Oxford University Press, 1991). For tripartite race relations, examples include Los Angeles, San Francisco, and Tampa; see Nancy Hewitt, "'The Voice of Virile Labor': Labor Militancy, Community Solidarity, and Gender Identity

among Tampa's Latin Workers, 1880–1921," in Ava Baron, ed., *Work Engendered: Toward a New History of American Labor* (Ithaca, N.Y.: Cornell University Press, 1991), pp. 142–67; Michael Kazin, *Barons of Labor: The San Francisco Building Trades and Union Power in the Progressive Era* (Urbana: University of Illinois Press, 1987).

2. Ole Hanson, *Americanism Versus Bolshevism* (New York: Doubleday, 1920); Robert Friedheim, *The Seattle General Strike* (Seattle: University of Washington Press, 1964), pp. 173–74.

3. Alexander Saxton, *The Indispensable Enemy: Labor and the Anti-Chinese Movement in California* (Berkeley: University of California Press, 1971), pp. 270–78; Yuji Ichioka, *The Issei: The World of the First Generation Japanese Immigrants, 1885–1924* (New York: Free Press, 1988), pp. 99–102; Phillip S. Foner, *History of the Labor Movement in the United States*, Vol. III (New York: International Publishers, 1964), pp. 268–71.

4. Co-operative League of America, *Report of the Proceedings of the First American Co-operative Convention* (Springfield, Ill.: Co-operative Association of America, 1919); *Report of the Proceedings of the Second American Co-operative Convention* (Cincinnati, Ohio: Co-operative Association of America, 1920). For evidence of widespread reportage in the labor press of cooperatives in Seattle, see, e.g., Little Rock, Arkansas, *Union Labor Bulletin*, 12 September 1919; *Railway Carmen's Journal* Vol. XXIV, No. 8 (August 1919), p. 1256. My thanks to Eric Arnesen for these two clippings.

5. Leo Troy, *Trade Union Membership, 1897–1962* (New York: National Bureau of Economic Research, 1965), p. 8.

6. For an example of this dynamic, see Bruce Nelson, *Workers on the Waterfront: Seamen, Longshoremen, and Unionism in the 1930s* (Urbana: University of Illinois Press, 1988).

7. Steven Fraser, "Dress Rehearsal for the New Deal: Shop-Floor Insurgents, Political Elites, and Industrial Democracy in the Amalgamated Clothing Workers Union," in Michael Frisch and Daniel Walkowitz, eds., *Working Class America* (Urbana: University of Illinois Press, 1983), pp. 212–55. On the transformation of the CIO in the forties and early fifties, see Nelson Lichtenstein, *Labor's War at Home: The CIO in World War II* (Cambridge: Cambridge University Press, 1982); Kim Moody, *An Injury to All: The Decline of American Unionism* (New York: Verso, 1988), pp. 17–69; Toni Gilpin, "Left by Themselves: A History of the United Farm Equipment and Metal Workers Union, 1938–1955," Ph.D. Diss., Yale University, 1992, esp. pp. 279–80; Stanley Aronowitz, *Working Class Hero: A New Strategy for Labor* (New York: Pilgrim Press, 1983); Judith Stepan-Norris and Maurice Zeitlin, "'Red' Unions and 'Bourgeois' Contracts," *American Journal of Sociology* Vol. 96 (March 1991), pp. 115–20.

8. Michael Massing, "Detroit's Strange Bedfellows: The Auto Workers' New Partnership with Management," *New York Times Magazine*, 7 February 1988, pp. 20–27 and 52 and cover photograph.

Index